Business Elites and Corporate Governance in France and the UK

French Politics, Society and Culture
Series Standing Order ISBN 0–333–80440–6 hardcover
Series Standing Order ISBN 0–333–80441–4 paperback
(*outside North America only*)

You can receive future titles in this series as they are published by placing a standing order. Please contact your bookseller or, in case of difficulty, write to us at the address below with your name and address, the title of the series and the ISBN quoted above.

Customer Services Department, Macmillan Distribution Ltd, Houndmills, Basingstoke, Hampshire RG21 6XS, England

Business Elites and Corporate Governance in France and the UK

Mairi Maclean
Professor of European Business
Bristol Business School
University of the West of England

Charles Harvey
Professor of Business History and Management
Strathclyde Business School
University of Strathclyde

Jon Press
Professor of Business History
Bath Spa University

Foreword by
Sir Adrian Cadbury
Former Chairman of Cadbury-Schweppes
Chairman of the UK Committee on the Financial Aspects of Corporate Governance

First published 2006 by
PALGRAVE MACMILLAN

Palgrave Macmillan in the UK is an imprint of Macmillan Publishers Limited, registered in England, company number 785998, of Houndmills, Basingstoke, Hampshire RG21 6XS.

Palgrave Macmillan in the US is a division of St Martin's Press LLC, 175 Fifth Avenue, New York, NY 10010.

Palgrave Macmillan is the global academic imprint of the above companies and has companies and representatives throughout the world.

Palgrave® and Macmillan® are registered trademarks in the United States, the United Kingdom, Europe and other countries.

ISBN–13: 978–1–4039–3579–3 hardback
ISBN–10: 1–4039–3579–3   hardback

This book is printed on paper suitable for recycling and made from fully managed and sustained forest sources. Logging, pulping and manufacturing processes are expected to conform to the environmental regulations of the country of origin.

A catalogue record for this book is available from the British Library.

Library of Congress Cataloging-in-Publication Data
Business elites and corporate governance in France and the UK / Mairi
    Maclean, Charles Harvey, Jon Press; foreword by Adrian Cadbury.
        p. cm. – (French politics, society, and culture series)
    Includes bibliographical references and index.
    ISBN 1–4039–3579–3 (cloth)
        1. Businesspeople–France. 2. Businesspeople–Great Britain.
    3. Elite (Social sciences)–France. 4. Elite (Social sciences)–Great Britain.
    5. Corporate governance–France. 6. Corporate governance–Great Britain.
    I. Maclean, Mairi, 1959- II. Harvey, Charles, 1950- III. Press, Jon, 1953-
    IV. Series.
    HC276.B87 2006
    338.60941–dc22   2005054418

Printed and bound in Great Britain by
CPI Antony Rowe, Chippenham and Eastbourne

Contents

List of Tables and Figures

Tables

viii *List of Tables and Figures*

Figures

Acknowledgements

Many people have helped, directly and indirectly, with this book. In the first place, we wish to thank the Leverhulme Trust, for funding a two-year Leverhulme Research Fellowship. We also wish to express our gratitude to Sir Alec Reed, who, through Reed Charity, funded a pilot project at Royal Holloway, University of London. Interviewees who gave so freely of their time are especially deserving of thanks. In particular we wish to thank Xavier Barrière, Human Resource Director, Air Liquide; François-Régis Benois, French Senate; Pierre Bilger, former PDG of Alstom; Sir Adrian Cadbury, former Chairman of Cadbury-Schweppes and Chairman of the UK Committee on the Financial Aspects of Corporate Governance; Dr George Cox, former Director General of the Institute of Directors; Iain Gray, General Manager and Managing Director, Airbus UK; Larry Hirst, CEO, IBM UK; Sir Digby Jones, Director General of the Confederation of British Industry; Jean-Claude Le Grand, Director of Corporate Recruitment, L'Oréal; Agnès Lépigny, Director of Economic Affairs, Mouvement des Entreprises de France; Rémi Lallement of the Commissariat Général du Plan; Senator Philippe Marini, French Senate; Dr John Mellor, Chairman, Foundation for Independent Directors; Peter Orton; Chairman of HIT Entertainment; Louis Sherwood, Director, HBOS; Per Staehr, Chairman of Bombardier Transportation, UK; Mike Street, Operations Director, British Airways; Jean-François Théodore, CEO, Euronext; Lord William Waldegrave, Managing Director, UBS, and former Cabinet Minister; as well as those who preferred to remain anonymous. We are especially grateful to Sir Adrian Cadbury for taking time out of his busy schedule to write the Foreword to this book. We wish to thank Professor Mark Casson, University of Reading, for his perceptive comments. The support of David Boughey, Susan Godfrey and Huw Morris was invaluable. The staff of the Bolland Library processed and obtained numerous library loans. The research assistance of Holly Combe was greatly appreciated, and, previously, that of Roberta Anderson, Sally Dobbie, Alexandre Buisson, Margaret Taylor and Edmond Tchibota. Thanks are due to Alison Howson of Palgrave Macmillan for her kind assistance in the production of this book. Finally, we would like to thank our families for their love and support.

MAIRI MACLEAN
CHARLES HARVEY
JON PRESS

List of Abbreviations

ABI	Association of British Insurers
AFEP	Association Française des Entreprises Privée
AFG	Association Française de la Gestion Financière
AGF	Assurances Générales de France
AGM	Annual General Meeting
AMF	Autorité des Marchés Financiers
ASFFI	Association des Sociétés et Fonds Français d'Investissement
BASD	Business Action for Sustainable Development
BAT	British-American Tobacco
BCCI	Bank of Credit and Commerce International
BNP	Banque Nationale de Paris
BP	British Petroleum
BT	British Telecom
CAC-40	Cotation assistée en continu (top 40 French companies by market share)
CalPERS	California Public Employees' Retirement System
CBE	Commander (of the Order) of the British Empire
CBI	Confederation of British Industry
CBP	Code of Best Practice
CDU	Christlich-Demokratische Union
CEO	Chief Executive Officer
CFO	Chief Financial Officer
CGE	Compagnie Générale d'Electricité
CMF	Conseil des Marchés Financiers
CNPF	Conseil National du Patronat Français (now MEDEF)
CNRS	Centre Nationale de Recherche Scientifique
COB	Commission des Opérations de Bourse
CSR	Corporate Social Responsibility
DTI	Department of Trade and Industry
EADS	European Aeronautics, Defence and Space Company
EAP	Ecole des Affaires de Paris
EBRD	European Bank for Reconstruction and Development
EC	European Community
ECGI	European Corporate Governance Institute
ECJ	European Court of Justice
EdF	Electricité de France
ENA	Ecole Nationale d'Administration

ENS	Ecole Normale Supérieure
ESC	Ecole(s) Supérieure(s) de Commerce (or ESCAE)
ESCAE	Ecole(s) Supérieure(s) de Commerce et d'Administration (or ESC)
ESSEC	Ecole Supérieure des Sciences Economiques et Commerciales
EU	European Union
FDI	Foreign Direct Investment
FESE	Federation of European Stock Exchanges
FIBV	International Federation of Stock Exchanges
FRC	Financial Reporting Council
GATT	General Agreement on Tariffs and Trade
GdF	Gaz de France
GDP	Gross Domestic Product
HBOS	Halifax Bank of Scotland
HEC	Ecole des Hautes Etudes Commerciales
HEFCE	Higher Education Funding Council for England
IC	Imperial College
ICMG	International Capital Markets Group
IEP	Institut d'Etudes Politiques
IMF	International Monetary Fund
INSEAD	European Institute of Business Administration
IoD	Institute of Directors
ISC	Institutional Shareholders Committee
ISS	Institutional Shareholder Services
ITV	Independent Television
KCL	King's College London
KCMG	Knight Commander (of the Order) of St. Michael and St. George
LBS	London Business School
LIFFE	London International Financial Futures Exchange
LSE	London Stock Exchange
LVMH	Moët Hennessy Louis Vuitton
M & A	Mergers and acquisitions
MBA	Master of Business Administration
MBE	Member (of the Order) of the British Empire
MEDEF	Mouvement des Entreprises de France
NAPF	National Association of Pension Funds
NED	Non-executive Director
NHS	National Health Service
NIC	Newly industrialised countries
NRE	Nouvelles Régulations Economiques

NYSE	New York Stock Exchange
OBE	Officer (of the Order) of the British Empire
OECD	Organisation for Economic Cooperation and Development
PDG	Président-Directeur Général
PPR	Pinault-Printemps-Redoute
PS	Parti Socialiste
RAE	Research Assessment Exercise
RATP	Régie autonome des transports parisiens
RBS	Royal Bank of Scotland
RPR	Rassemblement pour la République
SBF	Société des bourses françaises
SEC	Securities and Exchange Commission
SEITA	Société nationale d'exploitation industrielle des tabacs et allumettes
SME	Small and medium-sized enterprises
SNCF	Société Nationale des Chemins de Fer
SNECMA	Société nationale d'étude et de construction de moteurs d'aviation
SOX	Sarbanes-Oxley Act
UAP	Union des Assurances de Paris
UCL	University College London
UGC	University Grants Committee
UMP	Union pour un Mouvement Populaire
UN	United Nations

Foreword

By Sir Adrian Cadbury

It is a great pleasure to be invited to write a foreword for a book which I read with considerable interest and enjoyment. It is a study of the ways in which businesses in France and Britain are being governed at a time when companies in both countries are having to adapt to *la mondialisation*. The book's analysis and findings are important for a number of reasons. One is precisely because the research behind it links governance structures and systems with those who activate them. It is that combination which determines how corporate power is exercised in both countries. Power is the issue. Public concern over accountability for the exercise of that power helps to account for the speed with which corporate governance has moved up the political and business agenda. The emergence of large multinational companies, apparently subject to no single jurisdiction, raises inevitable questions over the nature and extent of their accountability.

By taking two countries similar in the size and structure of their business systems, but with different historical and cultural backgrounds, the authors are able to compare the varied ways in which their leading companies are responding to change. In doing so they lay bare the factors which influence the actions and motives of British and French board members. A broader set of international comparisons could not explore the detailed differences in the thoughts and actions of these leaders which are the essence of this study. The book's fascination lies in the window which it opens on the lives of the individuals in both countries, who at the time of writing held the reins of power. How did they arrive at these positions, what motivates them, how far were they advantaged, and in what ways are the French and British elites similar and in what ways different?

Britons may well find it difficult to believe that their country has a business elite, conscious as we are of the role of the *grandes écoles* in France. These mainly historic institutions were after all established to forge an elite and to train a governing class, able to move effortlessly between the public and private seats of power. The book brings out the relatively narrow base from which that class is formed and the degree of uniformity in their training for their future positions. It starts with a few select Paris schools and it requires talent and determination for provincial contenders to enter the top stream at a later stage. Intermarriage between elite families assists in their hold on power, and the family as such plays a stronger part in French companies and in the building of networks than would be true in Britain.

The authors' analysis does, however, bring out a greater degree of interconnection between the members of those identified as the business elite in Britain than might be expected. There is a pattern of schools and universities which recur in the backgrounds of those at the head of British enterprises. To have gone to the same school or to have studied at the same university, however, is a relatively weak tie, unless those who did so have other interests in common. But as the authors explain weak ties have their strengths, for example in building extended networks. What those members of the British elite with a shared educational background, even though following a variety of courses, did gain from that experience were confidence, connections, and an entry card into society and the world beyond business. This contrasts with the more specialised French focus on maths and science and on exam results, the outcome of which is the consequent brotherhood (overwhelmingly) of those who studied at the *grandes écoles*.

Whatever the differences between the educational experiences of the French and British elites, their ability to perpetuate themselves, while being open to the entry of fresh blood, is well documented. At the same time, the book makes clear the influence of history and culture on the ways in which the leading companies in the two countries are governed. The strength of the director network between companies and the ties between business and the state are that much more powerful in France. The prevalence of interlocking directorships, even if waning, makes it hard for members of French boards to recognise possible conflicts of interest or to act on them. Equally, the influence of the state on business was clear to those of us who represented British industry in Brussels. UK representatives pressed the case for their industries, regardless of the policy of whatever government was in power. Our French counterparts seemed more inclined to represent their government than their industry.

The book, however, covers the full range of issues related to business elites and corporate governance in the two countries and it does so with clarity and authority. Against that background, it is interesting to consider how far a process of convergence is likely to take place, given the distinctive nature of the French and British approaches to these matters.

To take the formation of business leaders first, will aspiring chief executives increasingly look to an elite class of international business schools as a necessary step to senior positions? Already leading business schools from around the world are planting their campuses, or are planning to do so, in Asia and Europe. The best will be research-intensive and multinational in terms of staff, students and the nature of their courses. The specialised higher degree they will be able to offer could form a natural progression from the broad degree syllabuses of British universities. This could be matched by a sharper differentiation between the universities favoured by those aiming for leadership and the rest. The more students and their families have to contribute to the cost of university education in the UK, the more demanding they will become over the quality and nature of the courses they attend.

If this kind of pattern takes shape, it will face the *grandes écoles* with difficult choices. How far will institutions established to train a cadre for leading positions in business and government in France, be able to provide the international element in education which is already being sought and will become even more sought after in the future? However, there will surely be no sudden changes in an elite educational system which has strong historical roots and has served the nation well. This potential tension between national traditions and international imperatives will no doubt be resolved in a uniquely French fashion.

In the field of corporate governance there is already a degree of convergence worldwide. The distinction between the Rhenish view of the role of companies in society and what is somewhat misleadingly referred to as the Anglo-Saxon view, a distinction vividly drawn by Michel Albert in *Capitalisme contre capitalisme*, is becoming blurred. The requirement for companies everywhere to provide the resources for economic growth and to meet the growing burden of retirement are setting international standards for the return on corporate assets. At the same time, companies, especially the multinationals and those which are becoming dependent on outsourcing, are acutely aware of the risks to their reputations, if they fail to be seen to be accepting their responsibilities to society. It is noteworthy, in parenthesis, that the French use the same word for company and for society.

Convergence is taking place, but it is largely reflected in outcomes, in British and French businesses having to meet the expectations of their investors, in particular their international institutional investors. There is no necessity for their structures and processes of governance to converge and I fully accept the authors' conclusion: *'Viewed in this light, over a long-term period, further convergence is likely. Our research over the period 1998-2003, however, has pointed overwhelmingly not to the convergence of the French and British business systems, but rather to the persistence of national distinctiveness, to the strength of cultural reproduction, despite globalisation, and more than a decade of corporate governance reform.'*

I wish to finish by stressing the importance of *Business Elites and Corporate Governance in France and the UK* as a work of reference. In addition to its own inherent merits, it provides the benchmark against which future developments in this field will be measured.

Solihull
August 2005

1

Business Elites and Corporate Governance in France and the UK

'It is true that liberty is precious – so precious that it must be rationed.'

Lenin

This book is a cross-national study of business elites and corporate governance in France and the UK. It examines corporate governance from a comparative standpoint, and looks beneath the surface, beyond the application of formal rules and regulations, at the exercise of power and authority in two distinct national business systems. It explores key issues concerning business elites, their networks, recruitment, reward, reproduction, and commonality of membership of organisations against the backdrop of an increasingly global economy. The book aims to shed light on the mechanisms that govern the stability and regeneration of business elites in both countries in the face of far-reaching change. Change has been driven by globalisation and heightened competition on the one hand, and an increasing focus on matters of corporate responsibility, accountability and transparency on the other. Are the old systems breaking down, and, if so, are we witnessing the emergence of European and international business elites? Are we observing a convergence in matters of corporate governance, in which Britain is often perceived as leading the way?[1]

The twin themes of business elites and corporate governance are inextricably bound. Yet this is a relationship that is often overlooked, and few studies have sought to relate corporate governance, an issue that has come very much to the fore in recent years, to the recruitment and functioning of business elites. It is argued that the relationship between business elites and corporate governance is central to the manifold ways in which power and authority are exercised in modern corporations. To understand boards

1

better, we need to know more about the mindsets, predilections and behaviours of those who sit on boards. Elite corporate networks can be seen to extend beyond business into government and other realms within society – especially in France where business and politics are closely related – exercising power and influence in numerous areas of public life. Corporate governance has been defined variously as 'the system by which companies are run',[2] or 'the mechanisms by which companies are controlled and made accountable',[3] or more specifically as 'the ways in which suppliers of finance to corporations assure themselves of getting a return on their investment'.[4] Such definitions, however, do not reflect the fact that each nation has a system of corporate governance in its own image, moulded over time by the particular capitalist creed to which it adheres,[5] reflected in the number of national codes now in existence.[6] Few nations would accept a one-size-fits-all approach to corporate governance, as evinced by the difficulties experienced by the European Commission in setting up a European Union (EU) company statute. The cultural specificity of corporate governance is a point to which we shall return. In this book, we define corporate governance as the legitimating mechanisms, processes and codes through which power and authority are exercised by business elites. In defining elites, we follow the definition put forward by Tom Bottomore, who defines them simply as 'functional, mainly occupational, groups that have high status (for whatever reasons) in a society'.[7] This leads us, for the purposes of this study, to identify members of the business elite as the upper tier directors of the top 100 companies in France and the UK respectively.

Corporate governance has undergone significant change in recent years, on both sides of the Channel, as elsewhere. This has resulted in a plethora of governance reports in a general drive towards greater openness and accountability – most notably, as far as Britain and France are concerned, the Cadbury [8] and Viénot Reports,[9] which have spawned numerous others. The 1992 Cadbury Report in particular was a landmark in thinking on governance, whose influence cannot be played down.[10] It successfully focused corporate minds on matters such as regulation, responsibility and reporting to shareholders; board effectiveness, structures and procedures; auditing and accountability. It struck a chord in France in the wake of some embarrassing business scandals, propelling the role of top management out of public complacency and on to centre stage. This led directly to the 1995 Viénot Report, which paved the way towards further reform. Is corporate governance in France now converging on the British model, traditionally more geared to shareholders' concerns? The word 'British' is used here advisedly, in preference to

'Anglo-American'. The governance systems that obtain in Britain and the
US are in fact quite distinct, despite widespread perceptions to the contrary, Britain having a unitary board, whereas in the US the board is
essentially a non-executive body, normally with just the president and
chief executive being linked to the operational parts of the business.[11]

Reform and increasing regulation have not, however, stemmed the tide of
financial scandal, as the recent cases of Enron and WorldCom amply
demonstrate. Nor has the advent of company committees designed to ensure
good governance – remuneration, audit and nomination committees – led to
greater self-control in the setting of directors' salaries and emoluments, as
the example of Vivendi-Universal underscores. Jean-Marie Messier,
Vivendi's former chief executive, enjoyed the use of a £15 million apartment
on New York's Park Avenue. On being ousted by the board in July 2002, he
attempted (unsuccessfully) to negotiate a severance package that would
include the luxury flat. As Stefan Kirsten, Chief Financial Officer (CFO) of
ThyssenKrupp AG put it: 'There is no corporate governance code in the
world that can guarantee ethical behaviour on the part of board members.
Greed has no part in management competencies. Ultimately, it is always
going to be down to the people involved to breathe life into the principles of
corporate governance'.[12] Or, as Pierre Bilger of Alstom has commented:
'[Corporate governance] does not mean that decisions will be better, but
they will be better documented'.[13] This book engages with each of today's
pressing debates on governance and the exercise of power, which are issues
of wider public interest. These include appropriate management remuneration, the role of independent directors in corporate life, business regulation,
ethics and corporate social responsibility.

Conceptual framework

The rising interest in matters of corporate governance in both practitioner
and academic circles has spawned numerous research studies – economic,
legal, institutional, financial, administrative and political. What has been
missing, however, is a comparable interest in the ways in which the
structures, systems and processes of a governance regime are forged and
function through interactions with members of the business elite. It may
seem an obvious point, but people – company directors – are part-and-
parcel of any governance regime, and a practical understanding of corporate governance requires an understanding of their predilections and
collective behaviour.

A governance regime, when viewed holistically, may be conceived as a
pyramid, existing on three levels, each interrelated (as originally articu-

lated by Maclean in *Economic Management and French Business*).[14] The most visible and easily apprehended features are its formal practices, rules and regulations, shown in Figure 1.1 as close to the pinnacle.

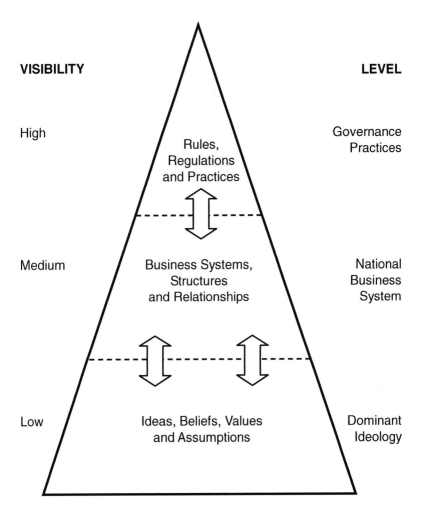

VISIBILITY

LEVEL

High

Rules,
Regulations
and Practices

Governance
Practices

Medium

Business Systems,
Structures
and Relationships

National
Business
System

Low

Ideas, Beliefs, Values
and Assumptions

Dominant
Ideology

Figure 1.1 Elements of a governance regime

In legal or constitutional terms, we might think of the ways in which companies are set up and dissolved, the composition of boards of directors and the ground rules for financial reporting. Each of these is relatively simple to observe and document. Conversely, underlying ideologies, assumptions and deeply held values, on which rules and practices draw, are positioned closer to the base of the pyramid, being much more difficult to circumscribe and pin down. Like an iceberg, that which cannot be seen is often the most important part, and the most treacherous to ignore. Business systems, structures and relationships mark the middle ground, linking unseen ideologies to the more easily apprehensible rules and regulations.

Each of the layers in Figure 1.1 – organisational, systemic and ideological – is of course an abstraction. However, the distinction made between the features of a governance regime that are clearly seen, partially seen and largely unseen is a valuable one. The annual reports of quoted companies, nominally open and transparent, are the means by which corporations report on their activities within the strictures of the law and prevailing conventions (the top layer). Yet a deeper ideological understanding is clearly required to decode their messages fully, to dig beneath the chosen rhetoric to reveal the hidden beliefs and values that lie behind (the bottom layer), the 'cultural baggage' in Hofstede's terms, of which the authors themselves may not even be aware.[15] It follows that changes at the uppermost level, such as changes to corporate governance practices introduced in the wake of key governance reports, are only ever likely to be stable if matched by parallel changes in assumptions, values and beliefs at the ideological level. Endogenous pressures, such as executive compensation and the lure of stock options, discussed in the chapters ahead, are certainly powerful motors for change at the apex. But for genuine root-and-branch changes to occur, parallel changes to the dominant ideology are a *sine qua non* for successful change at the organisational level.

Research foundations

This book, in response to the identified need to view corporate governance holistically, is based upon extensive cross-national comparative research (see Appendix 1 for a technical note on sources and methods). The aim of all comparative studies is to derive meaning – to see things more clearly – by comparing and contrasting the size, substance and features of one entity or system with another. By comparing the corporate governance regimes of France and the UK, from an elite as well as an institutional perspective, we aim to demonstrate crucial differences between two national business systems and the reasons why these differences persist in the face of strong pressures to harmonise and converge.

The research has two main elements. The first is quantitative and

founded upon the creation of a database of the organisational and governance characteristics of the top 100 companies in France and the UK,
together with 'life, career and network' profiles for the directors of
selected companies. There are 2,291 business leaders included in the
database, who in turn are associated with more than 25,000 organisations
around the world. The database reveals the commonality of membership
of organisations such as schools, universities, *grandes écoles* and *grands
corps*, as well as the company links and reciprocal mandates underlying
the exercise of power in both countries. It enables systematic analysis of
the collective membership and 'multi-positional' character of business
elites as highlighted by Bourdieu.[16] High-profile members of the elite, for
example, often participate in public, private and charitable organisations
in the cultural, educational, governmental and sporting arenas as well as in
the corporate world (see Chapter 6).

For this study, a 'census date' of 1 January 1998 was selected to ascertain
organisational and individual membership of the corporate elites of France
and the UK. The top 100 companies in each country were identified as
possessing the greatest amounts of 'corporate power', defined by their
'command over resources' – financial, physical, human, intellectual, social
and symbolic (see Appendix 1). Membership of the business elite was
confined to individuals with decisional authority at the summit of top 100
companies. In the UK, the main board stands conspicuously at the head of
companies, and members of the elite can be identified straightforwardly as
the executive and non-executive directors who sit on the main board. In
France the situation is more complex. Top companies have more varied
forms of ownership, legal constitution, governance structures and stakeholder representation, and typically there is little overlap between the mainly
non-executives who sit on boards of directors (*le conseil d'administration*)
or supervisory boards (*le conseil de surveillance*) and the executives who sit
on executive boards and executive committees. Moreover, the size and
composition of each of these 'directorial entities' varies considerably from
company to company. We found ourselves in need of pragmatic and realistic
decision rules for who constituted the equivalent of a UK main board
director and who did not. Accordingly, we chose to include in the database
all members of French boards of directors or supervisory boards other than
honorary members and employee representatives, whose rights and standing
are limited, along with all inner-circle executive directors with responsibilities for such matters as finance and operations, often designated as members
of an executive board (as opposed to second-tier executive directors often
designated as members of an executive committee).

Data were gathered from a wide range of publicly available sources on each of the 2,291 people identified as belonging to the business elites of France and the UK in 1998. In addition, a more in-depth study was conducted of the 200 most powerful individuals from amongst this group – 100 affiliated to French companies and 100 to UK companies. A power index was calculated for this purpose by first dividing the corporate power of individual companies between the directors who have command over the resources of a particular company. The 'shares' of corporate power attributed to individual directors vary according to the role played by the director in the company. In the UK, for example, a Chief Executive Officer (CEO) is deemed by 'rule of thumb' to have twice the amount of power in the company as other executive directors serving on the main board. A French Président-Directeur Général (PDG) in comparison is deemed to have three times the power of his fellow executive directors by virtue of his serving as both CEO and chairman of the board. In both countries, executive directors are held to exercise much larger shares of corporate power than non-executive directors, other than company chairmen who have a special role to play with respect to corporate governance. Once the corporate power of individual companies is divided up and attributed to individual directors, the total power attributable to a business leader can be calculated and presented as an index simply by adding together the power stakes each person has in one or more top 100 companies.

Table 1.1 The business elites of France and the UK in 1998

| | France | | UK | |
	No.	%	No.	%
Population				
Men	1,206	95.60	993	94.57
Women	54	4.40	57	5.43
All	**1,260**	**100.00**	**1,050**	**100.00**
Top 100 Directors				
Men	98	98.00	99	99.00
Women	2	2.00	1	1.00
All	**100**	**100.00**	**100**	**100.00**

Notes: The data relate to 2,291 individuals, of whom 1,031 were directors of UK top 100 companies, 1,241 were involved in French top 100 companies and 19 were involved in both French and UK companies.

The broad features of the business elites of France and the UK in 1998 can be seen in Table 1.1. The French elite is somewhat larger that the British as a consequence of the peculiarities of the system of corporate

governance in operation in that country. What is most striking, however, is
the extent of male domination in both countries. Taking the elite groups as
a whole, women made up barely one-in-twenty of the total in either
France or the UK, and the situation is even more pronounced when the top
100 directors in either country are considered (see Chapter 5).

The collective biography presented in this book offers not just a syn-
chronic snapshot at a particular point of time, but also a diachronic
exploration over time, emphasising duration while seeking to avoid the
'pitfalls of purely statistical studies of social groups'.[17] We have undertaken studies of the social backgrounds and careers of members of the
business elite and have tracked developments with respect to top 100
companies and top 100 individuals between 1998 and 2003 (and in some
cases beyond). By retracing individual destinies in the context of networks, interest groups, and ideological and educational solidarity, this
prosopographical study is also longitudinal, allowing us 'to integrate the
individual and the event into social history'.[18] Numerous questions may be
addressed. For example, by 2003, which companies retained their independence and position as a leading player? How many had been the object
of a merger? What were the major trends in governance in the two countries – what changed and what remained constant? Likewise, what happened to the directorial cohorts of 1998 – how many people stayed and
how many moved on? What happens to elite executive directors when
they leave a top 100 company? Above all, the database allows privileged
insights into the cohesion and integration of French and British business
networks as they confront the new global economy, at the dawn of the
third millennium. Ezra Suleiman suggests that such networks may prove
to be sufficiently robust to withstand globalisation; particularly the close-
knit business networks typical of France, compared to which British 'old
boy' and American 'ivy league' networks are dismissed as 'a joke'.[19] The
database provides 'hard evidence' for such relationships and networks,
with some startling results (see Chapter 6).

Numerous quantitative analyses are supported by the database relating
to corporate governance as well as to members of the business elite. The
top 100 companies in each country are profiled with respect to their
governance characteristics. For example, have they introduced an audit
and remuneration committee, as recommended by the Cadbury and Viénot
Reports, or a nomination committee, seen as useful but less essential?
Does board membership confirm the continuation of reciprocal mandates,
a longstanding feature of French business? Is the situation in Britain really
that different, or are what seem on the surface to be distinctive national
traditions merely reflective of small differences in institutional arrange-

ments? Differing and changing perceptions of independence in France and Britain are also explored. Can the independence of non-executive directors be audited and certified, as the former investment banker Derek Higgs, author of the government-sponsored Higgs Review, maintains?[20] Or is it essentially all to do with the individual and his or her capacity to exercise sound judgment, 'a matter of attitude and wallet and nothing else'?[21]

The second main element of our research is qualitative and founded on a series of in-depth interviews with governance experts and prominent members of both national elites. These semi-structured interviews were envisaged as enriching 'encounters' between informants and interviewer, raising questions and issues more fundamental than those typically of interest to journalists and shareholders.[22] Interviewees included PDG, Chairmen and CEOs, and directors of leading French and British companies, such as Air Liquide, Alstom, L'Oréal, HBOS, IBM (UK) and British Airways, as well as Lord Waldegrave, a former Cabinet Minister and now a City-based managing director of the European investment bank, UBS. They included the directors of leading European or international companies prominent in France and Britain, such as Airbus and Euronext, the company formed by the merger of the Paris Bourse with the Dutch and Belgian stock exchanges in 2000, and Bombardier, a world leader in transportation engineering, one of Alstom's main competitors. Leading experts in corporate governance also participated in the study. These included Sir Adrian Cadbury, author of the Cadbury Report, generally recognised as the 'founding father' of corporate governance in the UK and elsewhere, and Senator Philippe Marini, author of the 1996 Marini Report.[23] Other interviewees in the UK include the Directors General of the Institute of Directors (IoD) and the Confederation of British Industry (CBI), and in France directors at the Mouvement des Entreprises de France (MEDEF)[24] and the Commissariat Général du Plan.

The effort and commitment required of participants was not negligible, not least in giving at least an hour of their time and often much more. In-depth interviews, described by Burgess as 'conversations with a purpose', can be demanding of interviewees who are brought to reflect on aspects of their lives, careers and motivation – which some directors may not be used to.[25] Bourdieu writes, however, of the '*joy of expression*' that interviewees may experience, as well as the opportunity '*to explain themselves* (in the most complete sense of the term) that is, to construct their own point of view both on themselves and on the world and fully to delineate the vantage point within this world from which they see themselves and the world'.[26] As a consequence, interviews that may have been time-limited in advance often exceeded their allotted time. Bourdieu also comments on the need for the interviewer to participate actively and engage with the interviewee, 'to "acknowledge reception" ... or to show interest and to offer agreement with certain points of view'.[27] He contrasts this type of maieutics with the sterile, purportedly neutral approach adopted in opinion polls or questionnaires, which he sees as serving 'to *impose* a problematic': far from being neutral in their effect, they hijack opinions and give them social existence.[28] The need for a more participative style on the part of the interviewer is underscored by the fact that the interviewees in the current study are elite members, for whom it is inappropriate to apply a stock 'stimulus-response' mode of questioning, a point made by Kadushin in his study of the French financial elite in the mid-1990s. 'Interviews with elites', he observes, 'can never follow a strict "stimulus-response" model that assumes the validity of responses depends on exact adherence to the verbatim text of a question. Elites often demand an interpretation of the question and a certain conversational style'.[29] The rewards, however, certainly repay the efforts. The interview data presented in this study complement the data drawn from other sources and have enabled the authors to drill down and explain some of the features and patterns revealed through the database-centred quantitative study.

Corporate governance in comparative perspective

This is not the place to consider in detail the economic and business structures of France and the UK. However, the basis of any comparative study requires some explanation, and equally it is important to establish an appropriate context for subsequent analysis. Why select France and the UK as the two national jurisdictions for a cross-national study of corporate governance? The answer comes in three parts. First, the justification of any comparative study in the social sciences is that through a process of systematically comparing and contrasting the characteristics of two or more systems or entities, we come to see patterns and processes in sharper relief, opening up the possibility of generalisation and the identification of key explanatory variables. The requirement is that the entities being compared fall within the same broad category or type, as there is little point in comparing entities that are so radically different as to make the exercise trivial. France and the UK plainly satisfy this requirement. Both have mature capitalist economies operating within sophisticated legal and democratic political systems. They have evolved in tandem over a long period, and since the onset of industrialisation in the eighteenth century both countries have experienced sustained though not revolutionary periods of economic growth and structural change, punctuated by the same major wars and similar ideological struggles. This commonality within the broad sweep of history, set against enduring cultural, governmental and social differences, has for long excited the interest of comparative social scientists.

The second point to make is that the present similarities in size and structure between the French and UK economic and business systems are pronounced, making the two countries natural choices for a two-way cross-national study of business elites and corporate governance, which is made all the more enticing by the physical proximity and enduring cultural and political rivalry of the two countries. Table 1.2 makes the point simply and eloquently: France and the UK, both leading economic powers and closely integrated within the international economy, have near equal populations, national incomes, and standards of living, as measured by gross domestic product (GDP) per capita.

Table 1.2   Comparative economic indicators for France and the UK, 2003

	France	**UK**
Population (million)	59.6	59.2
Gross Domestic Product (US$ billion)	1,764	1,795
Gross Domestic Product per Head (US$)	29,294	29,795

Note: At current prices.
Source: Economist Intelligence Unit, *France Country Profile 2004* and *UK Country Profile 2004*.

The comparison becomes all the more alluring when attention is turned from broad economic aggregates to a consideration of the characteristics of the corporate economies of the two countries. The numbers presented in Table 1.3 bear testimony to the outcome of a long period of corporate growth – partly organic and partly through mergers and acquisitions – that began prior to the Second World War and has continued since, driven by the pursuit of economies of scale and scope. Again, a number of striking similarities emerge. The top 100 companies in France and the UK respectively employ, on average, very similar numbers of people and have similar levels of turnover. Even the figures for total capital employed are broadly comparable, although the capitalisation of French companies is far more varied than that of their UK counterparts. Only with respect to pre-tax profit are there manifest differences between France and the UK, with UK companies ostensibly far more profitable. This intriguing difference may be explained on the one hand by the extraordinarily high profitability of the British financial sector, which distorts the picture to some degree, and on the other hand by the greater pressures faced by UK business leaders to deliver immediate returns for shareholders. French business is marked, in contrast, by a wider stakeholder approach, a belief in the 'social interest' of the firm: that the firm exists also for the good of its employees and the community, as well as for the benefit of owners and shareholders. On balance, however, the impression gained from Table 1.3 is one of level pegging between the top 100 companies in France and the UK in 1998 at the start of our study period.

Table 1.3 Indicators of size of top 100 French and UK companies in 1998

		French Companies	UK Companies
Total Capital Employed (M€)	Median	4,562	4,890
	Mean	9,298	7,236
	Standard deviation	15,783	7,258
Turnover (M€)	Median	4,562	5,552
	Mean	8,507	8,906
	Standard deviation	9,465	10,305
Pre-Tax Profit (M€)	Median	106	701
	Mean	254	1,156
	Standard deviation	480	1,299
Employees (No.)	Median	22,572	37,098
	Mean	45,065	46,089
	Standard deviation	54,061	41,813

Notes: Complete data series exist for UK companies, and for French companies for turnover and employees. Data are available for total capital employed for 84 French companies and for pre-tax profit for 86 French companies.

The third point to make with respect to the selection of France and the UK as comparator nations is that while there may be similarities between their economic and business systems, on closer inspection these similarities can be seen to conceal equally striking and deep-seated structural differences. Table 1.4 emphatically confirms this point.

Table 1.4 Distribution of corporate power by industry group amongst top 100 French and UK companies in 1998

Industry Group	No.	France % Share of Corporate Power	No.	UK % Share of Corporate Power
Construction	3	1.96	0	0.00
Financial Services	2	4.87	19	23.47
Food and Drink	12	4.49	10	8.64
IT and Business Services	6	1.45	3	1.77
Manufacturing	28	26.98	15	13.46
Media, Consumer Services and Products	9	6.68	11	9.91
Oil and Gas, Mining and Materials	14	13.35	9	16.55
Retailing	15	14.81	11	9.92
Transport and Distribution Services	5	5.51	7	4.71
Utilities and Telecommunications	6	19.91	15	11.58
	100	**100.00**	**100**	**100.00**

Note: See Appendix 1 for details of the definition and estimation of corporate power.

There are many fascinating insights to emerge from this analysis, which highlights differences in the distribution of corporate power in the two countries. For present purposes, however, it is sufficient to highlight three issues. First, it is clear that large manufacturing companies have been better placed in France than in Britain to survive the challenges of heightened international competition. Witness for example the contrast between the collapse of the British-owned motor vehicle industry and the continued success of the French manufacturers, Renault and PSA Peugeot Citroën. France is the second-largest manufacturer of motor vehicles in Europe, and fourth in the world. The automotive sector accounts for almost 7 per cent of French GDP, and employs 300,000 people, producing some 3.64 million vehicles in 2002.[30] Another telling example is provided by the Queen Mary 2, Cunard's state-of-the-art luxury cruise liner. This flies the British red ensign, but was built in France at St. Nazaire by Alstom, despite the UK's long seafaring tradition, with historic docks on Clydeside, Tyneside, and in Belfast. Secondly, the weight and significance of the financial services sector within the corporate economy of Britain finds no counterpart in France. Thirdly, the rise of French utility companies from bread-and-butter domestic businesses to acquisitive multinational enterprises such as Electricité de France (EdF) is confirmed by their command of a large share of corporate power, almost 20 per cent, which is not matched in Britain. What is plain is that the corporate economies of France and the UK have evolved along very different lines, resulting in different national structures, trajectories and priorities. One of the main aims of this book it to explore how and to what extent such differences can be explained with reference to the functioning of business elites and corporate governance in the two countries.

Corporate governance, accountability and society

Since the Cadbury and Viénot Reports, companies have included explicit discussion of corporate governance in their annual reports and accounts, a condition of their continued listing in the UK since 1993, on the basis that companies should comply or explain. Leading French companies are increasingly listed on the London Stock Exchange (LSE) – seven by the year 2000, Alstom, Danone, Euro-Disney, Lafarge, Saint-Gobain, Thomson CSF (now Thales) and TotalFinaElf[31] – and are therefore subject to the same conditions. By comparing the annual reports of 1998 and 2003, we have been able to chart the rise of corporate governance in the top 100 firms of Britain and France over a five-year period. Governance, of course, has existed as a practical reality for as long as there have been companies, as evinced by the novels of Dickens, Balzac and Zola. But as an explicitly discussed topic in annual reports and accounts, we can observe its rise as a relatively recent phenomenon.

What exactly do companies mean by corporate governance in their annual reports? Broadly speaking, they focus on how the board operates and functions, how it is managed, and how it communicates with shareholders. This approach, while frequently revealing, is essentially one of conforming to regulatory standards or prevailing stakeholder expectations. In this study, we go beyond these confines, following in the academic tradition beginning with Berle and Means, to consider matters relating to the location and exercise of power and authority, examining corporate governance as a genuine social phenomenon.

Ever since companies grew large enough to warrant the appointment of salaried managers to run them, bringing about a separation of ownership and control, problems of governance potentially have existed. In brief:

The inability of the financier to observe the behaviour of managers gives rise to the problem of moral hazard. Managers may divert resources to their own personal ends, and, as Adam Smith expressed it, look with less 'anxious vigilance' over the shareholders' wealth than they would do over their own.[32]

The 'managerial revolution' observed by Berle and Means in the US in 1929, caused by a growing dispersal in shareholdings, was deemed to be incomplete due to the continuing influence exerted in the boardroom by minority shareholders, often relatives of the founding entrepreneurs.[33] As share ownership became increasingly dispersed, so, it was argued, would the divorce of ownership and control near completion, allowing managers to act unchecked. Principal-and-agent issues may arise, with executives able to substitute their own managerial goals for the profit-maximising goals of company owners,[34] leading in turn to a potential abuse of power to the benefit of managers, no longer acting in the best interests of owners or employees. Agency theory places the board at the centre of corporate governance, serving as a means of monitoring corporate management (agents) and holding it accountable to shareholders (principals).[35]

Agency theory, while highlighting a fundamental problem of corporate governance, is not sufficient as a theoretical apparatus for our purposes. Three main limitations are apparent. In the first place, agency theory, predicated on the assumption that both principals and agents are self-serving, does not confront the social realities of the boardroom or the milieu in which business leaders operate. The perspective is narrow and correspondingly the motivations of individual actors and the dynamics of real-time decision making are ignored.[36] Secondly, ownership and control are not sharply separated in many companies and national business systems. In France, for example, we can observe the continuation down to the present of extensive family and state ownership, in contrast to the UK. Thirdly, many governance crises stem not from conflicts between rational actors but from deficient boardroom cultures and practices. Indeed, the potential for abuse or recklessness on the part of top management in large corporations has been confirmed in recent years by a succession of business scandals, making investors and other stakeholders much more sensitive to the significance of what, for them, is at stake. Business elites, by virtue of their command over vast resources, have the power both to create and to destroy value on an unprecedented scale. A badly thought out mega-merger, for example, in which an acquirer pays a high price for asserted but unrealisable synergic gains, can cause the market value of the business to melt away, leaving shareholders, pensioners, employees and governments exposed to the long-term consequences. This phenomenon is a feature of corporate capitalism across the world: big mistakes, whether or not allied with hubris, corruption and deceit, are very difficult to identify from the outside, even by skilled analysts.

In 2000, prior to the collapse of Enron, the management guru Gary Hamel described the energy giant as a 'radical new business model', which had 'achieved the almost magical mix of entrepreneurship with the ability ... to get things done'.[37] In 2002 the company was ranked fifth in the world, according to *Fortune Magazine*, which compiles annual rankings of the top 500 US firms based on revenue. One year later it had disappeared from the list, as indeed had the telecom company WorldCom, in 42nd position in 2002.[38] WorldCom counts as one of the biggest corporate frauds in US history (the firm had improperly recorded $11 billion in its accounts),[39] and Enron as the biggest collapse in corporate history (the company collapsed into bankruptcy with debts exceeding $16.8 billion).

Recognition that management failings are difficult to identify in real time, when they are actually occurring, caused us to study the top 100 French and UK companies over a five-year period from 1998 to 2003. As a general rule, the basic financial structures within well-managed companies tend to be fairly stable, predictable, even within a context of growth. The cost base of such firms is observably well managed, revenues are consistently strong, and profit levels are of an order that enables retention of earnings while paying dividends. A good level of retained earnings is generally the foundation for sustained growth, other than in companies that grow swiftly through acquisition, in which case financial structures are more volatile and difficult to read year-on-year. The many stable, well-managed, financially secure companies in our sample exude a real sense of confidence in their strategy and leadership. They may be moving dynamically into new markets, but there is a sense of confidence that top management has made the right choices. As Collins and Porras demonstrate in *Built to Last*, they are focused and have continuity of purpose.[40] This in turn enables them to inspire the confidence of shareholders and other stakeholders and to develop a positive reputation, which in itself is a major trading strength and source of stability.

A number of companies in our sample had all these characteristics at the beginning of our study period but had lost them by the end, demonstrating in the process that the actions of business elites have a significance fully equivalent to those of more prominent political elites. Vivendi, for example, formerly Compagnie Générale des Eaux, a French water, sewage and general services group in existence for 148 years, and earning almost a billion euros in profit each year (€823 million in 1998, see

Appendix 2), was previously one such company. However, its €30 billion acquisition in December 2000 of Seagram, the Canadian-owned drinks and entertainment group controlled by the Bronfman family, triggered a multibillion shopping spree on the part of its chief executive Jean-Marie Messier. This brought the former giant to the brink of bankruptcy eighteen months later, amid debts of €33 billion.[41] The Bronfman family, which had emerged from the sale of Seagram to Vivendi with a 6 per cent stake in the new group, saw the value of its shares plummet from $5.4 billion to less than $1 billion. The family was subsequently forced to witness the auction of its collection of more than 2,500 works of art, including works by Picasso, Rodin and Rothko, which Vivendi had inherited at the time of the takeover. Phyllis Lambert, daughter of family patriarch Samuel Bronfman, called the sale 'part of a Greek tragedy'.[42]

Value destruction on the scale achieved by Vivendi-Universal has severe consequences for all stakeholders in the business. Most immediately, as financial analysts downgrade their estimates of the worth of the enterprise, shareholders see the value of their investment plummet. This is not just a disaster for super-wealthy families like the Bronfmans. In the UK, pension funds and other institutional investors hold large parts of the equity of top 100 companies on behalf of a multitude of small investors, and, when the market capitalisation of a business crumbles, collective misery ensues. The UK telecommunications and electrical equipment manufacturer Marconi had a market capitalisation of £35 billion in 2000. It had a cash mountain accumulated over decades by the legendary Arnold Weinstock (when the business was still known as General Electric or GEC), but by the end of 2002 the company had lost a staggering 96 per cent of its stock market value.[43] The story here is one of a company embarking on an ill-fated strategy of transformation from old economy company to new era digital technology provider. The losers were not the directors, the people who devised and implemented a strategy that retrospectively seemed naïve; they escaped financially unscathed, while shareholders saw the value of their assets virtually wiped out overnight. An equally spectacular collapse in market value afflicted Alstom, the French engineering giant, following a series of unanticipated events, including the bankruptcy of a major cruise-ship customer, Renaissance, which led to massive contingent liabilities. The share price fell from a high of €34 in January 2001 to less than one euro by March 2003.[44]

Pensioners likewise are frequently victims of the failings of top management. Company pensioners lost an estimated $64 million in the WorldCom accounting scandal. In August 2003, the state of Oklahoma filed charges against the company and six of its former executives, including the former CEO Bernie Evers and former CFO Scott Sullivan, in an effort to make the company and its officers accountable for their actions and thus gain restitution for its citizenry.[45] Pensioners have similarly lost out at Marconi, where huge debts have inevitably devalued promises made to them when the business was financially sound.[46] They were not the victims of corporate fraud – as were the Mirror Group pensioners, defrauded of their pensions by Robert Maxwell (who treated pension funds as company assets to be plundered to bolster other parts of his ailing empire).[47] Rather, they were victims of poor decision making on a monumental scale.

Boardroom decisions may also have far-reaching consequences for employees, who can find themselves out of a job. This is more likely to be the case in Britain, where declaring redundancies is relatively easy, than in France, where workers enjoy far greater employment protection. When Jean-Hugues Loyez, former head of the French company Castorama, resigned in 2002, Kingfisher, which had just won control of the do-it-yourself chain, was forced to pay him as much as £780,000. French employment law dictated the size of the payoff, setting a figure of four times his annual salary.[48] Enron employees fared less well. In 2001 the energy trader employed some 21,000 workers in more than 40 countries.[49] Its collapse left thousands of employees penniless, and resulted in the suicide of a former executive. Marconi's workforce was similarly decimated, falling from 71,763 in 1998 to 14,000 in 2003.[50] In 2003, the future of Alstom's 110,000 employees in 70 countries across the world hung in the balance, as the French government battled to save the ailing giant (see Chapter 3).

Corporate failure on a grand scale also has enduring consequences for government. The collapse of leading firms erodes the tax base of the nation, directly and indirectly: directly through lost corporation tax, and indirectly through taxes on employment which are no longer paid. It has implications, too, for the balance of payments. That this has remained consistently negative in the UK since the early 1980s is a direct consequence of large numbers of foreign exchange generative firms going out of business each year. In December 2004, Britain's trade deficit reached record levels, as did government borrowing. In other words, the bottom line is that the behaviour of business elites, through the way in which they exercise power and authority, affects us all. The collapse of a company the size of Alstom would have serious consequences in and beyond France. Business elites are integral to the operation of modern capitalist societies, and their impacts are numerous and generalised.

Why, then, is it only in quite recent times that people have started talking about governance? Why has it become such a phenomenon and such a hot topic? The answer lies in the extraordinary concentration of economic power we are witnessing today. It lies in the fact that these companies have become very big and very conspicuous, through merger and acquisition and through organic growth. The larger and more conspicuous they become, the clearer it is that they touch all our lives. Secondly, as we have become increasingly aware of how much power top business people wield, and how their actions impact upon us in myriad ways, we have not always liked what we have seen. We have witnessed extraordinary greed, 'fat cat' style remuneration through inflated executive salaries and lucrative stock options, even when companies have performed badly. The public does not like the rashness of the Enrons, Marconis or Vivendis, or the apparent rapacity of executives such as Philippe Jaffré, PDG of Elf, seen to have profited handsomely through stock options when Elf was taken over by TotalFina SA in 1999.[51] Such behaviour seems neither to be inspired by a humanistic concern for fellow man nor by a sustainable business strategy. On the contrary, it appears in these extreme cases to be driven by the greed and personal ambition of powerful individuals. In the UK, an enduring image of such greed was provided by Cedric the pig, brought to the 1995 British Gas annual general meeting (AGM) as the mascot for protesting small investors, outraged at CEO Cedric Brown's 71 per cent pay rise despite poor company performance. Cedric has become a lasting symbol of executive 'snouts in the trough'. At the time, it tended to be the unions who expressed concern over 'fat cat' pay. Large investors chose to ignore the noisy row at British Gas. Now, however, the City is increasingly concerned to ensure that high remuneration packages should reward good performance. Shareholders have the right to vote on directors' pay, and they are increasingly using it, as companies such as Royal & Sun Alliance, Reuters, Granada, Barclays and Corus learned in the 2003 round of AGMs.[52]

Matters reached a head in May 2003 at the AGM of GlaxoSmithKline, the world's second largest drugs company (the product of a mega-merger between Glaxo Wellcome and SmithKline Beecham).[53] Here, the company suffered a humiliating defeat at the hands of investors, who successfully foiled a resolution by the board to award CEO Jean-Pierre Garnier a massive $24 million (£15 million) payout in the event of his losing his job.[54] A 'golden parachute' of such magnitude would be reward for failure on an unprecedented scale. Anti-establishment protestors were quick to point out that such a sum could pay for a year's treatment for 100,000 HIV victims with Retrovir, the company's drug that postpones the onset of AIDS.[55] However, outrage was not confined to corporate outsiders. Peter

Montagnon, head of investment affairs at the Association of British Insurers (ABI) argued that 'Pay-offs as large as this ... are liable to do grave damage to the reputation of companies which pay them and undermine the ability of companies to give fair rewards for performance'.[56] The board of GlaxoSmithKline was forced on this occasion to climb down,[57] appointing Deloitte & Touche to review its remuneration policy. The vote had been a narrow one, with a tiny majority of 50.7 per cent of investors voting against the company's pay policy, while institutional investors abstained in vast numbers. This has led the UK Department of Trade and Industry (DTI) to consider outlawing abstentions, as part of its general reform of governance practices.[58]

In short, the general public sees such behaviour as an abuse of the power and trust granted to the senior officers of major companies. It explains why annual reports and accounts are used to convey a sense of openness and sound governance procedures. The message from directors is clear: we follow the rules and we do things properly here. Such statements are an assertion and proclamation of legitimacy. There may be a regulatory requirement to comply with codes of corporate governance, but nowadays companies feel the need to do more to reassure existing and potential investors that the value of their investment will not be destroyed either through ineptitude or mendacity. Institutional investors in particular have begun to take a more proactive role in ensuring that companies are well managed and that the highest standards of governance apply. Collective pressures, normative 'isomorphism', the tendency of one organisation to follow the lead of another, have thus proved to a major force for change in corporate governance in both France and the UK.[59]

The book in brief

This chapter has sought to set the scene for what follows by exploring the importance of corporate governance as a rising social phenomenon of the twenty-first century, and exploring the links between corporate governance on the one hand and business elites on the other. The dual methodology underpinning the book has been explained. Chapter 2 builds upon this foundation. It takes the form of an in-depth review of the theoretical and empirical literatures on business elites. Our analytical approach and theoretical framework are explained, and the nature and sources of elite power and authority are explored with reference to the concepts deployed by Bourdieu, Foucault and others.

Chapter 3 is essentially historical and comparative in nature, looking back at the evolution of corporate governance in Britain and France since

1945. As such, it is concerned with the economic, business, political and cultural history of Britain and France in the post-war era. Included in the discussion is an exposition of the dimensions of the French and British national business systems.[60]

Chapter 4 focuses on the education of business executives in the two countries, comparing and contrasting the ways in which elites are recruited and trained. Education clearly holds one of the keys to the reproduction, and hence the stability, of business elites. This chapter lays bare the stratification in education systems on both sides of the Channel, which reinforces elite solidarity while justifying the maintenance of the elite at the pinnacle of society. It considers pressures to create an 'Ivy League' style elite of top-ranking universities in the UK, the so-called 'Russell Group'. This situation is not unlike that which obtains in France, where universities are *de facto* second-class citizens to the elite cohort of leading *grandes écoles.*

Chapter 5 focuses on the interface between elite careers and lifestyles, examining such matters as career patterns and types, formative experiences, elite bonding and solidarity, honours, rewards and motivation. We consider what it takes to make a high-flying career and entry into what we call 'the field of power', wherein members of the business elite mingle freely, as equals, with elite individuals from other fields such as politics, the law, education, and culture. The chapter includes discussion of the roles and representation of women in the boardroom in both countries.

Chapter 6 examines business networks, aiming to bridge the discussion between business elites and corporate governance. It goes to the heart of how national business systems really work by deploying the methods of social network analysis. Social and cultural institutions are theorised as meeting places wherein actors create the capacity to mobilise power and systemic pressure. The chapter includes a discussion of the critical role played by the state, which particularly in France acts as a lynchpin, and shows how power is exercised, channelled and constrained in both countries.

Chapter 7 broadens the discussion to examine national business systems and corporate governance against the backdrop of the global economy. The concluding chapter reviews and reconsiders the main arguments and issues raised in the book, and aims to provide a challenging and definitive interpretation of the different ways in which power and authority are exercised across business and political networks in France and the UK. Against the backdrop of the evidence presented in the book, we offer some final thoughts on big issues of the day such as business regulation, ethical leadership, and executive pay.

Conclusion

There are difficulties inherent in any cross-national study in the social sciences, and the present study is no exception. Common and logically grounded categories are required for comparisons to be valid and meaningful, but this is not always a simple matter when the categories themselves relate to disparate systems replete with different emphases and meanings. It follows that gathering truly comparable data is often problematic. In our case, the standardised nature of corporate reporting in the UK meant that creating a consistent and complete data set was a relatively simple matter, but the same was not true for France, where for many companies we had a long, arduous and not always entirely successful search to locate the required data. What kept us going in the search was the prospect of understanding more about the role played by business elites and corporate governance in the functioning of two distinct national business systems. Both the French and UK systems are to some degree path dependent, creatures of their own making, and prone to self-reproduction. Yet in each case the old order must confront the challenges of the new global age, while at the same time protecting its own interests. The outcome of this battle royal is not easy to predict. What we do know is that the actions and activities of business elites of both countries will be fundamental to national economic performance. Effective governance has become a *sine qua non* for continued faith in the competence and integrity of our corporate elites.

2
Theoretical Perspectives on Business Elites and Corporate Governance

'Every real inquiry into the divisions of the social world has to analyse the interests associated with membership or non-membership'.

Pierre Bourdieu[1]

This chapter examines the main theoretical ideas that underpin the analysis and discussion that follows in the remainder of the book. We draw extensively on the writings of numerous authors, notably Foucault, Bourdieu, Scott and Granovetter, and present our own theoretical perspectives on business elites and corporate governance.

In their examination of the workings of power and authority in the modern world, both Bourdieu and Foucault are equally illuminating. Both are concerned with the practices and mechanisms of domination, the 'polymorphous techniques of power', as Foucault put it, which abound in human living.[2] One of Foucault's key contributions to the debate on power and authority in the modern age was to recognise that 'modernity does its work in the micro-physics of daily life'.[3] In *Discipline and Punish* in particular, he explores the disguise of power through apparently neutral institutions whose control mechanisms are internalised by the individuals they seek to dominate.[4] The symbolic 'Panopticon' moves imperceptibly inside the individual, where it continues its work, unseen, its physical manifestation, the all-seeing watch-tower, now superfluous.[5] Unlike Foucault, however, whose natural preserve is the autonomous and transcendent system, whether of language, knowledge or the science of sexuality, Bourdieu's 'reflexive sociology' is grounded in reality, consistently geared to actual social spheres – of elite schools and the state, or academia, or cultural taste and distinction.[6]

One danger in building upon the theoretical foundations laid by Bourdieu is that his conceptual apparatus is grounded in predominantly French social spaces and realities. To apply his conceptual tools within a British or international context might be viewed as problematic. Bourdieu himself points to the dangers inherent in exporting his ideas into different social settings. His ideas, he fears, 'have little chance of being grasped without distortion or deformation', being ripped 'from the constellation of which they are but elements'.[7] There is, as Tournier claims, 'no translation without alteration'.[8] Our view, however, is that the work of Bourdieu, as it moves from empiricism, to theory and self-reflexivity, proceeding by trial and error, and purporting to create conceptual tools through *bricolage* as opposed to a Foucauldian grand theory,[9] lends itself in particular to comparative research despite its apparent cultural specificity. In this we follow Scott, who has called for more comparative studies to reinvigorate the debate over management control, pointing out that research on relations between firms has been slower to develop in Europe than in the US.[10]

The remainder of this chapter is organised around five main questions. First, we ask, what are the main qualities and characteristics of membership of elite groups generally and of business elites in particular? Secondly, what is the special role played by members of business elites that legitimises the high levels of power, status and reward accorded to them? Thirdly, how does someone acquire and demonstrate the capabilities and behavioural qualities that single them out for recruitment to an elite business group? Fourthly, how do business elites reproduce and regenerate themselves when their membership, at the individual level, is constantly changing? Finally, what is the relationship between elite business groups and the mechanisms, processes and codes that make up a modern corporate governance regime?

Bourdieu, social stratification and business elites

The writings of Bourdieu are marked, like those of Foucault,[11] by a tendency to perceive binary oppositions in all aspects and strata of social life, populated by dominant or subordinated agents. Oppositions such as masculine/feminine, noble/common, inheritors/parvenus, old/young, white/black, operate as underlying cognitive structures. The initial act of cognition, however, is essentially one of *mis*-recognition, recognition of an order that exists also in the mind.[12] Nobility exists, for example, for and by those nobles or commoners who are able to perceive and to recognise it, due to their situatedness in a world organised according to such structuring principles.[13] Here, the influence of structuralism is detectable in Bourdieu's work, at the centre of which lies the sacred/profane dualism articulated by Durkheim, though it lacks, perhaps, the grey areas of uncertainty in human agency which exist between the realms of possibility and impossibility, outside the dichotomous binary order conceived by Bourdieu.[14]

All symbolic systems – whether culture or language – are sources of domination, helping to fix and preserve social hierarchies. Bourdieu shares Foucault's view that power is exercised from innumerable points, and that it is inherent in other types of relationship, such as economic processes. Both agree that power comes not only from above but is also supported from below, so that power depends on those who bear its effects, on rulers and ruled in equal measure.[15] The relationally embedded nature of power, however, causes it to be misunderstood by those held in its grip, as Bourdieu explains:

> Without turning power into a 'circle whose centre is everywhere and nowhere', which could be to dissolve it in yet another way, we have to be able to discover it in places where it is least visible, where it is most completely misrecognized – and thus, in fact, recognized. For symbolic power is that invisible power which can be exercised only with the complicity of those who do not want to know that they are subject to it or even that they themselves exercise it.[16]

Bourdieu is perhaps particularly well qualified to speak for both dominant and dominated categories, having experienced the 'habitus' or 'life world' of both in his career: from provincial, lower-middle-class social origins, he ascended to the apex of the academic pyramid.[17] Born in 1930 in the Béarn region of South-Western France, the son of a farmer turned postman, Bourdieu proved to be an industrious, able pupil, eventually entering the prestigious Ecole Normale Supérieure (ENS) in the rue d'Ulm in Paris. This, the most academic of the Parisian *grandes écoles*, had a policy of opening its doors to a small number of academically gifted recruits (including Georges Pompidou, who overcame his peasant origins to become President of France).[18] The ENS has served over the years as a breeding ground for French intellectuals, including as former students Althusser, Bergson, Deleuze, Derrida, Durkheim, Foucault, Jaurès, Lévi-Strauss, Merleau-Ponty, Nizan, Sartre and Touraine. Here, however, lacking the social and cultural capital of his peers, Bourdieu was made to feel an outsider. Set apart by his provincial origins, denied the 'unselfconscious belonging of those born to wealth, cultural pedigree and elite accents',[19] he saw himself as a frustrated 'oblate'.[20] This experience of alienation instilled in him a desire for revenge against the institutions to which he owed his success, angered by the gulf between their professed ideals and ingrained prejudice against the lower classes.[21] He criticised their role as institutions of social reproduction[22] – indeed, it was as a 'crisis of reproduction' that he viewed the events of May 1968.[23] In particular, he objected to the university mandarins who determined the curriculum and did little empirical research while acting as gatekeepers to aspiring academics by controlling access to the higher echelons of academe.[24]

After graduation in 1951, Bourdieu began teaching in a *lycée* outside Paris, and in 1955 he was sent to do military service in Algeria. Here, finding that the agrarian society of Kabylia had much in common with the peasant community of Béarn, he began social scientific research as a self-taught ethnographer, an experience which later informed his thinking on issues of social domination.[25] Opposed to the French war in Algeria, he left and took up sociology, which at the time enjoyed little prestige and academic recognition in French universities. But this also presented Bourdieu with the freedom to elaborate his own theories and research methods. He went on to found his own academic *avant-garde*, creating a school, a Centre for European Sociology and, in 1975, a journal to promote his own brand of sociology – theoretical, yet empirically researched.[26] In 1981, his academic achievements were crowned by his election to the Chair of Sociology at the Collège de France, joining the ranks of Raymond Aron and Claude Lévi-Strauss. In the 1990s, having established his position at the pinnacle of French intellectual life, his international renown spread, facilitated by the translation into English of a growing number of his major works, and by regular visits to the US, Japan and elsewhere in Europe. He was extraordinarily prolific in the course of his career, publishing over 30 books and 350 articles by the time of his death at the age of 71 in January 2002. His body is interred in the prestigious Père Lachaise Cemetery in North-East Paris, alongside writers Marcel Proust and Oscar Wilde, singers Edith Piaf and Jim Morrison, composers Bizet and Chopin, and artists Delacroix and Modigliani – a prodigious achievement for the provincial boy from Béarn. Only the Panthéon confers greater honour.

Bourdieu's dual status as outsider-insider is a further point in common with Foucault, both being provincial outsiders excluded from the Parisian social elite, their writing imbued with an anti-institutional *esprit de critique*.[27] The Collège de France is a highly prestigious institution, but it is arguably marginal, not mainstream. Bourdieu's status as outsider within the academic community was underlined by the fact that he lacked a *doctorat d'Etat*, the fundamental qualification for a university chair, which meant that his career lacked one vital element of state-conferred legitimacy and personal distinction: he could not, for example, preside over a committee for the *soutenance* (viva voce) of a doctoral thesis. This absence of an exemplary manifestation of symbolic capital must have stung Bourdieu, for whom the state is the key instigator of symbolic violence in society partly because of its power to *name*, to confer upon an individual or group 'its social titles of recognition (academic or occupational in particular)'.[28]

Bourdieu's personal history, experience and feelings were fundamental to his interpretation of the social processes that order society.[29] The field concept is pivotal to his thinking. Modern society is portrayed as highly differentiated and stratified,[30] characterised by specialisation and the progressive splitting of fields into sub-fields, resulting in an order characterised by a complex web of interweaving fields, 'differentiated social microcosms operating as spaces of objective forces and arenas of struggle … which refract and transmute external determinations and interests'.[31] Fields do not have hard and fast boundaries but are defined relationally, one to another, within a nested configuration. The field of art, for example, can be divided into numerous sub-fields such as fine art and decorative art, which in turn may be divided and sub-divided.[32] Boundaries between fields are permeable, but within fields there exists a degree of autonomy from the external environment. There is tacit acceptance by actors – whether institutions, organisations, groups or individuals – of the rules of competitive engagement within the field. There are numerous lines of power linking actors within what Bourdieu views as a hierarchically stratified space of dominant and subordinate positions.

This view of society, at once divided vertically into fields and sub-fields and horizontally into social strata, is illustrated in Figure 2.1 with reference to the field of medicine. When viewed vertically, the field divides into specialisms such as cardiology, orthopaedics, urology and oncology. A legal, professional and institutional framework supports the medical field as a whole, and professional autonomy is maintained within recognised sub-fields by means of specialist professional organisations, journals, conferences and learned societies. Authority as a doctor stems from the professional fluency achieved through mastery of the life-worlds of field and sub-field, not simply accredited technical proficiency. When viewed horizontally, the field divides into three main strata – doctors at the top, nurses in the middle, and support workers at the bottom – delineated by field boundaries that cannot be infringed: nurses cannot become doctors.

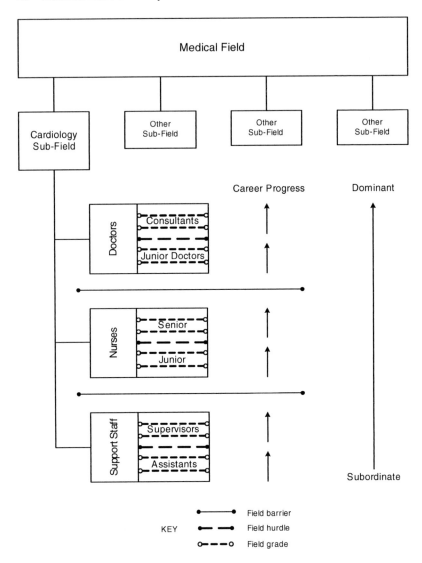

Figure 2.1 The stratification of fields exemplified

Within the main strata there are sub-strata marked by field hurdles that an actor must overcome in order to progress to higher positions, and also field grades that denote seniority. Membership of elite groups within the field of medicine comes with the highest level of financial reward, the exercise of leadership within professional bodies and medical organisations, command over extensive resources, and the award of major state and professional honours. Stratification arises in the medical field, as in all fields, because actors possess different amounts of capital. Members of the elite within any field are capital rich and can apply this in a variety of ways to maintain their dominant position. In this way, they reap the rewards of capital accumulation, control, legitimacy and distinction. One of Bourdieu's main contributions to contemporary sociological thought is the identification of four types of capital, the possession of which is the ultimate source of power in society, as illustrated in Figure 2.2.

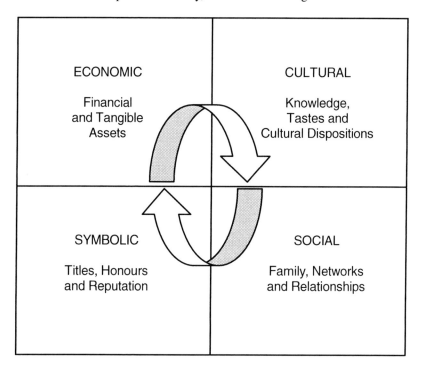

ECONOMIC

Financial
and Tangible
Assets

CULTURAL

Knowledge,
Tastes and
Cultural Dispositions

SYMBOLIC

Titles, Honours
and Reputation

SOCIAL

Family, Networks
and Relationships

Figure 2.2 Bourdieu's four types of capital

Economic capital, in its various guises, is the main source of power and basis of stratification within industries. In contrast, at the other end of the spectrum, cultural capital is the predominant source of power and distinction within the intellectual field, which embraces the arts, literature and education. Cultural capital, the practical command of knowledge domains, may be acquired formally through education but equally may be assimilated through personal experience. Thus, children from the upper classes have their life chances enhanced through regular involvement in culturally rich activities.[33] They also have access through family and friends to social capital, relationships that are frequently instrumental to success in professions such as law and medicine, which stand mid-spectrum between the economic and intellectual master fields.

It follows that domination within any field or sub-field is contingent on possession of the right quantities and combinations of economic, cultural and social capital. To some degree, each of these is transmutable, because economic capital, which Bourdieu considers the dominant form, can be used within limits to purchase cultural and social capital, and in like manner possession of the latter may lead to the accumulation of economic capital. In all fields, legitimacy, the acceptance of domination by the subordinated, is signified by possession of a fourth kind of capital, symbolic capital, in the form of possessions, qualifications, titles, honours and such like. This Bourdieu summarises as 'the capital of recognition accumulated in the course of the whole history of prior struggles (thus very strongly correlated to seniority), that enables one to intervene effectively in current struggles for the conservation or augmentation of symbolic capital'.[34] The historical context of power struggles is important, informing current dynamics and moulding the present context for power and influence.[35]

In business only a small minority of people enjoys the distinction of recruitment into the elite: elevation to the board of a top 100 company is coveted by the many but achieved by the few. Appointment to the board brings with it, individually (for executives) and collectively (for executives and non-executives), tremendous power by virtue of the company's command over extensive resources. Large corporations are the dominant actors, nationally and internationally, within the economic field and its innumerable sub-fields (industries and the divisions and sub-divisions within them). Business leaders might not recognise the value of Bourdieu's theory of capital at first sight, but when translated into the more familiar terminology applied in Figure 2.3 the relevance of the core ideas to their direct experience becomes readily apparent.

The top 100 companies of Britain and France command very extensive resources. Many have assets valued in billions of euros and employ tens of thousands of people (see Appendix 2, Tables A.2.1 and A.2.2). Their assets can be divided into four distinct types, broadly equivalent to the classification suggested by Bourdieu. The tangible, most visible, assets of a business are its systems and facilities, which in turn are an outward expression of its capacity to organise activities and routinely execute large numbers of transactions. Without tried and tested routines and physical infrastructure, a company cannot prosper.

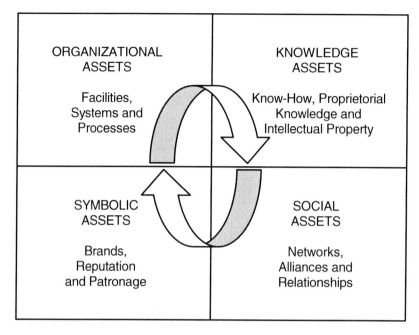

ORGANIZATIONAL ASSETS	KNOWLEDGE ASSETS
Facilities, Systems and Processes	Know-How, Proprietorial Knowledge and Intellectual Property
SYMBOLIC ASSETS	SOCIAL ASSETS
Brands, Reputation and Patronage	Networks, Alliances and Relationships

Figure 2.3 Capital transformation in business

Equally, however, domination of markets, whether at home or internationally, depends on the possession of large amounts of other forms of capital. Pharmaceutical and other high technology companies are founded on their ownership of intellectual property rights, accumulated through heavy investment in research and development. Know-how, in systemic and process terms, likewise requires investment to create the capabilities needed to retain a commanding position in highly competitive markets. This applies just as much to low technology firms like the internationally expansive French food preparation and catering empire, Sodexho, as to a mass car manufacturer like Renault. Sodexho is an example of a business that depends crucially on the quality of its networks and alliances to win contracts across the world: the company has operations in 70 countries, and achieves 80 per cent of its turnover outside France.[36] Such networks and alliances are a form of social capital just as much as the privileged relationships many French firms enjoy with the state, the significance of which is demonstrated by the preparedness of government to rescue ailing businesses like Alstom. Finally, the trading strength of all top companies depends to a greater or lesser extent on the possession of symbolic capital in the form of brand and reputation.

The power wielded by corporate elites is a function of command over corporate resources, over the organisational, knowledge, social and symbolic assets of the business. Financial assets – cash and near cash resources – are depicted as arrows in Figure 2.3. Cash is generated through the deployment of organisational, knowledge, social and symbolic assets, and in turn the business invests in each of these for the purposes of regeneration and development. Companies are forever transforming themselves in this way, and the primary role of a board of directors is to devise and implement strategies that will lead to capital growth, strengthening the business and creating value by distributing surplus funds and increasing its share price. This is a far from static process. Enacting a strategy involves numerous moves, the deployment of resources, the creation of new capabilities, and the transformation of one form of capital into another on a continuing basis. The acid test of any corporate elite is how well it manages this dynamic process, as measured by value created or value destroyed.

What, then, qualifies someone for membership of the corporate elite within a top 100 company in France or the UK? The answer, simply, is that the candidate must have already accumulated a sufficiently high level of personal economic, cultural, social and symbolic capital to warrant appointment to the board of a major company. Discussions amongst existing members of the elite, in nomination committees or with top head-hunters, may not always follow an exacting methodology, but they do ask the right questions and set exacting standards. These questions relate to track record, relevant knowledge and experience, personal qualities, connections in and beyond business, and personal reputation and standing. Whatever the particular strengths of an individual appointed to a top 100 company board, they must already have achieved an appropriately high level of distinction within their field, and the personal dispositions and behaviours needed to function effectively alongside others in a strategic leadership role.

Business elites in the field of power

Making and enacting strategy may be the most fundamental responsibility of corporate elites, but the social reality confronting directors of top 100 companies is in fact far more textured, varied and complex than this definition of role might suggest. As George Cox, until recently Director General of the Institute of Directors (IoD) and previously head of Unisys Europe, suggests: 'Strategy is essentially boring; if it changes all the time, it's not a strategy; what matters most is the tactics, everything that has to be done to deliver the strategy'. In the UK, for example, board meetings typically involve two classes of activity. First, the board receives and discusses a series of high-level operational reports and projections relating to such matters as sales, finances and human resources. This provides the big picture for all directors and enables ideas to be collected and necessary day-to-day decisions made. Secondly, there are special reports and major discussion items pertaining. to projects and programmes intended to deliver strategic change. A boardroom is thus a paradoxical place: on the one hand the emphasis is on control, while, on the other, strategic change necessitates deliberately upsetting the existing order in pursuit of fresh goals and ambitions.

Consider the case of Vodafone, the British-based mobile telephony company, whose strategy is to build a technologically sophisticated communications network to provide unrivalled services for its customers in all parts of the world. Enacting this strategy has required remarkable consistency of purpose and massive investment. For the directors, innumerable decisions have had to be made concerning the organic growth of the network, alliances and service agreements with other major telecommunications companies, and the acquisition of major companies outside the UK, including Mannesmann of Germany, a traditional engineering and telecommunications company, at a cost of £83 billion in 1999.[37] Monumental decisions such as these cannot be taken lightly. They involve sophisticated calculations and judgements on the part of directors, and these have to be taken without losing sight of everyday imperatives such as the management of cash flow, legal challenges, and employment relations across a myriad of national jurisdictions.

The reality of life at the top of the corporate tree is that it is both extremely demanding and rewarding. Corporate elites – like government ministers, top civil servants, senior judges, university vice-chancellors, military leaders, and others at the pinnacle of their field – inhabit what Bourdieu refers to as 'the field of power'. By this he means something more than membership of the uppermost stratum of society, the highest level in all fields combined. Rather, the field of power is a social space in which members of different elite groups freely mingle, recognised by one another as social and positional equals. Elite legitimacy – the right to rule – stems not simply from acceptance on the part of those lower down, but also the conferment of due recognition by those on a par. The conferment of top state honours by governments or honorary degrees by universities are powerfully symbolic of this process of elite recognition, or indeed denial (as confirmed by the pointed rejection of British citizenship to Harrods boss Mohammed Al-Fayed).[38]

	Owner-Directors	Manager-Directors
Executive Directors	Economic Cultural Social Symbolic	Cultural Social (Symbolic)
Non-Executive Directors	Economic Symbolic (Social)	Social Symbolic (Cultural)

Figure 2.4   Predominant forms of capital possessed by directors of top 100 companies

   Legitimacy and recognition within the field of power, as a director of a top 100 company, stems from different sources in different cases. In Figure 2.4, two distinctions are made: the first between directors who enjoy significant ownership rights in the business and those who do not; the second between executive and non-executive directors. This gives four possibilities. Owners with executive responsibilities, family capitalists, common in France but not in the UK, typically are high-profile individuals, blessed of abundant economic, cultural, social and symbolic capital. They are wealthy, knowledgeable, well connected, and their family name is symbolically significant. These executives contrast with the manager directors, common in the UK, appointed to run the business on behalf of the shareholders. They are rich in cultural and social capital, knowledgeable about the business, its environment, and the arts of leadership and strategic management. They have extensive business networks, and some, though a minority, are high-profile individuals with extensive symbolic capital. Owners who serve as non-executives, again a common type in France, may not have the knowledge needed to run a major business.

Their position is legitimised by possession of significant economic and symbolic capital and their role is primarily concerned with the management of personal or family wealth. Finally, non-executive directors without significant ownership rights, effectively part-time top managers, are legitimised in their role by their extensive social and symbolic capital, and their possession of generic cultural capital relevant to high-level decision making. Such people, drawn from a wide spectrum within the elite, within and outside business, move fluently across the field of power, at home and internationally, making connections and lending authority to the board by virtue of their personal authority and distinction.

The formation of elite qualities and capabilities

The view of society put forward by Bourdieu is essentially one of change and contestation within regulating and self-reproducing structures. In this world, few things are exactly what they appear at first sight. Material and symbolic power are intertwined, making it difficult for actors, as practical strategists, intellectually to transcend their situational understanding of the world. Much of human behaviour is the product not of conscious decisions and independent action, but of 'habitus', conceived by Bourdieu as the ingrained and socially constituted dispositions of social classes that lead actors to make choices and decisions that reproduce existing social structures and status distinctions. As Thompson explains, habitus gives individuals a sense of how to think, feel and act in their daily lives, orienting their actions and inclinations but without precisely determining them. It gives them a 'feel for the game', a practical sense (*le sens pratique*) of what constitutes appropriate behaviours in the circumstances, and what does not. Thus, he argues, habitus is less a state of mind than a state of body, in which posture, mannerisms, accent and virtually every tiny movement of an individual indicate the repository of embedded dispositions that have become, as it were, 'natural'.[39]

Habitus is the means by which life chances are 'internalized and converted into a disposition'.[40] It is thus 'one of the mediations through which social destiny is accomplished'.[41] Habitus serves as a binding force between various fractions within a class, leading to common though not orchestrated action on the basis of categories of 'perception and appreciation' that are themselves produced by an observable social condition.[42] In this way, habitus serves to reconcile the co-existence of subjective and objective conditions within society. The objective conditions of existence include the consumption of goods, which may be valued more for their social meaning than for their functional utility.[43] Furnishings or ornaments, for example, are 'instruments of a ritual',[44] trivia or paraphernalia which nevertheless confer distinction (see Chapter 5).[45] The preservation of social order, of the continued acceptance of domination by the subordinated, does not require members of the ruling elite to think or act alike.[46] It is sufficient that there are homologies between fields that lead dominant actors to share similar dispositions across domains.[47] The 'circular circulation' of information within elite circles that share social origin and education contributes to homogenisation and political conformity[48] – to what the French term 'la pensée unique'.

The practical value of Bourdieu's thinking stems from the insight that people who rise through society into elite positions do so both by consciously acquiring personal capital (qualifications, experience, connections) and by unconsciously assimilating knowledge and dispositions through habitus. He conceives of habitus as a 'structuring structure', a mechanism for social reproduction, which is central to his understanding of such matters as education and taste. For our purposes, the idea that membership of a social institution can serve unconsciously to form the potentialities of an individual actor is an important one. It suggests that the life chances of individuals are forged uniquely, and in no small measure, through their membership of a series of institutions, of which family, educational institutions, and corporate and professional organisations are the most fundamental.

The family

Bourdieu shares with Foucault a preoccupation with the family as the key component in the workings of society and the economy, and the main site of social reproduction. As Bubolz points out, the family is the primary source and builder of social capital, 'supplying the "glue" that helps other parts of the social-economic system to hang and function together'.[49] Bourdieu explores the notion of the family as *constructing* social reality, while, through the use of such words as 'house, home, household, *maison*, *maisonée*', seeming merely to describe it.[50] 'In the social world', he writes, 'words make things, because they make the consensus on the existence and the meaning of things, the common sense, the *doxa* accepted by all as self-evident'.[51]

The family is the primary means whereby capital and power of various guises are transmitted and reproduced from one generation to the next. It plays a key role in reproduction strategies, transmitting economic, cultural and symbolic privilege, first and foremost the symbolic capital of the family name. Among the executive class in particular, Bourdieu notes that the family is instrumental 'not only in the transmission but also in the management of the economic heritage, especially through business alliances which are often family alliances'.[52] Pointing out that *grand bourgeois* and aristocratic dynasties tend to weather revolutions very well, Bourdieu likens them to 'select clubs':

> Bourgeois dynasties function like select clubs; they are the sites of the accumulation and management of a capital equal to the sum of the capital held by each of their members, which the relationships between the various holders make it possible to mobilize, partially at least, in favour of each of them.[53]

Marriage thus becomes in Bourdieu's eyes a 'strategy' – though at times functioning more subconsciously than consciously – designed to ensure 'the perpetuation of the patrimony'.[54]

An illustration is provided by the marriage in 2003 of Kate Rothschild, heiress and scion of one of the most powerful banking families in Europe, to Ben Goldsmith, son of the late Sir James Goldsmith, who made his fortune in finance and groceries. Their alliance was billed as 'the society wedding of the decade', uniting two of Europe's richest dynasties.[55] In 2004, what was described as a 'historic merger' (a business term) was cemented by the arrival of their baby Iris Goldsmith. Bourdieu regards such unions of human affection with sound business sense as exemplifying 'class-fraction endogamy'. It is the nexus of endogenous relationships that characterise elite French business networks, discussed in Chapter 6. Bourdieu observes that 'the structure of the circuit of matrimonial exchanges tends to reproduce the structure of the social space', whether by 'the free play of sentiment' or 'deliberate family intervention'.[56] The married couple is, Foucault explains, 'attuned to a homeostasis of the social body, which it has the function of maintaining'.[57] As 'the keystone of alliance',[58] he argues, the conventional family is 'an integral part of the bourgeois order',[59] giving rise to 'a *deployment of alliance*: a system of marriage, of fixation and development of kinship ties, of transmission of names and possessions'.[60]

Being brought up in a family rich in economic, cultural, social and symbolic capital is formative of tastes and personal dispositions. Cultural practices in essence are reflective of underlying class distinctions, serving as subtle yet powerful forms of social distinction. Lifestyles give practical expression to the symbolic dimension of class identity. Tastes stem not from internally generated aesthetic preferences, but from the conditioning effect of habitus and the availability of economic and cultural capital.

Each social class or fraction of a class has its own habitus and correlative set of cultural practices.[61] This leads Bourdieu to conclude that relative 'distance from necessity' is the main determinant of habitus and the formation of tastes and preferences.[62] Those in the uppermost strata of society, free from material constraints, develop an aesthetic disposition characterised by 'the stylization of life', the primacy of form over function, and manner over matter.[63] In contrast, the working classes are seen to privilege substance over form, the informal over the formal, and the immediate over the deferred. By way of a myriad of cultural practices, dominant factions thereby distance themselves from the subordinated, affecting a sense of casual superiority and social distinction. The exercise of taste thus serves to reinforce the right to rule.

Educational institutions

Educational institutions operate as structuring structures at two levels. Their explicitly stated purpose is to increase the cultural capital of individuals. But schools and universities are not all the same, and it is perhaps through their implicit role in helping to differentiate between individuals that they have their greatest impact on future careers. Education, like other fields, is highly stratified, and attendance at an elite institution is one of the surest of all mechanisms for career advancement.

In the UK, school league tables for educational attainment demonstrate variations in student performance between individual schools and classes of institutions, which remain remarkably consistent over time. At the top are the most prestigious independent (so-called 'public') schools, and these are followed in the pecking order by a raft of other, somewhat less prestigious, independents. Some government-funded schools achieve slightly better results than the lowest performing private schools, and these typically are of the highly aspirational grammar school type that prizes high academic achievement, often sending students to elite universities. Beneath these schools are other state schools offering a general-purpose 'comprehensive' education. In France, the situation is somewhat different in that 'private' schools are independent of state control on religious grounds, education in France being secular as a matter of principle. The most prestigious schools, in particular the bourgeois Parisian *lycées*, Louis-le-Grand, Saint Louis and Henri IV, may select their entrants, but are nevertheless 'public' in the sense that they are owned and run by the state, drawing their pupils from the locality.

The higher education systems in France and the UK are likewise very different, but in both countries a high degree of stratification prevails, confirmed by numerous league tables that distinguish between the elite, the middle order and the rest, composed in the UK of institutions once designated as polytechnics and colleges of higher education. The elite, predictably, consists of Oxford and Cambridge and a few other institutions that boast the best-qualified students, the highest level of student performance, superior infrastructure and resources, and the most important and prestigious research. In France, elite education developed outside the university system.[64] Here, the elite institutions are not the universities, but specialist *grandes écoles* like the Ecole Nationale d'Administration (ENA), Polytechnique, or Sciences-Po, clustered in Paris, with the provincial business and management schools providing a second order, viewed by Bourdieu as minor institutions leading to middle management positions. The highly selective system of the *grandes écoles* contrasts with almost free university entry for anyone with the *baccalauréat*, or 'bac' as it is commonly known, acquired by three-quarters of all school leavers. This, of course, obscures the fact that selection has taken place already through the choice of *bac*, the maths and physical sciences option being reserved for the most gifted pupils;[65] and that it will take place again at the end of the first year, with many new university students being eliminated at this point. But it is seen as vital to maintain public confidence in the notion that everyone has an equal chance of success. In recent years a small number of universities, such as Aix-en-Provence, Paris II-Panthéon Assas and Paris IX-Dauphine, have introduced candidate selection. They are now competing with the provincial graduate management schools for students while charging much reduced tuition fees. (see Chapter 4).

The benefits of an elite education are legion. Besides the cultural capital acquired through study, there are the enduring benefits assimilated through time spent in an elite academic environment. These include the rigours of intellectual exchange, the setting of high personal standards and expectations, team working skills, the formation of refined tastes and preferences, the accumulation of cultural knowledge, and the personal dispositions and skills needed to move confidently in society. Added to all this is the symbolic capital conferred on graduation from an elite institution, a lasting signifier of intellectual and cultural distinction.

Corporate and professional organisations

Top 100 companies in both France and the UK recruit large numbers of graduates, often to fast-track development programmes, and often selectively from a small number of elite institutions. However, graduate programmes are not the only means of making rapid career progress in either country: it would not be in the best interests of any firm arbitrarily to limit its management 'gene pool', and many successful firms have found it wiser to take a more flexible approach to the recruitment of individuals into the managerial hierarchy. Large corporations are themselves powerful structuring structures, developing individuals explicitly through training and implicitly through habitus to meet the specific needs of the business. They seek to recruit the most talented people, and some initially may be more privileged than others with respect to training, but in the longer term it is being seen to perform well – adding greatest value to the business – that counts most when it comes to promotion.

As practical strategists, potential future members of the elite must quickly learn how to play the corporate game. We saw earlier how, in a professional field like medicine, actors accumulate capital and advance their careers in accordance with field-wide rules of the game. In large corporations, the broad principles of capital accumulation are the same, but the rules must be interpreted locally and specifically. This means seeking out roles and assignments that will yield most in terms of knowledge accumulation, network development, recognition and reputational gain, and proven experience of delivery. There are risks as well as rewards at every stage. Accepting leadership of a high-profile project, for example, might lead quickly to rapid capital accumulation if all goes well or if difficulties can be overcome, but equally the stock of an executive can fall significantly if a project fails or has to be rescued. It is for this reason that leadership of projects that are symbolically important for a company are often dismissed as a 'poisoned chalice' by executives less inclined to take risks.

It would be wrong, however, to depict the processes of personal capital accumulation and career development as simply a matter of rational calculation. Careers within large corporations depend not just on what an individual does, but also on how the individual is perceived. What matters in building a reputation, in establishing the trust of those in more powerful positions, is to be seen as a 'corporate insider': someone committed and with the best interests of the company at heart; someone in tune with the culture, norms and values of the organisation; someone who will make sacrifices (usually involving time or personal convenience) in the wider corporate interest; someone who has assimilated the right dispositions and behaviours, such that they are seen as fitting representatives of the business to the outside world. These qualities are the product of responsiveness to habitus, of a willingness to accept the disciplines of a specific corporate culture.

Regeneration, continuity and cultural reproduction

Corporate culture has been defined in popular terms as 'how things are done around here' and 'the social glue that holds the organisation together', and more formally as 'the deeper level of basic assumptions and beliefs' that condition how organisational members typically interact day-to-day and respond to particular behavioural cues.[66] Culture is not easily pinned down, observed or explained. Yet the realities of culture and its resilience are widely recognised and understood by organisational actors. In particular, it is acknowledged that attempts to change organisational cultures, with a view to improving performance, often end in failure.

In order to understand why corporate cultures are so resistant to change, often surviving multiple changes in organisational leadership, it is necessary to understand the processes involved in cultural reproduction within organisations. Our own theoretical position, building on the ideas of Bourdieu summarised above, are expressed in the model presented in Figure 2.5.

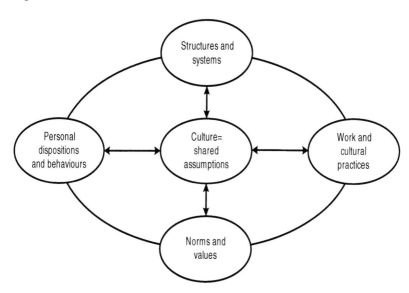

Figure 2.5 Culture and cultural reproduction

In this, culture is defined conventionally as residing in the 'common assumptions' of organisational members, which are forged through personal engagement with four intimately related components of the organisation. First, it is through interaction with the main operating systems and processes of the organisation that members first learn 'how things get done around here'. In control-oriented organisations, for example, there are typically multiple levels of approval and rigorously enforced, often inflexible, procedures for such matters as costing and bidding. Secondly, assumptions about how to get things done are formed through involvement with the work and cultural practices of longer-serving colleagues. Work practices involve such things as levels of consultation and information sharing with peers and superiors. There is an obvious direct link with the operating systems and processes that establish the framework in which work practices evolve. Cultural practices, on the other hand, are voluntary yet obligatory, covering all the symbols and rituals, large and small, of organisational life. Thirdly, when recently recruited members have dealings with established colleagues, especially when decisions have to be made, they quickly learn the norms and values that prevail in the organisation, setting boundaries and conditioning future actions. Fourthly, there is the formative experience of inter-personal exchanges with colleagues, of their personal dispositions and behaviours, which are related but different, more rounded and expressive, from the revelation of norms and values. Language, conversation, humour and style are important and inform in turn such things as styles of communication, the conduct of meetings, and human interaction and support more generally.

What is telling about the model is not just that culture is formed systemically, but equally the insight that culture is formative of the system. Cultural reproduction is the product of the two-way interaction between system components and assumptions held in common by organisational members. It is through assumptions that members perceive a natural order and ways of doing things. When organisational improvements are made or innovations introduced, the overwhelming tendency is to achieve fit with the accepted order, in conformance with the 'organisation in the mind'. This, then, is the nature of culture and cultural reproduction.

What is the importance of these theoretical insights to the reproduction and regeneration of corporate elites? The first point to make is that all top 100 boards have their own unique micro-culture that reflects, and is intimately related to, the culture of the organisation as a whole. Shell, with dual Anglo-Dutch board structures that have persisted over many decades, is illustrative in this regard: some of the oil giant's current difficulties have to do with the fact that for many years the business has been run like a club. There is, we assert, a strong tendency towards cultural reproduction at board level. Periodic elevation of senior executives to the main board is essential for regeneration, but it is at the same time an act of reproduction. These corporate insiders are steeped in the culture of the organisation.

Existing members of the elite thus tend to recruit new members forged in their own image, standard bearers of tradition, a source of continuity rather than a force for change, just as certain French corporations have traditionally favoured a particular *grand corps*. This general principle applies even to non-executives who, in general, are recruited because they conform to norms set by the board, and if they do not, the prevailing board culture imposes its own disciplines to produce conformance.

Enron and other major scandals have exposed the dangers inherent in cultural conformance at board level in recent years. The problem of 'group think' is widely recognised, and from time to time a board will, in a drive to improve performance, take the decision to appoint a Chief Executive Officer to 'transform' the organisational culture. Bold moves such as these may succeed if the changes made are sufficiently widespread and robust, but often even the boldest initiatives meet with fierce resistance, and the culture reasserts itself. Martin Taylor, for example, was welcomed as a change agent as CEO of Barclays; but after a few years he felt worn down by the weight of cultural resistance encountered, and he elected to leave. This comes as no surprise in light of the theory of cultural reproduction outlined above.

Business elites and corporate governance

The sociologist John Scott has produced a large corpus of work on corporate elites and the rise of big business in Britain, the US and elsewhere. He follows Alfred Chandler in pointing out that 'managerial capitalism', marked by the increasing separation of ownership and control in large enterprises, had its origins in the US in the 1860s in transportation, manufacturing and distribution. The sheer size of the US economy, and the creation of businesses that could reap economies of scale and scope by operating nationwide, meant that companies had to look for capital outside the immediate circle of founding entrepreneurs. By taking advantage of limited liability status, companies were able to draw on a wide pool of investors who felt at ease trading ownership rights through the medium of a stock exchange. The effect was to distribute corporate ownership ever more widely, away from founding families, as businesses grew big first through national expansion and later internationally. Already, by 1914, US companies were active in Europe and Asia, and their international expansion continued apace in the twentieth century as they exploited the technological and commercial knowledge accumulated at home. Chandler acknowledges the same tendency in Britain, but argues that the displacement of owner-managers by corporate-managers took place more gradually, thereby slowing the rise of the corporate economy and lessening industrial dynamism, as firms remained wedded to pre-modern structures and attitudes.[67] According to this thesis, it was only after a series of merger waves following the Second World War that managerially dominated enterprises displaced family firms at the hub of the British economy.

The Chandler thesis, told and re-told in his three master works – *Strategy and Structure*, *The Visible Hand*, and *Scale and Scope* – has been hotly contested; though the essential thrust of his argument remains intact.[68] Scott makes the point that the separation of ownership from control has never become as complete, even in the US, as was predicted by Berle and Means in 1929.[69] On the contrary, companies may still be subject to significant influence by founding families, even when they possess a relatively small block of shares, especially since family shareholdings invariably go hand in hand with representation on the board.[70] Moreover, Scott argues, the trend towards the separation of ownership and control has been frustrated in practice by the concentration of voting power in the hands of a relatively small number of financial institutions, which he terms a 'constellation of interests'.[71] Contrasting the shareholdings of the top 20 shareholders in Union Pacific in the years 1937 and 1980 respectively, Scott notes that the size of the stake which they owned actually increased during this time from 14.47 per cent in 1937 to 22.43 per cent in 1980, while the number of families included in the top 20 shareholders more than doubled, from two in 1937 to five in 1980.[72] Thus, Scott observes in the US:

> a transition from personal possession by particular families and inter-ests to impersonal possession through an interweaving of ownership interests. But this transition was not a simple unilinear movement. Fam-ily ownership and family influence persist in many areas of the econ-omy.[73]

Control through a constellation of interests has likewise become the dominant form of corporate control in the UK, with as many as 100 of the top 250 British firms included in this category by 1976.[74] Institutional shareholders such as banks, insurance companies, pension funds and investment trusts have consistently increased their grip on UK equity since that time, owning an estimated 75 per cent of the total capitalisation of the London Stock Exchange by the early twenty-first century. This leads Scott to conclude that in the UK economic power is concentrated in the hands of a small, self-aware and exclusive group: a unified business class, whose continued existence depends on its ability to manage the corporate economy.[75] Scott and Griff draw on the work of Wright Mills, who demonstrated how the period from the 1920s to the early 1950s witnessed the further consolidation of the American upper classes through 'managerial reorganization', as propertied families joined forces with the managers of corporate property to form 'a more sophisticated executive elite'.[76]

The power of the wealthy has been reinforced in turn by the growth of inter-corporate relations, which may be personal, capital or commercial, with personal and capital relations forming the key 'control relations' in which firms are enmeshed.[77] Above all, Scott is concerned with the interlocking directorships and shareholdings that bring firms and individuals closer together within the field of power. An interlocking directorship may be said to exist whenever one person is a director of two companies, thus creating a social relation between the two firms, which creates in turn the potential for information exchange and coordinated action. By the same token, through multiple board memberships, 'inner circle' directors[78] who are united through kinship and friendship have access to 'a complex web of social relations'[79] which Scott and Griff refer to as 'kinterlocks'. Thus, 'people meet as kinsmen, friends, co-directors, and as colleagues of kin and friends, and each relation reinforces the others to produce multiple, and multi-stranded, personal relations'.[80]

There have been numerous studies of corporate interlocks in Britain and France. In 1976, Scott found that three-quarters of the top 250 British companies had board level connections.[81] Large British companies possessed an average of 4.3 interlocks, with two individuals holding six or more directorships, but with no company having more than 30 interlocks.[82] In the French system, links between firms have often been characterised by an exchange of executive directors who become non-executives within associated organisations.[83] In the 1970s, the two largest financial groups, Paribas and Suez, were key power players. In 1977, for example, it was found that as many as 220 of the 250 largest French firms were bound together through varied interlock patterns into a single unit. In the late 1980s and early 1990s, Paribas and Suez were superseded by UAP (Union des Assurances de Paris) – a spider at the centre of a large web of affiliations that now forms part of AXA. These affiliations, Kadushin observes, are reinforced by the fact that members of the French business elite serving as directors on multiple boards were more likely to have attended the 'right' schools, and to be members of the 'right' clubs. Such schools (for example Louis-le-Grand and Janson-de-Sailly) and clubs, often possessing a political dimension, functioning rather as policy circles (such as Le Siècle, Club des 100, Entreprise et Cité, Association Française des Entreprises Privées, Jean Moulin, Echange et Projets, Fondation Saint

Simon and Galilée), thus come to serve as 'proxies' for membership of the upper social classes (see Chapter 6).[84]

The research of Scott and others who have focused on the social networks that bind national business systems together has three important implications for corporate governance. First, their work confirms that elite business groups do not have complete freedom of action, but rather operate under a socially negotiated compact with more or less remote owners and their representatives. At one extreme, when ownership is highly dispersed and the voice of owners is little heard, the main sanction on management – at least in the UK, though less so in France – comes through the threat of a takeover bid, a challenge from another management team. At the other extreme, when ownership remains concentrated and the voice of founder or family is strong, management must satisfy owners directly, face-to-face, that its course is true and performance satisfactory. In the majority of cases, however, the 'constellation of interests' or network view of the relationships that typically exist between owners and managers suggests something different. Institutional investors, by their nature, are 'spread-betters' with numerous investments. They may demand information and access to management, and from time to time they may issue challenges, but by and large their interests are best served by leaving management to manage. In return for large financial rewards, they expect good performance from a board of directors and from individual members of the corporate elite. If value creation is strong and evident, institutional investors will give the appearance of passivity. It is only at times of apparent poor performance that networks in the field of power become fully activated. When a crisis ensues, as in 2004 when Marks & Spencer was subject to a takeover bid from the entrepreneur Philip Green, the incumbent board must actively defend its record and demonstrate its on-going fitness for office. It is at such times that the compact between owners and managers is tested, sometimes breaking down, and leading, symbolically, to loss of office for one or more individuals, as demonstrated by the August 2004 operational crisis at British Airways, which saw numerous flights cancelled and the reputation of the airline damaged.

The second implication for corporate governance of research into ownership patterns and social networks is that institutional investors have the most significant of all vested interests in the implementation of comprehensive codes of practice. Large individual shareholders and family groups can always demand information and action from top management. Institutional investors, however, typically with lower single-digit percentage equity holdings, must rely on management to be open and forthcoming with information. It is essential for them to have financial and other crucial data disclosed and reported on an agreed basis in order for them to make sound investment decisions. The crisis at Shell in 2004 surrounding the overstatement of oil reserves serves to underline the point. In this case, institutional investors felt aggrieved that accepted reporting conventions were flouted, and that this in turn might be traced back to more general governance failings within the company. At Shell, as elsewhere, the perception is that corporate governance is not just about rules and conventions, but also about having the right balance of power within board teams. Hence the rising interest in the roles of chairmen and non-executive directors as a counterweight to the authority of full-time executives.

Finally, research into elite networks serves to highlight the importance of personal and organisational interactions to the preservation of distinctive national systems of corporate governance. Companies adopt standards and conventions not simply because they are obliged to do so by regulators, but also because they learn from others what is deemed to be acceptable. This process of normative isomorphism, for example, could be seen at work in the conduct of the review of the role and effectiveness of non-executive directors conducted in 2002-03 by Derek Higgs.[85] In this case, the announcement of the review triggered a wide-ranging conversation within the field of power on governance principles and practices. This was fed into the committee in the evidence presented by large firms, professional bodies, associations like the Confederation of British Industry and the IoD, and influential individuals with a special interest in corporate governance. A consensus gradually emerged around issues like the appointment of independent directors that ultimately led to changes in the combined code on corporate governance for UK companies. What is important, however, is not the fact that some changes were made to the code, but that the fundamental approach to corporate governance in the UK – that compliance is voluntary and not enshrined in legislation – was once more affirmed. Within national business systems, just as within organisations, the forces of cultural reproduction, while not sufficiently strong to deny all change, preserve that which is fundamental, of the essence, even sacred.

In studying elite networks among the French and British business communities, we have found the work of Mark Granovetter to be especially illuminating. In a seminal and oft-cited article on the paradoxical 'strength of weak ties', Granovetter pinpoints the value of low-density networks as a powerful source of knowledge on which the individual may draw in order to realise, for example, a job opportunity.[86] Viewed in this light, the fact that an individual's acquaintances are less likely to be socially involved with one another than his or her friends or family accords them a particular usefulness, allowing informal, interpersonal contacts to function as a bridge to more distant parts of a network.[87]

However, we have found elite cohesion to be achieved very differently in France and the UK. In France, where networking is supported and facilitated by the state for those who meet its exacting requirements, through august state institutions, the ties that bind the French business and, indeed, political elite tend to be institutional and strong. Family ties are also important, and in many leading listed companies, such as L'Oréal or Michelin, family ownership still dominates. In the UK, on the other hand, networking is first and foremost a social requirement for business executives who wish to make their mark. Here, the ties that bind the British business elite are largely social in nature and relatively weak, conforming more closely to Granovetter's notion of weak ties than the tightly networked French economy. It is an interesting paradox that cohesion should be achieved in different ways, socially and institutionally, in two different national business systems (see Chapter 6).

Conclusion

We have sought in this chapter to elaborate the theoretical framework and perspectives that inform the discussion in subsequent chapters. It is through theory that we achieve coherence and completeness in the explanation of social phenomena, but theory without the corroboration of empirical data is of little value, and indeed can be misleading rather than informative. What is required is that the predictions of theory are validated through appeal to the data, and if they are not then we must accept the limitations of theory or seek improvement in some way.

In the theoretical world we have sketched out, the most basic constructs are those of field, sub-field and strata: society is seen to divide and sub-divide vertically into fields and sub-fields, and horizontally into strata. Elite groups form the uppermost strata within fields and sub-fields. Membership of the corporate elite, for the purposes of this study, is confined to the directors of the top 100 companies that dominate the economic field in France and the UK respectively. These are the social actors who within business have tremendous power and authority, stemming from their command over huge resources, classified by Bourdieu as economic, cultural, social and symbolic. In business, as in other fields, each of these types of capital has specific forms and expressions, but in all fields it is possession of large amounts of capital that enables elite actors to dominate. Those with less capital experience, to a greater or lesser degree, subordination within their field or sub-field. To rise from a subordinate to a dominant position is difficult but not impossible, given the right strategy and the on-going conversion of one type of capital into another. There is fluidity and movement in the system.

Individuals as well as organisations are blessed with different amounts of capital. In general, those at the top in business – elite individuals, members of elite groups – are personally well endowed with variable amounts of economic, cultural, social and symbolic capital. This is a condition for recruitment to membership of the corporate elite. It requires aspiring individuals, over the course of their careers, to pursue strategies, consciously or sub-consciously, that lead to the accumulation of significant amounts of personal capital. Some individuals have a better starting point than others in this quest. They may inherit significant economic capital or assimilate cultural and social capital through membership of social institutions. Families, educational institutions and corporate and professional organisations are each structuring structures that shape the behaviours and personal dispositions of their members. Membership of these institutions is also a lasting source of symbolic capital. It is by getting the most out of membership of families, educational institutions and corporate and professional organisations that individuals add to their stock of capital and position themselves for recruitment into the corporate elite.

Our theoretical position is not deterministic. Actors can do well or badly depending on how well they play the game. Of particular importance in large companies is the need to master organisational culture. Individuals who rise most rapidly through the ranks are those who assimilate most quickly and effectively the behaviours and dispositions needed as a corporate insider. One aspect of cultural reproduction is that established elites tend to recruit new members in their own image, and, once they become a member of an elite group, a whole new world opens up. This we refer to as the field of power, the social space in which members of elite groups from different fields and sub-fields meet on an even footing to debate and resolve issues of mutual concern. Those who move fluently in the field of power as acknowledged leaders are showered with honours and rewards from all quarters. These are the ultimate rewards of social distinction.

3

Governance Regimes in Comparative Perspective

'Making money through others is the surest way of getting fat'.

Zola [1]

The change that has taken place over the past decade in the structure of companies and their boards has been nothing short of dramatic. By 2003, ten years after the implementation of what became known as the 'Cadbury Code' in the UK, codes of best practice had been drawn up by a wide spectrum of countries. These embraced not only Western Europe and North America, but also former Communist nations of Eastern and Central Europe as they prepared to join the European Union (EU) in 2004, in addition to Latin America, South Asia, Africa, Australasia and the Far East. [2] Global and pan-European institutions, such as the World Bank, the International Monetary Fund (IMF), the Commonwealth, the Organisation for Economic Cooperation and Development (OECD), and the European Bank for Reconstruction and Development (EBRD), likewise jumped on the bandwagon. So too did institutional investor organisations, [3] publishing their own sets of guidelines for sound standards in business and corporate practice. [4] This represents a resounding endorsement of the Code of Best Practice published by the Cadbury Committee in December 1992 under the title of *The Financial Aspects of Corporate Governance.* [5]

It is noteworthy that some of the wording used in British codes has been adopted worldwide, underlining the international relevance of the work of the Cadbury Committee and its successors, Greenbury, Hampel and, more recently, Higgs, [6] 'addressing practical governance problems, and providing needed guidance, rather than being well-meaning but basically uncalled-for interventions'. [7] As a direct result of the introduction of notable corporate governance reforms, boards have been growing in strength relative to management, and investors are now holding their boards accountable, in a manner that would have been unthinkable in the early 1990s.

The Cadbury Report, as it became known, defines corporate govern-ance as 'the system by which companies are directed and controlled'.[8] In *Corporate Governance and Chairmanship*, Sir Adrian Cadbury notes that the term 'governance' may be traced back to the fourteenth-century English author, Geoffrey Chaucer, deriving from the Latin *gubernare*, meaning 'to steer'.[9] The French word for 'rudder', *gouvernail*, originates from the same root. Yet although corporate governance has been with us since companies assumed their present form – ever since companies grew large enough to require salaried managers to manage them, introducing a separation between ownership and control – and despite the many decades of governance research since Berle and Means,[10] it is only really since the early 1990s that matters of corporate governance have come to the fore. As Sir Adrian Cadbury observes, looking back on the 'somnolent boards' and relative calm of the corporate scene in the aftermath of the Second World War:

> It was understandable that corporate governance was on no one's agenda. It was a time of reconstruction worldwide, the problem was shortage of supplies and any remotely competent company could keep its shareholders satisfied. I did not, as a sales representative, have to sell Cadbury's chocolate to my customers in the early 1950s, I had to ration them.[11]

One consequence of the 1948 Companies Act in post-war Britain, as Toms and Wright observe, was to foster a lack of transparency, after company directors lobbied for reduced disclosure for reasons of commer-cial secrecy. The 1962 Jenkins Report aimed to achieve greater account-ability, but it was not until the 1967 Companies Act that executive pay was made public in the UK, while other emoluments were not disclosed until further legislation in 1976.[12]

The Cadbury Report was not the first governance report to be written. It was pre-dated in the US by the Treadway Report, produced five years previously by the Treadway Commission, a US panel charged with examining fraudulent financial reporting, which contained 11 recommen-dations regarding audit committees.[13] It was pre-dated, too, by the 1977 Bullock Report in the UK, which was concerned with changing the power balance within boards, arguing in particular for the appointment of employee directors.[14] But in its impact as a trail-blazer, setting in motion a chain of reforms of ultimately global impact, establishing key principles upon which successive committees have built, it was of groundbreaking importance. It crystallised the debate in Britain and beyond, concentrating corporate minds on matters of regulation, responsibility and communication with shareholders; board effectiveness, structures, procedures and remuneration; auditing, transparency and accountability.[15] It outlined a 'code of best practice' to which all listed companies registered in the UK were urged to adhere, embracing the duration of directors' service contracts, interim reporting, the effectiveness and perceived objectivity of audit, and the role of institutional investors (specifically regarding the disclosure of their policies on voting rights). Listed companies were required to make a statement as a condition of their continued listing on the London Stock Exchange about their compliance (or reasons for non-compliance) with the code in annual reports published from June 1993. It recommended that a successor body be set up to review the implementation of the code. The Committee on Corporate Governance, referred to as the Hampel Committee after its chairman, Sir Ronald Hampel, was established in November 1995. Its preliminary findings were published in August 1997 and its final report the following year.

This chapter examines in comparative perspective the historical development of governance patterns in France and Britain, exploring the root causes behind the new emphasis on corporate governance. It considers matters of executive pay; ownership and control; the role of the state; board structures and composition; business cultures and decision-making; the rise of investor activism and international share ownership; and responsibilities to stakeholders. It compares and contrasts the organisational, systemic and ideological attributes of the French and British national business systems. Key corporate governance reports are included in the discussion: namely, the Cadbury, Greenbury, Hampel and Higgs reports[16] in the UK, and the Viénot, Marini, Viénot II and Bouton reports in France,[17] as well as the Nouvelles Régulations Economiques (NRE) of 2001,[18] which led to the *loi de sécurité financière* of 2003. The chapter questions where power lies in both countries in the first decade of the twenty-first century, and summarises the major changes that have taken place over the past decade as a direct result of corporate governance initiatives.

Historical background and underlying causes

The underlying causes of the new concern with corporate governance since the early 1990s were noticeably similar in both countries. The 1998 AFG-ASFFI Report on corporate governance cites the following factors as instrumental in bringing the French to focus on governance issues: privatisation; the increasing presence of foreign shareholders, particularly US pension funds; the emergence in France of the concept of pension funds; and the desire to modernise the Paris financial market.[19] To this list may be added the takeover mania triggered by the creation of the European Single Market in 1992, and a long list of much-publicised business scandals on both sides of the Channel.

Privatisation

Privatisation has played a critical role in underscoring the need for sound corporate governance. Far-reaching privatisation programmes were implemented in both Britain and France in the 1980s and 1990s.[20] In the UK, this entailed not only the privatisation of companies which belonged naturally in the private, commercial sector, such as Jaguar, but also, more controversially, the sale of public utilities – telecommunications, gas, water, electricity and the railways – which, given their monopoly status and the attendant difficulties of introducing genuine competition, many saw as the natural preserve of the public sector. In France, public service is endowed with special meaning. Despite extensive privatisation, the French public sector remains one of the largest and most fiercely protected in Europe. It is only relatively recently that attention has turned there to the major public utilities, due to the need to satisfy, albeit belatedly and minimally, successive EU directives on the liberalisation of energy markets.[21] Union entitlement to a percentage of Eléctricité de France (EdF) / Gaz de France (GdF) income for pension funds is the reason commonly cited for the alleged difficulties concerning privatisation, restructuring or market access in France.[22]

In Britain, the 1995 Greenbury Report on directors' remuneration swiftly followed the Cadbury Report. In the mind of the British public, corporate governance had become synonymous with executive pay. This was largely due to the publicising by the media of inflated pay awards, share options and substantial bonuses to senior executives, often made with scant regard to company performance. A 1994 study of Britain's top 169 companies showed that while average earnings in these companies rose by 17 per cent between 1985 and 1990, directors' pay rose by as much as 77 per cent in real terms.[23] Public outrage was at its most acute when the executives concerned came from privatised utilities, enjoying near-monopoly markets, and acquiring millionaire status 'not because they built up the business through their entrepreneurial flair, not because of personal risk, not because of any special contribution to performance, but because they happened to be in the right place at the right time'.[24] The public image of the heads of Britain's privatised utilities was now, indelibly, one of 'fat cats', an image that has persisted, extending to other captains of industry. In mitigation of this rather bleak picture, however, it may be argued that, with the exception of privatised utility companies, where increased profits and share options may derive from monopoly power in product markets rather from enhanced board performance, executive share options may have the potential to bring about a greater alignment of shareholder and executive interests.[25]

Privatisation continued in the UK with the arrival in 1997 of Tony Blair's New Labour government, which, having jettisoned 'clause four' of Labour's constitution on nationalisation, pursued elements of privatisation in what were previously seen as integral public-sector activities. These included the prison service, the postal service, the National Health Service (NHS), schools, universities, air traffic control, motorways, and the London Underground, often through increasing use of 'public private partnerships'.

The Cadbury and Viénot Reports

The Cadbury Report struck a chord in France in the wake of a number of embarrassing business scandals, propelling the role of top management in major business failures out of public complacency and on to centre stage. It prompted the setting up of a working party on the mission, composition and functioning of the board of directors (*le conseil d'administration*): an arguably narrow remit, but nevertheless a fundamental one. This was set up by the French employers' association, the Conseil National du Patronat Français (CNPF, renamed the Mouvement des Entreprises de France, MEDEF, in 1998), in conjunction with the Association Française des Entreprises Privée (AFEP), under the chairmanship of Marc Viénot, then head of Société Générale. This resulted in the first Viénot Report (1995). Hitherto, matters of corporate governance had been largely ignored in France, such that there was no French equivalent of the term, a direct translation of the English, 'gouvernement d'entreprise', being adopted for convenience. Some company heads had long enjoyed a form of absolute power, aptly described as 'un pouvoir de pharaon', a pharaoh's power.[26] The significance of the Viénot Report, which consisted of a short, 24-page pamphlet produced by an independent, non-governmental working party, therefore went beyond appearances. It represented a much-needed attempt to grapple with key governance issues, arguably all the more important in France due to the long-standing tradition of state involvement in industry (*dirigisme*), diminishing individual accountability, while reporting to shareholders was negligible. In short, the Viénot Report of 1995 stimulated the first serious debate on corporate governance in France. In so doing, it sought to establish counterpoints to the enormous power of the Président-Directeur Général (PDG) who serves as both Chairman and Chief Executive Officer (CEO) of many French companies. To this end, it boldly urged the removal of the cross-shareholdings that had formed the bedrock of France's particular brand of capitalism since the 1960s. Nomination and remuneration committees were proposed, as was the appointment of at least two independent non-executive directors (NEDs), with the recommendation, in accordance with the Cadbury Report, that all of this be achieved through the initiatives of directors and shareholders rather than through legislation. Hard on the heels of the Viénot Report came the first official government response to the problems of corporate governance in France in the form of the 1996 Rapport Marini, *La Modernisation du droit des sociétés*, commissioned by the former prime minister, Alain Juppé. Written by Senator Philippe Marini, the report was published 30 years after the enactment of France's 1966 company law, which had been conceived in a former era and was now badly in need of modernisation.

Takeover mania

The speculative excesses of the takeover wave of the late 1980s and early 1990s led some sound businesses down dubious paths, culminating for some in a 'bonfire of vanities'[27] when inappropriate financial structures collided with the recession of the early 1990s. Merger mania had been galvanised in Europe by the need for businesses to prepare for the 1992 Single Market, and had reached fever pitch by the late 1980s. In 1991-92, however, the European takeover bandwagon slowed considerably, when firms which had overstretched themselves in order to acquire the critical mass deemed necessary to compete in the harsher environment of the new Europe, found themselves saddled with debt, or an undigested prey, which often had to be discarded. Some of the most celebrated acquisitions by French firms in the 1980s were sold in the 1990s to reduce debt at a time of rising interest rates and a general economic downturn.[28] It is interesting to note that the fortunes of British and French firms took rather different turns during this time, for while British firms accounted for some 18 per cent of cross-border takeover targets in the late 1980s, by 1991 French companies had become (together with US companies) the most active cross-border acquirers in Europe.[29]

This has much to do with the differing attitudes to takeovers that have traditionally prevailed in these two countries. In the UK (as in the US), takeover activities have been generally welcomed as providing a necessary discipline that works in shareholders' interests, facilitating where necessary the replacement of inefficient management by a more effective management team better able to add value.[30] A convergence of interests between management and shareholders is thereby fostered, at least in theory, as boards are alerted to the need to achieve a high level of performance. The downside is that by focusing attention on the share price, the use of takeover activity as a stick to beat poor management may encourage short-termism at the expense of long-term growth, with profits distributed as dividends rather than ploughed back into the company to fund future investment. A recent study of takeover activity, however, has challenged the notion that takeovers help to solve fundamental agency problems in large corporations. Gugler argues that, on the contrary, only the most blatant abuses of managerial discretion are corrected, with incumbent managers seemingly able to 'squander a third of the firm's value before the threat of displacement becomes serious'.[31] He concludes that the market for corporate control should be just one control measure alongside other devices, including shareholder monitoring and supervisory boards.[32]

Traditionally, the situation in France with respect to takeover activity has been rather different. Until relatively recently, it would have been almost impossible to see the share price ever sparking a takeover battle. Large French firms have sought since the 1960s to arm themselves to the hilt with a battalion of takeover defences, including crossed shareholdings (where corporate allies hold major stakes in one another), *autocontrôle* (a large proportion of a quoted company's shares being held safely by its own subsidiaries) and shareholder pacts. *Autocontrôle* was outlawed in 1991, but crossed shareholdings survive. Notable alliances include Air Liquide and l'Oréal; Air Liquide and Sodexho; Alcatel and Société Générale; Alcatel and Vivendi; AXA and BNP; AXA and Schneider; BNP and Renault; BNP and Saint-Gobain; BNP and Vivendi; LMVH and Vivendi; and Vivendi and Saint-Gobain.[33] It is argued here, however, that the main form of protection for incumbents comes not from crossed shareholdings but rather from interlocking directorships, which our research has shown to be twice as prevalent in France as in the UK (as discussed in Chapter 6). The combined effect of these weapons has been to shield management from potential challenges from outside investors and to impede share movement, encouraging a 'reciprocal complacency' designed to protect the *status quo* by preserving intact the establishment network – a sort of 'nomenklatura'[34] – which has long held France's large companies in its grip. In Anglo-American terms, managerial failure has been allowed to continue uncorrected, with the main threats to the position of an incumbent PDG often coming from investigative journalists or investigating judges rather than corporate predators.

More recently, however, there are signs that this may be changing, not least because of the growing presence of US institutional investors in the share capital of French firms. In 1997, the proportion of share capital in the companies of the CAC-40 (France's top 40 listed companies by market value) held by foreign investors stood at 35 per cent.[35] Foreign mutual funds were now in a powerful position to influence and monitor management methods and decisions, and to make their voices heard, encouraging a new shareholder activism, strengthening the hand of the board *vis-à-vis* company executives.[36] The higher profile accorded to the share price as a result has been coupled with a greater willingness to punish poor performance.[37] The market for corporate control has become more rigorous, as evinced by the hostile takeover of the investment bank Paribas by the Banque Nationale de Paris (BNP) in 1999 to form BNP-Paribas, France's largest bank, scuppering a would-be friendly merger of Paribas with BNP's rival Société Générale in the process.[38] What was interesting about this hostile takeover was that it was a purely French affair. Banks that had previously co-existed in cosy complacency (even to the extent, on occasion, of colluding to fix financial results)[39] were now rivals engaged in fierce competition for supremacy. On the other hand, the Franco-French nature of the consolidation was not coincidental. The French banking sector has remained tightly guarded, with foreign banks deterred from investing in France due to the well-known dislike of hostile takeovers on the part of successive French governments, coupled with the protectionist nature of French employment law.

Business scandal

A plethora of much-publicised business scandals on both sides of the Channel injected a new urgency into the debate on corporate governance. In 1990, the directors of Guinness were found to have bought up large numbers of their own shares four years previously in a hostile bid for Distillers. Several, including CEO Ernest Saunders, were jailed. The Maxwell affair, which came to light in December 1991 after the death of Robert Maxwell, and hit the headlines periodically over the next few years, saw thousands of Mirror Group pensioners defrauded of their pensions. Pension funds had been treated as company assets to be plundered to bolster other parts of the ailing Maxwell Empire.[40] Despite a long and expensive trial, Maxwell's sons, Kevin and Ian, avoided prison sentences.

The collapse in 1991 of the Bank of Credit and Commerce International, a Middle Eastern bank licensed to operate in the UK, proved to be a similar catalyst. British local authorities had been advised to bank with BCCI on a (misguided) government recommendation, with the Western Isles alone losing almost £50 million when the bank collapsed owing more than £10 billion. The repercussions of the affair were far-reaching. The liquidators Deloitte & Touche fought hard for the bank's creditors, led by the Three Rivers District Council, managing to claw back 75 pence for every pound lost. Even the Bank of England became a target, accused of supervisory failure and dishonesty.[41] Many of the scandals that have been examined as part of this research have their roots in the past, as new standards and ways of doing things collide with older, less stringent regulatory practices.

Polly Peck, a company 'founded on little more than hot air',[42] foundered amid charges of false accounting, the scandal spiced by large donations to Conservative Party funds. When the affair came to trial, its CEO, Asil Nadir, jumped bail, absconding to northern Cyprus.[43] The fact that the accounts of such firms had given no indication of the parlous state of their finances called into question the trust that could be placed in annual reports and accounts.[44] In February 1995, Barings, Britain's oldest merchant bank, was brought to its knees by the unauthorised activities of one rogue trader, Nick Leeson, a futures trader in Singapore, who lost $1.4 billion in derivatives trading. The episode exposed the extent to which otherwise reputable institutions could rely on risky, unregulated, but potentially lucrative activities to sustain core business operations.[45] Singapore's local inquiry into the Barings collapse, published in October 1995, went beyond that produced by the Bank of England, suggesting that Leeson's fraudulent trading was deliberately covered up at the top.[46]

In France, business scandal grew thick and fast during the Mitterrand years. In the 1980s, scandals involving Carrefour (1986), Société Générale (1988) and Pechiney (1988) turned these companies into household names. In the 1990s, business improprieties forced half a dozen Cabinet ministers to resign, with several ending up behind bars, their downfall indicative of the venal potential created by the close contacts between business and politics in France.

Business leaders, however, have paid a far higher price than that paid by any politician. By 1996, the year of Mitterrand's death, the bosses of several top French companies were under investigation for fraud or corruption, including those of Saint-Gobain, Bidermann, Bouygues, SNCF, Paribas, EdF, Auchan, GMF and Renault.[47] Others were already serving prison sentences, the head of Schneider (Didier Pineau-

Valencienne) and BTF (Bernard Tapie) being the most infamous. As Hayward remarks: 'it is ironic that whereas Mitterrand frequently and perhaps sincerely expressed his contempt for a money-motivated society, he presided over a dramatic change in official morality in which his own entourage played a conspicuous part but which reflected a much more pervasive social and cultural phenomenon'.[48] Events after his death, however, cast doubt on that sincerity, when venality revealed itself rather closer to home, with his son, Jean-Christophe, and *alter ego*, Roland Dumas, finding themselves mired in the Elf affair in which Mitterrand himself was seemingly implicated.

The Pechiney and Société Général scandals of 1988 underline the interconnection between business and politics in France, a symbiotic relationship allowing old-style collusion to be put to unethical use. The purchase in November 1988 of the American National Can subsidiary of the US firm Triangle by the state-owned aluminium and packaging group, Pechiney, gave rise to one of France's most famous insider-trading scandals. Alain Boublil, the *directeur de cabinet* of the late Pierre Bérégovoy, then Finance Minister, had encouraged Pechiney in the purchase as a means of achieving critical mass. That Pechiney was then a public-sector company, and therefore not normally permitted to indulge in acquisitions according to government rules, slowed the acquisition process while at the same time increasing the number of officials involved in the decision-making process, thus expanding the potential for insider dealing. On the same day that Chairman Jean Gandois secured the government's agreement to proceed with the acquisition, a businessman with close links to the Parti Socialiste (PS), Max Théret, bought 32,000 Triangle shares in his own name, whilst a close personal friend of President Mitterrand, Roger-Patrice Pelat (best man at the Mitterrands' wedding), purchased a further 20,000 shares through an investment company, having set up a business in Panama through which to launder the profits. For a moment it seemed as though the President himself might be under threat. Interviewed on television, Mitterrand spoke movingly of a friendship born in a prisoner-of-war camp, and vehemently of the corrupting influence of money. As Routier observes, 'the wound was too visible for him not to emerge cleansed from the experience, amnestied from the only insider dealing of which he had allowed himself to be guilty – that of friendship'.[49] Pelat was never seen again at the Elysée.

The Société Générale scandal consisted of an ill-fated government-backed attempt to break up the 'hard core' of the newly privatised bank through a raid on the company's shares orchestrated by Georges Pébereau, former head of Compagnie Générale de Eléctricité (CGE), who was close to Bérégovoy. This allowed friends of the socialist government to reap large profits through access to confidential information concerning upcoming transactions.

By far the greatest scandal of the period, however – the collapse of Crédit Lyonnais in 1993 – was rooted not in corruption but in incompetence, questioning in spectacular fashion the ability of establishment elites to function as efficient captains of industry in a world no longer limited by French borders, where the rules were no longer fixed in advance by the state. As one of the largest and most spectacular bankruptcies in French history, its repercussions have swept over the years, leading to the resignation in October 2003 of Jean Peyrelevade as Chairman, as further instances of alleged malpractice continue to come to light.

It is noteworthy that many of the business scandals that have filled the pages of French newspapers often had their origins in earlier times, when French business leaders were freer to steer their ships as they saw fit. Several, indeed, have based their defence on the 'French tradition of easy money at high levels of state'.[50] Loïk Le Floch-Prigent, former head of Elf and, later, SNCF, claimed at his trial in spring 2003[51] that he and his fellow defendants were victims of a corrupt and long-standing system, sanctioned at the very top, in which Elf served as a slush fund to reward friends and allies of the state.[52] Le Floch-Prigent, his deputy Alfred Sirven, and André Tarallo, Elf's 'Mr Africa', spoke for the first time, and with disarming sincerity, of the way in which state assets were used to buy influence and contracts in Africa: in Angola, Cameroon, Congo and Gabon. As Le Floch-Prigent put it:

> Clearly in most petrol-producing countries it is the head of state or king who is the real beneficiary. The Elf system had been at the heart of the French state for years. It was not so much secret as opaque. The President of the Republic (François Mitterrand at the time) didn't want anyone to say, 'Elf is giving money to Cameroon.' So the money went to the names that the heads of these countries designated. If it sometimes ended up in an orphanage then I am very happy. But let's say it didn't always end up in an orphanage.[53]

All three senior executives were found guilty of embezzlement, having amassed personal fortunes totalling $350 million by top-slicing illicit slush funds run by the company. Commissions were paid to African leaders and French political parties. Their co-defendants included as many as 34 other Elf executives and private middlemen, in one of the largest trials of its kind. In all, 14 former Elf officials and associates were given jail sentences, 16 were given suspended sentences, and seven were acquitted. Although corporate financing of political parties was outlawed in France in the late 1980s, Le Floch-Prigent and Sirven made it clear that Elf's slush funds also went to French political leaders (approximately €44 million). Le Floch-Prigent claimed that when he became head of Elf, in 1989, the money had benefited mainly the right-wing Rassemblement pour la République (RPR). Mitterrand, a member of the PS, asked him to 'balance things out'.[54] The defendants nevertheless refused to name names in court, despite initial threats to do so, while the court, though tough on the Elf 'gang', betrayed a marked reluctance to pursue matters further. Significantly, they were not pressed for further details of political beneficiaries, nor were any politicians called to give evidence.[55]

That leading politicians and their entourages did benefit from kick-backs was already implicit in the arrest of Jean-Christophe Mitterrand in December 2000, on suspicion of arms trafficking and money laundering. Jean-Christophe (nicknamed 'Papamadit', or 'Daddy said') had served as his father's Elysée advisor on Africa from 1986 to 1992, and had been on Elf's payroll as a 'consultant' from 1992 until his father's death. He is suspected of having used his influence in Africa to secure two arms deals, worth more than $500 million, destined for the Angolan regime of José Eduardo dos Santos in 1993-94. Jean-Christophe admitted receiving $1.8 million in a Swiss bank account in 1997-98, claiming that $700,000 of this was his own, despite having claimed unemployment benefit that year. After spending Christmas in jail, he was bailed in January 2001 for €760,000, a sum his mother, Danielle, described as a 'ransom'.[56] The German Christlich-Demokratische Union (CDU) headed by Mitterrand's close ally, Chancellor Helmut Kohl, also allegedly benefited from Elf largesse. The CDU is said to have received a €37 million kickback in 1992 over Elf's purchase of the Leuna oil refinery, designed to bolster Kohl's chances of re-election in 1994, which both leaders viewed as indispensable to the continued construction of Europe. Despite his subsequent banishment from the party, Kohl always refused to say where the money had come from.[57] Notably, he was not called as a witness at the trial.

In a similar vein, Pierre Bilger, the former PDG of Alstom, was charged in May 2003 with 'abus de biens sociaux' for having allegedly authorised payment of €793,000 to Pierre Pasqua, son of the then Interior Minister, Charles Pasqua, in June 1994 – at a time when kickbacks to politicians were commonplace and even, some might say, expected. The money was intended to secure the agreement of the Interior Minister for the transfer of the headquarters of Alstom's transport company from Nanterre (Hauts de Seine) to Saint-Ouen (Seine Saint-Denis). Bilger insisted that he had acted in the best interests of the company and that Alstom's shareholders had not been disadvantaged.[58] To avoid becoming a figure of scandal in the eyes of company employees and investors – 'for the hundred thousand Alstom employees whom I have had the honour to manage and for the shareholders, whether or not they work for Alstom, who have had faith in me'[59] – in August 2003 Bilger repaid the €4.1 million he had received on leaving office, the first time a golden parachute had ever been repaid in France.[60]

Meanwhile, Jean Peyrelevade – previously seen as one of France's more progressive PDG, with a reputation for being his own man, willing to stand up to the government – has been condemned for what he knew, or did not know in 1998 about the purchase of Executive Life in 1991, two years before he joined Crédit Lyonnais, then under state control. The bank had secretly purchased the California-based insurance company using a consortium of shareholders as a front – despite the fact that, according to Californian law, banks were prohibited from acquiring local insurance companies. The French were keen to avoid a trial, which might result in the bank losing its US licence, and an out-of-court settlement worth $585 million came close to being clinched in September 2003. However, President Chirac personally vetoed the deal, because it did not include immunity from prosecution for his close friend, François Pinault. The latter, France's third richest man, a billionaire entrepreneur and former timber merchant whose holding company, Artémis, controlled Europe's main non-food retailer, Pinault-Printemps-Redoute (PPR), had helped to finance the acquisition of Executive Life by purchasing a portfolio of junk bonds.[61] In March 2004, Pinault paid €274 million in fines to settle the litigation against him.

In his resignation statement, Peyrelevade insisted: 'I do not remember anyone drawing my attention to the conditions of acquisition, which proved to be open to criticism, of Executive Life. I did not understand that there could be any problem in this regard before the 31st December 1998'.[62] The fact that Peyrelevade did not take over as boss of Crédit Lyonnais until 1993, two years after the acquisition, made little difference. The US regulator intervened personally to request that Peyrelevade resign, 'in order', Peyrelevade explained, 'to disassociate my own case from that of the bank'.[63] The new system, in which US institutional investors play a large and growing role, stared, unforgiving, at the sins of the old. The events of 2001-02, with the collapse of Enron and WorldCom in particular, have irrevocably changed people's attitudes in the US to corporate governance. As Ross Goobey, chairman of the International Corporate Governance Network and former head of Hermes Pensions Management has observed: 'Increasingly, the clients are asking their managers to get involved'.[64] The implications of this involvement for the management of top French companies are obvious, and far-reaching.

Executive remuneration

In 1995, the Greenbury Report turned the spotlight in the UK on the perceived problem of excessive rewards for senior management. A decade of scrutiny of directors' pay by remuneration committees had, by all appearances, failed to curb exorbitant pay awards. It may even have encouraged them. There is, after all, a natural logic to this. Since the non-executive members of remuneration committees are normally executive directives elsewhere, it is in their interests to sanction pay increases, of which they themselves are likely to benefit, reciprocally, in their own companies. At the same time, such advice as they do receive is likely to 'talk up' pay awards. As one study explains:

> Too few Remuneration Committees, even when composed entirely of non-executive directors, take the stance that they should pay as much but no more than is necessary to senior people. Rather they take the advice of the Chairman and CEO, sometimes supplemented by outside data provided by the Human Resource Director or by compensation consultants who have been hired by the Chairman or CEO. The mere presence of non-executives on the Remuneration Committee does not solve the Principal Agent problem. It may not be in the interests of non-executive directors (who are themselves almost always executive directors in major companies) to keep down levels of executive pay. On the contrary. When non-executive directors are themselves very highly paid within their own companies it can be positively in their interests to close the gap by recommending big increases in other companies' level of pay.[65]

While the relationship between pay at the top and that of the average employee was once fairly stable in the UK, there has been a growing detachment between the two. With globalisation, international benchmarking, especially against the US, has become commonplace. Thus, executive pay in the US is often cited as a reason for paying British executives more, on the (mistaken) premise that the higher salaries available there will lure away top executives. Yet, as Sir Adrian Cadbury argues, such 'international comparisons are only valid if all the other factors, like tax, are taken into account and they are often not relevant to those who choose to cite them'.[66]

A 1995 study of international governance regimes by the International Capital Markets Group (ICMG) observed that executive remuneration was not at the time a major issue in France, nor, indeed, Germany or Japan, where a balance of what was deemed socially acceptable and fair according to company performance was seen to apply.[67] France's draconian privacy laws have long kept the pay of individual executives out of the public domain. Any journalist who infringed personal privacy in this way could be thrown in jail. French privacy laws, writes Béatrix Le Wita, are the ethnologist's *bête noire*: 'private life, in [French] society, is that which is legally entitled to escape outside scrutiny', a salient difference with the UK, where lack of privacy is viewed as the unavoidable price of celebrity.[68] With the publication of the Greenbury Report in the UK, to which French business leaders looked increasingly for guidance in matters of corporate governance, and the growing presence of US pension funds amongst the shareholders of major French companies, pressure on them to disclose the pay packages of senior executives increased. That it continued to be resisted was assisted in part by the fact that Marc Viénot, the author of two governance reports, who was seen as the conscience of France's corporate elite, did not believe that the remuneration of senior executives should be made public, despite the fact that transparency was one of the key recommendations of the second Viénot Report.[69] Revealing the pay of top executives, he claimed, would serve only to help competitors lure them away with the offer of higher pay. While Americans liked to boast about their salaries, he argued, the French did not: 'what other profession in France has to reveal salaries?', he asked, adding that it was hard to 'justify the discrimination' against the PDG.[70] It is true that such disclosure goes against the grain of the culture of discretion that has long prevailed in France, where it is simply not done to flaunt one's wealth. Herein lays a familiar double standard: while to *inherit* wealth is regarded as noble, to be seen to *acquire* it is viewed as far less seemly. Interestingly, in the ten years since the publication of the first Viénot Report, executive remuneration in France has increased sizeably.[71]

The publication of the second Viénot Report in 1999 was followed by new legislation in the form of the NRE on 15 May 2001. This obliged companies to disclose in annual reports the total remuneration, including stock options, of their top ten senior executives – collectively, not individually.[72] Whereas in 2000, only six PDG of the CAC-40 companies disclosed their salaries, by 2001 almost half had done so (46 per cent). By 2002, 95 per cent of leading companies had complied with the new law, and just two (Michelin and Sodexho) continued to refuse.[73] That said, only 20 chose to provide detailed information concerning the fixed and variable components of executive pay. The 2002 Bouton Report likewise insisted on the importance of transparency of remuneration.[74]

France has displayed a certain 'cultural resistance' to corporate governance measures.[75] Full implementation of the 1995 Viénot Report was not achieved until 2002, and several firms, most prominently Michelin, have displayed a 'tradition of silence' on the subject.[76] Yet there has been a conspicuous willingness to increase incentives and rewards in what might be termed a 'creeping Americanisation' of French business culture with regard to executive pay. A growing number of firms in difficulties are making large pay-offs to senior executives associated with business failure. In the light of this, French deputies held an inquiry into executive pay in October 2003. Both Pierre Bilger, who had reimbursed his €4.1 million pay-off, and Jean-Marie Messier, who had battled at an American tribunal to secure one of $20.5 million from Vivendi,[77] gave evidence.

While the average pay packet of a CAC-40 PDG in 2002 amounted to €1,825,000 (including fixed and variable components), the highest salary was awarded to Lindsay Owen-Jones of L'Oréal, who in 2002 won the accolade of 'manager of the year', the first time this had been awarded to a non-French national. Owen-Jones was top earner both for fixed and variable pay, receiving €5,552,000 in total.[78] When, in an interview with Jean-Claude Le Grand, Director for Corporate Recruitment at L'Oréal, it was mentioned that Owen-Jones was the best paid CEO in France, he retorted, 'Yes, and he is badly paid! I worry when people are badly paid!'[79] Le Grand added that he expected an international market for executive pay to be established in the end. Obviously such a market would in all likelihood be influenced by the situation in the US, and might be expected to exacerbate the growing detachment of top executive salaries from that of the average company worker, as in the UK.

That said, the ethics committee of MEDEF has argued that executive pay should enhance solidarity within the firm, not detract from it: 'Remuneration policy must be measured, balanced, equitable and reinforce solidarity within the firm'.[80] MEDEF insisted that while 'the market is one point of reference ... it cannot be the only one'.[81] One member of the ethics committee, Madame Agnès Lépinay, Director of Economic, Financial and Fiscal Affairs at MEDEF, and a member of the 2002 Bouton committee, explained at interview that the intention had been to establish a more secure ethical position than that contained in the Bouton Report.[82]

All too often in the UK, the link between performance and remuneration has been similarly tenuous. There are too many examples of the top executives of large firms performing badly while rewarding themselves handsomely for their efforts. While MG Rover made substantial losses from 2002, its directors – who had bought the company in 2000 for just £10 – rewarded themselves handsomely, setting up a £13 million trust fund for their own pensions.[83] Corus, the Anglo-Dutch steel group born of the merger of British Steel with Hoogovens in 1999, watered down the link between performance and bonuses in 2003, increasing the maximum bonus paid to directors from 50 per cent to 60 per cent of salary. At the same time, it was announced that 1,150 British workers were to lose their jobs by 2005, on top of 6,000 previously announced. The latest round of cuts involved redundancies at several of the company's smaller plants in the UK (Rotherham, Tipton, Llanwern, Teeside and Scunthorpe). Most dramatically of all, it signalled the end of steel making in Sheffield, once the heartland of steel production in the UK.[84] Similarly Boots, the health and beauty group, offered its new CEO, Richard Baker, a guaranteed bonus worth 50 per cent of his £625,000 salary, irrespective of performance, in addition to a £644,000 'golden hello'.[85] The concept of a 'guaranteed bonus' is something of an oxymoron, yet such devices for boosting executive pay are becoming more commonplace. This flies in the face of guidelines published in December 2002 by the National Association of Pension Funds (NAPF) together with the Association of British Insurers (ABI) to the effect that remuneration committees should acknowledge the possibility of executive failure when drawing up contracts, and mitigate pay-offs. Cable & Wireless took the NAPF's advice in June 2003, when its former CEO's pay-off on leaving the company was reduced to six months' salary and a £500,000 boost to his pension fund. Since Wallace could have demanded as much as £1,162,000 in salary and £643,000 in pension, the cut was hailed as a victory for shareholder activism. But it still amounted to a reward of £887,500 for a man who had presided over a significant decline in the value of the telecommunications firm.[86] Niall Fitzgerald, former Chairman of Unilever, has described excessive rewards to ousted bosses as a 'potential cancer' holding society in its grip.[87]

One of the reasons for rising levels of executive pay, sometimes in the face of poor performance, is the fact that the main reference point for pay is not performance but company size. One US study established that 'firm size accounted for eight times more variance in CEO pay than did firm performance'.[88] It is nevertheless hard to avoid the view that self-seeking behaviour has become 'institutionalised' at the highest levels. It cannot help that in Britain leading politicians, Cabinet Ministers and MPs, who ought to be setting the tone, have bumped up their own pensions while those of most workers have been squeezed. In 2001, MPs voted to grant themselves a 25 per cent rise in their guaranteed final salary scheme – already the second most generous pension scheme in Britain after that of BP.[89]

The importance of ownership

The divorce of ownership and control highlighted in the 1920s by Berle and Means in the US, where the control of founding families decreased as firms expanded, did not occur to the same extent in Europe, where they have continued to play an important role. Jones and Rose note the continuing importance of the family firm in Europe in the 1990s,[90] when between 75 per cent and 99 per cent of enterprises in the EU were family firms.[91] Whilst often small, these nevertheless accounted for some 65 per cent of business turnover in the EU and 66 per cent of total employment.[92]

Table 3.1 Ownership of top 100 companies in France and the UK in 1998

Ownership	France No.	UK No.
Public Company – Dispersed Shareholding	22	95
Public Company – Concentrated Shareholding	42	5
Dominant Family Shareholding	15	0
Dominant State Shareholding	15	0
Co-operative Enterprise/ Groupement d'Intérêt Économique (GIE)	6	0
	100	**100**

Note: A company with a dispersed shareholding is defined as no single shareholder or shareholder group holding 20% or more of equity. A company with a concentrated shareholding is defined by a single shareholder or shareholder group holding 20% or more of equity. A dominant family or state holding is 20% or more of equity.

As Table 3.1 demonstrates, family ownership continues to matter much more in France than in Britain, 15 of the top 100 French companies in 1998 being family-dominated, against none of the top 100 British companies.[93] While 95 of the British top 100 companies were public companies with dispersed shareholdings, this applied to just 22 of the top 100 French firms. Franks and Mayer found in 1995 that 84 per cent of the top British listed companies had no shareholder holding more than 25 per cent of the voting equity.[94] Britain differs further from France as one of only two countries (together with Switzerland) where stock market capitalisation exceeds annual GDP.[95] The legal forms of company are also more varied in France. Whereas 99 of the top 100 British companies in 1998 were public limited companies, with one mutual company being the exception that confirms the rule, 83 of the top 100 French companies were *Sociétés anonymes*, seven were *enter-*

prises publiques, four were cooperatives, three were *sociétés en com-mandite par actions*, two *Groupement d'Intérêt Economique* and one company an *Association (loi 1901)*.

Liliane Bettencourt provides an example of the enduring nature of family control in leading French firms. She is the daughter of Eugène Schneider, a French chemist who developed a formula for hair dye and, in 1907, founded L'Oréal. Madame Bettencourt holds 53.7 per cent of the shares (through the family holding company Gesparal) in what is now a global enterprise, the world's largest cosmetics maker by sales.[96] Jean-Claude Le Grand recounted how business analysts had regularly sought to convince Madame Bettencourt to distribute her wealth across several companies, rather than put all her eggs in one basket. This she refused to do, preferring to affirm her faith in the family firm.[97] With a fortune estimated at £9.1 billion, she is believed to be France's richest person, and the 12th richest in the world.[98]

There is some disagreement over whether the persistence of family ownership in France has been largely beneficial or harmful. The debate over the impact of the persistence of family capitalism is, of course, long in the tooth. David Landes' powerful thesis ascribes the disappointing performance of the French economy before 1945 to its atomistic structure and the predominance of inherently conservative family capitalism.[99] Similarly, Chandler insists that it was precisely the prevalence of personal capitalism in the UK – dominated by 'gentlemen', the sons of founding entrepreneurs, and 'players', salaried managers who aspired to become gentlemen – which let down the British economy until well after the Second World War, impeding the development of the long-term industrial capabilities needed to achieve domestic and international success.[100] Growth, he claims, was not the main goal of the personally managed British firm, even the most efficient of which sought a gentlemanlike co-operation rather than the aggressive price competition more typical of American firms, preferring current income to reinvestment in the business. Despite the limitations of this thesis,[101] Chandler's point that British family firms were slow off the mark when the new industries were born, at huge cost to the economy, is to some degree persuasive.[102]

Chadeau, on the other hand, argues that the growth of large family-controlled firms in France between the wars was hindered 'less by a conservatism born of personal capitalism than by market limitations'.[103] Moreover, many performed well, successfully penetrating international markets. L'Oréal, for example, has operations in 59 countries, having expanded into the US, Latin America and Asia. The company has what it terms three 'creativity' centres, in Paris, New York and Tokyo, with a portfolio of 17 international brands, including Lancôme, Maybelline and the Japanese Shu Uemura.[104] L'Oréal has enjoyed enormous stability in its hundred-year history, having had only four PDG during this time. The fourth, Lindsay Owen-Jones, was appointed head of the firm in 1988, a prodigious achievement for a foreigner from a lower-middle-class background whose studies at Oxford were in literature.[105] The company's success confirms the conclusions of a recent study by the Ecole des Mines, according to which a combination of family ownership and professional management provides the best corporate model for France, 'uniting wisdom and dynamism'.[106] Indeed, contrary to the logic of the Chandler thesis, there is no evidence that companies like L'Oréal, Michelin, Sodexho (Bellon family) and LVMH (Arnault family) have had their investment and internationalisation plans curtailed due to family ownership.

Stability, however, has at times been compromised by the difficulties of succession in the typical French family firm.[107] French succession law is complex and financially penalising. Many family firms that have gone into liquidation have done so following the death of the founding member. However, many others have used financial vehicles such as investment trusts to retain family control. Hermès International, for example, is one of the French luxury goods manufacturers to remain family owned. The firm went public in 1993 (under pressure from some of the family) but retained over 80 per cent of its equity in the hands of 56 members of three founding families, the Dumas, Guerrand and Puech families, descendants of the founder Thierry Hermès.

The use of the holding company in particular, which crystallised in the inter-war years, and which was explicitly designed to allow the parent company to control or influence a group of associated companies without, however, assuming full control of these, has enabled families to 'have their cake and eat it' by reconciling expansion with personal control.[108] Scott notes that in 1971 one-half of France's top 200 enterprises remained in family hands, with most families enjoying majority or dominant minority control, while in 1987 Morin found that 57 per cent of the 200 largest privately-owned French companies had a single individual or family as majority shareholder. Family control by means of the holding company, bolstered by crossed shareholdings which proliferated in the post-war period, gave rise to a uniquely French style of capitalism, 'capitalism without capital', as it has been dubbed. This was dominated by an oligarchy of families – a closed aristocracy, traditionally reluctant to admit newcomers[109] – whose all-embracing influence extended beyond the major businesses to the Banque de France, the Paris Stock Exchange and even the press, 'weighing heavily on the destiny of France'.[110]

In the 1970s, this extended family of associated enterprises featured two big godfathers – Suez and Paribas – creating rival financial empires that dominated the corporate landscape. Crédit Lyonnais and Union des Assurances de Paris (UAP) sought to replace them in the early 1990s, seeking to emulate German-style links between banks and firms (an idea promoted by the late Pierre Bérégovoy, called *bancindustrie*). Strategic alliances were promoted between the banking and insurance sectors (UAP fostered a relationship with BNP, and Crédit Lyonnais with Assurances Générales de France (AGF), termed *bancassurance*), but the endeavour failed. Crédit Lyonnais went bankrupt in 1993; UAP was acquired by its rival AXA in 1996; while AGF was swallowed up by the German insurer Allianz in 1998.

The real 'revolution' in ownership, at least in the latter part of the twentieth century, and especially in the US and UK, has been in the escalation in shareholdings by financial intermediaries, a replacement of individual shareholders by institutional shareholders – banks, insurances companies, occupational pension funds, and pooled investment vehicles, such as unit trusts – leading to the control of large enterprises by what Scott and Griff term 'a constellation of financial interests'.[111] By 1981, insurance companies and pension funds held 20.5 per cent and 26.7 per cent respectively of shares in British firms, as against 8.8 per cent and 3.4 per cent in 1957, while share ownership by individuals fell from 65.8 per cent to 28.2 per cent of market value over the same period.[112] By 2000, according to Bloch and Kremp, individuals or families continued to hold sizeable holdings in France (more than 50 per cent), with non-financial firms and holdings the second most important category of owners (more than 30 per cent). Financial firms and foreign firms each owned approximately 3 per cent of the capital, while the state was by now a relatively modest shareholder.[113] In marked contrast, individual share ownership in the UK stood at just 20 per cent of the UK equity market in 2001, down from 50 per cent in the early 1960s.[114]

The value of British pension funds quadrupled during the 1980s due to the explosion in occupational and personal pension schemes, fuelled by government incentives and tax concessions to shift the burden of pensions away from the social security system on to the private sector. Under Margaret Thatcher, the link with the rise in average earnings was broken; henceforth the state pension would increase in line with inflation, which had fallen considerably. The collective value of British pension funds rose from £8 billion in the late 1970s to an estimated £650 billion by 1997, equal to 68 per cent of annual GDP.[115] They were hit hard, however, by the subsequent removal of the tax credit by Chancellor Gordon Brown, and scandals such as endowment mis-selling and the near-collapse of Equitable Life further dented public confidence.

In France, the picture is different. In 1997, fledgling pension funds represented a tiny 4 per cent of GDP, totalling no more than $50 billion.[116] While 75 per cent of the British labour force was covered by a privately funded pension scheme (50 per cent by occupational pensions and 25 per cent by personal pensions, both voluntary), in France private coverage was limited to less than 10 per cent of the workforce.[117] Funded pensions have clearly won the argument in Europe over pay-as-you-go schemes, owing to projected demographic difficulties.[118] Laws have been passed in several EU member states, including France, to pave the way for pension reform. The French, however, remain strongly attached to their state-run pension scheme, whereby those in work pay directly for those who are retired. The scheme is notably generous: a teacher with 37.5 years of contributions will retire on not less than 75 per cent of his or her final salary. Many *regimes spéciaux* apply, according privileged terms to, in particular, SNCF, RATP, EdF and GdF employees. The concern is that unfunded pension liabilities will progressively drain government finances, despite the modest reforms introduced by the Raffarin government in 2003 (which aimed to bring public-sector workers in line with those in the private sector, increasing the number of years employees needed to work to qualify for the full state pension).[119]

Shareholdings in French firms by non-residents – often US institutional investors – are nevertheless increasing fast. In the late 1990s, US pension and mutual funds sought to invest their capital internationally, targeting firms in continental Europe, buying up released equity as government and non-financial firms reduced their involvement in non-core business sectors, thereby inducing a trend shift in shareholding classes.[120] By 1998, the Californian public-sector employees' pension fund, CalPERS, the biggest public pension fund in the US, had significant holdings in all of France's top companies, while US mutual funds Templeton and Fidelity chose to target specific firms. By 1998, Maréchal found that non-residents held as much as one-quarter of the equity of French listed companies.[121] Morin, as mentioned, put this figure as high as 35 per cent.[122] By 2000, foreign ownership of the equity of the top 40 companies had reached an average of more than 40 per cent, a record among the world's leading industrial nations. The most international firm by ownership of the CAC-40 was TotalFinaElf (renamed Total in 2003), with 65 per cent of its equity in the hands of non-residents. In second place was Dexia (55.7 per cent), while in third place was Suez Lyonnaise des Eaux (55 per cent, following its takeover of Générale de Belgique).[123] This rise in international share ownership is helping to promote international standards of corporate governance. Foreign investors clearly do not want to invest money in companies with poor governance standards.

Institutional investors have not tended in the past to seek a close relationship with the management of the firms in which they chose to invest. But ownership brings responsibilities. With the shift in the pattern of share ownership in favour of institutional investors, exit has to some extent given way to voice as a means of expressing dissatisfaction with top management. There are two reasons for this, as Sir Adrian Cadbury clarifies. Firstly, boards can no longer disregard the views of major shareholders, especially when there is consensus between them. Secondly, there are powerful motivations for investors to use their influence on boards to improve the performance of their portfolios. Now that holdings are larger, as Georg Siemens, former chairman of Deutsche Bank puts it, 'If you cannot sell, you must care'.[124] Shareholder activism is encouraged by the NAPF, which proposes having a shareholder representative on the board, and which in 2003 ran numerous shareholder campaigns. In April 2003 alone, the NAPF recommended 32 annual general meeting (AGM) abstentions – but only four no votes.

An illustration of the extent to which investing institutions can be prepared to stay and fight for the best deal for their clients is nevertheless provided by a groundbreaking lawsuit launched by CalPERS against the New York Stock Exchange. The pension fund sued the NYSE and several member firms for $155 million for turning a blind eye to illegal trading practices (known as 'front running'). The lawsuit, which followed criticism of the $190 million severance payment made to Dick Grasso, former head of the exchange, sought damages for all shareholders who had invested in equities since 1998, as well as for pensioners. As Sean Harrigan, president of the board, explained:

> We are filing today a landmark lawsuit to recover losses and to right a serious wrong that exists at the New York Stock Exchange. That wrong concerns the specialist trading system. The lawsuit alleges that the exchange looked the other way when these rules were violated. We intend to seek recovery of every single dollar lost.[125]

The implications of the case extend well beyond the US. Such investors have important holdings on both sides of the Atlantic. In 2003, following the successful merger of the television companies Carlton and Granada to create a single ITV company, big investors including Merrill Lynch Investment Managers and Fidelity, angered by the 2002 fiasco of ITV Digital, launched a 'coup' against the former Carlton head, Michael Green, to prevent him from taking over as CEO of the new corporation. Meanwhile, at BSkyB, where 30-year-old James Murdoch, son of Chairman Rupert Murdoch, became the youngest CEO of a FTSE 100 company, leading shareholders, including Standard Life and Barclays Global Investors, concerned about his lack of experience, fought the board over his appointment. Standard Life issued a statement to express its disappointment, adding: 'This highlights our ongoing concerns about corporate governance at BSkyB'. Options for large investors included pressing for further corporate governance reform at the company, or refusing to endorse the appointment of James Murdoch as director, or approve the re-election of non-executive directors, a course of action favoured by NAPF.[126]

The job of non-executive director has also became more demanding, as evinced by the plight of 15 former directors of Equitable Life who were sued for negligence for £1.7 billion by the company's new board.[127] It was alleged that from 1993 to 2000 they failed to safeguard the interests of investors and policyholders. In 1999, with long-term interest rates in decline, the board took the decision to renege on promises of guaranteed annuities. The idea that promises to policyholders should be insured for £200 million had been briefly mooted at a board meeting, but was rejected as too expensive. The House of Lords' ruling in 2000 that the mutual should honour its guarantees to 70,000 policyholders subsequently blew a £1.5 billion hole in its finances, forcing the company to close to new business.[128] It appeared that non-executive directors at Equitable Life were unable to stand up to its charismatic managing director, Roy Ranson (1991-97), described by Lord Penrose in his report, published in March 2004, as 'autocratic', 'aggressive' and 'manipulative'.[129] The Cadbury Report defines independence as meaning that directors 'should be independent of management and free from any business or other relationship which could materially interfere with the exercise of their independent judgement'.[130] Independence of mind and the ability to challenge executives depends as much on individual character as on the absence of any commercial relationship with the company. Board minutes reveal that the ending of the guarantees on guaranteed annuity policies at Equitable Life was broached only once in a meeting. Directors were apparently satisfied by Ranson's assurances that there was no problem. As Wheatcroft writes: 'To have pressed the matter might have been to upset Mr Ranson and it seems clear that upsetting Mr Ranson was something that people at Equitable Life were keen to avoid'.[131] This again underlines the importance of effective board functioning to good corporate governance.

One final major change in shareholding patterns has been the evolving role of the state, particularly in France, where its participation as a shareholder has declined dramatically over the past 25 years. From its peak in 1981-82, when, following the socialist nationalisation programme, the public sector embraced 24 per cent of employees, 32 per cent of sales, 30 per cent of exports and 60 per cent of annual investment in the industrial and energy sectors,[132] the state has became, according to Bloch and Kremp, an 'unimportant' shareholder.[133]   Yet amongst the top 100 French companies in 1998, 15 possessed a dominant state shareholding (with seven officially designated 'entreprises publiques'), as against none in the UK (see Table 3.1).[134] Business organisations in the UK have a legal duty to act at all times in the best interests of shareholders, to maximise shareholder value, even though at times this may contravene the long-term interests of the company. In France, the British obsession with shareholder value is replaced by a wider concern with the 'social interest' of the firm, as enshrined in the *arrêt Freuhauf-France* of 22 May 1965. Henri Weber defines this as a belief in the common weal uniting the interests of workers and employers; a belief that economic and social affairs cannot be separated; and an expectation that employers should pay attention to their responsibilities as well as to their rights.[135] Whereas the British government has long since abdicated any responsibility it once may have had for the survival and prosperity of British industry, *dirigisme* is alive and well in France, where underlying values, attitudes and beliefs have changed comparatively little.

The cases of Alstom and Bombardier provide graphic illustrations of the contrasting attitudes that characterise the two countries.[136] When, in September 2003, Alstom was on the brink of bankruptcy, with estimated debts of €5 billion, the state was only too keen to put together a rescue package which involved a capital injection of €3.4 billion, and would have seen it emerge with 31 per cent of the company's shares. In the event, the European Commission vetoed the restructuring package, on the grounds that it breached state aid rules, and another was put forward in its stead. According to the new, renegotiated deal, Alstom's 30 creditor banks accepted a €3.2 billion rescue plan, while the French government ploughed €1.5 billion in short-term aid into the company, exchanging a direct stake in Alstom for a 20-year, €300 million eurobond, convertible into shares should the Commission agree.[137]   But whether the rescue package ultimately involved an infusion of equity, a subsidy or a direct stake in the company is ultimately immaterial. As Charkham pertinently remarks, 'The point is the investment, not its classification'.[138] Alstom was safe, and its thousands of employees, in France at least, breathed a sigh of relief. The 10,000 or so workers Alstom employed in the UK did not, however, enjoy the same protection. Fearing widespread job losses, Derek Simpson, the general secretary of Amicus, bemoaned the British government's attitude, and regretted that it was not more like the French:

> [Alstom's UK workers] still face the sack in the New Year simply because it is easier and cheaper to get rid of British workers. Our people have been sacrificed to keep the French afloat … We would like our government to act in the same way, rather than allowing 2,500 manufacturing jobs a week to disappear from this country.[139]

The sentiment that, in this inexorable erosion of British manufacturing industry, a portion of blame should lie with the British government, was confirmed in an interview with a top-ranking director of Bombardier Transportation, who admitted that, while train manufacturing was more expensive in Germany than in the UK, and while British productivity was higher, in a straight choice between closing plants in Germany or Britain, Britain would be chosen. This was due to the fact that the German government had made it clear that if a single German plant were shut down, Bombardier would never sell another train carriage in Germany: 'Close down in the UK', a German industry minister exhorted, 'not in Germany!' The director concerned, a former Danish naval officer who used nautical analogies to illustrate his points, concluded that the British were not as good at 'rowing the boat' as the Germans or French:

> The Brits … are following the rules to the letter, and we are seeing much more flexibility on the continent. I don't think we will ever be able to export trains to Germany, and still our government is importing freight from Germany to the UK for the South, and I think that for an industry which is mainly sponsored by taxpayers' money, I think it's a disgrace.[140]

This attitude on the part of the British government was plainly visible in its failure to offer MG Rover anything more than sticking plaster, in the form of a £6.5 million loan, when the company collapsed in April 2005, leading to the closure of the Longbridge plant, at a potential loss of 20,000 jobs in the West Midlands.[141] The EU questioned the loan; but the attitude of the French government in a similar position is often to carry on regardless. As Nicolas Sarkozy, then Finance Minister, put it when faced with the crisis at Alstom: 'It is not a right of the state to help its industry. It is a duty'.[142] The fact that Alstom had been bailed out by the French state without the prior approval of the European Commission prompted a year-long EU investigation into the terms of the Alstom rescue package. Sarkozy, however, remained committed to saving the engineering giant, stating in May 2004 that he would do everything in his power to prevent its break-up.[143] In the event, he successfully negotiated a four-year deadline for Alstom to enter into a partnership with another private-sector firm. While the Commission favoured the German Siemens, the French government had its sights on a partnership with the French nuclear group Areva, the company formed by the merger of Cogema, Framatome and CE Industrie in 2002.[144]

Board structure and composition: where does power lie?

As currently configured, power in the modern corporation lies primarily not with large institutional investors, despite the advances these have made in recent years with respect to ownership and influence, or with small shareholders, who are likely to be widely dispersed and geographically spread, but rather with the board of directors. As Tricker asserts, 'Power lies with the incumbent board'.[145] That said, France and Britain display marked differences in this regard.

In the first place, as the second Viénot Report highlights, the French situation appears to be unique in Europe: since 1966, French companies have had the option of single board (*conseil d'administration*) or a two-tier board (*conseil de surveillance* and *directoire*)'.[146] The former is considered to be based on the British board of directors, while the latter is fashioned on the German Vorstand/Aufsichtsrat model. Nevertheless the unitary model, as it has evolved in France, is very different from British practice. Members of the *conseil d'administration* are all non-executive with the exception of the PDG, who serves as both the president of the *conseil* and as the most senior executive. The PDG, who must own a substantial number of shares in the company, is thus an extremely powerful figure. The two-tier system, on the other hand, grants full executive authority to a management board (*le directoire*), but this is monitored by the supervisory board (*le conseil de surveillance*). Members of the supervisory board are shareholders appointed at the shareholders' general meeting, and they also appoint the management board and its president. The president of the management board – who is not obliged to own shares in the company – is thus accorded a lower profile than the PDG.

In practice, the vast majority of French listed companies prefer the unitary system precisely because it permits strong leadership.[147] In 2003, as many as 72 per cent of top 100 French companies continued to use the unitary structure, down slightly from 75 per cent in 1998, as Table 3.2 highlights. The French situation displays an extraordinary concentration of power in the person of the PDG, in whom sole executive authority is vested – reflective of the long-standing French tradition of the centralisation of power in an individual or institution, characteristic of Colbertism, Bonapartism or Gaullism (at times alternating with periods of weaker institutions as in the Fourth Republic), and which the Revolution of 1789 did not change but rather confirmed. According to law, the PDG is elected by the board, which is appointed by the shareholders. In law, shareholders holding more than 50 per cent of voting rights can appoint 100 per cent of board members. In practice, it is the PDG who has tended to handpick the board (and on occasion even his own successor),[148] a process likened by Jean Peyrelevade, former PDG of UAP and Crédit Lyonnais, to the election of the Communist Party in North Korea![149] Once appointed, the PDG is king. He (it is usually he) dominates the board. As Peyrelevade insists, 'Power in the boardroom, as everyone knows, is not for sharing!'[150] Such is the authority of the PDG that the law stipulates no criteria at all for the terms and conditions of his employment. Article 98 of the French company law of 1966 entrusts boards with 'the most extensive powers to act in any circumstance in the name of the company'. Yet article 113 uses precisely the same phrase to define the extensive powers of the PDG, giving rise to a fundamental confusion, regarding the PDG and the company itself as effectively indivisible, one and the same.[151] The functions of chairman and CEO have been united in his role since 1940, a hangover from the Vichy regime.

Moutet points out that this supreme authority and the notion of a power which is not for sharing owe much to the First World War, which glorified the image of the captain who leads his men on attack from the front, values which continue to be instilled by the military-style Ecole Polytechnique, where many of France's 'captains of industry' are educated (see Chapter 4).[152] Indeed, Moutet observes that the unquestioned authority of the foreman in the workplace, the intermediary between management and employees, derives from the same source: the total obedience that had to be shown to be army sergeant in the trenches of the First World War.

Table 3.2 Board structures of top 100 companies in France and the UK in 1998 and 2003

Structure	France		UK	
	1998	**2003**	**1998**	**2003**
Unitary Main Board (UK unitary)	-	-	100	100
Conseil d'Administration + Comité Exécutif (French unitary)	75	72	-	-
Conseil de Surveillance + Directoire (French dual)	25	28	-	-

Note: In some cases, the data for 2003 relate to a successor company.

The French system has nevertheless begun to show signs of change. A rash of corporate scandals has encouraged leading French *patrons* to share strategic decision-making amongst a small group of top company executives. Increasingly, the PDG no longer takes decisions in isolation but as part – albeit the most important part – of a small executive board. This consists normally of the PDG, the chief financial officer (CFO) and a third executive, entitled in the case of Alstom 'Chief Executive Vice President'.

Moreover, there has been some pressure to separate the functions of Chairman and CEO which have traditionally been embodied in the role of the PDG. The second Viénot Report viewed the two-tier system as expensive and inefficient, and this in part explains the relatively slow rate of change demonstrated in Table 3.2. Given the rather vague definition of 'independence' employed, the composition of the supervisory board has not always been such as to ensure its independence from the management board and major shareholders.[153] The Report therefore advocated a change in the law to allow the functions of Chairman and CEO, united in the role of PDG, to be separated. This was enacted in the NRE law of May 2001. By December 2002, 15 of France's top companies had elected to separate responsibilities at the top. Several bastions of family capitalism opted for separation, including Accor, Casino, Lagardère, Michelin, Peugeot and PPR.[154] But the division of the two roles may be revoked and is thus reversible.[155] This occurred in the case of Alstom, when, in March 2003, Patrick Kron, then CEO, became PDG on the resignation of Pierre Bilger from his position as Chairman, reuniting the two roles and returning to the *status quo*. Suez likewise reunited the functions of Chairman and CEO in the person of Gérard Mestrallet.

Overall, the conduct of non-executive French board members has tended to be overwhelmingly compliant with the wishes of the PDG, especially since he in turn may well be a board member of their own organisation (see Chapter 6). While the NRE limited the number of directorships an individual could hold to five (or four for a managing director or member of a supervisory board), one year after its enactment several directors exceeded this number by some way. Jean Peyrelevade held seven directorships, and Michel Pébereau and Jean-Marie Messier six each.[156] Such incestuousness was more likely to breed a cosy complacency than any tendency to rock the boat.

That said, there are signs that a small number have become more willing to speak out. Claude Bébéar, the powerful former chairman of AXA, for example, who served on the board of Vivendi Universal, is known to have campaigned for the removal of Jean-Marie Messier as its head.[157] There is other evidence that board members in France were becoming more independent. The 2002 Bouton Report defined an independent director as entertaining 'no relation at all with the company, its group or management, which might compromise the exercise of his judgement'.[158] The Report recommended in particular that the proportion of independent directors on the main board should increase from at least one-third, as recommended by the second Viénot Report, to one-half.[159] In 2002, seven CAC-40 companies achieved this aim, while five exceeded it: Air Liquide, Alstom, AXA, Lafarge and Schneider. Some, however, continued to flout the recommendation, with several companies – Capgemini, EADS, Renault and Sodexho – having only one independent director, and one (TF1) having none at all.[160] The second Viénot Report also specified proportions of independent directors for key company committees, namely that they should comprise one-third of the audit committee, one-half of the remuneration committee, and one-third of the nomination committee. With a large number of CAC-40 companies exceeding these recommendations, the independence of these key governance committees has increased, ostensibly at least, by 55 per cent, 83 per cent and 44 per cent respectively since 2001.[161] The second Viénot Report further recommended that directors' periods of tenure be reduced from six to four years.

Two months prior to his resignation as Chairman of the Board at Alstom in 2003, Pierre Bilger explained the growing role of the board in the nomination process that led to the appointment of his successor, CEO Patrick Kron:

Normally you would say that a Board has no importance apart from to remove a CEO and to appoint a new one. That is probably the most important aspect of a board. In our case, probably 15 years ago there would have been some consultation with the French government. Obviously, in my case, when I was appointed in 1990 there was no consultation at all. Times have changed from this point of view. With the increasing role of the board in the nomination process, the criteria have become more objective. A board has always got to justify a decision it makes, has always got to bear in mind that at some point in time, especially when you are listed in the Paris and New York Stock Exchange, as we are, somebody could ask how you took that decision, which steps have you taken to reach a decision. This means that in this case it took more than 18 months, we started in September 2000, which means more than two years, to find the right person. We appointed a headhunter; we carried out a review of what our external and internal options were, we submitted a short list to a psychological analyst, etc. Not only to protect ourselves, but also for the benefit of the shareholders. This professional approach is clearly incompatible with external interference.[162]

In Britain, the unitary board of directors, consisting of both top executives and non-executive directors, has been the norm for many years. Indeed, so ubiquitous has it become that there is little prospect of alternative forms being adopted. The concept of a two-tier board has been denounced by the Institute of Directors (IoD) as unnecessary and potentially destructive of the unified vision of strategy which the unitary board allows.[163] Another reason why it would be likely to encounter fierce resistance from business leaders is that it is often equated with worker participation, which has been a feature of the German supervisory board model since the 1970s.

That is not to say, however, that UK boards have remained untouched by the corporate governance agenda. As in France, the combination of the roles of Chairman and CEO attracted criticism. The Cadbury Report promoted the separation of responsibilities at the head of listed companies, in order to achieve a balance of power and authority, 'such that no one individual has unfettered powers of decision'.[164] As Sir Adrian Cadbury has expressed it, no one person is wise enough on his or her own: '*Nemo solis satis sapit*'.[165] Already by 1998, 91 of the top 100 UK companies had separate Chairmen and CEOs, and the number was to rise to all 100 by 2003-04.

Much of the attention in the UK has focussed on the role of the non-executive director. In Britain, stress had long been laid on the independence of non-executive directors: in a recommendation contained in the Watkinson Report of 1973; by Pro Ned, the association which promotes the presence of non-executive directors on boards, founded in 1982; by the Cadbury Report; and most recently by the Higgs Review. This was launched following high-profile corporate collapses in both the UK and the US, implicit in which was the suggestion that non-executive directors were failing to attach sufficient importance to their monitoring role. Published in January 2003, the review aimed to 'let in some daylight' on the role of the non-executive director and the workings of the board.[166] It expanded the definition of 'independence' provided by the Cadbury Report, based on the notion that 'all directors have to take decisions objectively in the interests of the company'.[167]

The Higgs Review proved to be contentious, however, arousing widespread criticism from chairmen and non-executives alike. It had argued that independent directors should meet at least once a year on their own;[168] that they should hold regular meetings with major shareholders, and that these should be specified in the annual report.[169] It argued, further, that company chairmen should be banned from heading the nomination committee, to be chaired instead by an independent director,[170] a proposal rejected by 87 per cent of chairmen in a Confederation of British Industry (CBI) poll.[171] Further recommendations included the barring of chief executives from becoming chairmen of the same company,[172] while no individual was to hold more than one FTSE chairmanship.[173] Non-executive directors were likewise angered by the review, which some interpreted as an attempt to turn them into 'corporate policemen', while seeking to limit their tenure to two terms of three years.[174] To be well informed, directors would have to undergo induction and professional development, while their performance should be evaluated annually.[175] Sir Adrian Cadbury welcomed this emphasis on training, admitting in an interview that this was an issue about which he felt very strongly:

> It seems to me quite extraordinary that it should appear to be the one job in the world for which people don't feel they need to be trained. And I know that, because one of the outcomes of the [Cadbury] Report was that we started a new training course. But we didn't really get a vast number of people wanting to come on it, so it was not the understanding, I think, of our board members.[176]

This was similar to the situation in France, where moves to encourage the training of non-executive directors were tentative and largely unsuccessful. Although training was recommended by the Bouton Report, it remained voluntary: 'Each director should benefit, if he deems it necessary, from complementary training on the specificities of the enterprise, its businesses and sector of activity'.[177]

Although the Higgs Review did not propose an age limit for directors, implicit in it was the suggestion that company boards needed new blood, the Cadbury Report having warned against a loss of board vitality should non-executive directors remain on the board too long.

Table 3.3 Age profiles of the business elites of France and the UK in 1998

	France		UK	
	Female	**Male**	**Female**	**Male**
Population				
% under 30	1.9	0.2	0.0	0.1
% 30-39	18.5	3.6	5.3	0.9
% 40-49	38.9	24.4	24.6	20.3
% 50-59	29.6	43.7	54.5	49.4
% 60-69	5.6	21.6	17.5	28.2
% over 70	5.6	6.6	0.0	1.2
Mean Age	48.2	54.9	52.5	56.1
Standard Deviation	11.2	9.2	7.2	6.1
Top 100 Directors				
% under 30	0.0	0.0	0.0	0.0
% 30-39	50.0	1.0	0.0	0.0
% 40-49	0.0	19.4	0.0	9.2
% 50-59	50.0	40.8	0.0	66.3
% 60-69	0.0	30.6	100.0	24.5
% over 70	0.0	8.2	0.0	0.0
Mean Age	48.5	57.1	58.0	55.1
Standard Deviation	14.9	8.4	-	6.1

The evidence presented in Table 3.3 confirms the commonly held view that boards are heavily populated by experienced people aged 50 and above. There is little to choose between France and the UK with respect to the mean age of directors, but it is conspicuous that in France a small minority of relatively young people do find themselves in powerful positions. Some of the women in the sample in particular have advanced quickly through the ranks, although this phenomenon, as will be shown in Chapter 5, is exaggerated due to the appointment of young female relatives to the boards of family-owned firms. In France, also, it is more common for the careers of high-profile directors to be lengthened by their retention as non-executives on the boards of companies with whom they have enjoyed a special relationship. Take, for example, Marc Viénot, who served as Directeur-Général Adjoint, Directeur-Général and PDG of Société Générale between 1973 and 1997 before continuing as a non-executive *administrateur,* or Réné Thomas, who stepped down from an executive role at BNP in 1993, but retained a seat on the *conseil d'administration* until his death ten years later. Overall, however, the established pattern for boardroom recruitment is one of staid uniformity, which explains the impulse of reformers in both France and the UK to increase diversity amongst the population of non-executive directors.

Far from 'widening the gene pool' of non-executives, however, as Derek Higgs had hoped, as many as one in two British directors claimed that they would not seek re-election if the review's recommendations were implemented. Altogether, as many as 70 per cent of non-executive directors polled in an FTSE 250 survey (commissioned by the City law firm Norton Rose) were found to be against its proposals.[178] One interviewee, Lord Waldegrave, was sceptical as to the numbers of appropriately qualified, potential non-executive directors able to do the job effectively.[179] Such widespread criticism led to a watering down of the review's proposals by the Financial Reporting Council, the private-sector body responsible for overseeing changes to the Combined Code. In particular, the recommendation that chairmen should be banned from chairing nominations committees was speedily dropped. It was recognised, too, that a third term, though not automatic, was nevertheless acceptable for independent directors,[180] a concession which, in Sir Adrian Cadbury's eyes, made sense: 'I'd be horrified at the feeling that … at point x you cease to be independent. In my view independence is far more a state of mind than it is how long you've been on a board. I worry about prescription'.[181]

One of the most striking critics of the role of the non-executive director has been the Morrisons supermarket chain. Alone amongst Top 100 companies, it did not have any non-executive directors at all in 1998. The annual report and accounts for 1998 stated bluntly that 'The company does not have any non-executive directors and the board is currently of the opinion that there is no commercial benefit in appointing them'. By the time of the 2004 Report, in the wake of Morrisons' £3.35 billion acquisition of Safeway, the company's position had weakened to the extent of having a single non-executive director – David Jones, the Chairman of Next, who joined the Morrisons board in May 2004. One year on, shareholders threatened to revolt unless Chairman Sir Ken Morrison agreed to improve corporate governance at the supermarket group by admitting a further four non-executive directors into the boardroom, one of whom could eventually succeed him.[182] Days later he bowed to pressure from investors, relaxing his grip on the day-to-day running of the company.[183]

The French agree that independence is first and foremost a mindset. According to head-hunters Korn Ferry, 'real independence ... is more a question of character and personal ethics than a simple problem of formal criteria'.[184] The problem is that French non-executive directors cannot be classified as 'independent' to the same degree as their British counterparts, since they often have a personal stake in the company: it is mandatory for large corporate shareholders, known as *actionnaires de référance*, to provide a board member. Traditionally, these have accounted for at least two-thirds of the board (which range in size from three to 24 members). Our research has revealed the average size of the directorial team at France's top 100 companies to be around 18, including 6 executives and 12 non-executives (see Table 3.4). There is far more variation amongst top French companies than amongst British ones (with a standard deviation of 6.03 for French boards and 3.25 for British boards). While the size of the former can be excessive – even reaching 40 in some cases[185] – the latter display greater isomorphism, normally including around 12 members, 6 of whom are normally executives and six non-executives. Sir Adrian Cadbury likewise observed a decline in the size of British boards around the turn of the century, citing the example of the board of Marks and Spencer, which in 1998 numbered 21 members, but which by 2002 had shrunk to 14.[186]

Table 3.4 Size and composition of directorial teams of top 100 companies in France and the UK in 1998

| | France | | UK | |
	Mean	Standard Deviation	Mean	Standard Deviation
Executives	6	3.32	6	2.11
Non-Executives	12	4.93	6	2.30
All	**18**	**6.03**	**12**	**3.25**

Conclusion

The current debate on corporate governance, which this chapter has sought to illustrate and explain from both the French and British perspectives, has been fuelled by the notion that good corporate governance must

ultimately lead to better performance. The link between corporate governance and firm performance, however, is notoriously difficult to demonstrate. Attempting to prove that such a relationship does exist, as Johnson
et al. suggest, is like trying to find a unicorn: 'there can be two general
rationales for our failure to "discover" this legendary species. First, this
animal simply does not exist. Second, we have not searched in the right
place, at the right time, with the right equipment'.[187] But as Gillies and
Morra point out, common sense tells us that there *is* such a link: 'The fact
that various empirical macrostudies in corporate governance have been
unable to identify it does not mean that this relationship does not exist'.[188]
The apparent tenuousness of the link between governance and performance was seemingly confirmed in 2005 by a FTSE corporate governance
league table, designed to help investors to choose or avoid companies
according to their governance practices, and to monitor their performance
in meeting best practice.[189] The league table accorded poor rankings to
some blue-chip companies such as Tesco, the first British retailer to break
through the £2 billion annual profit threshold, but ranked just 91st out of
100 according to governance criteria.

It is important to bear in mind, moreover, that the rash of corporate scandals, including those of Vivendi, Enron and WorldCom, which pointed to
abuses of power by high profile leaders, occurred *after* many of the corporate governance initiatives discussed in this chapter were introduced.
However, as standards have been driven up, many of the old ways of doing
things have been found to be wanting. In the French case, the closeness of
business-government ties is clearly implicated. As one British interviewee
put it, 'where the government ends and where the banks begin [in France] is
still extremely obscure'.[190] This is coupled with a longstanding tradition of
illicit rewards at the highest political levels. In January 2004, the former
Prime Minister Alain Juppé, President of the governing Union pour la
Majorité Présidentielle (UMP), was given a suspended prison sentence of 18
months for 'illegal conduct and activities'. The guilty verdict shocked the
political community – up to a point. As Lerougetel has observed, 'Cynics
say that the sole crime of Juppé was to get caught. In these circles, cynicism
is so advanced that even getting caught is no longer a crime'.[191] Juppé was
tried alongside 26 co-defendants. This culture is deeply rooted and enduring,
as confirmed in February 2005 when the Finance Minister Hervé Gaymard
was forced to resign after setting up home in a luxury Paris apartment paid
for by the government, to which he was not entitled because he already
owned several properties.[192]

That said, the present chapter has outlined many changes to governance
practices in France, particularly in recent years. These include greater

transparency in annual reports and accounts on matters of corporate governance; greater openness regarding the remuneration of senior executives; a more widespread separation of functions at the top; greater evidence of shared decision-making at executive level; and greater stress on the independence of non-executive directors. The combined pressures of investor activism, media invasiveness and public outrage have combined to push French companies down the path of reform. Under threat of increased regulation, the British approach to corporate governance, of voluntary compliance with agreed norms and standards, has proved ever more appealing to French business leaders.

Yet it would be wrong to conclude that France and the UK are heading inexorably towards a common model of governance. The reforms introduced in both countries, in response to similar pressures, while superficially alike, will continue to impact differentially because of more fundamental differences in national business systems and elite ideologies. This chapter has demonstrated, for example, how different patterns of ownership, cultural forces and institutional traditions may conspire to generate very different responses to corporate crises. In France, the closely bonded business and political factions of the ruling elite typically rally together to ward off major threats to the immediate national interest, whereas in Britain there is general acceptance of the punishing consequences of corporate failure. The underlying causes of such differences, reflexive and deeply rooted, are explored in successive chapters through extensive comparative analysis of the making and functioning of two distinctive national business elites.

4
Social Origins and the Education of Business Elites

'The people who have the best schools are the leading people: if not today, they will be tomorrow'.

Jules Simon, 1865 [1]

This chapter builds upon the theoretical exploration of elites conducted in Chapter 2. The starting point for what follows in this and later chapters is the argument that business careers are the product of multiple 'structuring structures' and the capacity of individuals, as practical strategists, to master the rules of the corporate game. We eschew any form of determinism. Neither in France in nor the UK is it possible to predict whether someone at an early stage in life will reach the top. There are simply too many variables to contend with, many relating to circumstances, and many others relating to personal qualities. This is not to say, however, that there are no observable regularities in recruitment to the elite. Numerous studies have shown that individuals from more privileged social backgrounds, with an elite education, are more likely to succeed than less privileged individuals. Yet, even so, there is a great diversity of experience. Many high flyers have shown a remarkable propensity to overcome adversity, and our own research adds weight to the evidence that business elites are regenerated through the recruitment of individuals who have started out in life from towards the lower end of the social spectrum. [2]

The importance of education to the study of elites is twofold and to a degree paradoxical. On the one hand, education is widely acknowledged as one of the principal mechanisms for elite reproduction, as a powerful means by which families from the upper strata of society advantage their offspring. On the other hand, education is the main source of opportunity for those born into families lower down the social order, serving as a primary mechanism for personal capital accumulation and upward social mobility. In this chapter, we examine this duality, which legitimises the rhetoric of meritocracy deployed by the ruling class while at the same time perpetuating the practices of social inequality and disadvantage. To this end, the chapter compares and contrasts the ways in which business elites are educated in France and Britain. It reflects on the historical development of education, particularly of elites, in the two countries, and examines the current situation. It considers previous studies of elite education in Britain and France, and their relevance today, examining some of their main conclusions in the light of findings from our own research.

We live in a socially stratified world. In both France and the UK, in all fields of activity, there is a hierarchy of positions running from the most dominant to the most subordinate. Education is no exception, and the very fact of its stratification makes it a key structuring structure, serving as a primary gateway to privileged business positions. It is through education that the recruitment of elites takes place, and that elites are replenished and renewed. In Britain, annual league tables published in broadsheet newspapers bear witness to the jockeying for position in which British universities are almost constantly engaged. Actual positions may vary, but invariably top of the list are Oxford and Cambridge, followed closely by University College London (UCL), Imperial College London (IC), the London School of Economics, London Business School (LBS) (the Oxbridge-London triangle as it is known), and widely esteemed provincial universities like Birmingham, Bristol, Durham, Edinburgh, Glasgow, Leeds, Manchester, St. Andrews and Warwick.

In France, the most prestigious establishments are the leading *grandes écoles*, identified by Bourdieu as 'avenues to the highest social positions'. These include the Ecole Polytechnique, known as 'X', geared to grooming France's captains of industry; the Ecole Normale Supérieure (ENS) in the rue d'Ulm, described as 'the seedbed of France's high intelligentsia', which Bourdieu himself attended;[3] and the Ecole Nationale d'Administration (ENA), which produces high civil servants and cabinet ministers, and which has arguably replaced the ENS as the most prestigious form of higher education in contemporary France.[4] Other leading schools include the Institut d'Etudes Politiques de Paris ('Sciences-Po'), the Ecole Centrale des Arts et Manufactures, and the engineering schools, the Ecole Nationale Supérieure des Mines de Paris and the Ecole Nationale Supérieure des Ponts et Chaussées. To these may be added the leading business schools, including the Ecole Supérieure des Sciences Economiques et Commerciales (ESSEC), the Ecole des Hautes Etudes Commerciales (HEC), and INSEAD (European Institute of Business Administration), which Marceau compares to Harvard.[5] Of the Ecoles Supérieures de

Commerce or ESC, the provincial business and management schools, which Bourdieu considers minor institutions leading to middle management positions, 'refuges for dominant-class youth ... unable to gain access to the academically most selective *grandes écoles* and yet who refuse the alternative of going to less prestigious university faculties',[6] that of Lyon, the oldest,[7] is generally recognised as top of the list.[8] The provision of different pathways to success recognises that there are different categories of inheritors of power. This ensures, in turn, 'the *pax dominorum* indispensable to the sharing of the spoils of hegemony'.[9]

The original findings presented in this chapter are based upon the analysis of data relating to 2,291 directors of the top 100 companies in Britain and France in 1998. Within this, we focus in particular on the top 100 most powerful directors in each country in 1998, typically the CEOs and Chairmen at the summit of the corporate hierarchy who engage most vigorously in what Giddens terms 'elite circulation' – the 'phenomenon of multiple holding of elite positions (as in interlocking directorships, or where political leaders hold business appointments)'[10] – who function as something of 'an elite within an elite'.[11] In effect, they constitute a 'super-elite', occupying, as Wright Mills puts it, the 'strategic command posts of society'.[12]

The social foundations of elite careers

From theory we can predict that individuals from the upper echelons of society will, through habitus and formal education, be more likely to accumulate the cultural and social capital prized by companies than their more numerous counterparts lower down the social order. This prediction has been confirmed in practice in numerous elite studies: individuals from privileged social backgrounds are highly 'over-represented' in elite positions relative to their numbers in society. It is clear, to state the obvious, that coming from a 'good' family, having a 'good' education at a prestigious school followed by attendance at a 'good' university are all related positively to subsequent career success. Lord Waldegrave of North Hill, for example, who came from the landed upper class, being the younger son of the 12th Earl Waldegrave, provides an interesting illustration of someone benefiting greatly from cultural and social capital laid down early in life. He attended Eton followed by Oxford, subsequently becoming a Cabinet Minister under Margaret Thatcher before embarking on a business career. Following the loss of his parliamentary seat, he settled upon a portfolio career, working as a journalist for the *Daily Telegraph* and becoming a non-executive director of the Bristol & West

Building Society. He was then headhunted to join the investment bank Dresdner Kleinwort Benson in an executive capacity, moving to the Swiss-owned UBS as a Managing Director five years later in 2003. When asked about the particular skills he brought to his current role, he pointed out that he was not an investment banker in a strictly technical sense, but rather someone with the seniority and social skills needed to move in elite circles, being at one level 'a salesman for a product I have to understand enough about to be able to present it'.[13] It mattered, he thought, to be on a par, an equal in terms of experience and standing, with business leaders taking very big decisions, seeing things strategically rather than technically, and advising accordingly.

Similarly, in France, there is a prescribed route which may enhance the individual's chances of success, through the *classes préparatoires* followed by entrance to a *grande école* of renown, then admission to a *grand corps* and perhaps a ministerial cabinet, as exemplified by Jean-François Théodore, CEO of Euronext. Théodore attended the Lycée Louis-le-Grand, graduating in 1968 from Sciences-Po, one of the brightest jewels in the crown of French higher education, and from the Ecole National d'Administration (ENA) in 1974. He joined the French Treasury the same year, becoming its Deputy Director (under Jean-Claude Trichet), before being appointed CEO of the Paris Bourse in 1990, and CEO of Euronext, formed by the merger of the stock exchanges of Paris, Brussels and Amsterdam, in 2000. Viewed in this light, the French system appears overwhelmingly meritocratic: a good passage through the right places will help to propel the individual towards a successful career. However, the fact is that coming from a 'good' family will boost the individual's chances significantly, at the very least pointing the way to what may be possible. For Théodore, joining the French civil service always seemed to be 'the natural choice': his father, an early entrant to ENA after the war, became responsible for managing the National Debt at the Treasury, while his mother was one of France's first female judges.[14]

In classifying the super-elite by social origins, we have adopted a typology based on four social classes – upper, upper-middle, lower-middle and lower – as described in Appendix 1. The upper class consists of a small minority of families with substantial wealth and a large income based on inheritance or a parent occupying a leading position in society. Upper-middle-class families are defined as having one or more parent with a prestigious job and high earnings, and constitute a relatively narrow section of the population, though broader than the upper class. This class we take as broadly similar to Halsey's middle or service class of 'professional, managerial and administrative occupational groups'.[15] The lower-middle class is comprised of a swathe of families with middling incomes and a comfortable but far from lavish lifestyle, like Halsey's 'non-manual employees, small proprietors, self-employed artisans … lower-grade technicians and supervisors of manual workers'.[16] Families with modest or low incomes, again forming a broad section of the population, are defined as lower-class, such as industrial and commercial manual and clerical workers in unskilled or semi-skilled positions. In practice, having little hard evidence on family income, we had to make judgments about social origins on the basis of parental occupations (our main discriminator), schooling, place of residence, and family lifestyle descriptions from a variety of sources including self-reports from elite members. The results are presented in Table 4.1.

Table 4.1 Social origins of top 100 directors of French and UK companies in 1998

Social Class	France (%) (n=94)	UK (%) (n=91)
Upper	42.55	35.17
Upper-Middle	34.04	28.57
Lower-Middle	19.15	25.27
Lower	4.26	10.99

Note: See Appendix 1 for note on classification of social origins.

It can be seen that in both countries, a large majority of those who had made it to the very top in business in 1998 (77 per cent in France and 64 per cent in the UK) came from upper- and upper-middle-class families, which together would have comprised no more than 15 per cent of all families. Table 4.1 provides evidence of considerable upward social mobility from the lower-middle class, but relatively few individuals in the top 100 business leaders in either country came from the lower class, which constitutes the largest segment of society. The table suggests that upward mobility through a career in business may have been more frequent in the UK than in France, but the observed differences between the two distributions are not statistically significant. This indicates that the similarities between France and the UK with respect to the reproductive capacities of elites are stronger than any differences that might exist. In both countries, those raised in upper- and upper-middle-class families are far more likely to accumulate, through everyday experience and education, the cultural capital needed to succeed at the highest levels; not least the understated outward confidence and cultural sophistication so evident in men like William Waldegrave and Jean-François Théodore.

The fact that 'continuity of familial status between generations' is one of the main features of elite reproduction noted by Halsey and other researchers, does not deny the possibility of considerable upward mobility for a minority from the lower orders, especially the lower-middle class.[17] One of our interviewees, George Cox, made a fortune from the sale of his own information technology business, Butler-Cox, before going on to run Unisys in Europe and later the UK Institute of Directors (IoD). His father was a porter and his mother a waitress. He had the good fortune, however, to gain entry through competitive examination to a UK grammar school. He went on to study engineering at Queen Mary College, University of London, before embarking on a long business career. This story is not atypical of children from lower-class backgrounds making good. Of the ten UK top 100 directors from lower-class backgrounds, nine attended a grammar school or won a scholarship to attend an independent school before progressing to university or taking a professional qualification. Derek Wanless, for example, who in 2002 declared that he was 'not scared to betray his working-class northern roots',[18] attended the Royal Grammar School, Newcastle, and Cambridge University, where he studied mathematics. He held a scholarship from the National Westminster Bank while at university, and joined the bank immediately on leaving university, rising through the ranks to become CEO in 1992. Sir Terry Leahy, CEO of Tesco, grew up on a council estate in Liverpool, in a prefabricated house, something that, he admits, differentiates him from the heads of most large companies.[19] He attended St Edward's, a high-achieving Catholic grammar school, and later UMIST in Manchester, where he read management science. Halsey's conclusion, having surveyed the evidence on social mobility, that the social order in Britain is 'neither completely open nor rigidly caste-like' is certainly confirmed by our findings.[20] He goes on to point out that stratification and inequality in terms of financial and status rewards have remained a constant feature of society in later modern Britain, but that the elite is effectively regenerated by the movement upwards of some and the downwards movement of others. In most cases, but not always, those that have moved upwards, like George Cox and Derek Wanless, had the advantage of an extensive, high-quality education. Those that move downwards in the social order, by the same token, tend to be the least educated.[21]

This general proposition holds just as true for France as it does for the UK. However, the institutional mechanisms of social differentiation, of which educational systems form an important part, are nationally specific and culturally distinct. In both countries, the present is very much a creation of the past, not in a slavish or remorseless manner, as numerous changes can readily be observed, but enough to demonstrate significant path dependency and cultural reproduction.

Education, social stratification and the 'legitimating illusion'

Bourdieu argues that elite French educational establishments are one of the primary mechanisms for the preservation and perpetuation of privilege. Education, as a societal structuring structure, is the main subject of several major works, in particular *The State Nobility* (1994).[22] In *The Inheritors*, Bourdieu and Passeron document what they see as the continued over-representation of upper- and middle-class students in French universities, despite the official postwar policy of expanding educational opportunity. Bourdieu exposes the stratified nature of the French education system; and while his ideas may be considered 'Francocentric', we have found them in practice to be 'irrepressibly universalizing in analytical intent and reach'.[23] In *The State Nobility*, Bourdieu builds on the ideas outlined in *Distinction* (1984),[24] to explain the logic and mechanisms of social domination in a complex, capitalist society, and the means by which it dissembles and perpetuates itself, deeply embedded within the French system of class, culture and education.

Habitus, we saw in Chapter 2, is one of the primary means by which life chances are internalised. It also has an external dimension, in what Bourdieu terms 'bodily *hexis*' – that is, a way of being in social space: the physical dispositions, attitudes and gestures that develop in individuals due to their relationships with particular fields.[25] Key features of bodily *hexis* are language and accent. Variations in vocabulary, intonation and accent indicate different ranks in the social hierarchy. Elsewhere, Bourdieu explores the production and reproduction of 'legitimate language', the theoretical norm against which all linguistic performance is judged, and which is policed by grammarians and teachers, who threaten the legal sanction of academic failure.[26] Through pronunciation, characteristic turns of phrase, slang (itself implying a common set of values), deportment or shared ways of interacting, occupancy of a particular position in the social hierarchy is confirmed or denied.[27] Desirable French accents tend to be Parisian and bourgeois, while in the UK, so-called 'received pronunciation' centres on the South-East of England. As Bourdieu notes, at very high levels of education, 'where the qualities associated with the academic image of excellence are most insistently required, the opposition between Parisian and provincial origins (... lastingly inscribed in habitus as accent) takes on critical importance'.[28] Bourdieu's own accent was provincial, from the Languedoc region of South-West France, distinguishing him from the majority of his fellow-students and academic colleagues in Paris. The linguistic field is thus structured by power relations founded on the unequal distribution of linguistic capital (or opportunities to assimilate linguistic resources), which has implications for differing degrees of authority on the part of speaking subjects.[29]

While once the Church sanctified the feudal lord's possession of large areas of land, riches and weaponry, in contemporary society, Bourdieu argues, the education system has taken over this role of the sanctification of social divisions. The graduation ceremonies of leading British (and American) universities resemble ceremonies of religious ordination. These are 'rites of passage', sometimes conducted in Latin, where the graduand is 'dubbed' by the university chancellor in the same way as a monarch bestows a knighthood. The similarity is not wholly arbitrary, for it is through the elite schools, 'institutions entrusted with the education and consecration of those who are called to enter the field of power', that society produces its new nobility.[30]

In the UK, the classification of degrees is an intrinsic part of the process – though the class of degree obtained arguably matters less than its provenance. Iain Vallance, for example, the former CEO of BT, was awarded a third-class degree in English by Oxford. Degree classification is the UK is paralleled in France by the strict rank order produced for each *concours* or entrance examination. Such grading implies unbiased objectivity, disguising the social reproduction function of education, which Bourdieu sees as its main function, and which it causes to be misrecognised.[31] Students are graded according to their cultural capital, determined largely by birth and upbringing: 'behind the impeccable appearance of equity and meritocracy, ... [is] a systematic bias in favour of the possessors of cultural capital'.[32] For Bourdieu, the two key principles of social hierarchy that shape and inform the struggle for power, giving access to positions of power, and determining the life chances of individuals and groups, are economic capital (property, income, wealth), which he considers the 'dominant principle of hierarchy', and cultural capital (educational qualifications, knowledge and culture), which he calls the 'second principle of hierarchy'.[33]

Cultural capital, though deriving primarily from the family, through which it is inherited and passed down, has the advantage of seeming to reside in the person of the bearer, suggestive of a 'true *social essence*', as cultural capital is converted into good academic performance.[34] Educational credentials, such as a university degree, help to structure and hierarchise the social order by presenting inequalities that arise between individuals as the inevitable result of differential amounts of talent, application and achievement. They have the virtue of seeming to endow pre-existing differences in cultural capital with a meritocratic seal of approval, while guaranteeing the transmission of inherited cultural capital from one generation to the next.[35] The word 'credentials' itself possesses religious overtones, being derived from the Latin verb *credere*, meaning 'to believe'. Academic labels are able to transform or transmogrify social labels through a process akin to 'social alchemy'. Coming from a teacher or a university, Bourdieu insists, academic judgments are accepted and internalised by the recipient.[36] In this way, 'academic verdicts take on the weight of destiny', asserting themselves and being experienced as 'absolute, universal and eternal'.[37] The result is that academic taxonomies come between the recipient and his or her 'vocation', influencing individual career trajectories, and supporting the *status quo*:

> The academic taxonomy, a system of principles of vision and division implemented at a practical level, rests on an implicit definition of excellence that, by granting superiority to the qualities socially conferred upon those who are socially dominant, consecrates both their way of being and their state.[38]

Subjective aspirations and objective chances are thus closely aligned in a self-fulfilling prophecy. A successful socialisation strategy, Bourdieu claims, is one in which agents serve as accomplices in their own destiny.[39] Educational selection is ultimately often self-selection. While upper-middle-class students tend to anticipate academic success by virtue of their social advantages, many working-class students, lacking cultural capital, resign themselves to limited horizons. Those working-class students who perform well academically – as Bourdieu did himself – nevertheless bear the mark of their lack of cultural capital, since they lack the broad cultural knowledge typical of their well-to-do counterparts.

In summary, Bourdieu seeks to expose what he terms 'the legitimating illusion', by presenting the education system in what he sees as 'the true light of its social uses, that is, as one of the main foundations of domination and of the legitimation of domination'.[40] He effectively demonstrates that democratisation through education is ultimately a myth.[41] Cultural capital is reinforced rather than redistributed through the educational system, which thus performs a social reproduction function.[42] Educational credentials assume a similar social function – of legitimate exclusion or inclusion – to nobility titles in feudal society, a function they fulfil all the more effectively for their apparent objectivity:

> All strategies of reproduction fulfil inseparably functions of inclusion and exclusion which contribute objectively to maintaining the *numerus clausus* of reproducible agents, either by limiting the biological products of the class so that they do not exceed the number of positions whose possession conditions the maintenance of the class (fertility strategies), or by excluding from the class a part of the biological products of the class, in this way discarded to other classes or kept at the fringes of the class in an ambiguous or amputated status (we may think, for example, in the case of the aristocracy of the *ancien régime*, of the enforced celibacy of daughters relegated to religious institutions or the departure of younger brothers to the army).[43]

In short, the academic meritocracy forms a type of nobility, grounded in the idea of 'natural' rights and abilities, which effectively conceals inherited cultural advantages.[44]

Education and elitism in France

In France, where the 1789 Revolution technically abolished legal class structures, the view nevertheless persisted that *culture générale* was not for the masses, a view shared and promoted by Enlightenment philosophers such as Rousseau, who argued in his novel *Emile* (1762) that the poor had no need of education.[45] Despite the revolutionary ideal of *égalité*, the full development of the human mind was seen as fitting for only a select few: inherent in French thinking on education was the notion of two cultures, one for the offspring of individuals of distinction, and another, more concerned with regulation, for the masses.

The 1833 Law on Public Education (the Guizot law) improved primary education and literacy levels, in a country where illiteracy was widespread.[46] Guizot himself, as Minister for Public Instruction (1832-37), was concerned with the moral aspects of education, believing that the masses, as yet unprepared for freedom, could nevertheless be prepared for freedom through education. But concern for progress superseded concern for individual liberty. France's defeat at the hands of Prussia in 1871 was interpreted as exposing severe weaknesses not just of a material nature but also in her education system. Jules Simon, Minister for Education, believed that education could help maintain French pre-eminence in the world. A democracy that had rid itself of a hated monarchy and aristocracy was arguably more sensitive to notions of privilege and the preservation of privilege than one that had not. The education system to which it gave rise was liberal, but not democratic, as the so-called reforms of the 1880s and 1890s contributed to the further restriction of access.[47]

Despite overtly espousing an egalitarian ideal, many political leaders of the late nineteenth century subscribed to the view that it was through an elite education that the privileged would prepare themselves for leadership in society.[48] The liberal professions and higher reaches of the French civil service took full advantage of the great Parisian *lycées*: Janson, Condorcet, Louis-le-Grand, Saint-Louis and Henri IV, 'from which they went not only to Sciences-Po but also to Polytechnique'.[49] Vaughan points out that the 'contradiction between the republican postulate of state efficiency and the revolutionary ideal of social equality could perhaps only be resolved by legitimating educational disparity'.[50] In this way, meritocratic selection and elitist classification went hand in hand.

The Fourth Republic inherited a system in which, while the basics were available for all, secondary and higher education remained the preserve of an elite.[51] Writing in 1946, Camus remarked that the French education system had changed little over the years: 'the world is changing and with it both people and France itself. Only French education remains the same. So we teach our children to live and think in a world which has already passed away'.[52] By the time of the Liberation in 1944, there was nevertheless a growing recognition in France that the path to social ascent lay in education, for which there was a new and increasing demand. France, which, according to Majault, in the nineteenth century had 'altered education only in details, remade it in the decade after 1959'.[53] Government spending on education doubled from 7.12 per cent of the national budget in 1914 to 15.9 per cent by 1964, while teachers and administrators employed by the Ministry of Education increased from 252,323 in 1951 to 509,922 in 1963,[54] accompanied by an expansion in pupil numbers from 6.4 million in 1940 to 9.2 million in 1960.[55] University students exploded in number from 79,000 in 1939 to 598,000 by 1968.[56] It is against this background that Bourdieu and Passeron, pointing to the continued over-representation of upper- and middle-class students in French universities, suggest that education, far from encouraging upward social mobility, works in fact to reinforce the existing social structure by bolstering existing differences in culture, status and wealth.

As an institution, the *grandes écoles* have amply fulfilled their ostensible function of producing an elite of knowledge while, at the same time, justifying the position of that elite at the pinnacle of society. Some schools, such as Polytechnique and the ENS, were established in revolutionary times, in 1794 and 1795 respectively, to provide the state with trained administrators and teachers. Twelve, including the Ecole des Ponts et Chaussées (1747), predated the Revolution, originating under the *Ancien Régime*. Others, such as the Ecole Centrale (1829), are products of the Napoleonic system. Concerned with administrative efficiency, Napoleon sought to instil a sense of loyalty to his regime while institutionalising the recruitment of elites, desiring that those who graduated from the *grandes écoles* should be men 'deeply devoted to [his regime] … whom he could use wherever the demands of its service would render them useful'.[57] The hallmarks of these schools, even before the Napoleonic era, were selection, vocationalism and service to the state.[58] Above all, they strove to be fundamentally meritocratic. To gain entry, applicants had to demonstrate both ability and effort. But in practice this meritocratic ethos favoured the sons of the Parisian bourgeoisie. Daumard's study of Polytechnique from 1815 to 1848 found no more than 14 students being admitted from *les classes populaires*, most of these being the offspring of petty officers, Ministry or prison *concierges*, and only one the son of a worker. By contrast, 62 per cent of Polytechnique students came from a privileged background, and one in five came from the capital.[59] The low pay of entrants into administrative jobs made economic self-sufficiency essential.[60] The revolutionaries who founded Polytechnique and the ENS failed to anticipate what Suleiman terms the 'entrenchment' of French elites along class lines.[61] The entrance examination, designed to identify the most deserving students, in fact tested cultural knowledge more than natural ability, functioning as a mechanism of confirmation rather than of genuine selection. As Granick observes, attendance at a *grande école* became 'restricted to sons of independent businessmen, company directors, free professionals in independent practice, and government civil servants', the sons of manual workers, employees, and farmers having been disqualified from the race at the beginning.[62]

The ENA, established in 1945 in response to the discrediting of the old elite,[63] which was seen as having let France down during the Second World War, strove to break with tradition by ending the dominance of well-born Parisian-educated candidates. But while recognising that

Sciences-Po, which hitherto had trained the higher echelons of the civil service, 'is scarcely accessible other than to well-to-do students domiciled in Paris', ENA continued nevertheless to draw its students from the affluent classes, despite initial efforts to widen participation by establishing seven satellites in the provinces.[64] Paris and its surrounding area remains the primary birthplace of French business leaders. A 1968 study of the French business elite by Hall and de Bettignies found that not only were the PDG of large French companies most likely to be born in the Paris basin – almost 40 per cent of their sample of 159 PDG were born in the capital or its vicinity – but that this also applied to the occupants of top positions in the largest corporations in general.[65] Our own research reveals that this has changed very little over 30 years. As Table 4.2 demonstrates, as many as 38 of the top 100 French directors in 1998 came from the Île-de-France. The Eastern region, in second place, produced 10. Business leaders were least likely to hail from the South-West or North-West, with just six each. This contrasts with a far greater geographical spread in the case of British directors, almost one-quarter of whom (24) came from outside mainland Britain. That said, as many as 30 UK directors came from London and the South-East.

Table 4.2 Region of upbringing of top 100 directors in France and the UK in 1998

Region	Directors of French Companies No.	Region	Directors of UK Companies No.
Central	7	London	14
Île-de-France	38	Midlands	11
Eastern	10	North-East	7
North-East	8	North-West	8
North-West	6	Scotland	11
Northern	9	South-East	16
South-East	7	South-West	4
South-West	6	Wales	1
Outside Mainland France	5	Outside Mainland Britain	24
Not Known	4	Not Known	4
Total	**100**		**100**

Tradition, coupled with the rigidity of the examination structure, militated against the professed democratisation of ENA.[66] In Suleiman's eyes, the open competition, which admits fewer than one candidate in ten, ensures the preservation of the dominant social type.[67] Thus, as many as

79.8 per cent of ENA students came from an upper-middle-class back-ground (*cadres supérieurs*) in 1993, while 10 per cent were middle-class (*cadres moyens*), and only a tiny 2.4 per cent working-class.[68] This supports the findings of Hall and de Bettignies 25 years previously: three out of every four PDG from their sample were from the upper and upper-middle classes. More than 40 per cent were themselves the sons of business leaders, rising to 51.4 per cent for the PDG of the largest firms, revealing a tight correlation between parental occupation and personal career success.[69] Plainly, 'to him that hath, more shall be given'.[70] Citing François Bloch-Lainé, Suleiman describes ENA as 'a machine for classi-fying people'.[71] He reserves particular criticism for the Mitterrand presi-dency (1981-95). The socialists, who might have been expected to widen access to elite establishments, failed to reform the *grandes écoles* system, perhaps because they recognised that ultimately it served their interests: 'once installed at the helm of the state, the left realised just how important it was for it, if it wanted "to endure", to rely on the existing machinery and, in this way, on the administrative machine and on the elite'.[72]

The results presented in Table 4.3 provide compelling evidence of how little things have changed in France over the years. The pathway to the top in whatever chosen field could not be more clearly marked for the chil-dren of upper- and upper-middle-class families. A singularly French phenomenon is that children of the upper- and upper-middle classes, no matter where they are born and raised, are clustered together as young adults in the top lycées, particularly in and around Paris: the top ten most frequently attended schools alone accounting for 35 per cent of known school attendances of the directors of the top 100 French companies in 1998. The predominantly upper- and upper-middle-class families, who have the financial means to get their children into these schools, qualify-ing for admission by ownership of a local residence in sought-after areas, make educational choices with reference to tried and tested institutional status pathways. The top lycées are meticulous in preparing candidates for entry into a *grande école* like Polytechnique. Just four Parisian *grandes écoles* – Polytechnique, IEP Sciences-Po, ENA and HEC – account for a remarkable 39 per cent of the 1,357 known higher education attendances of the French business elite of 1998. The children of families lower down the social order, no matter how able, do not have such ready access to knowledge regarding educational and career pathways. They are not debarred from participation, as competitive examinations are open to all, but only those with the requisite knowledge, resources and confidence can work the system to full advantage.

Table 4.3 Schools and higher education institutions most frequently attended by members of the French business elite of 1998

Rank	Institution	Frequency of Attendance	% of All Known Attendances
Schools			
1	Lycée Louis-le-Grand, Paris	79	9.42
2	Lycée Janson-de-Sailly, Paris	55	6.56
3	Lycée Saint-Louis, Paris	37	4.41
4	Ecole Sainte-Geneviève, Versailles	32	3.81
5	Lycée Carnot, Paris	25	2.98
6	College Stanislas, Paris	16	1.91
7=	Lycée Buffon, Paris	12	1.43
7=	Lycée du Parc, Lyon	12	1.43
7=	Lycée Henri IV, Paris	12	1.43
10	Ecole Saint-Louis-de-Gonzague, Paris	10	1.19
	Other	549	65.43
	Total Known Attendances	**839**	**100.00**
Higher Education			
1	Ecole Polytechnique	163	12.01
2	Institut d'Etudes Politiques (IEP), Sciences-Po, Paris	160	11.79
3	Ecole Nationale d'Administration (ENA)	125	9.21
4	Ecole des Hautes Etudes Commerciales (HEC)	82	6.04
5=	Paris I-Panthéon Sorbonne	65	4.79
5=	Paris II-Panthéon Assas	65	4.79
7	Ecole des Mines de Paris (ENSMP)	53	3.91
8	Harvard	36	2.65
9	Ecole Centrale	33	2.43
10	Institut Européen d'Administration des Affaires (INSEAD)	22	1.62
	Other	553	40.75
	Total Known Attendances	**1,357**	**100.00**

Passage through ENA or another leading *grande école* may serve also as a prelude to joining a *grand corps*, such as the Inspection des Finances, the Corps des Mines or the Corps des Ponts et Chaussées, the pinnacle of France's civil service elite, accession to which depends on the rank obtained in the final examinations. Suleiman describes the *grands corps* as 'placement bureaux', pointing out that no one ever entered the Inspection des Finances to inspect finance, or the Corps des Mines for a career in mining.[73] Some *corps* are more prized than others. Kosciusko-Morizet contrasts the happiness of a young engineer from the Corps des Mines with the despondency of one from the inferior Corps des Ponts et Chaussées, who, having obtained a lower ranking in the final examination, is disconsolate because he is not an *ingénieur des Mines*.[74] Each *corps* is governed by a council, and occasionally by an individual 'chef du corps' who serves as its conscience.[75]

Like the *grandes écoles*, the *grands corps* often function as forms of extended family, fostering an *esprit de caste*. Suleiman cites the president of one of France's largest industrial companies as saying, 'when we look for talented people we do not place ads in newspapers or anything like that. We go to our corps and we try to find someone who fits the job we're trying to fill',[76] not dissimilar to Freemasonry, or the way in which a family business might aim to 'keep it in the family'. Our own study of the top 100 most powerful business leaders in France in 1998 identifies 15 Inspecteurs des Finances and 13 members of the Corps des Mines, including (in 2005) Thierry Desmarest, PDG of Total, Louis Schweitzer, PDG of Renault, Jean-Louis Beffa, PDG of Saint-Gobain, and Jean-René Fourtou, PDG of Vivendi. Possession of a symbolic mark of distinction of this magnitude is a potent signifier of 'fitness for high office', and, by the same token, this implies that the French upper managerial strata remain relatively closed to 'ordinary' recruits into middle management.[77] Rival *grands corps* and *grandes écoles* often compete with one another for power within the structures of government, seeking to further the interests of members of the group,[78] just as Wright Mills depicted competing institutions battling for power within the government and leading socio-economic interest groups in the US.[79]

The bonds of friendship forged at the *grandes écoles* and *grands corps* are often cemented, as Bourdieu observes, through marriage, when graduates marry the sisters and daughters of their colleagues, giving rise to a tightly knit oligarchy. By establishing the occupation of the fathers-in-law of their sample of business leaders, Hall and de Bettignies demonstrate that marriage is very much an 'intra-class affair', with 75 per cent of their sample having wives belonging to the same social class.[80] Marriage is fundamental to the perpetuation of economic power on the part of business elites. Our own research reveals that almost all of the super-elite are married (with just two elite directors from both the French and British top 100 power indices remaining single), and further, that their mean number of children exceeds national averages, the mean number of offspring of top 100 French and British directors being 2.9 and 2.4 respectively.

That the offspring of political, administrative and business elites go on in their turn to be educated by members of the intellectual elite, and are initiated through their education into a network of power and influence, ensures their survival and the preservation of the *status quo*. Successful 'marriage strategies' and 'succession strategies' allow a combining of 'the secondary profits provided by matrimonial exchanges between families of company heads with the advantages gained through corporate ties'.[81] Bourdieu highlights an important dialectic relationship between the formal and informal, as informal familial relations feed and support the strictly economic networks of the circulation of capital, such that 'a network of family relations can be the locus of an unofficial circulation of capital that enables the networks of official circulation to function and in turn blocks any effects of the latter that would be contrary to family interests'.[82] Each individual has a share by proxy in the symbolic capital possessed by each member of the group, whether family or *grand corps* or other signifier of high distinction. The maximisation of this capital depends in particular, according to Bourdieu, on the degree of integration of the group.[83] In this way, elite cohesion, nurtured by a similarity of social origin and cultural background, is enhanced by the *grandes écoles*, the *grands corps*, and successful marriage strategies, which come together to function as a virtuous circle reinforcing elite solidarity.

It should be noted, however, that public acceptance of this highly selective system designed to serve existing French elites and their offspring, while masquerading as a meritocracy, depends, in part, on the reverse side of the coin: the maintenance of the right of entry to the university system for all who leave secondary school with the *baccalauréat*. It is clear that the high prestige accruing to the *grandes écoles*, which have assumed responsibility for the training of the elite, and to which the children of the elite were plainly attracted, has influenced the status of French universities to their detriment.[84] The highly selective system of the *grandes écoles* contrasts with the right of entry to the university system for anyone with the *bac*. This, of course, obscures the fact that selection has taken place already through the choice of *baccalauréat*, of which there are more than 20 options, with 'le bac C', the maths and physical sciences option, being reserved for the most gifted pupils.[85] And that it will occur again later, at the end of the first year at university, when many new students are discarded. But it is important to maintain public confidence in the fact (even if this is essentially a fiction) that everyone is given a chance of success. As Suleiman points out, public acceptance also depends upon the exercise of an element of discretion by the elite: as noted by Mosca and Pareto, it ill behoves an elite to flaunt its privileges.[86]

Education and elitism in the UK

It is tempting to believe that education in the UK is somehow less elitist and divisive than in France. The reality, however, is more complex. Disraeli once observed that Britain is ruled not by an aristocracy, but rather by the 'aristocratic principle': 'an aristocracy which absorbs all aristocracies'.[87] Education in 'elementary' schools only became compulsory following the 1870 Education Act, and the school leaving age remained at 11 until 1921, when it was raised to 14. The provision of secondary education remained patchy, confined to a limited number of church schools and a broad swathe of socially graduated, independent fee-paying schools, the most illustrious being the grand 'public' boarding schools such as Eton, Harrow, Winchester, Marlborough and Charterhouse. A national system of state secondary schools began to take shape after 1902. Entry to state grammar schools was selective, based on a competitive examination at the age of 11, and local authorities paid for the places of successful candidates. Demand for grammar school places far exceeded supply. Political pressure for reform increased during the Second World War, and the 1944 Education Act, introduced by Butler, Minister of Education in Churchill's coalition government, introduced free schooling at secondary level on a universal basis. The means of realising universal access was to create large numbers of secondary modern schools for children of lesser academic ability than those selected for grammar schools. A number of secondary technical schools were also created, for which entry was also selective, and these became identified as broadly equivalent to grammar schools. At the age of 11, all pupils in the state primary system took a competitive examination, and, depending on their results, they were channelled into a grammar, secondary modern or secondary technical school. The system was further reformed after 1964, when the newly elected Labour government set about replacing the tripartite system with comprehensive secondary schools to which all children would go. The comprehensive system became dominant in the 1970s, but even three decades later a considerable number of grammar schools remained in place, although their powers of selection had been weakened somewhat over the years.

Most members of the UK business elite of 1998 grew up within a highly stratified system of secondary education with three main tiers: a narrow top tier of elite 'public' boarding schools; a middle tier composed of grammar schools and lesser fee-paying 'independent' schools (boarding, day and mixed); and a broad bottom tier of secondary modern schools. This is the system under examination in the classic 1980 study of education and social mobility conducted by Halsey, Heath and Ridge, using data relating to 8,000 men aged between 20 and 59 in 1972: 13 per cent of respondents were from the upper and upper-middle classes, 31 per cent were from the intermediate or lower-middle classes, and 56 per cent were from the lower classes.[88] One of the main results was to confirm that the education system tended to reproduce patterns of inequality across generations, since children from the higher social classes were disproportionately represented in higher status schools, the first and second tier independent and grammar schools of the system described above. Likewise, children from the lower social classes were disproportionately represented in lower status schools, the secondary modern schools and their precursors. In fact, 71.9 per cent of upper- and upper-middle-class children attended 'selective' higher status schools, compared to 39.7 per cent from the lower-middle classes and 23.8 per cent from the lower classes; conversely, just 28.1 per cent of upper- and upper-middle-class children attended lower status secondary modern or comprehensive schools, compared to 60.3 per cent and 76.3 per cent of children from the lower-middle and lower classes respectively. The conclusion drawn by Halsey and his colleagues was that the UK education system, while providing good opportunities *individually* for a minority of children from the lower classes, effectively worked to benefit the upper- and upper-middle classes *as a whole*. Education serves simultaneously as a vehicle for the reproduction and regeneration of elites. The system enables a relatively limited number of fortunate children from the lower classes to prosper through the accumulation of cultural and social capital, while preserving the advantages enjoyed by children from the upper reaches of society.

The results of our own research broadly confirm the conclusions drawn by Halsey et al. The top 10 most frequently attended schools by the directors of the top 100 UK companies in 1998, listed in Table 4.4, are all independent fee-paying schools, and the most heavily represented of all are the four great public schools of Eton, Winchester, Harrow and Marlborough. Foremost amongst these is Eton College, which Rubinstein defines as '*predominantly* a school for the sons of the bona fide elite'.[89] In a study conducted by Whitley in 1971 of connections amongst the British financial elite, 80 per cent of the sample was found to have attended a fee-paying school, while 34 per cent attended Eton alone.[90] Such schools featured less prominently when the education of the directors of large industrial firms came under scrutiny: 34 of the 261 directors for whom data were available attended Eton (13 per cent), with two-thirds attending fee-paying schools.[91] In the Wakefords' study of the secondary and higher education of those holding elite positions in the UK in the early 1970s, 13 per cent of elite positions were found to be held by former Etonians and 14 per cent by the alumni of five further elite schools. The results reported in Table 4.4, when set against the findings of earlier studies, suggest some loosening of the private schools' grip on UK boardrooms, echoing the results of a recent US study by Cappelli and Hamori, but confirming nonetheless that attendance at a top independent school is an enduring source of career advantage.[92]

Table 4.4 Schools and higher education institutions most frequently attended by members of the UK business elite of 1998

Rank	Institution	Frequency of Atten-dance	% of All Known Attendances
Schools			
1	Eton College	33	6.59
2	Winchester College	13	2.59
3=	Harrow School	11	2.20
3=	Marlborough College	11	2.20
5=	Ampleforth College, York	6	1.20
5=	Charterhouse School	6	1.20
5=	Shrewsbury School	6	1.20
5=	Glasgow Academy	6	1.20
9=	Malvern College, Worcestershire	5	1.00
9=	Rugby School	5	1.00
	Other	399	79.62
	Total Known Attendances	**501**	**100.00**
Higher Education			
1	Cambridge	119	16.21
2	Oxford	97	13.22
3	Harvard	47	6.40
4	Manchester/UMIST	23	3.13
5	London School of Economics	21	2.86
6	Glasgow	18	2.45
7	Imperial	16	2.18
8	Birmingham	15	2.04
9=	Edinburgh	14	1.91
9=	London Business School	14	1.91
	Other	350	47.69
	Total Known Attendances	**734**	**100.00**

The Wakefords found a more concentrated pattern of attendance with respect to higher education, with Oxford and Cambridge graduates holding 50 per cent of all elite positions.[93] Whitley's studies of the financial and industrial elites found that two-thirds of industrial directors who attended university were alumni of Oxford or Cambridge. The percentage of Oxbridge-educated financial-sector directors was even higher at 87 per cent.[94] These studies, conducted in the early 1970s, are now rather dated, but our own study again confirms the continuing pre-eminence of Oxford and Cambridge, while nevertheless underscoring the fact that this is less pronounced than previously, accounting for 29.4 per cent of higher education institutions most frequently attended by British directors of 1998. When London is included in the picture, however, this rises to 39.1 per cent (including attendances at UCL and King's College London (KCL) of 1.5 per cent and 1.23 per cent respectively, which do not feature in the top 10 higher education institutions, lying in thirteenth equal and fifteenth equal positions respectively).

Traditionally, the universities of Oxford and Cambridge have provided higher education to the offspring of the elite, in what Perkin describes as 'a peculiarly English version of meritocracy, which assumes that the most meritorious go to Oxbridge'.[95] Curiously, a prosopographical study of the students of Oxford University from the sixteenth to the nineteenth centuries nevertheless finds that from 1570 to 1630, students describing themselves as the sons of 'plebeians' formed the largest single element among the student body, representing some 50 per cent of all matriculants. By the late nineteenth century, however, the sons of 'gentlemen' formed by far and away the largest category of students, followed by those of 'esquires' and 'clergy', with almost no sons of plebeians matriculated. Both Oxford and Cambridge came to play a pivotal role in class and cultural reproduction. The liturgical character of graduation ceremonies observed by Bourdieu is not fortuitous: the teaching body of Victorian Oxford was wholly Anglican and mainly clerical. The extent of clerical control over the university is apparent in the fact that, of 545 scholarships awarded in 1850, only 22 of them were based on merit. Similarly, of 25,000 enrolments in the first half of the nineteenth century, 40 per cent were ordained.[96] According to Vaughan and Archer, the Oxford colleges were fundamentally undemocratic, intent on preserving 'religious intolerance, social exclusivity, and academic traditionalism',[97] being 'created, regulated and endowed by private munificence, for the interest of certain favoured individuals', as Sir William Hamilton put it.[98]

It was only in the nineteenth century that the seeds of a truly national system of higher education were sown that led the breaking of 'the centuries-old duopoly, reinforced by religious tests, of Oxford and Cambridge.'[99] However, it was not until the foundation of University College in 1826 that Londoners had access to a university institution. This marked the beginning of the University of London, formally established in 1836, as a collection of semi-autonomous colleges. In Scotland, universities in Glasgow, Aberdeen and Edinburgh joined St Andrews, which had been founded in 1411. A series of local movements followed across the UK to set up university colleges in other large cities, beginning with Owen's College in Manchester in 1851, which became the Victoria University of Manchester in 1880. New university institutions took root in the coming decades in Birmingham, Liverpool, Leeds, Bristol and elsewhere. The government provided recurrent funding for the first time in 1889 and arrangements became formalised through the establishment in 1919 of the University Grants Committee, the forerunner of today's Higher Education Funding Councils. Full-time student numbers in higher education grew slowly from 25,000 in 1900 to about 50,000 in 1939.[100] A concerted effort was made to increase the scale of the system after the Second World War, at first by adding new departments and faculties within existing institutions and, following the Robbins Report of 1963, which stressed the need for growth and greater social equity, by granting university status to colleges of advanced technology.[101] A short time later other colleges were grouped together to form polytechnics, ostensibly with a vocational focus, and in 1992 these too were granted university status. The result was an explosion in student numbers from 77,000 in 1947, to 170,000 in 1966 and 261,000 by 1980. By 2004 there were 1.87 million undergraduates and postgraduates studying in the UK, 1.61 million home students and 260,000 from abroad.[102] Correspondingly, the proportions of those attending university increased dramatically in the course of the twentieth century: from just 1 per cent in 1900 to 4 per cent in 1962 to 7 per cent in the late 1970s.[103] By 2004, the percentage of school leavers entering university had swollen to 35 per cent.

One of the consequences of mass higher education in the UK has been an increase in social differentiation and stratification. The formation of London University and the establishment of civic universities like Manchester, Birmingham, Bristol, Leeds, Liverpool and Sheffield created a genuinely differentiated alternative to Oxford and Cambridge in terms of curriculum and teaching methods at a time when only a small minority of the population could contemplate attending a university. It is for this reason that the older Scottish universities and the nineteenth- and early twentieth-century English and Welsh universities were able to establish themselves as socially respectable members of an elite club, geographically spread across the country and of increasing significance nationally. They were in place before the rise of mass higher education, and this conferred upon them elite status. Those that came later had to fight harder to build their reputations, but those with particular resource advantages and sound strategies like Warwick were able to compete in terms of reputation with the civic universities, and indeed with Oxford and Cambridge. However, the former polytechnics, which became universities in 1992, have found it much harder to compete for resources and reputation, and have become identified, along with the weaker members of the previous generation of 'new' universities, as lower-tier institutions far from the cutting edge of knowledge. The upper-tier institutions, meanwhile, have increasingly overtly identified themselves with the language and symbols of elitism, ritualised by the state through devices like the Research Assessment Exercise, used to legitimise the granting of research funding on a highly selective basis.

The institutional and cultural forces that promote elitism and stratification remain as powerful in the early twenty-first century as they had been 30 years earlier, notwithstanding the rhetoric of 'opportunity through education' deployed by politicians of all hues. Writing in the early 1970s, Frances and John Wakeford observed that British universities already 'with money' were blessed with more money by government. In 2004, Oxford and Cambridge benefited from endowments estimated to amount to almost £500 million each, with no other university coming close. Edinburgh University took third place with £156 million, while King's College and UCL occupied seventh and eight positions with endowments of £88 million and £78 million respectively.[104] Yet these universities also receive the lion's share of research funding, echoing Marceau's thesis regarding the French education system that 'to him that hath, more shall be given'. Speculating on the relationship between the power structures within the university sector and those operating in society at large, the Wakefords put their finger on one of the quintessential issues affecting British universities: 'Why is money offered, by whom, and, perhaps more significantly, when and why is it refused?'[105] The fundamental divide in the British university sector highlighted by the Wakefords in 1974 has not been healed, despite three decades of 'social progress', and despite the advent in 1997 of a supposedly left-of-centre 'New Labour' government:

Those universities already closely allied to traditional elite groups have the resources to nurture and transmit to their students 'high culture', the scholarly pursuit of 'pure' knowledge and fundamental scientific enquiry, and the conservation of accumulated knowledge and experience, 'uninhibited and unfettered by any extraneous considerations whatsoever' … whether social, political or dogmatic. Several writers have noted the strength of … the 'London-Oxford-Cambridge Axis'. Other universities, whose resources and relationships with both the polity and the economy reflect a very different degree of internal quality determination, are faced with a real dilemma: should they primarily strive to emulate the elite universities or should they rather adopt an alternative model ... staffed by and recruiting, socialising and certificating for a 'service class'? What influences the decisions a university makes in the face of this dilemma, and what effects will its resolution have on the future of higher education in Britain?[106]

The historical development of higher education in the UK goes a long way towards explaining the patterns of university attendance observed in our research on the UK business elite of 1998. For the generation with which we are concerned, attending Oxford or Cambridge vested the individual with significant symbolic capital, irrespective of his or her chosen subject. It formed a natural entrée into the corridors of power of public- and private-sector institutions. However, other 'legitimate' educational options were available, and while the likes of Imperial College, UCL, KCL, the London School of Economics, Sheffield, Manchester, Durham, Birmingham, Bristol, St Andrews, Glasgow or Edinburgh may not have enjoyed quite the same level of kudos as the Oxbridge colleges, attending one of them still served as a significant marker of distinction. Moreover, there were well-regarded options for further study outside the university system. At a time when university places were scarce and the practice of university attendance not yet commonplace, many young people sought recognised professional qualifications from bodies such as the Institution of Chartered Accountants and the Chartered Institute of Bankers. Since examinations were open to university graduates and non-graduates alike, the opportunity existed to lay the foundations for a business career without the requirement to sacrifice earnings for three or more years.

The range and perceived quality of higher and professional educational choices available in the UK between 1950 and 1980, when the system was opened up but not yet 'massified', suggests that while Oxford and Cambridge might be dominant as elite 'structuring structures', we would nonetheless expect to see individuals from other higher and professional educational backgrounds reaching the top. This challenges to some degree the established stereotype of the late twentieth-century business leader as upper- or upper-middle-class and educated at an elite public school followed by Oxford or Cambridge.[107] Scott, for example, identifies a core business stratum founded on family control and financial influence, kinship and privilege,[108] and Stanworth and Giddens see company chairmen as 'an elite within elite'. And whereas Perkin estimates the upper class to embrace just 3 per cent of the population,[109] Stanworth and

Giddens found that as many as two-thirds of their sample of 460 top executives was upper-class and only 1 per cent (5 chairmen out of 460) working-class.[110] Looking further back, Crouzet concludes that the notion of the self-made man as fuelling the Industrial Revolution is spurious; essentially the upper and upper-middle classes drove industrialisation, he insists.[111]

Rubinstein, however, is strongly critical of studies on elite recruitment in the UK (including those by Scott, and Stanworth and Giddens)[112] for what he sees as their tendency to conflate attendance at a public school with membership of an existing elite, such that attendance at one of the sought-after Clarendon schools followed by Oxbridge is often taken at face value as evincing substantial family wealth and high status:

> Almost invariably [such studies] take the secondary and tertiary educa-
> tional qualifications of an elite position-holder as *prima facie* evidence
> of his childhood social position with education at a fee-paying school
> or a university normally taken as evidence of the high status and con-
> siderable family wealth of the elite position-holder. As a result they
> conceal the true extent of social mobility, based upon merit, into Brit-
> ain's most prestigious and powerful positions, conceal the considerable
> degree of change, particularly in the economic status of the position-
> holders' families, and conceal the true nature, dimensions and degree of
> fluidity within Britain's so-called 'Establishment' during the past cen-
> tury.[113]

In obscuring the realities of social mobility, Rubinstein points out that the above studies rely on a circular argument, whereby 'attendance at a public school and Oxbridge indicates considerable wealth and high status, while the family wealth and high status of the man in question is proved by the fact that he attended a public school and Oxbridge'.[114] This equa-tion of attendance at an elite institution or institutions with the accumula-tion of wealth and privilege has the effect of conflating 'the scions of bona fide aristocrats and plutocrats with the sons of very ordinary and often virtually poor persons, certainly with no connection whatever to privilege, who attended the same sorts of school, into a spurious "Establishment" hallmarked by an equally spurious homogeneity'.[115] Close examination of the make-up of four elite groups studied by Rubinstein – permanent under-secretaries in the civil service, Church of England bishops and archbishops, the vice-chancellors of English and Welsh universities, all from the period 1880-1970, and the chairmen of the largest British industrial companies, as identified by Stanworth and Giddens (1890-1970)

– reveals, on the contrary, that these were drawn disproportionately from the lower-middle classes. Their emergence as members of the elite depended, in Rubinstein's view, not on money and connections but rather on hard graft and sheer talent – on 'IQ plus effort'[116] – such that achieving a starred first at Oxbridge was akin to 'discovering that one's father was somehow unsuspectedly in Burke's Peerage'.[117]

Hannah, who points to the declining numbers of public school and Oxbridge alumni amongst the chairmen of Britain's top 50 companies from 1979 to 1989, supports Rubinstein's argument.[118] Nicholas, however, dismisses such views as overly optimistic 'pro-meritocratic revisionism', claiming instead that becoming a member of the British business elite is still 'largely determined by the interconnected characteristics of a wealthy family and a prestige education', and further, that 'the [British] business elite has become increasingly homogenous', against, perhaps, the expectations of a century and a half of far-reaching socio-economic change.[119] In our own view, the connections between family background and access to a prestigious education identified in 1980 by Halsey et al., and the consequences for social reproduction, remain strong. Yet there can be no doubt that the offspring of some families of modest means do take advantage of educational opportunities and do rise to prominence in the world of business.

In Britain, elitism remains multi-faceted and subtle in its expressions. Stanworth and Giddens make the point, for example, that the continued use of aristocratic titles – often used as a reward for business success – points to 'the continuation of the trappings and symbols of an old order into modern times'.[120] The award of such titles and honours in contemporary Britain is bound up with power and control. It is veiled in secrecy, a necessary part, perhaps, of the 'legitimating illusion'. As Snow observes, governments remain 'happy to use the honours systems to do what politicians have done since medieval times: dish out hierarchical class-based honours to lock key elements of the body politic into position'.[121] The 'aristocratic principle' identified by Disraeli as infusing all aspects of British society is seemingly alive and well.[122]

Education and elite recruitment

Our own research has confirmed the expected concentration of top company directors in establishments of repute, in both France and the UK, as detailed in Tables 4.3 and 4.4. A useful summary of our findings on place of study is provided in Table 4.5. Each country has several thousand secondary schools and hundreds of places of higher learning, yet attendances at both the secondary and tertiary levels are concentrated in relatively few institutions. The French and UK patterns are remarkably similar for higher education, with five institutions accounting for well over 40 per cent of attendances in both countries. Twenty institutions account for more than 70 per cent of attendances in France and 67 per cent of attendances in the UK. As might be expected, concentration levels are lower for schools, but when the total number of schools is considered the results are impressive. In France, just five schools account for 27 per cent of attendances and 20 schools account for 43 per cent of all known attendances. There is a significant difference between France and the UK. In the latter, there is a lesser degree of concentration, yet five schools still account for 15 per cent of attendances and 29 per cent of directors attended one of the top 20 most frequently attended UK schools.

Table 4.5   Concentration of attendances at French and UK educational institutions by directors of top 100 companies in 1998

Institutions	France (% of Known Attendances)	UK (% of Known Attendances)
Higher Education		
Top 5	43.77	43.82
Top 10	59.20	54.31
Top 20	71.00	67.39
Schools		
Top 5	27.18	14.78
Top 10	34.57	20.38
Top 20	43.15	28.74

It can be concluded that, in both France and the UK, place of education is a major factor in identifying present and future members of the business elite. Polytechnique alone accounts for 12 per cent of all known attendances of top 100 company directors in France, with Sciences-Po and ENA close behind, accounting for 11.8 per cent and 9.2 per cent of attendances respectively. Nine of the top 10 most frequently attended establishments of higher education are in the Paris basin, the exception, interestingly, being Harvard. There is not the same geographic concentration of attendance in the UK, as Table 4.4 confirms, with universities up and down the country, including two in Scotland, represented in the top 10. However, Oxford and Cambridge hold similarly hegemonic positions to Polytechnique and Sciences-Po, accounting in turn for 16 and 13 per cent of known attendances. Harvard, which regularly sits atop of lists of the world's elite universities, features prominently in third place with 6 per cent of attendances. This is accounted for partly by US citizens sitting on UK boards and partly by the popularity of Harvard Business School as a place for aspiring members of the UK business elite to study.

The reputation of the top Parisian *lycées* for preparing young people for admission to Polytechnique and Sciences-Po serves as a magnet for upper- and upper-middle-class families. The Lycée Louis-le-Grand in the Latin Quarter accounts for 9.4 per cent of all known attendances by French directors of the top 100 companies, with Janson-de-Sailly close behind at 6.6 per cent. As Table 4.3 demonstrates, nine out of the top ten establishments favoured by the elite are clustered in the Paris basin, the exception being the Lycée du Parc in Lyon. The prominence of a handful of elite educational establishments located in and around Paris is revealing. Most capital cities are culturally heterogeneous, places of in-migration, where mobility increases heterogeneity.[123] In the French case, however, the Parisian schools and *grandes écoles* are the seedbed of aspiring *patrons*, central to the reproduction and regeneration of the establishment. There is no counterpart in Britain. The top British schools, like the top universities, show a wider geographical spread, including one in Scotland, Glasgow Academy. Leading public schools feature prominently, with Eton accounting for 6.6 per cent of all known attendances.

The fact that attendance in educational institutions is highly concentrated in both France and the UK should not disguise equally important differences between the two systems. Two of the most important of these are highlighted in Table 4.6. The first relates to the subjects future members of the business elite elected to study in higher education. In France, the impression is of a two-horse race. Equally dominant are engineering and science subjects that require a high degree of competency in mathematics, and subjects related to business and economics.[124] Professional subjects like law are also seen as a fitting academic background for a career in business. The same broad pattern is repeated in the UK, where engineering and science subjects and business and economics related subjects make a very strong showing along with law, but here there is a far greater tolerance in business for people with academic backgrounds in the arts, humanities and social sciences.

Table 4.6 Known higher education backgrounds of elite directors in France and the UK in 1998

	France (n=671)		UK (n=511)	
	No.	%	No.	%
HE Discipline Group				
Arts, Humanities or Social Sciences	20	2.98	83	16.24
Business, Economics or Administration	293	43.67	180	35.23
Science, Engineering or Medicine	300	44.71	177	34.64
Professional	58	8.64	71	13.89
Highest HE Qualification				
Doctorate	74	11.03	56	10.96
Higher Degree	540	80.48	144	28.18
First Degree	57	8.49	311	60.86
HE Institutions Attended				
Elite	567	84.50	416	81.41
Non-Elite	104	15.50	95	18.59

Notes: See Appendix 1 for a note on the classification of discipline groups, qualification levels and status of institutions attended.

The second main difference revealed in Table 4.6 concerns the amount and level of higher education experienced by French and UK top 100 directors. It appears at first sight that far more business leaders in France possess a master's degree than in the UK, but it could be argued that this finding is more reflective of terminological rather than substantive differences between the two cadres. The typical pattern in France is for an aspiring member of the elite to leave school and spend two years in *classes préparatoires* before taking the entrance examination for a *grande école*, and this is counted as part of their higher education. Then, in a senior institution like Polytechnique, students graduate after three years with a *diplôme*, which is held to be the equivalent of a higher degree. Thus, simply by having graduated in the 'normal' way, members of the French business elite may appear better educated than their British counterparts. However, the story does not end there. Many aspiring members of the French elite do not rush straight from higher education into a job, as is typically the case in the UK. Rather, they move between elite educational institutions and read for additional qualifications, sometimes full-time and sometimes part-time. Indeed, we record a mean attendance figure of almost exactly two higher education institutions for top 100 company French directors compared to 1.4 for their UK counterparts.

The differences in the educational experiences of French and UK business leaders are confirmed by our more detailed study of the super-elite of the top 100 most powerful directors in France and the UK in 1998, the results of which are presented in Table 4.7. With a mean age of 56, the typical member of the super-elite was educated at secondary level in the 1950s and was in higher education or professional training in the 1960s. At this time, the most prestigious secondary schools in France were the Jesuit-run independent schools and the state-run *lycées*, and their counterparts in the UK were the independent schools of various types and the state grammar schools. The *lycées* and grammar schools offered a rounded, high-quality academic education and prepared the best students for entry into the elite strata of higher education. Only the best students in France progressed to a *lycée* and in the UK, the majority of students were excluded from grammar school and sent to a less academic, non-selective, secondary modern school.

Of those members of the super-elite for whom we have data on secondary education and who were not educated abroad, the vast majority had a 'selective' secondary education – 97 per cent in France and 95 per cent in the UK. In France, as for our full sample, most went on to study either a business related discipline or a science and engineering related discipline at a *grande école*. Some studied law and only very few chose the arts, humanities or social sciences. Ninety gained a qualification equivalent to a master's degree or above, and 68 won qualifications from at least two elite institutions, the most common paths being from Polytechnique to the Ecole des Mines (11) and either Paris I (Panthéon Sorbonne) or Paris II (Panthéon Assas) to Sciences-Po (9). The pre-eminence of Polytechnique and Sciences-Po is confirmed by the fact that 37 of the super-elite attended the former and 23 the latter. Eight graduates of Polytechnique or Sciences-Po, or both, stood at the very summit of French business in 1998, as a PDG of one of the country's top ten enterprises: Gérard Mestrallet of Suez, Jean-Marie Messier of Vivendi, Serge Tchuruk of Alcatel, and Thierry Desmarest of Total attended Polytechnique; Michel Bon of France Télécom, Philippe Jaffré of Elf Aquitaine, and Louis Schweitzer of Renault attended Sciences-Po; and Jean-Louis Beffa of Saint-Gobain attended both.

In the UK, the route from school into higher education was somewhat less predictable in terms of both origins and destination. The majority of the UK super-elite went to private schools, of which the most frequently attended were Eton and Shrewsbury (three each).

Table 4.7 Educational profiles of top 100 directors in France and the UK in 1998

	France	UK
Type of School		
Independent	15	43
French *Lycée* or UK Grammar	69	30
Other State School	3	4
Overseas	4	14
Not Known	9	9
Higher Education		
Elite Institution	88	62
Non-Elite Institution	3	12
None	8	25
Not Known	1	1
Education Type		
Arts, Humanities or Social Sciences	2	12
Business, Economics or Administration	42	26
Science, Engineering or Medicine	44	27
Professional	4	29
School Only	7	5
Not Known	1	1
Highest Qualification		
Doctorate	10	6
Higher Degree	80	23
First Degree	2	45
Professional Qualification only	0	20
School	7	5
Not Known	1	1
Executive Management Education		
Yes	33	16
No	66	83
Not known	1	1

Note: See Appendix 1 for definitions and classifications.

The majority of the remainder went to a grammar school, the starting point to the top for 60 per cent of the directors with a lower- or middle-class family background. Fewer of the UK directors went into higher education than their French counterparts (74 compared to 91), and those that did spent less time engaged in study; just 29 of them being awarded a higher degree. Many more UK directors had no exposure to higher education (25 compared to 8), a similar proportion to that observed by Windolf in 1993,[125] but in compensation, many took a demanding part-time professional course in accounting or banking. The university graduates, like their French counterparts, clustered in business or engineering and science-related disciplines. However, as for our full sample, many more studied in the arts, humanities and social sciences than in France, and they were spread more evenly across a greater number of institutions, with the lead players – Oxford and Cambridge – educating 13 and 11 graduates respectively. Oxbridge graduates occupied CEO positions at three of the UK's top ten companies in 1998: Mark Moody-Stuart at Shell, Edmund Browne at BP, and Martin Taylor at Barclays. This contrasts with the out-and-out dominance of Polytechnique and Sciences-Po graduates of top positions in France, especially when it is considered that four CEOs of the top 10 companies – John Bond at HSBC, Bill Cockburn at British Telecom, Peter Ellwood at Lloyds TSB, and Dino Adriano at Sainsburys – never attended university. When the analysis is widened to include the CEOs of the top 20 UK companies in 1998, the same pattern is repeated: Oxbridge graduates occupied four positions, other elite university graduates occupied eight positions, non-elite university graduates occupied two positions, and those with no university education occupied six positions. Five of the six non-university educated CEOs hold professional qualifications: three – John Bond of HSBC, Peter Ellwood of Lloyds TSB, and Peter Birch of Abbey National – are Fellows of the Chartered Institute of Bankers, and two – Dino Adriano of Sainsburys and Brian Moffat of British Steel – are qualified accountants.

In neither France nor the UK was a postgraduate qualification in management a requirement for membership of the super-elite. It is only in recent decades that European countries have attempted to bridge the gap in management knowledge between themselves and the US. In this, France was for long ahead of the UK, HEC having been founded in 1881, ENA in 1945 and INSEAD in 1957, whereas the London Business School was established as late as 1964, admitting students for the first time in 1966. The majority of the top 100 directors were educated before the massive expansion in executive education of recent times, and it is not surprising therefore that relatively few hold an MBA degree (three in France and ten in the UK). However, 28 members of the French super-elite attended ENA. Of the 16 UK directors with a postgraduate education in management, nine attended Harvard, confirming the enduring prestige of US business schools.

Finally, analysis of the relationship between the social origins and education of top 100 directors is more revealing for the UK than for France. This stems from the fact that there is such a high degree of uniformity of educational experience in France at both secondary and tertiary levels.

Nearly all members of the French super-elite attended a prestigious *lycée* or independent Catholic school, and nearly all members attended at least one top-tier *grande école*. The consistency of the educational starting point for the highest-flying business careers is regular and predictable, making further statistical analysis unrewarding.

Table 4.8 Percentage distributions by social origins of types of schools and universities attended by the top 100 directors of UK companies in 1998

	Parental Class		
	Upper	Upper Middle	Lower Middle and Lower
School			
Independent	92.0	56.5	20.0
Grammar	8.0	43.5	72.0
Secondary Modern	0.0	0.0	8.0
Total	**100.0**	**100.0**	**100.0**
	(n=25)	(n=23)	(n=25)
University			
Elite	84.4	61.6	39.4
Non-Elite	6.3	19.2	15.2
None	9.3	19.2	45.4
Total	**100.0**	**100.0**	**100.0**
	(n=32)	(n=26)	(n=33)

Notes: Excluded from consideration are directors for whom there are missing data, and in the case of schools those who were educated outside the UK.

In the UK, however, there is far greater variability in both the social origins and educational histories of top 100 directors. From Table 4.8 it can be seen that those from the upper reaches of society almost invariably attended a fee-paying school. The upper-middle class, composed of senior professionals and the top levels of management in the public and private sectors, confronted a choice between an independent and a grammar school education. In fact, a small majority favoured a state education, confirming the finding of Halsey et al. that children from better-off families heavily colonised the grammar schools. Some of the future directors from a lower- or lower-middle-class background attended an independent school by way of a scholarship or parental sacrifice, but a large majority went to a grammar school. Just two attended a secondary modern school.

From school, those from the upper class predominantly went on to elite universities spread across the UK and abroad, but with significant clusters in Oxford (7) and Cambridge (6). A handful went on to non-elite universities or began a career straight from school. Those from upper-middle-class backgrounds were less likely to attend an elite university, although 16 out of 26 did so, with very small clusters in Birmingham (2), Cambridge (3) and Oxford (2). Five went on to non-elite universities like Aston and City, and another five went straight into work. A minority of those from the lower and lower-middle classes went to an elite university: 13 of them, spread across 12 universities, with only Manchester receiving more than one. Fifteen of the people in this category, just three fewer than those who went to university, began their career directly on leaving school. Three of them entered high street banks and became professionally qualified as a Fellow of the Chartered Institute of Banking. Nine more qualified as accountants, and rose to the top in UK business through mastery of the finance function.

Overall, elite institutional pathways – family, school and higher education – can be seen to differ markedly in France and the UK. Yet there are equally profound similarities. In both countries education plays a pivotal role in the recruitment and selection of elites, and hence in their reproduction and regeneration, and the stability of society. Institutions, according to Giddens, while nationally distinct and qualitatively different, commonly function as a 'switchboard' in the distribution of individuals in society; the process of socialisation within them serving as a currency that secures access to elite pathways and positions.[126] The social contacts made in these establishments are clearly important, but so too are the learned demeanours and assimilated behaviours (acquired both consciously and unconsciously) that distinguish those individuals who attend such establishments, who are assumed to have certain dispositions and qualities of character (often 'ascribed' rather than necessarily 'achieved').[127] Frequently, such assumed personal characteristics rest on the most traditional of values.[128] Appropriate behaviours thus serve as shorthand to confirm a common value system.[129] Equally, the absence of expected behaviours, or the inability to display them, may eliminate candidates *a priori*, marking them out as ineligible for selection.

Education is central, too, to the legitimation of elites in society, whose privileged position is justified through merit, 'social selection on the basis of ability plus effort'.[130] This is especially the case in France, where the institutionalised training of elites is accepted by both rulers and ruled – the former prizing it for its efficiency, the latter accepting it as a form of legitimate differentiation, since the state clearly requires talented individuals to run it.[131] Yet it also applies, albeit to a lesser extent, to the UK. The 'pervasiveness of a meritocratic basis of promotion' is affirmed by Rubinstein in

Elites and the Wealthy in Modern British History throughout the highest reaches of the British elite structure.[132] Donald Coleman's celebrated thesis was precisely that the 'cult of the gentleman' in second or third generation elites specifically opened the way to new men, who earned the right to be included through merit, enabling 'the "practical man", the Player, … to cross the social divide and become a Gentleman'.[133]

Current examples, drawn from our own research, include George Cox, whose parents believed that their children should go to university at a time when only 5 per cent of the population did so: 'Although nobody in my family had ever been to university, my parents believed that was what their children should do, and their attitude was very much that you could achieve what you wanted to do. I think that made a great influence on our attitude'.[134] Lindsay Owen-Jones, PDG of L'Oréal, who was raised in a lower-middle-class family from Liverpool, likewise distinguished himself at an early age through access to an elite education. As the only son in the family, he went to Oxford and then to INSEAD, the leading business school at Fontainebleau, after which he joined L'Oréal, rising to become its head at the age of 42.[135]

A good education at an elite university, of course, does not guarantee that someone will rise to the top in business or any other field. It serves as a primary structuring structure and has enduring value as a social discriminator. As Giddens reminds us, any analysis of elite recruitment must therefore be tempered by what he terms 'the mediation of control', an examination of the actual use of power by individuals and organisations.[136] Not all who are called can ultimately be chosen.

Conclusion

This chapter has compared and contrasted the education of business elites in France and the UK, reflecting on the historical development of education, particularly of elites, in the two countries. Bourdieu may have written specifically on France and the French education system, but the 'structuring structures' he identified there, though differing in detail in the two countries, have been found to be equally relevant on both sides of the Channel. His writings shed light on the logic and mechanisms of social domination in a complex, capitalist society, and the methods by which it conceals and perpetuates itself, rooted within the systems of class, culture and education. Though the overall thrust of changes to the education systems of France and Britain has been, broadly speaking, in the direction of openness and inclusiveness, with some evidence, supported by our research, that the recruitment of business elites has become gradually more open over the years, nevertheless whilst undertaking this study we have been startled by the degree to which elitism still applies, by the extent to which the structuring structures shoring up elitism and privilege continue to function, while often dissembling themselves as structures of democratisation. Indeed, it is when framed as strategies to facilitate the social advancement of the masses that such structures perform at their best, apparent disinterestedness proving to be an excellent guise – as Bourdieu expresses it, 'on the hither side of calculation and in the illusion of the most "authentic" sincerity'[137] – masking the cynicism that often underlies attempts at so-called inclusiveness. For example, the most recent endeavour by the British government to move to a mass higher education system by introducing variable top-up fees, whilst ostensibly democratic, is likely to be elitist in its effects.[138] The struggle for resources and reputation waged by competing universities in a mass system of higher education will only increase pressures for stratification and the continuance of elitism: the already dominant will continue to dominate. As in the past, disproportionate numbers of children from the richest and most knowledgeable families are likely to come out on top, as recipients of a prestigious education at an elite university, with a sound foundation for an elite career.

In a similar vein, the French education system, while overtly espousing an egalitarian ideal, nevertheless legitimates educational disparity by virtue of an ostensibly meritocratic system. The *grande école* diploma obscures the socio-cultural criteria companies employ in the recruitment of business elites, while implying that merit is the sole consideration.[139] In this way, the system works to strengthen social divisions by bolstering existing differences in culture, wealth and status. It reinforces rather than redistributes cultural capital, and performs a crucial function of social reproduction. As Gaetano Mosca put it more than a century ago:

> In all countries of the world those other agencies for exerting social influence – personal publicity, good education, specialized training, high rank in church, public administration, and army – are always readier of access to the rich than to the poor. The rich invariably have a considerably shorter road to travel than the poor, to say nothing of the fact that the stretch of road that the rich are spared is often the roughest and most difficult.[140]

Thus, even in the third millennium, the easy access of the rich and privileged to particular fields or spheres of influence contrasts with the rocky road travelled by the majority of the less well-off.

5

Elite Careers and Lifestyles

'Taste classifies, and it classifies the classifier'.

Bourdieu [1]

The advantages of an elite education were enumerated in the previous chapter, where it was demonstrated that a large proportion of those who actually reach the top in business, especially in France, have enjoyed the benefits of attending elite schools and institutions of higher education. There is nothing mystical about the process. Graduating from a top institution with a top qualification is a rite of passage that signals to potential employers high levels of personal ability, potential and prestige. In other words, it is easier for a person with an elite education to get started on a fast track career with a 'blue chip' employer than for those educated at less prestigious institutions. Once in employment, moreover, other advantages come to the fore. Some stem from the inner confidence that comes from personal identification with the ruling elite, of knowing the rules of the game, of having the right instincts and cultural reference points. Others stem from the enduring value of 'brand' association, of being recognised by others as 'one of them', the product of an institution known to imbue future leaders with the right values and personal dispositions, rendering them conventionally safe, reliable and trustworthy.

Yet, notwithstanding these undoubted advantages, a good education in a prestigious institution offers no guarantee of reaching the highest levels in business or in any other walk of life. Thousands of people graduate each year from elite educational institutions, but only a small number of these actually rise to the very top in their chosen field. It is important to recognise that companies are themselves powerful structuring structures that are instrumental in forging careers and developing future members of the business elite. Those that advance most rapidly, through a combination of good fortune and good strategy, accumulate the cultural, social and symbolic capital needed to function effectively in strategic roles within organisations. To be seen as 'fit for high office' requires recognition of major accomplishments and abilities, to be seen as a serious player, as somehow vital to the long-term future of the organisation. The difficulties inherent in standing out and winning the approval of existing leaders mean that most people, with or without the advantages of an elite education, make relatively limited progress in their careers. Some, however, are singled out for successive promotions and increased rewards by the perceived excellence of their everyday performance. They have learned through cultural assimilation how to win powerful supporters. It is these 'corporate heroes', who actively seek and achieve distinction, either within a single company or by moving between companies, who eventually enter the ranks of the business elite.

The processes of reputation building and personal capital accumulation can be seen in the career histories of many of our interviewees. Louis Sherwood is one example. After reading Classics at Oxford and taking an MBA at Stanford, he began his career in 1965 with the investment bank Morgan Grenfell. In 1968, he decided to leave what was considered to be a 'cradle to grave' job to work as personal assistant to James Gulliver, managing director of the food retail chain Fine Fare, a part of the Associated British Foods group controlled by the Weston family. In this capacity, Sherwood made important business connections and learned about retailing from the top downwards. When Gulliver left Fine Fare in 1972, Sherwood moved on, selling himself as a 'bright young retailer' to the business tycoon James Goldsmith, whose portfolio of interests covered tertiary banking, property and Cavenham Foods. His drive and energy made an impression on Goldsmith, and in 1977 he was asked to chair the executive board responsible for sorting out the affairs of the near-defunct Slater Walker Bank. This was a first-class opportunity, and in recognition for a job well done Goldsmith appointed him Senior Vice President of the Grand Union food retail chain in the US, where, aged 36, he was placed in charge of business development. Grand Union was a turnaround project and Sherwood's role was pivotal and high profile. It led to his recruitment in 1985 as President and second in command at the rival supermarket chain, Atlantic and Pacific Tea. Three years later he was headhunted to return to the UK as Chairman and CEO of Gateway Food Markets. Gateway was taken over in 1989, and Sherwood, aged 48, changed tack and decided to use his reputation and extensive connections to build a career as a portfolio non-executive director. Numerous appointments followed, including chairman of the television company HTV, director of the insurance company Clerical Medical, and director of HBOS, formed in 2001 by the merger between the Halifax Building Society and the Bank of Scotland.

Louis Sherwood's career illustrates some of the principles of personal capital accumulation referred to above. He invested first in an elite education, in the UK and the US, making him a natural 'transatlantic', and then early in his career he repeatedly left the 'safe zone' to take on new challenges, accumulating cultural and symbolic capital in the process, as with Slater Walker. He developed an extensive personal network, not only in retailing, but also in the City of London and New York financial circles. At an early age he had dealings with the Bank of England and important entrepreneurs and financiers. He was recognised for his intellectual gifts, as a strategist with a fine eye for detail, who could assess risks and could be counted upon to deliver good results. The name of Jim Wood, his boss first at Cavenham and later at Grand Union and Atlantic and Pacific, appears repeatedly during his account of the early part of his career – implying a high degree of mutual trust and respect between them, and highlighting the importance to elite careers of influential sponsors, who serve as role models, mentors and providers of opportunities. Once proven in his own right, Sherwood's network and reputation made for a smooth career transition from specialised executive to generalist non-executive.

In what follows, we explore in greater depth the factors underpinning elite careers. The focus is on the super-elites of French and British business: the 100 most powerful directors in each country in 1998 (see Tables A.2.3 and A.2.4 of Appendix 2). These are people who have enjoyed the most illustrious careers, and stand at the very summit of their respective business systems. Our analysis is supported by the results of a survey of the career experiences of the 2,291 individuals who make up our entire sample, and by qualitative material drawn from interviews and case studies. The wealth of data available enables us to consider from a comparative standpoint how members of the elite first entered the business world, the routes they took to the top, and the actual experience of elite careers. It also enables us to look in some depth at why so few women have made it into the boardrooms of top 100 companies in France and the UK, and at the relationships that exist between elite careers and lifestyles.

A breakdown of the business super-elites of France and the UK in 1998 is presented in Table 5.1. The majority, as might be expected, in both France (81) and the UK (82), hold senior executive positions such as Président-Directeur Général (PDG) or Chief Executive Officer (CEO). Some are dedicated executives – 29 in France and 37 in the UK – and largely confine their business activities to their substantive post. Others hold one or more non-executive directorships with other top 100 enterprises in addition to their main role. The practice of executives holding multiple non-executive directorships is much more common in France than in the UK, and in terms of governance practices differentiates the two systems. Power brokers like Philippe Jaffré, former PDG of Elf, Michel Bon, former President of France Télécom, Serge Tchuruk of Alcatel, Gérard Mestrallet of Suez and Jean-Louis Beffa of Saint-Gobain were all 'hard wired' into other French top 100 companies (often through the privatisation process of the late 1980s and 1990s) in a way that is uncommon, though not unknown, in the UK, where it is seen as good practice to avoid 'excessive' concentrations of power. This said, in the UK, as in France, the holding of multiple non-executive directorships by 'portfolio non-executives' is justified on the grounds of inter-company learning and experience sharing. In 1998, Jean Peyrelevade and Antoine Bernheim shared the French portfolio non-executive record with seven top 100 directorships each, compared with just four top 100 directorships each for the three UK joint record holders, Colin Marshall, Michael Angus and Christopher Harding, although the three did hold six non-executive chairmanships between them.

Table 5.1 Breakdown by type of involvement of top 100 directors with top 100 companies in France and the UK in 1998

	France (No.)	UK (No.)
Executive Director only	29	37
Executive Director with a single Non-Executive Directorship	19	30
Executive Director with two or more Non-Executive Directorships	33	15
Non-Executive Director only (one or more)	19	18
Total	100	100

Entering the business world

The concentrated elitism of the French system of higher education is paralleled in the way in which graduates and non-graduates of the system make their way into the business world, in turn magnifying the differences that exist between the business elites of France and the UK, and indeed the governance regimes of the two countries. In France, business leaders who have made it to the very top – the super-elite in our study – began their business careers from three main starting points, as reported in Table 5.2. The first group of very highly educated and academically well-qualified individuals went virtually directly into government service, often attending the Ecole Nationale d'Administration (ENA), the French civil service school. Many of these became specialists in economics and finance and earned the title Inspecteur des Finances. Others entered the service of the state as technical specialists, scientists and engineers, who frequently style themselves 'ingénieur', a mark of high status. Examples include Jean-Louis Beffa, PDG of Saint-Gobain, Thierry Desmarest, PDG of Total, and Jean-Martin Folz, CEO of Peugeot-Citroën. Others embarked on a more general administrative career at home or in the Foreign Service. In this, as Windolf's analysis confirms, France is unique amongst the major industrial nations.[2]

Table 5.2 Career profiles of top 100 directors in France and the UK in 1998

	France	**UK**
Corporate	41	84
Enterprise to Corporate	9	2
Public Administration to Corporate	49	3
Law to Corporate	0	6
Media to Corporate	0	2
Politics to Corporate	1	1
Academia to Corporate	0	1
Sport to Corporate	0	1
	100	**100**

Notes: This table tracks how people found their way into a director role in a top 100 company. People who entered the corporate sector at an early age and worked their way up are classified as having a corporate only career profile. Other people, who spent a significant time earlier in their career working in another field, are classified as having moved into the corporate sector. Those who founded a company or who helped in making a small enterprise into a top 100 company are classified as having moved from the enterprise sector into the corporate sector.

The second group, a little smaller than the first, entered directly into business and consists of two main types. The first is a member of a founding family with controlling or residual ownership rights. These people are surprisingly numerous in France: in the top 100 directors alone there are nine business leaders, in addition to nine founding entrepreneurs, who owe their position to family, including such well-known names as Michel-Edouard Leclerc, François Michelin, Pierre Peugeot, Martin Bouygues, Patrick Ricard and Serge Dassault. They are descendants of the founders of the business and their wealth and status are intimately tied up with its continued success. Professional career managers are the second type of director to have begun their careers in business. There are 32 of these, including several single company men like Claude Bébéar, Chairman of AXA, who joined the company in 1958 aged 22, and Lindsay Owen-Jones, the British PDG of L'Oréal, who joined the company in 1969 aged 23.

The third group, consisting of just nine people, is made up of individuals who started a company or joined it when small. Prominent amongst this group of entrepreneurs are Gérard Mulliez, who founded the retailer Auchan in 1961, Pierre Bellon, who founded the catering group Sodexho in 1966, and François Pinault, who in 1963 founded the company that was to become the international fashion house Pinault-Printemps-Redoute (PPR). Some of these businesses have already become family dynasties similar to L'Oréal and Michelin, wherein a family investment company holds a controlling interest and is represented on the board by selected family members. In June 2004, for example, the Bellon family held 38.7 per cent of the equity of Sodexho and was represented on the board by five members in addition to PDG Pierre Bellon.[3] Likewise, the Arnault family held a 46 per cent stake in LVMH, while Marc Ladreit de Lacharrière held two-thirds of the equity of Fimalac.

The distribution of top 100 career profiles in France is the product of history and the capacity of organisations – business and non-business – to structure careers by both inclusion and exclusion. The legacy of interventionism in France is underscored by the fact that so many current business leaders were shaped in terms of their knowledge, networks, mindsets and personal dispositions by working for the state. When privatisation came (in 1986), or the state otherwise loosened its grip on business organisations, these were the people who naturally took on the mantle of business leadership, as insiders, trusted instruments of public policy. The training, experience and connections of such people are seen to be of such value within the private sector that they are legitimate candidates for top positions even in companies without any history of state involvement. Some of these genuinely private-sector companies, like Michelin, Bouygues and Leclerc, are family controlled, but in many others ownership is widely dispersed. In these companies, the culture is one of recruiting and retaining the best talent available, and invariably 'the best' is defined historically and conventionally as being educated at a *grande école* or elite university, reinforcing the dominant pattern of elite reproduction.

This conclusion is further reinforced when consideration is given to the group of entrepreneurs who do not conform to the standard pattern. Just one member of this group was raised in the Île-de-France, compared to 38 of the full sample, and similarly none was educated at an elite *lycée*. Four out of the nine had no higher education at all, and only one attended Polytechnique. Members came mainly from outside the Parisian mainstream. Five were born and raised in northern France, which is surprising, as just nine of our top 100 directors came from the region. What stands out is that the entrepreneurial group was relatively free from the homogenising structuring structures that typically have shaped the French business elite. Yet it is equally important to recognise that members of the group did not hail from socially disadvantaged backgrounds. Six came from the upper class, two from the upper-middle class, and one from the lower-middle class. Their families had often been in business and accumulated considerable capital. Rather than taking flight from their background, these people set out to create more wealth, building upon the achievements of their parents. Having sufficient wealth and being free from dominant social mores, they created the potential to generate substantial new wealth by founding or developing a business of their own. In this venture, they were continuing in a long-established tradition of French families building and retaining control of substantial business empires.

The pattern for entry into the business world depicted in Table 5.2 is very different for the UK than for France. The pathway taken by 84 of the UK top 100 directors was to embark on a business career straight after leaving school or university. There is little evidence of continued family involvement in top 100 UK companies, with the odd exception such as the food and family retailer Morrisons. Andrew Buxton, chairman of Barclays, may have descended from that famous banking family, but his family connections were not his major source of power. Indeed, the UK has evolved as the corporate economy *par excellence*, in which ownership and control are profoundly separated and directors are appointed as agents for a plethora of shareholders. There is very limited state involvement in the business sector other than in formerly state-owned organisations such as the Post Office. The most typical pattern, followed by 50 of the 84 career executives in our sample, is to have progressed up the management hierarchy of the company they first joined on leaving school or university. Typical are the oil barons: Sir Mark Moody-Stuart joined Shell in 1966 aged 26 after completing his doctorate at Cambridge; his colleague Philip Watts joined the company at 23 after taking his master's degree; likewise, Edmund Browne of BP entered the oil business straight from university.

Set against this high level of conformity to the norms of 'organisation man', business in the UK does have a track record of admitting selected individuals from other fields to the inner circle of corporate life as non-executive directors. Law is the biggest provider, with six of the top 100 UK directors in 1998. Five of the six were in non-executive roles, and include well-known individuals like Peter Sutherland, Sydney Lipworth and Martin Jacomb. Top lawyers such as these have particularly valuable skills and knowledge, adding intellectual weight and authority to board-room deliberations. They also have extensive social and symbolic capital. Each came from an upper- or upper-middle-class family, was independently educated and went to an elite university, either in the UK or abroad.

The small number of top 100 directors with backgrounds in public administration contrasts sharply with the situation in France. Sir Peter Middleton of Barclays and Lord Wright of Richmond both enjoyed high-flying careers in the civil service, at the Treasury and Foreign Office respectively, before moving in retirement into the corporate world. They are, however, exceptions, and their move into business took place at the end of their careers, not in mid-career as is common in France. Likewise the transitions of Jan Leschly from international tennis star to CEO of SmithKline Beecham, and Martin Taylor from financial journalist to CEO of Barclays, are exceptions that do little to cast off the impression of staid uniformity with respect to admission into corporate life in the UK. Moreover, just two people managed to make it into the top 100 by virtue of playing a central role in the creation of a major enterprise, compared to nine in France. After three years working for industrial magnate Lord Hanson, Gregory Hutchings purchased an 11 per cent stake in the light engineering company Tomkins in 1983, and through numerous acquisitions – large and small – he took the business within ten years from corporate minnow to giant conglomerate. His immediate contemporary Nigel Rudd, a grammar school educated accountant from a solidly working-class background, acquired control of the Williams foundry business in 1982, and, like Hutchings at Tomkins, built up a formidable top 100 enterprise by purchasing and restructuring struggling companies.

Routes to the top

There is a hidden danger in elite studies: in focusing upon those that have made it to the top, sight is easily lost of those that fell by the wayside. What choices did the high flyers make that differentiated them from their less successful contemporaries? How did the winners in the corporate game accumulate more capital of the right sort than their rivals for promotion within the corporate hierarchy? What is it that helps maintain momentum in a career when others begin to flag? These are the questions to which we now turn.

The wisdom or otherwise of an initial career choice inevitably varies according to demand patterns within elite labour markets, which in turn are reflective of both economic structures and social systems. In France, for example, the relatively heavy weight of manufacturing in the economy, and the continued direct involvement of the state in business, advantages those with backgrounds in engineering and the public sector; whereas in Britain there is a lesser demand for advanced technical knowledge and an in-depth understanding of the machinations of government. If we assume that the pool of individuals with a high level of ambition is filled with rational actors, then potential high flyers will make early career choices that are broadly aligned to national economic and social circumstances. Market signals have a powerful disciplining effect on potential candidates for membership of the national business elite.

Table 5.3 Career foundations of top 100 directors in France and the UK in 1998

	France	UK
General, Operations and Project Management	32	32
Engineering, Science and Technical	32	19
Finance and Accounting	9	27
State Policy and Administration	26	2
Marketing and Media	0	11
Law	0	7
Human Resources and Communications	0	2
Research and Academia	1	0
	100	**100**

Notes: This table classifies the main activities engaged in by future top 100 directors during the first decade of their career. In France, many future top 100 directors began their careers as government employees. These are distributed in the table within three categories according to function and orientation: engineering, science and technical; finance and accounting; state policy and administration.

In Table 5.3 we present the results of our research into the career foundations of the super-elites of French and UK business. The most marked similarity between the two countries is that almost exactly a third of both groups began their careers in operational and general management roles. Often these are people – bankers and retailers for example – who accumulate valuable knowledge through immersion in operational detail, moving periodically from role to role, gaining in experience and gradually moving up the corporate hierarchy. Mike Street, Director of Operations and Customer Services for British Airways, for instance, joined the company aged 15 and by the time of his retirement, after more than 40 years of continuous service, has an unrivalled knowledge of all aspects of the global air transport industry. Within any large organisation, people with their fingers on the pulse, who understand power relations seemingly intuitively, and who have woven a web of secure connections across the organisation, are prized for their capacity to take action and implement solutions to pressing problems. Because of the specificity of their knowledge, they often dedicate their careers to a single company, and are rewarded for this with regular promotions. In the UK, nearly two-thirds of directors with an operational background gained their first main board position with their first employer, compared to exactly half in France. The higher proportion in the UK is accounted for by the prevalence in the sample of bankers and retailers, often one-company employees, and the institutional practice of promotion to the top from within at large companies like BP, HSBC and Unilever.

In manufacturing and natural resource companies, many of those who eventually reach the top begin their careers in engineering or scientific roles, directly applying the high-level technical skills acquired through extensive higher education. Men like Sir Mark Moody-Stuart at Shell, Edmund Browne at BP and Richard Sykes at Glaxo set out as specialists but quickly acquired a more general knowledge of operations and strategic management, typically through the management of a subsidiary company. The same pattern is found in France but on a more extensive scale. Alain Joly at Air Liquide and Pierre Daurès at Electricité de France (EdF) are typical examples, as is Anne Lauvergeon, popularly known as 'Atomic Anne', who holds a doctorate in physics and in 2005 headed the nuclear engineering company Areva. These are all people who recognised at an early stage that to forge a top career they must move from an engineering role into a more strategic role. In the case of Anne Lauvergeon, she invested in learning how power and politics interact with business, and how to acquire the social capital needed to function effectively at the highest level. When she was just 32 years of age she worked as Deputy Chief of Staff at the French Presidency before moving three years later to a partnership with Lazard Frères. This experience prepared her for appointment as Senior Vice President at Alcatel and then as CEO of Cogema in 1999 and Areva in 2001.

Next to operations management, the most solid foundation for an elite business career in the UK is accounting and finance. There are several explanations for the exceptionally high esteem in which the finance function is held, and the widely held view that finance directors have the right credentials to become a CEO. First, the pressure brought to bear on management teams by investors to maximise returns on investments has elevated the status of financial information in decision-making. Secondly, the pivotal role of the City in the economic life of the UK has further elevated the standing of finance directors. Thirdly, accounting has had the benefit of powerful professional bodies that have successfully promoted the interests of members over many decades. Fourthly, business education was slow to develop in the UK, and a professional training in accounting for long served as a substitute qualification. Each of these factors offers a plausible part-explanation, but no single factor can explain the phenomenon. What is important is that the high status accorded to the finance function has become institutionally embedded, central to the mindset of business leaders and the micro-culture of UK boardrooms. This explains why 27 accounting and finance specialists, 25 of them professionally qualified but 14 of them without a university education', were amongst the top 100 most powerful UK directors in 1998. Unlike their general management counterparts, many of these people, because of the generic and transportable nature of their skills, moved around in search of their first major finance directorship, just five joining the board of their original employer.

Finance directors, of course, also enjoy high status in France, but their training is very different from the UK. All nine of the top 100 directors with a financial background were highly educated graduates, six attended ENA and three top business schools, and four styled themselves Inspecteurs des Finances, including Michel Bon of France Télécom and Jean-Marie Messier of Vivendi fame. This profound difference in institutional traditions could not be more apparent, and is confirmed by the fact that 26 other members of the French super-elite founded their careers in public administration, as policy-oriented generalists rather than financial or engineering specialists. This group includes high-profile reformers like Jérôme Monod of Suez-Lyonnaise des Eaux and Marc Viénot, author of the reports that have become the touchstone of the French corporate governance movement. In 1995, Monod launched a self-critical attack on France's business elite, reflecting that the privileged few, educated like himself at premier institutions such as ENA, 'are shuffled from one high level position to another with little risk of being accountable for mismanagement'.[4] Irrespective of whether this critique is valid or not, coming as it does from an insider, it highlights the social cohesiveness of the French business elite. Of the 26 members of the super-elite who began as public administrators, 14 graduated from Sciences-Po and 22 from ENA, and all attended at least one *grande école*. Seven of them served as executive directors of companies in which the state retained an interest (see Table 6.3 in Chapter 6), including Louis Gallois, PDG of SNCF, Louis Schweitzer, PDG of Renault, Jean-Dominique Comolli, PDG of Seita, and Jean-Cyril Spinetta, PDG of Air France. Three others – Christophe Blanchard-Dignac, Anne Le Lorier and Nicolas Jachiet – remained in post as top government officials, holding a portfolio of non-executive directorships as representatives of the state.

Three general observations emerge from our research with respect to top executive careers. The first is that the choice of early career path is critical, and that the choices available differ between national business systems. In France, most personal capital is accumulated through engagement with policy, strategy and general management, whether in the public or private sector. Finance, because of its centrality to decision making, is also an inner-circle discipline. The UK is similar in its preference for policy, strategy, general management and finance as top career tracks, but there is a cleavage between public- and private-sector careers. Public-sector management experience is not regarded in the private sector as equivalent to the mastery of business operations or a specialist discipline like accounting and finance or marketing. The second observation is that people who reach the top often attach themselves at an early age to successful companies in dominant sectors within a national (or potentially regional) business system. In France, a wide range of manufacturing enterprises continue to flourish, and industry groups like transportation engineering are national specialist clusters within the international economy. Banking, insurance and finance likewise represent a UK specialist cluster of global significance. The differing compositions of the French and UK national business elites are thus reflective of two different structural and institutional pathways to economic growth. The third observation is that the more organisation-specific the personal capital accumulated during a career, then the greater the rewards of organisational loyalty in terms of career progression. It favours both individuals and organisations to promote from within into positions that demand an extensive command over context-specific industry and corporate information. In the UK in particular, but also in France, the evidence points to long-serving employees progressing into a high proportion of top executive positions.

A typical illustration is provided by the career of Iain Gray, Managing Director of Airbus UK. In effect, he is a one-company executive who joined the division of British Aerospace that was to become Airbus UK immediately on leaving Aberdeen University, where he had studied engineering. Like many other graduate engineers, Mr Gray had the option of making a career purely as a technologist with highly special-ised skills, but instead he progressively added strategic and general management skills to his technical competencies. This won him the reputation of someone who could handle complexity, technical and organisational, and could pull together the elements needed to deliver solutions for the business. He used his social skills, business knowledge and practical networking capabilities to accumulate the personal capital needed to engender trust in those above him, making him a natural choice for promotion when the opportunity arose. In his own words:

> You do create your own luck. I do remember very early on in my career being given the advice that said absolutely everybody in the organisation will be given a lucky break, they will be given an oppor-tunity, but 99 per cent of people will not recognise it as such when they get it. So, you know, part of it is luck, but part of it is recognis-ing that break when it comes along, and sometimes it can be quite obtuse in terms of seeing an opportunity and seizing it. … It can be quite simple things in life that happen almost on a daily basis that can provide big opportunities. A simple thing might be somebody sud-denly being asked to a meeting to take the minutes, and there will be two different kinds of people. One will go along grudgingly, not really wanting to do it, bit of a slog, they do the job, they don't get anything out of it. Another person would go along to the same meet-ing, would actively listen, take part in terms of taking notes of the meeting, pick up on things he didn't understand that were said in the meeting, and ask 'What did you mean when you said that?', and when he writes the minutes will actually put together an action plan and follow up an action plan. So you can see, out of a simple oppor-tunity, you can identify two completely different extremes in how somebody will seize that opportunity. So, when I say luck and oppor-tunities, I think it is about recognising the opportunities when they come along, and milking them, and really extracting from that oppor-tunity the maximum. I guess that's how I would characterise how I've developed my career.[5]

The need to seize opportunities and to 'see the bigger picture' is a theme reiterated in many of the interviews we have conducted. Another theme is 'finding yourself in the right place at the right time', as did Iain

Gray at Airbus, which over the past 30 years has emerged from the shadows to rival Boeing for leadership of the global air transport industry. In rapidly growing enterprises like Airbus, opportunities abound and create the potentiality for trusted, knowledgeable and strategically-oriented executives like Iain Gray to reach the highest levels in global business.

The route to the top, of course, is different for members of the family and entrepreneurial groups in our French and UK samples. Top executives like Michel-Edouard Leclerc, François Michelin and Martin Bouygues were in a sense 'born to rule' as successors to already prominent dynasties. Yet they did have to prove themselves: with executive colleagues, rival members of the family, employees, partners in business alliances and networks, customers and suppliers, political leaders, and not least with critical sections of the media. Legitimacy for such people is established through performance, and in almost all cases the requirement of stakeholders is that the 'chosen one' learns the business from within, working up through the management hierarchy alongside other executives. There is simply too much at stake for all checks and balances to be cast aside, and for this reason the executive careers of family members often resemble those of other top executives, although they tend to reach the boardroom at a much earlier age, typically in their mid-thirties.

The same is not true of founding entrepreneurs. These people in effect abandon at some point the notion of a conventional executive career in favour of the pursuit of the main chance. This approach invariably involves the accumulation and deployment of personal capital in innovative and unusual ways. Bourdieu views social change as the product of power struggles between dominant and subordinated factions; between established, senior members of a class and newcomers or challengers seeking to advance their fortunes and legitimacy.[6] As argued in Chapter 2, established members of the elite tend to pursue conservative strategies in defence of their assets, power and privileges, while aspiring factions pursue strategies that seek to reform the existing order.

The experience of George Cox is illustrative. The 'most redefining moment' of his career occurred when, as a young man in 1977, he left his then employer (the Devold Organization) to set up a consultancy business designed to keep companies abreast of developments in the fast-growing IT business:

I went back to the offices in New York [of the Devold Organization] with a very different plan of how the company was going to be developed. It would be a very high-level consultancy, in terms of working with big corporations at senior level, and would work both for major users of technology and major suppliers of it. We would also run a research programme to keep developing the idea the company already had, but designed to keep CEOs abreast of what was going on. To my great disappointment, Devold didn't buy the idea at all. I thought that this was a tremendous way to develop the business, and had to weigh up the possibility of taking the idea elsewhere with the fact that I liked the company and was well rewarded. Do I try to sell the idea somewhere else, or what do I do? In discussions with David Butler, a friend of mine who worked in the Frankfurt offices of the same company, we said: 'Why don't we just do it?' That was probably the most redefining moment of my whole career.[7]

The company formed by the duo, Butler Cox, included a research programme for large corporations, to which they would pay an annual subscription to be kept abreast of IT developments. Butler Cox continued to grow over the years to the point that it had more than 500 global corporations subscribing to it, with bases in several countries. It was eventually floated on the stock exchange in 1990, attracting a friendly offer from the Computer Sciences Corporation about a year later – and being sold for a sum that meant that neither partner would ever have to work again.[8]

What the Butler Cox story confirms is that newly formed companies that grow swiftly and strongly do so because of the attractiveness of what they have to offer. Their value proposition quickly finds favour in their chosen market, and the new organisation has the capital and leadership skills needed to manage a series of rapid transitions. Butler Cox was founded on the basis of the strategic knowledge of information technology and personal networks of Butler and Cox. The subscription scheme generated cash from the beginning, and this was reinvested in developing the company's brand, reputation and product portfolio. A virtuous cycle of growth ensued, which was maintained through excellence in strategic leadership. The reputations of the two principals in the business grew accordingly, and following the sale of the company carried George Cox to a top executive position in the global IT industry as Chairman and CEO of Unisys in Europe.

Many of the same processes in evidence at Butler Cox can be seen in the rise of top 100 companies in Britain and France such as Tomkins, Williams, Sodhexo and Accor. Each is associated with one or more entrepreneurial superstars – Gregory Hutchings, Nigel Rudd, Pierre Bellon, Paul Dubrule and Gérard Pelisson – and each successfully navigated the transition from small firm to giant enterprise. With growth came organisation building, the creation of a managerial hierarchy and the formalisation of governance structures. Entrepreneurs once renowned for their personal style and distinctiveness have become normalised with the business system as a whole, honoured and revered as national leaders, pillars of the establishment, and, paradoxically, as 'corporate men' themselves.

Elite careers

Writing in the *Harvard Business Review*, Cappelli and Hamori, on the basis of a study of ten most senior executives of each Fortune 100 company in 1980 and 2001 respectively, propose a radical change in recent decades in the composition of the US business elite: the new breed 'are younger, more of them are female, and fewer of them are educated at elite institutions. They're making it to the top faster and taking fewer jobs along the way. And they are increasingly moving from one company to another as their careers unfold'.[9] These are large claims, but when reference is made to the data, it is plain that while there is evidence of change in US business, there is also evidence of structural continuity: 89 per cent of top executives in 2001 remain men; a disproportionately high proportion was educated at elite private colleges; 45 per cent spent their entire career in one company; and the average age of a top executive was still 52 years. On this account, the forces of cultural reproduction remain as powerful in the US as in France and the UK.

In all comparative research, whether conducted over time or across space, similarities and differences between systems invariably can be found. The results presented in Table 5.4 relating to the main board appointments of the super-elites of French and UK business are typical in this regard. Confirmation is found for the supposition that high-flying business people generally make their mark early, with the directors of French companies winning a position on a top 100 company board around the age of 40 compared to 44 for their British counterparts. Much of this difference is explained by the fact that founders and family representatives have a lower mean age – 31 years in France and 36 years in the UK – than directors without significant ownership rights, and these are far more numerous in France than in the UK, as discussed above. When account is taken of this, there is no statistically significant difference in this respect between the countries. Equally, in both countries, there is no evidence that hopping between companies is the best means of securing a first appointment to a top 100 company board. When short-lived early career employments are discounted, it transpires that most executives are appointed to a main board of the company responsible for their first, second or third substantive post – 89 per cent in France compared to 88 per cent in the UK. However, as is often the case, this statistical similarity belies more subtle differences in the nature of elite careers in France and the UK. In the latter, the largest category is single employer at 41 per cent (24 per cent in France), whereas in France the largest category is two employers (47 per cent against 23 per cent in the UK). The UK result is explained by the corporate tradition of promotion to the top from within, echoing the situation in the US reported by Cappelli and Hamori. The French result, in contrast, stems from the fact that so many top executives spend the first part of their career as an employee of the state, as a member of the inner circle responsible for conceiving, implementing and overseeing national business and economic policies.

Table 5.4 Main board appointments of top 100 directors of French and UK companies in 1998

| | France | | UK | |
	Mean	Standard Deviation	Mean	Standard Deviation
Age on First Appointment as Top 100 Director	40.45	6.04	44.12	5.79
Number of Companies to First Top 100 Directorship *	2.22	1.20	2.13	1.20
Number of Top 100 Director-ships in 1998	2.73	1.64	1.86	0.89
Number of All Directorships in 1998	3.75	2.34	2.62	1.34

Notes: * This analysis is based upon the number of substantive employments of two years or more with distinct companies. The effect is to discount early career moves, multiple roles in an organisation or with subsidiary companies.

Appointment to the board of a top 100 French or UK company is the starting point for an elite business career. It is, by definition, something only very few business people can experience, opening up possibilities for reward and recognition that are extreme and potentially transforma-tional. As a board member, closely involved in resource allocation decisions regularly involving thousands of jobs and tens of millions of euros in investment funds, the reality of power is manifest. Top people lead busy lives, packed with meetings, often scheduled from dawn to dusk. They have the benefit of close personal support and abundant resources, but equally they are expected to perform routinely at a high level. They travel extensively, nationally and internationally, mingling on a daily basis with customers, suppliers and partners. Strategy and policy must be kept to the fore amidst a myriad of details and the taking of numerous routine and tactical decisions. The routines and rituals of executive life and the strictures of corporate governance, which delineate roles and specify rules, provide structure. This balance between intense activity and regulated order has been likened to 'living at the edge of chaos' and is consistent with the personal accounts of life at the top given by many of our own interviewees.[10]

All our interviewees regarded intelligence gathering – being well informed – as fundamental to fulfilling the strategic role of a top 100 company director, and this necessitates the active involvement of members of the elite with numerous other actors in the field of power from within and beyond the business world (see Chapter 6). This perceived requirement to have one's 'finger on the economic pulse' legitimates a variety of networking practices in both France and the UK, of which the holding of multiple directorships is one of the most important.

The dynamics of the careers of the business super-elites of France and the UK are captured in Table 5.5. This focuses upon how elite careers unfolded over the five-year period from 1998 to 2003. Each of the top 100 directors in 1998 was classified by type: executive only, executive with top 100 non-executive directorship(s), and non-executive only. Many of the French directors in the executive only category were relatively young, with a mean age of 49 compared to the mean age of 57 for all top 100 men. This explains why 15 of them progressed naturally into the category of executive holding additional non-executive appointments. Most, like Denis Ranque of Thomson-CSF and Pierre Gadonneix of Gaz de France, continued to lead their original company, while some, including Patrick Kron who moved from Imerys to Alstom in 2003, went from running a large company to CEO of a giant company, picking up non-executive appointments in consequence. Elite career progression of this type was much less common in the UK; a large majority of those originally in the executive only category that went on to non-executive directorships did so only after retiring as an executive. Prominent amongst this group were Sir Mark Moody-Stuart, who retired from Shell in 2001, subsequently becoming chairman of Anglo-American and a non-executive at HSBC and Accenture; Martin Taylor, who resigned as CEO of Barclays in 1998 before his election as chairman of W.H. Smith and as a non-executive director at Syngenta and international advisor to Goldman Sachs; and Ian Strachan, CEO of BTR from 1996 to 1999, who, following a short spell with BTR's successor company Invensys, went on to become a non-executive at Reuters, Rolls-Royce and Johnson Matthey.

Table 5.5 Career trajectories of top 100 directors within top 100 companies in France and the UK, 1998-2003

	France (No.)	UK (No.)
All Directors		
Retain status	47	29
Change status	53	71
Executive Director Only in 1998		
Retain status	7	5
Add Non-Executive Directorships	15	3
Become Non-Executive Directors only	3	24
Retired from Business	1	4
Deceased	2	1
Not Known	1	0
All	**29**	**37**
Executive Directors with One or More Top 100 Non-Executive Directorships		
Retain status	26	12
Become Non-Executive Directors only	20	33
Retired from Business	3	0
Deceased	2	0
All	**51**	**45**
Non-Executive Director Only in 1998		
Retain status	14	12
Become Executive Director with Top 100 Non-Executive Directorships	3	0
Retired from Business	3	4
Deceased	0	2
All	**20**	**18**

Of those in the category executive plus non-executive, more of the French company directors retained their status over the period 1998-

2003, reflecting the normality of this type of elite career in France. In the UK, where top executive careers are less prolonged, a large number of directors (33 compared to 20 in France) changed status to join the ranks of the career non-executives. Most of these, no longer with an executive base, inevitably slid down the super-elite league table as others ascended. Even so, with approximately 20 per cent of the top 100 directors in both countries in this category in 1998, it is evident that the most highly regarded business leaders, such as Claude Bébéar (the long-serving PDG then non-executive chairman of AXA) and Michael Angus (who made his career with Unilever), can extend their career long after giving up executive responsibilities. A particular phenomenon in the UK, because of the separation of the CEO and chairman roles, is for ex-CEOs to move on to hold a chairmanship and several non-executive directorships. Of the 12 people who retained their status as non-executives only between 1998 and 2003, 11 were chairmen and one a vice-chairman. In France, where the roles of CEO and chairman are often combined, the pattern is more complex. Five of those retaining non-executive only status were chairmen, one was a vice-chairman, and eight were simply holders of numerous regular non-executive positions.

The top 100 directors in both countries can be seen to have a wealth of social and symbolic capital acquired as a major player within the field of power over a sustained period. In consequence, they are faced regularly with opportunities to extend their career beyond retirement in a way that is not open to lesser actors, and, remarkably, between 1998 and 2003 only 12 of their number were completely lost to the system in France and only 11 in the UK. This interesting structural similarity can be seen from a different viewpoint in Table 5.6, which compares and contrasts turnover rates by role and industry group. The marked differences observed between industries results from specific corporate developments. In UK manufacturing, for example, high director turnover rates stemmed from boardroom turbulence at companies like Marconi and the merger of companies like BTR and Siebe to form Invensys. This contrasts with the general stability witnessed at corporate and industry level within the financial services industry. Overall, it can be seen that the number of people still holding the same position in 2003 as in 1998 was about half the population of 2,291 French and UK company directors. This does not mean that a half was lost to either system, but rather that many roles were re-cycled, with directors on different career trajectories moving between organisations. At one and the same time there was both stability (same people) and change (different roles) within the French and UK business systems.

Table 5.6 Turnover of directors of top 100 companies in France and the UK between 1998 and 2003

| | % of 1998 Directors Remaining in 2003 | | | |
| | France | | UK | |
Industry Group	Executives	Non-Executives	Executives	Non-Executives
Construction	66.67	56.52	na	na
Financial Services	75.00	61.76	60.53	42.37
Food and Drink	64.29	65.74	66.67	49.21
IT and Business Services	46.15	49.06	62.50	71.43
Manufacturing	53.30	40.18	37.08	34.44
Media, Consumer Services and Products	68.89	64.22	57.41	39.39
Oil and Gas, Mining and Materials	43.75	44.38	57.41	50.85
Retailing	45.57	55.65	54.88	45.61
Transport and Distribution Services	58.06	51.47	43.75	40.00
Utilities and Tele-communications	29.79	31.76	57.58	37.93
All Companies	**51.95**	**48.93**	**54.61**	**42.59**

Notes: Data refer to persons who were still directors of the same company in 2003, although they were not necessarily in the same role.

Women in the boardroom

The power elite, as presented by C. Wright Mills, was an all-male enclave, drawn from a narrow pool of individuals sharing common experiences, career patterns, backgrounds and mindsets.[11] Fifty years on, there is a new preoccupation with diversity in the boardroom, particularly in the UK since the publication in 2003 of the Higgs Review, which argued for a more open and transparent process of appointment of non-executive directors.[12] In practice, the stereotype non-executive – a 45-55 year-old male chief executive of a similar-sized company – still has currency, as we have seen above.[13] The reflex 'think manager, think male' persists,[14] despite increasingly strident calls for this to be rectified.[15] While, by 2003, some 30 per cent of British managers were female, only 6 per cent of non-executive directors in the UK were female.[16] The situation in France was comparable, with just 26 women occupying 30 directorships out of 590 in total on the boards of CAC-40 companies, equal to just 5.1 per cent.[17] We now turn to explore to what extent women have made inroads into the boardrooms of France and Britain, and consider differences regarding the age and role characteristics, formative career experiences and educational backgrounds of women directors in the two countries.

One of the main issues raised in the Higgs Review is that of diversity in the boardroom, referring to the under-representation in the UK of women and members of ethnic minorities at the highest levels in business.[18] Higgs found that non-executive directors in the UK were normally white, British, middle-aged men, with experience of serving on the board of a public limited company,[19] or as one journalist irreverently put it, 'pale, male and stale'![20] This general finding is confirmed by our own research.

Table 5.7 Main board membership by gender for the top 100 companies in France and the UK in 1998

	France		UK	
	No.	%	No.	%
Female				
Executive Roles	19	25.33	9	13.43
Non-Executive Roles	56	74.67	58	86.57
Total	**75**	**100.00**	**67**	**100.00**
Male				
Executive Roles	545	31.57	577	48.61
Non-Executive Roles	1,181	68.43	610	51.39
Total	**1,726**	**100.00**	**1,187**	**100.00**

Note: An individual may have been a member of more than one board. The survey covers 55 women and 1206 men in France and 57 women and 993 men in the UK.

As Table 5.7 reveals, in 1998 there were just 55 women serving as directors of top 100 companies in France and 57 in the UK, occupying 75 and 67 directorial roles respectively. In both countries, it is readily apparent that women still have a long way to go before collectively they make their mark as business leaders, although there are notable individual exceptions. These include the aforementioned 'Atomic Anne' Lauvergeon, who ranks 29th in our power index of the top 100 French business elite members, and was named in 2003 as one of the 50 most powerful women in international business in the magazine *Fortune*.

The culture and structures of big business in France and the UK would seem to be equally unwelcoming of women in top positions.[21] However, just as for male directors, there are interesting differences between the two groups of women. In France, a significantly higher proportion of women were in executive roles than in the UK, and the French women were younger than their UK counterparts, with a mean age of 43 compared to a mean age of 46. This difference reflects, on the one hand, an increasing supply of female graduates from elite French business schools; and, on the other hand, the determined effort made by a minority of French companies to promote more women. At L'Oréal, for instance, it is speculated that the successor to the current PDG, Lindsay Owen-Jones, will in all likelihood be a woman, possibly from Asia. As Jean-Claude Le Grand, Director of Corporate Recruitment, explained: 'We often say in the human resource department that an Asian woman will be CEO in the third millennium … It is the company's objective to have a female CEO'.[22] L'Oréal, however, still has some way to go in practice before it catches up with companies like the media giant Carat France, which in 1998 had three women executive directors, and Sodexho and Alcatel, which had two each. Not a single top 100 UK company had more than one woman executive director.

In both France and the UK, women directors can have more than a single role, although the practice is much less developed for women than for men, and, as might be expected, is more common in France than the UK. Thus in 2004, Anne Lauvergeon, in addition to being CEO at Areva, was also a non-executive director of Sagem, Total and Suez. When UK companies source female non-executives, they often look to women in executive positions in other organisations outside the top 100 companies, with 17 out of 57 women falling into this category. Baroness Dunn, for example, ranked 87th in our British super-elite in 1998, after serving as an executive director of John Swire & Sons Ltd attracted non-executive directorships at Marconi and HSBC. This is a natural recruitment strategy, given the general shortage of women with the kind of experience deemed necessary for a top board appointment.

One of the most striking differences between female directors in France and the UK emerges from a study of career foundations. Nowhere is the enduring importance of national cultural and institutional peculiarities more clearly revealed. It can be seen from Table 5.8 that 16 of the French women directors owe their positions on the board to family membership as representatives of family shareholding companies. They are in effect non-executive directors engaged in wealth management, and are far from being independent directors in the sense intended by Cadbury. Liliane Bettencourt at L'Oréal, for example, is believed to be the third richest woman in the world by virtue of her shareholding in the company. Now entering her 80s, she still attends board meetings, often accompanied by her daughter, Françoise Bettencourt Meyers, also a board member.[23] At Sodexho, the board had three young women directors in 1998: Astrid Bellon, just 26 when she became a director, Nathalie Szabo and Sophie Clemens, the three daughters of Pierre Bellon, the driving force and major shareholder of the business.

Table 5.8 Formative career experiences of women directors of top 100 companies in France and the UK in 1998

	France		UK	
	No.	**%**	**No.**	**%**
Ownership	16	29.1	0	0.0
General and Operations Management	12	21.8	17	29.8
Engineering, Science and Technical	3	5.5	2	3.5
Finance and Accounting	1	1.8	4	7.0
State Policy and Administration	7	12.7	6	10.5
Marketing and Media	3	5.5	12	21.1
Law	2	3.6	3	5.3
Human Resources and Communications	10	18.2	8	14.0
Research and Academia	1	1.8	5	8.8
	55	**100.0**	**57**	**100.0**

Notes: The same system of classification applies as for Table 5.5 with one exception. In this case, female family representatives on boards have been classified under 'ownership.'

Ownership is not a widespread qualification for holding high office in British business, given the generally dispersed nature of shareholding in public limited companies, either for men or women. However, there are routes to the top for women in Britain that are quite distinctive. Several British women have risen to prominence through the media or through achieving high office in national institutions, including universities. Women such as the economics journalist Frances Cairncross and more recently the business academic Sandra Dawson have attracted attention as outstanding individuals, operating at the top of their profession, and as such are seen as natural candidates for the role of non-executive director of a top 100 company, having served previously on other less prestigious boards.

Within the two countries there are also considerable similarities in the routes by which women enter top 100 boardrooms. General and operations management, as for men and for the same reasons, is a favoured route to the top. In contrast, even in France, engineering, science and technology is not a career path favoured by women, whereas, in stark contrast to their male counterparts, human resource management and communications is the second most important route in both companies for aspiring women executive directors. This is attributable perhaps to the fact that women do not need 'combat experience' – hands-on experience of the cut-and-thrust of doing business – to succeed in these areas.[24] However, there were signs of change; by June 2002 almost half of women executive directors in the UK were directors of finance, confirming our own finding that in the UK accounting and finance is culturally embedded as an effective route to the top.[25]

For non-executive directors, having held a top strategic or general management role in a major organisation, public or private, is seen as a fitting qualification for appointment to the board of a top 100 company. In both countries, this favours establishment figures from the banking sector and public services. In France, women like Anne Le Lorier, who ranks 86th in the French super-elite, are official government appointees who are still in public service, rather than ex-civil servants as in the UK, such as Rosalind Gilmore, a former senior official at the Treasury, or Dame Stella Rimington, whose career in the security service spanned 27 years, culminating in her appointment as Director General of MI5.

The same combination of similarity and difference applies when the educational backgrounds of women directors are considered, again reflecting the continued importance of institutional and cultural forces in both countries. As can be seen from Table 5.9, women directors on both sides of the Channel have in the main been educated at the higher level in elite institutions, *grandes écoles* in France and universities such as Oxford, Cambridge or Edinburgh in the UK. Anne Lauvergeon, for example, is a graduate of the prestigious Ecole des Mines and Ecole Normale Supérieure, while Rosalind Gilmore attended University College London and Newnham College Cambridge. The biggest difference between them relates to subject. In France, business and administration is the most common background, whereas in the UK the most common academic grounding is in arts, humanities and the social sciences. Dame Stella Rimington, for instance, read English Language and Literature at Edinburgh University.

At a general level, the small number of women directors of top 100 companies in France and the UK is indicative of institutional continuity, of the power of cultural reproduction in the sense intended by Bourdieu.[26] As theorised in Chapter 2, culture is simultaneously resident in and forged by institutional systems and processes, work and cultural practices, norms and values, and personal dispositions and routines. Boardrooms are places of conformity, requiring a common mindset and pattern of behaviours to form and execute policies. They are in themselves 'structuring structures'.

Table 5.9   Known educational backgrounds of women directors of top 100 companies in France and the UK in 1998

	France (n=29)		UK (n=45)	
	No.	%	No.	%
Subject				
Arts, Humanities or Social Sciences	5	17.2	22	48.9
Business, Economics or Administration	18	62.2	13	28.9
Science, Engineering or Medicine	3	10.3	8	17.8
Professional	3	10.3	2	4.4
Highest Academic Qualification				
Doctorate	3	10.3	8	17.8
Higher Degree	21	72.4	10	22.2
First Degree	5	17.3	27	60.0
Institutions Attended				
Elite	27	93.1	40	89.9
Non-Elite	2	6.9	5	11.1

The women who by 1998 had reached the pinnacle of corporate life in France and the UK were products of the system, a small minority with the capacity to deliver and behave in ways that conformed to long-established practices. Many women directors in the UK held or were awarded titles – for example, Baroness Dunn, Dame Stella Rimington, Lady Patten of Wincanton, Professor Sue Birley – which serve as markers of distinction, signifying institutional continuity and approval.[27] Kanter suggests that this institutional emphasis on homogeneity of background and conformity in behaviour springs from the need to reduce uncertainty in big, impersonal organisations, as ease of communication, hence social certainty, are favoured over the difficulties inherent in coping with difference.[28] As Zweigenhaft and Domhoff put it: 'the men atop their corporations [want] others around them with whom they are comfortable', what they term the 'comfort factor' proving to be a major force for conformity.[29] The logic of homologies, as explained by Bourdieu, is clearly at work here, as dominated fractions, in this case businesswomen, seek to challenge the dominant class, established male directors, competing for social space in pursuit of legitimacy and integration.[30]

Elite lifestyles

The predominantly masculine micro-cultures typical of boardrooms in France and the UK are sustained through a variety of mechanisms that together constitute the phenomenon of cultural reproduction discussed from a theoretical standpoint in Chapter 2. One aspect of cultural reproduction concerns personal dispositions and the ways in which these are formed and sustained, which in turn raises wider issues relating to lifestyles, social differentiation and personal distinction. Those who reach the very top in business almost invariably have about them an aura of confidence that stems from their acceptance as an equal of others at the pinnacle of society, from a variety of fields that collectively merge into what we call 'the field of power'. This sense of confidence, 'naturalness' and assumption of the right to rule is not something with which individuals, however talented, are gifted at birth, but rather is socially constructed, a product, laid down layer upon layer, of repeated success, recognition and upward social mobility.

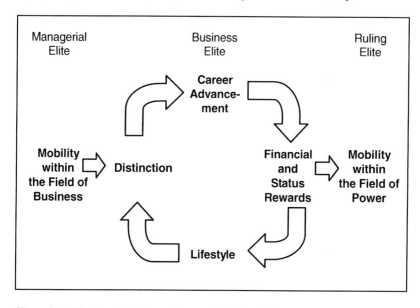

Figure 5.1 Lifestyle, distinction and upward social mobility

This process is modelled, in highly simplified form, in Figure 5.1. The model distinguishes between three elite groups at the uppermost strata of society and suggests a natural progression from membership of one group to another. Individuals accumulate capital in various guises and in various ways as they progress upwards through the managerial hierarchy. The financial and status rewards reaped as a result of career advancement enable individuals and their families to enjoy an ever more elitist lifestyle, and to cultivate a sense of social distinction, which in turn singles them out for further career advancement. Those who move from being senior executives into the boardroom join the business elite, and those who transcend the business elite move freely within the wider circle comprised of top politicians, lawyers, academics, civil servants, doctors and others that constitute the ruling elite. The most important implication is that the progress of an individual in their career is not simply a function of performance in role, but rather is intimately related to choice of lifestyle and the development of personal dispositions redolent of social distinction.

What is distinction? In English and in French the term has a double meaning, at once a classifying and social term, implying both 'difference' and 'distinguished character'. Distinction derives as much from what is concealed as from what is revealed,[31] being characterised by a degree of modesty, a refusal of excess, an 'ease within restraint' handed down through the generations.[32] It expresses and, at the same time, depends on the relative distance from economic necessity furnished by economic capital.[33] Taste, by extension, according to Bourdieu, is 'an acquired disposition to "differentiate" and "appreciate"' what is distinct.[34]

In Bourdieu's theory, patterns of consumption matter because the symbolic aspects of social life are inextricably bound up with the material conditions of existence. 'A class', Bourdieu writes, 'is defined as much by its *being-perceived* as by its *being*, by its consumption – which need not be conspicuous to be symbolic'.[35] The ownership of a home in a sought-after location, in the sixteenth *arrondissement* or in Kensington, serves as a lasting mark of superiority: 'a constant presence, unstated yet terribly insistent', as Le Wita puts it.[36] Burial plots are equally classifying, one among the great and the good at Père-Lachaise cemetery being the most sought after in Paris.[37] Symbolic systems structure reality. Though they themselves may be arbitrary, they are far from arbitrary in their social function, which is to reflect the structure of class relations.[38] Similarly, aesthetic values are socially constituted. Patterns of cultural consumption and production are determined by socio-economic structures. Intentionally or otherwise, culture is complicit in reproducing processes of social domination: 'art and cultural consumption', Bourdieu explains, 'are predisposed, consciously and deliberately or not, to fulfil a social function of legitimating social differences'.[39] We live in a 'world of ranked and ranking objects which help to define [taste] by enabling it to specify and so realize itself'.[40] Objects of mass production are far less desirable than those which are unique or whose production is restricted. The modern world, according to Gilles Deleuze, is one of simulacra.[41] The reproduction of an object further underlines the singularity and uniqueness of the original: the plethora of Impressionist reproductions, for example, renders the original paintings all the more rare and sought after. At the pinnacle of restricted production are works of art. Artistic and literary culture represent 'the form par excellence of disinterested culture, and consequently the most legitimate of the marks of distinction from other classes', which owe their great prestige to their apparent disinterestedness and cultural purity, and the distance from economic necessity that they imply.[42]

The two large sample surveys carried out by Bourdieu's research group, which provided the data for *Distinction*, were enormously wide-ranging in focus. Respondents were asked about their tastes, habits, knowledge and opinions relating to, for example, reading material, painting, photography, music, film, theatre-going, food, clothes, sports and home furnishing. Bourdieu argues that there are homologies of lifestyle. He draws parallels between taste in art and taste in food, wine or furniture. Lifestyles, comprising patterns of cultural consumption (food, drink, furniture, sport or leisure activities), appearance (clothing, hairstyle, make-up), bodily hexis (bearing, voice modulations) and the ritualisation of daily life (the family meal, special events), are imbued with values and cultural schemata. There is, Bourdieu argues, a 'correspondence between goods and groups'.[43] Taste is shaped by habitus, a 'present past that tends to perpetuate itself into the future'.[44] It functions as a form of social orientation, so that classes or fractions of classes choose what is effectively chosen for them. In effect, one excludes oneself, through 'a sense of one's place', from goods, persons and places from which one is excluded.[45] Seemingly trivial details – such as jewellery, silverware, or collections of ducks or china – are not trivial at all, but on the contrary the highly symbolic appurtenances that together make up what Foucault terms the man of modern humanism.[46] As Le Wita observes, 'trivia ... have a particular function, namely to create distinction'.[47] The apparently meaningless is often, in fact, extremely meaningful.[48]

For the present study, we decided to focus upon just four aspects of the lifestyles and potential sources of distinction of our interviewees and top 100 directors – family, sport, pastimes and charitable work – and we asked our interviewees about the extent to which their lifestyles had changed as their careers had progressed. In terms of family, as we saw in Chapter 4, the norm is for members of the business elite to be married and to have long marriages blessed by children. The impression of conventionality and family stability is reinforced by a divorce rate of just seven per cent among top French directors and 11 per cent among the British. In both countries nearly all the divorcees married again. The implication is that the symbols and rituals of married life – emphasising constancy, reliability and a belief in family values – are seen in themselves to bear witness to the fitness of a person to hold high office in business. (As Sir John Bond of HSBC put it, 'I'm married with three children and am dog-thoroughly boring'.)[49]

The results of our research into the sporting and other recreational interests of top 100 directors are presented in Table 5.10. The sociologist Clifford Geertz has described sport as a form of 'deep play', which gives expression to the most deep-rooted cultural values.[50] Sport is, in the words of Richard Holt, 'a story we tell ourselves about ourselves'.[51] For many of our participants, arguably the type of sport they had chosen to play dove-tailed neatly with the lifestyle they had elected to pursue, supporting Bourdieu's notion of lifestyle homologies. In both countries, engagement in sport by business leaders is widespread and clustered around socially stratified activities: golf, skiing, tennis and sailing alone account for 69 per cent of reported participation in France and 54 per cent in the UK. Field sports, rugby and swimming were also quite widely reported in each country, with contrasting national preoccupations only emerging with respect to relatively high British participation rates for walking and cricket.

Several interviewees enjoyed a variety of sports and remained involved in some long after their playing days were over. George Cox, an expert rower, coached the British team at two World Championships and became Chairman of Selectors for the 1980 British Olympic team. He tells an amusing tale of how he prevented Steven Redgrave from attending the Moscow Olympics:

> I named the team for the Moscow Olympics in 1980. It was a very tough year because Mrs Thatcher was urging the boycott of the Olympics because Russia had invaded Afghanistan – a bad thing to do in those days! A smaller team was sent than would otherwise have been the case, and one crew in particular, which had done very well in the junior Olympics, was to be left behind. At the time, it was my policy to tell the individuals who would and wouldn't be sent. I came to tell this tall, quiet and rather gangly kid that he wouldn't be sent, and that there would always be other Olympic Games for him to be involved in. That was Redgrave. I've gone through life as the man who didn't send Redgrave to the Olympic Games![52]

Sir Steve Redgrave went on, of course, to win a gold medal at each of the subsequent five Olympic Games.

Table 5.10 Recreational interests of top 100 directors of French and UK companies in 1998

	France		UK	
	No. of Reports	% of All Reports	No. of Reports	% of All Reports
Sporting				
Golf	20	19.05	28	18.06
Skiing	20	19.05	17	10.97
Tennis	19	18.10	16	10.32
Sailing	13	12.38	22	14.19
Walking	7	6.67	18	11.61
Hunting, Shooting and Fishing	6	5.71	7	4.52
Rugby	5	4.76	9	5.81
Swimming	4	3.81	3	1.94
Horse Riding	3	2.86	6	3.87
Football	2	1.90	11	7.10
Cricket	0	0.00	6	3.87
Other	6	5.71	12	7.74
All Sporting	**105**	**100.00**	**155**	**100.00**
Non-Sporting				
Music, Opera and Ballet	14	17.07	44	29.73
Books	20	24.39	22	14.86
Gardening	1	1.22	19	12.84
Art and Antiques	7	8.54	9	6.08
Theatre	1	1.22	15	10.14
Travel	4	4.88	12	8.11
Writing	13	15.85	0	0.00
Cars	3	3.66	6	4.05
Horse Racing	3	3.66	3	2.03
Other	16	19.51	18	12.16
All Non-Sporting	**82**	**100.00**	**148**	**100.00**

Sir Adrian Cadbury is also a rower, having been a member of the Cambridge rowing team as a student at King's College. Sir Adrian helps to run the Henley Regatta, where he still rows with fellow sportsmen from his student days that he counts among his closest friends – illustrating the bonds of friendship which participation in team sports can help to forge. He also acts as president of a West Midlands sports body, presiding over the Black Country Youth Games for several years.[53] Sir Mark-Moody Stuart, former Chairman of Shell, comes from a keen sailing family, owning a 32-foot boat that he sails up the River Orwell in

Suffolk, as well as a 49-foot boat he keeps in Turkey.

Many of the sports in which business leaders engage are quintessentially prestigious. In addition to those already mentioned, interviewees practised horse riding, scuba diving, gliding (one interviewee being chairman of a top gliding club) and horse racing, with one interviewee owning a string of high-class racehorses. Just as 'it is what you choose to buy – and what you shun – that says what class you are in', so the choices of sport and leisure activity are equally defining.[54] Jean-Claude Le Grand of L'Oréal combines playing football, one of the most mainstream sports, with polo, which he plays in Argentina and in France, at Rambouillet – one of the most elite and often prohibitively expensive sports due to the number of polo ponies, normally about five, needed for each player per game. (Not even Prince Charles, an avid polo player, keeps his own polo ponies, preferring, it is said, to borrow those of his friends!) Mr Le Grand sees this unusual combination of sporting activities as adding to life's rich pageant.[55]

Some observers emphasise the importance of sport in nurturing a common mindset in the organisation, something that again works against the advancement of women to the boardroom. Whereas men are trained from an early age to participate in competitive team sports – rugby, football and cricket in particular – most women are not.[56] Such sports foster in turn many of the skills needed for a successful business career: the development of individual skills in the context of helping the team to win, and of cooperative relationships with team-mates focused on winning, and coping with losing.[57] The importance of school sports in honing a competitive attitude is summarised in a comment from Sir Digby Jones, Director General of the Confederation of British Industry (CBI), who as a scholarship pupil at Bromsgrove School played 1st XV rugby, hockey and county cricket:

> Second place was no way. If you go to bed at night having discharged x amount of talent in the quest for competitiveness, good on you, and if you have not then you had committed a sin. That counted enormously, academically, in the sport field and drama class.[58]

Beyond this conventional perspective, it can be seen that playing sport at a high level is itself an enduring mark of distinction that can be brought to mind at will through a casual remark or telling an amusing story such as that related by George Cox. Larry Hirst, CEO of IBM in the UK, who has played soccer, cricket and table tennis at international level, related at interview how his sporting prowess helped lay the social foundations for his career with IBM. As a grammar school boy from a working-class background, it was through sport that he came to recognise the potency of class gradations and how these might be overcome, admitting to first learning 'about wine, food, and social behaviour' while on a cricket tour of the South-West of England. Later, having left Hull University with a degree in mathematics, and following a period as a salesman for Kodak, he joined IBM and quickly made an impression as a fiercely competitive team player. When asked how he rose so swiftly up the corporate ladder, sport was the first reason cited:

> Again, the sports thing has really helped me as well. The head of IBM at that time was Tony Cleveland, who is sports nuts. We put a team together to play against NatWest, who had their annual game at Eton. It was one of the best days of my life and a good story to this day. We turned up at the game and didn't know anybody. The NatWest bus pulled in, in their blazers and what have you, and I noticed that it didn't faze anybody. It didn't faze me because I was used to this my whole life. We batted first and got 375 for 3. We bowled in reverse order and we had them at 63 for 8 before tea. Eddy Nixon was the chairman and said: 'They're our bloody customer. What are your doing?' Tony Cleveland said: 'This is sport. If they can't take it I don't want to know'. We sat down in the changing room afterwards and we suddenly realised that we had 10 internationals, nine full county players, and six blues. I'd only been in the company six months and saw what a company I'd joined. Ever since that day I've always known that it wouldn't matter what challenge was set. I could turn out an orchestra tomorrow, a football team, a rugby team, a cricket team, and we'd take anybody on.[59]

Sport, it may be concluded, can offer three main benefits for ambitious executives. It serves as a proving ground, as a means of building personal confidence; it provides a mechanism for social bonding and the development of solidarity between individuals; and, perhaps most tellingly of all, it is an enduring source of personal distinction.

This said, many members of the business elite have found neither satisfaction nor advantage in sport, and sheer lack of competence would, in many cases, exclude it as a potential source of distinction. Many of the social advantages of sporting life – joining the 'right' club and associating with the 'right' people – can be attained through other cultural pursuits. In the UK, as may be inferred from Table 5.10, particular kudos attaches to involvement in the 'high' arts such as classical music, opera, ballet, theatre and fine art. In France, likewise, the possession of significant cultural capital is seen as a mark of social distinction: Jean-François Théodore, for example, has a subscription to the Paris Opera and attends a performance there every three weeks. Bourdieu regards visits to the theatre as a form of bourgeois art, which embodies frequently unrecognised power relations. A 1996 survey of London artgoers confirmed that these were largely middle-aged, middle-class and white.[60] Bourgeois art contrasts with the notion of 'art for art's sake', *l'art pour l'art*, characterised by its alleged cultural purity and rarity.

A significant difference between the French and UK business elites can be observed in relation to their interest in books. Reading is a widely enjoyed pastime in both countries. There is a big difference, however, when it comes to the production rather than the consumption of literary works. In France, being a published author is a mark of personal distinction, something that speaks 'elite'; 13 members of our super-elite fell into this category in 1998, and several more were published between 1998 and 2003.[61] Edmond Alphandéry was a leading academic economist before embarking on a career in politics that culminated in his appointment as Minister of the Economy between 1993 and 1995. He then served as PDG of EdF and as a director or advisor of numerous companies and state bodies while continuing to write prolifically on economic and monetary affairs.[62] Serge Dassault, an ex-fighter pilot and PDG of Dassault Aviation, is notoriously outspoken in his views on French economic and industrial policy, for example in his 2001 book *Un Projet pour la France*.[63] The essential theme of this and many of the other books written by businessmen is the competitiveness of the French industrial system and the position of France in the global economy. There is an intensely critical edge to much of the writing, but one that comes from an insider, an influential and critical friend, not an opponent. Dassault, for example, is a close personal friend of President Chirac. Respect for reading and writing amongst the French business elite, both as a source of pleasure and power, is a distinctive cultural phenomenon. One interviewee, Pierre Bilger, the former PDG of Alstom, who reads novels, essays and books of general interest, traces this back to his education: 'I used to read a lot, you have an exam called "Culture Générale", which is important. I read with pleasure'.[64] An equally distinctive passion of British directors is gardening, cited by 19 out of 100 members of the super-elite as a major recreational interest, compared to just one Frenchman.

Several of our interviewees collect works of art, such as contemporary paintings, Asian art and Buddhist art, although some preferred not to publicise their collections for insurance reasons.[65] François Pinault and Vincent Bolloré have created private art collections, with a view to

Elite Careers and Lifestyles 157

bequeathing these to their local communities in due course.[66] In addition
to collecting works by modern artists, one British interviewee had a
collection of letters by the author and dramatist Oscar Wilde. Some
interviewees were avid collectors, such as Lord Waldegrave, who collects
war memorabilia, or Sir Adrian Cadbury, who collects stamps, books,
clocks and what he describes as 'probably the only collection of old golf
tees which anybody has ever amassed'.[67] Iain Gray, Managing Director of
Airbus, admits to collecting stamps, postcards, model cars and things of
an aeronautical nature, while George Cox collects historical model planes.
One French human resource manager confessed simply to collecting
'good bottles of wine',[68] while Louis Sherwood, whose wife is French, is
a wine connoisseur who glories in the title 'Maître de la Commanderie de
Bordeaux à Bristol'.

Just as the symbolic capital conferred by works of art is all the more
powerful for its obvious distance from economic necessity, so too engaging
in charitable work attracts particular prestige in that it captures a comparable
profit of disinterestedness. Hoffmann suggests that involvement in voluntary
work is an essential aspect of the elite equation: 'far from being an innocu-
ous frill or mere outlet for conspicuous display, [it] is a vital part of that elite
matrix which includes the corporation, the law firm, and the executive
branch of the federal government'.[69] As many as 39 of the 100 most powerful directors in the UK in 1998 are known to have sat on one or more
charitable boards, and 48 have sat on the board of one or more educational
institutions. The comparable figures for the French super-elite are seven for
charitable boards and 30 for education boards. Sir Mark Moody-Stuart is a
Governor of Nuffield Hospitals, and President of the Liverpool School of
Tropical Medicine, as well as President of the Geological Society. Since his
retirement from Shell, he has become increasingly involved in two further
charities: the Violence Initiative and the Sussex Centre for Restoration
Justice.[70] Louis Sherwood, a director of HBOS, supports numerous charities
in Bristol, where he is a council member of Clifton College and an ex-
Master of the Society of Merchant Venturers, and in London, where he is a
trustee of the Hanover Foundation, which provides state-sector pupils with
one-on-one counselling and career advice.[71] Sir Adrian Cadbury likewise is
heavily involved in educational charities. His charitable work includes being
a member of the Kings' Chapel Foundation Committee and serving as
Chancellor of Aston University for a quarter of a century. Having been
brought up a Quaker, he regards Quaker beliefs and values as enormously
important, and has attempted within his business dealings to retain what he
regards as the core Quaker values, while accepting that life has changed a
great deal.[72]

Charitable work may demand considerable commitment from elite members, involving experiences that are themselves transformational. George Cox tells a fascinating story of his weeklong visit to the troubled Western part of the Congo in 2003 as Chairman of Merlin, the British equivalent of Médicins Sans Frontières, which sends medical teams to provide healthcare in trouble-spots around the world.[73] This was the first time a Merlin trustee had offered to go on a fieldtrip. Danger was ever-present, as Cox relates:

> We don't have hostage insurance, because we think that increases the likelihood of people being taken. There is no real infrastructure to the country, by that I mean no roads, railways, newspapers, televisions, banks, police force. To be honest, my fear wasn't that I'd be shot or taken hostage, but being stranded. The only real method of travel is by air and the planes will not enter an area that is coming under fire, so if fighting breaks out you're there for the duration. The instability makes you very nervous. There are seven main armies, but also much smaller groups. The groups are mainly made up of teenage boys, who are armed to the teeth ... If you pass drunken teenagers here you'd be a bit apprehensive. When they're armed to the teeth it's a different story. If they were to shoot you, there would be nothing that could be done about it. There's nobody to complain to, so you're acutely aware of how unstable the whole place is the whole time. Since I got back there was a massacre last week, very near to where I was.

The aspects of lifestyle and sources of social and personal distinction discussed here do not, of course, tell the whole story. It is inherently difficult to generalise about lifestyles and the transformations that come with business success, given individual differences in circumstances, perceptions and starting points in life. The most typical pattern is one of family stability amidst material plenty and a wealth of sporting and cultural pursuits. Easy circumstances often mean a second home in the country or abroad, for example. The Bilger family has a country house in Normandy, ideal for country walks and gardening, and within easy reach of Paris, previously having had one in Cannes, which proved too remote. Another interviewee spoke of his country retreat in Normandy as 'Le Manoir', the manor, keeping a photograph of it in his wallet, and confirming the importance in France of possessing a family seat, as observed by Le Wita.[74] Many others spoke of yachts, private airplanes, elite schools attended by offspring, glamorous family holidays and visits to the best ski resorts. Of the UK super-elite of 1998, 54 out of 100 were members of a prestigious private members' club, enabling frequent contact with celebrities and other members of the ruling elite. Extensive travel, for business and pleasure, is a central feature of many lifestyles. Like many HRM directors of global companies, Xavier Barrière, HRM Director of Air Liquide, travels as part of his job, but also holidays with his family, in Italy and Iceland. Jean-François Théodore enjoys discovering Asia on regular vacations with his wife.[75] Iain Gray, who has travelled extensively within Europe, Japan, India, Russia and the US, regards travel as 'very important' and 'one of the fascinations of the job'.[76]

The experience of extreme material affluence and cultural enrichment naturally varies according to the starting point and expectations of the individual. For those who come from upper- and upper-middle-class backgrounds, like Sir Mark Moody-Stuart, whose father, Sir Alexander, was a sugar plantation owner in Antigua, there may be little ostensible difference in living standard or lifestyle as a result of being a current member of the business elite, as life chances are transmitted down the generations. As Scott explains, 'patterns of family and household formation ... tie individuals together through bonds of marriage, partnership and parenting, ensuring that all members of a household share in the life chances and experiences that the dominant member enjoys by virtue of his or her occupational position'.[77]

In contrast to this group, which might assume the trappings of an elite lifestyle, are the extreme upwardly mobile individuals who, coming from a lower- or lower-middle-class background, have made their way to the top in business, the likes of George Cox, Peter Orton and Larry Hirst. For these people, their success in business has been nothing short of transformational for them and their families. The reflections of Larry Hirst when asked what his changed circumstances had meant for him, though extraordinary in the potency of the imagery, are not unusual:

I've seen the world geographically and everything contained in it ... I've met people that I never thought I would, and I'm not overawed by that. I've just sent some pictures of the Prime Minister and myself to my parents. It's not overly impressive, but for a Yorkshire boy like me it's been like a movie. I've been able to do things for my children that I thought were only in books when I was a child ... Clearly there are financial elements and the things that provides – car, home, nice wines, nice food ... but what else has it given me? I suddenly found that through this office, the company, and hopefully myself ... I could change things a little ... I could get involved with the inner city schools to fight bigotry in gender and racism. I have an opportunity to work

against all the things that I've had to fight against ... I tell them that
there is a way out ... When I started my Maths degree at university my
first letter from my Mum said: 'I hope the sums aren't too hard'. I have
this idea of an image in her mind of me sitting in front of pages and
pages of addition. I'm not being derogatory towards my family at all.
Within the degree of their comprehension they knocked down every
obstacle that they could for me, and those they didn't understand they
somehow overcame. I've now found a platform from which I can give
back.

As Larry Hirst perceives, both the legitimacy of the business elite and its
capacity for regeneration depend crucially on the admission of 'new
blood', of men and women who, while lacking the advantages of privilege, are nevertheless endowed with the talent, drive and intelligence to
seize opportunities, and so reach the summit of the corporate world.

Conclusion

This chapter has focused on the factors that make elite careers, and on the
interplay between careers and lifestyles. One of the main findings is that
in both France and the UK the co-existent and related 'structuring structures' of family, education and organisations have much in common, and
function in much the same ways. Yet, at the same time, we have charted,
measured and described equally fundamental cultural and institutional
differences between the business systems of the two countries. These relate to the enduring significance of the state and family ownership in
France compared to the near complete corporatism of business life in the
UK. This means that there are pronounced differences in career foundations and routes to the top in the two countries. Equally, the very nature of
elite careers, of the lived experience of business leaders, differs in significant ways.

We argue that both the similarities and differences between the elites and
business systems of the two countries are deeply entrenched and enduring.
This is an argument that emphasises institutional and cultural continuity. We
do not wish to suggest, however, that there is an absence of isomorphic
pressures or a lack of momentum towards convergence in governance and
business practices. Rather, we perceive the mechanisms of cultural reproduction to act as a brake on universal economic tendencies and the assertiveness of liberal economic ideas. This suggests gradual rather than radical
change and the continuation in Europe as elsewhere of a pluralism of
competing capitalisms, each with its own distinctive institutional and cult-

ural forms. In this formulation, nation states, as primary stakeholders, will continue to hold sway over the way in which globalisation unfolds. Business elites will continue to be forged to a considerable degree in the national image, the products of multiple nationally distinctive structuring structures, with mindsets attuned to the requirements of their own distinctive brand of capitalism. More women will gradually be admitted to boardrooms, but this in itself should not be read as a convergent tendency, since women as well as men will continue to reflect the commonly held values and assumptions of the national business elite.

We have portrayed elite careers and lifestyles as intimately entwined, and once again there are noteworthy similarities between France and the UK. Taste, according to Bourdieu, is a form of social orientation. Dependent on habitus, it operates subconsciously and subliminally as 'an acquired disposition to "differentiate"'.[78] Habitus works by adjusting expectations to life chances, as individuals effectively exclude themselves from goods and places from which they are, to all intents and purposes, excluded. Being 'bourgeois', Le Wita suggests, means mastering a whole system of words, gestures and objects, *comme il faut*, which together comprise a defined culture, as *being* becomes equated with *being perceived*. There are, in Bourdieu's eyes, homologies of lifestyle, correspondences between groups and goods, the pieces of an individual's life fitting together as a jigsaw, and the evidence presented here goes a long way towards confirming that – but this is not the whole story. Adonis and Pollard speak of 'middlebrow tastes accompany[ing] middlebrow lives' which came into being from the 1950s, a sort of 'average lifestyle' in Harold Perkin's words, 'home-centred, family-oriented, servantless'.[79] Many of the lifestyle choices observed are in the cultural mainstream, reflecting a considerable degree of conformity with contemporary tastes and social norms. As John Scott argues:

> Tastes and preferences are no longer so strongly governed by fixed social standards. They are 'lifestyle choices' for which people have an individual responsibility and for which they are judged by others. Lifestyles are inherently pluralistic, and people make a series of lifestyle choices that need not be integrated into any single, overarching style of life.[80]

Nevertheless, the rise in top executive salaries and bonuses over the past decade, discussed in Chapter 3, has been such as to bring about an increasing gap between high and low earners in many organisations.[81] Self-serving decisions in the boardroom have elicited public rage, especially when these display a wanton disregard for company performance.[82]

Identified by Monks as 'the real "smoking gun"',[83] the current staggering levels of CEO pay create the possibility for some business elites to experience a super-wealthy lifestyle which, like that enjoyed by premiership footballers, has long since spiralled out of reach, and out of touch, of the so-called 'average lifestyle' referred to above.[84]

6
Networks, Power and Influence

Je te tiens
Tu me tiens
Par la barbichette.
Le premier
De nous deux
Qui rira
Aura une tapette.

Anon.

Corporate governance is viewed here as the legitimating mechanisms and processes through which members of the business elite exercise power and authority. Power, however, is a quintessentially relational phenomenon. 'The fundamental concept in social science', wrote Bertrand Russell, 'is power, in the same sense in which energy is the fundamental power in physics'.[1] It is, according to Max Weber, the ability to enforce one's will in the face of opposition: 'the probability that one actor within a social relationship will be in a position to carry out his own will despite resistance'.[2] In short, power gives someone the means to do something they could otherwise not have done.[3] The definition of elite members given in Chapter 1 may thus be refined to denote those who 'individually, regularly and seriously have the power to affect organisational outcomes'.[4]

Of course, as Chapter 2 has shown, there is considerable potential for power to be misrecognised. Not all who are subject to influence are fully conscious of its hold, or their place in the structures of which they are part. Power, moreover, is not a static phenomenon. Power relations may ebb and flow over time, depending on the outcomes of struggles, past and present, for the conservation or augmentation of symbolic capital by incumbent elites or parvenus.

This chapter bridges the discussion of business elites and corporate governance. It examines how power and authority are wielded in business and how corporate systems are bonded, organisationally and socially. The national business systems of France and the UK are analysed from a social network perspective, highlighting major and enduring practical differences, which in turn have implications for corporate governance. We are concerned here with the 'field of power', the social space in which members of elite groups from different fields and sub-fields meet on an even footing to debate and resolve issues of mutual concern. Social and cultural institutions are theorised as meeting places, wherein actors create a capacity to mobilise power and apply pressure. These include business associations, clubs, public bodies, sporting occasions and events, and, most important, the boardrooms of top 100 companies themselves. Scott's use of the term 'constellation of interests' to denote the concentration of power in the hands of a relatively small group of associated financial institutions, is relevant here, focusing attention on the networks, formal and informal, which bind together the business elites of both countries, albeit in different measure.[5] The chapter considers the prevalence and consequences of interlocking directorships, and reflects on the importance of family networks. It includes a discussion of the critical role played by the state, particularly in France, where it acts as a lynchpin, and with which the business world has managed to weave strong ties.[6] Finally, we are concerned here with the endogenous and exogenous activities of directors, and with their boundary-spanning activities, the external ties that make directors more valuable to their organisations.[7] In brief, the chapter explores the social reality of how power is applied, channelled and contained in both countries.

Directors and corporate interlocks

Managerial elites, Pettigrew argues, are a much-neglected topic of academic study.[8] While the central activity of the business elite is manifestly its boardroom role, this area of research remains under-investigated. Boards, moreover, are not uniform; on the contrary, they are variegated and complex, with some directors enjoying more influence than others. The practical difficulties of examining corporate elites – foremost amongst which are obvious problems of access – militate against closer scrutiny of the organisational sociology of boards.[9] On the one hand, this throws into sharp relief the value of our database of top French and British business leaders as a research tool. But on the other hand, and paradoxically, problems of access in obtaining interviews with corporate elites may also illuminate to some degree the very networks we are keen to examine, as one elite contact leads to another through personal recommendation, demonstrating the central importance of 'who one knows'. In this way, for example, an interview with the Director General of the Institute of Directors led to another with the CEO of one of the boards on which he serves, while in France, an interview at L'Oréal was used to facilitate another with a director of an allied company, Air Liquide, and contact with a third at Lafarge. Success, or otherwise, in securing an interview through personal recommendation often depended, *inter alia*, on the measure of influence wielded by the recommending party. In contrast, cold calling, letters requesting interviews sent without elite member endorsement, were far less likely to meet with success.

Board members, of course, may be internal to the company, full-time executive directors or, alternatively, external, part-time, non-executive directors. There is also a third category of directors known as 'grey' directors, who have some link, actual or previous, with the organisation, perhaps as relatives of corporate officers, retired executives, consultants or lawyers, or enjoying substantial business relationships with the company.[10] Such affiliated directors lack real independence.[11] Corporate governance in France has moved increasingly towards nominally independent boards with a majority of seemingly outside, independent directors, since the first Viénot Report introduced the concept to French boardrooms. The second Viénot Report (1999) recommended that at least one-third of directors be independent, while the Bouton Report (2002) increased the recommended quota to half. In reality, however, many of these so-called 'independent' directors are themselves CEOs. As Yeo et al. are at pains to stress, 'When firms exchange their CEOs, these CEO outside directors are not truly independent outside directors. They are, in fact, grey directors'.[12]

In Chapter 5, it was demonstrated that members of the business elite in both France and the UK often hold several board level positions simultaneously within different companies. When these roles are contained within a defined set of companies, as with our top 100 French and UK companies, interlocking directorships are formed, which serve as ties binding the national business system together. The practice is very common in France, where in 1998 the mean number of top 100 directorships held by members of the business elite was 2.73 compared to 1.86 in the UK (see Table 5.4). If all directorships are considered, including companies outside the top 100, the figures rise to 3.75 and 2.62 respectively.

The results of our research on interlocking directorships amongst top 100 companies in France and the UK in 1998 are presented in Table 6.1. An interlock is formed when two companies have one or more directors in common, and the more directors there are in common, the stronger the relationship between the two companies. Since a company may have more than one set of interlocking directorships, it may be conceived as existing at the centre of a network of associated companies. These networks join together to form the entire corporate network, bound by links of differing strength, with various nuclei of power and influence formed by clusters of closely associated companies. The results presented in Table 6.1 are stunning and expose a profound difference between the business systems of France and the UK.

Table 6.1 Company-to-company networks in France and the UK in 1998 established through interlocking directorships

Company	Number of other Top 100 Companies with Directors in Common			Total No. of Associated Companies in Network	Total No. of Directorships in Associated Companies
	Number of Directors				
	1	2	3 or More		
French Companies					
1 AXA	20	8	4	32	57
2 Suez Lyonnaise des Eaux	19	6	2	27	37
3 BNP	17	5	4	26	39
4 Vivendi	18	3	3	24	35
5 Saint-Gobain	18	3	2	23	33
6 Schneider Electric	17	3	1	21	30
7 Bouygues	17	1	2	20	25
8 Total	16	3	0	19	22
9 Pechiney	17	2	0	19	21
10 LVMH	12	5	1	18	25
11 France Télécom	14	4	0	18	22
12 Rhône-Poulenc	16	2	0	18	20
13 Lagardère	13	3	1	17	22
14 Thomson-CSF	14	2	1	17	21
15= Aérospatiale	11	2	3	16	24
15= Alcatel	11	4	1	16	24
17 Renault	10	6	0	16	22
18 Air Liquide	7	7	1	15	24
19 Elf Aquitaine	11	3	1	15	20
20 Alstom	13	2	0	15	17
Average for French Top 100 Companies	**6.84**	**1.28**	**0.42**	**8.54**	**10.96**

Table 6.1 (continued) Company-to-company networks in France and the UK in 1998 established through interlocking directorships

| Company | Number of other Top 100 Companies with Directors in Common | | | | Total No. of Directorships in Associated Companies |
| | Number of Directors | | | Total No. of Associated Companies in Network | |
	1	2	3 or More		
UK Companies					
1 General Electric	13	1	0	14	15
2 British Airways	13	0	0	13	13
3 Diageo	11	1	0	12	13
4 Marks & Spencer	12	0	0	12	12
5 HSBC	9	2	0	11	13
6= British Telecom	11	0	0	11	11
6= Reuters	11	0	0	11	11
6= Rio Tinto	11	0	0	11	11
6= Unilever	11	0	0	11	11
10 Standard Chartered	9	1	0	10	11
11= Bass	10	0	0	10	10
11= British Aerospace	10	0	0	10	10
11= British Petroleum	10	0	0	10	10
14 Cable & Wireless	7	2	0	9	11
15 Barclays	8	1	0	9	10
16 Boots	8	1	0	9	9
17= Allied Domecq	8	0	0	8	8
17= NatWest	8	0	0	8	8
17= Whitbread	8	0	0	8	8
17= Williams	8	0	0	8	8
Average for UK Top 100 Companies	**4.72**	**0.17**	**0.00**	**4.87**	**5.02**

At the heart of the French business system are the dominant enterprises in manufacturing, services, natural resource and finance that are pivotal to the French economy. Companies like AXA, Suez, BNP, Vivendi and Saint-Gobain have extensive networks, frequently sharing more than one director, and incorporating more than 20 companies in each case. Heading the French list of interlocks is AXA, with reciprocal ties to as many as 32 companies, more than twice the number of interlocks displayed by the top British company, General Electric, which has ties to 14 companies. Not all French companies have extensive networks, but even towards the bottom of the league table it is evident that French companies place a high value on the connectivity that comes from being part of a dense social network. Correspondingly, the mean number of associated companies in top 100 French company networks is 8.5, supported by 11 directorships.

The situation in the UK is very different. Certainly, there are companies like British Airways, Diageo, British Telecom (BT), and HSBC that have reasonably extensive interlocking director networks, but these are smaller than those of any of the 20 most extensively networked French companies. AXA has almost four times as many interlocks as the most highly networked British company, General Electric (involving 57 directorships as against 15). The situation in Britain is also more uniform than in France, with nearly all companies having some interlocking directorships, but without the extremes of the French system. The mean number of associated companies in top 100 UK company networks is 4.9, supported by 5 directorships, approximately half the density of the typical French network, confirming the earlier findings of Windolf.[13] Very few companies have more than one director in common, reflecting the British view that good corporate governance means not being identified too closely with the fate and fortunes of other companies, nationally or internationally. This broad pattern is confirmed by the results presented in Table 6.2. This reveals that the top five most highly networked companies in France in 1998 had three times the number of interlocking directorships than their UK counterparts. For the top 25 companies in each country the ratio narrows to 2.5 to 1, for the top 50 companies to 2.4 to 1, and for the top 100 companies to 2.2 to 1.

Table 6.2 Frequency and distribution of corporate directorship interlocks in France and the UK in 1998

Most Highly Networked Companies	France		UK	
	Mean No. of Interlocks	% of All Interlocks	Mean No. of Interlocks	% of All Interlocks
Top 5	39.60	18.07	13.20	13.15
Top 10	31.80	29.01	12.10	24.10
Top 25	24.64	56.20	9.96	49.60
Top 50	18.78	85.68	7.82	77.89
Top 100	10.96	100.00	5.02	100.00

The differences that exist in this regard between French and UK companies are not only quantitative. Equally important are differences with respect to the individual directors who function as corporate interlocks. In the UK tradition, as discussed in Chapter 5, current executive directors, including CEOs, do not always serve on the boards of other leading companies, and in some cases they are actively discouraged from doing so. When they do serve in a dual capacity, as executives with non-executive responsibilities elsewhere, they tend strictly to limit the number of external engagements. In 1998, for example, Edmund Browne, CEO of British Petroleum (BP), served only on the board of SmithKline Beecham, while Peter Bonfield, CEO of BT, was vice-chairman of ICL-Fujitsu and a non-executive director of Zeneca. It is often only as an executive career is drawing to a close that an individual will actively seek non-executive positions with other leading companies. Accordingly, chairmen and non-executive directors, most commonly one-time executive directors, who hold several directorships both of top 100 and other companies, take up a large part of the burden of networking. Research conducted by Hemscott in July 2002, which fed into the 2003 Higgs Review on the role and effectiveness of non-executive directors, revealed that 10 per cent of non-executive directors held two non-executive directorships, with 7 per cent also holding an executive directorship. Altogether 282 individuals held both executive and non-executive director posts in UK listed companies, while as many as 13 per cent of chairmen held more than one chairmanship.[14] In the British view of corporate governance, these relatively strict informal limits on multiple directorships help to keep a distance between the executives and non-executives of different companies.

The situation could not be more different in France, where the PDG of top companies are amongst the most heavily used instruments of formal networking, routinely sitting on the boards of numerous allied companies, each holding one another, as the rhyme says, 'par la barbichette'. In 2002, three members of our super-elite held six directorships of leading companies: Jean-Marie Messier, Jean Peyrelevade and Michel Pébereau. Four more top executives held five directorships; eight held four; 15 held three; and a further 57 held two. Important relationships supported through having influential directors in common included those between Air Liquide and L'Oréal (Edouard de Royère and Lindsay Owen-Jones), Air Liquide and Sodexho (Edouard de Royère and Pierre Bellon), Alcatel and Société Générale (Serge Tchuruk and Marc Viénot), Alcatel and Vivendi (Serge Tchuruk and Jean-Marie Messier), AXA and BNP (Claude Bébéar and Michel Pébereau), AXA and Schneider (Claude Bébéar and Henri Lachman), BNP and Renault

(Michel Pébereau and Louis Schweitzer), BNP and Saint-Gobain (Michel Pébereau and Jean-Louis Beffa), BNP and Vivendi (René Thomas and Jean-Marie Messier), LVMH and Vivendi (Bernard Arnault and Jean-Marie Messier), and Vivendi and Saint-Gobain (Jean-Marie Messier and Jean-Louis Beffa).[15]

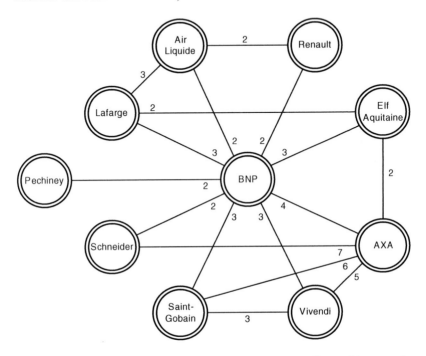

Figure 6.1 Business elite ties in 1998: the French corporate directorship network exemplified

The relationships formed between executives involve more than a series of bilateral exchanges, as can be seen from Figure 6.1. This opens up a window on the French corporate network from the perspective of BNP, which is depicted at the centre of a group of ten major companies, each of the others being linked to BNP by a minimum number of two directors. Besides these links, there are numerous others between companies in the group, creating a genuine social network as opposed to a series of bilateral relationships. AXA, for example, has seven directors in common with Schneider, six with Saint-Gobain and a further five with Vivendi, all of which are associated with BNP. In this snapshot of just a small part of the French corporate network, important nuclei of influence are exposed, including the triangle formed by AXA, Vivendi and Saint-Gobain involving 14 directors who meet regularly at meetings and events hosted by one another, and the AXA-Schneider-BNP nexus which has 13 closely associated directors.

This aspect of the French national business system, like many other defining attributes, is a product of institutional history. Integral to the reconstruction and subsequent growth of the French economy since the Second World War have been the guiding principles of corporate stability, economies of scale and scope, the creation of technological and managerial capabilities, internationalisation, and the fostering of economic growth through collaboration between the state and private enterprise. These principles have found different expression at different periods in recent history, as Maclean demonstrates in *Economic Management and French Business*, ranging from planning to nationalisation to privatisation.[16] However, the threads of policy have remained intact. A national consensus has existed over decades around the need for France to have well-founded companies with the size and resources needed to ride out difficult times and compete in international markets. This has led in turn to corporate restructuring on a grand scale, massive capital investment, especially in manufacturing industry and economic infrastructure, and the systematic development of technological and managerial capabilities. The long-term mission of this partnership between the state and business has been to attend to the national economic interest. State ownership and funding consequently have not been seen as taboo, and likewise companies have been encouraged to see their fates as tied together and interdependent. From this point of view, cross-shareholdings and interlocking directorships have been viewed as complementary devices for encouraging collaboration and retaining control of industry in the right (French) hands.

In its modern, most recent, expression, this doctrine of mutuality between the interests of the state and business has flexed towards cohesive action through corporate strategies and national policies, and away from direct intervention and blatantly uncompetitive behaviour. The old system of cross-shareholdings is still in evidence, as illustrated in Figure 6.2, again with reference to BNP, but this has begun to melt away, and is generally seen as ineffective and inappropriate to current business needs. The crossed shareholdings illustrated here between Vivendi and Saint-Gobain, in which BNP in turn had stakes, are substantial. In reviewing the policies of the top 100 French companies, however, as they evolved between 1998 and 2003, what stands out is the intention of companies to apply financial resources more directly in support of strategy, rather than dissipating them purely for defensive reasons.

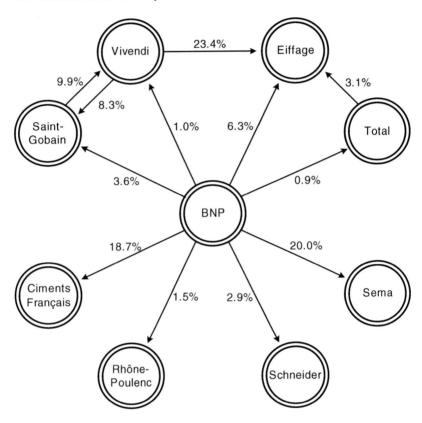

Figure 6.2 Ownership ties in 1998: the French corporate shareholding network exemplified

The implication of this change in direction, we believe, is not that France is preparing to abandon the distinctive practices that have been the hallmarks of its national business system. In our view, consensus and coordination increasingly have come to depend on the effective operation of elite business networks, diminishing the importance of ownership networks and concentrating power in the hands of the super-elite.

Implications of interlocking directorships

There is no shortage of justifications for members of the business elite having multiple roles in different companies. In the UK context, where the practice is relatively limited, four main arguments are advanced.

First, it enables companies to keep their 'ear to the ground', to understand better major developments within the corporate sector, the political realm, and the external environment more generally. Secondly, it enables best practice to spread more rapidly between companies, as in the case of corporate governance. The adoption of improved corporate governance mechanisms in France has been accelerated by UK business leaders like Sir William Purves, who while Chairman of HSBC also sat on the board of Alstom. Thirdly, engaging in high-level debates in different contexts and settings is said to sharpen the thought of business leaders and assist in the formation of a consensus around critical issues. Sound arguments, advanced by different people at different times, can help sway important decisions, for instance concerning legislation and regulations, at the national and international levels. Fourthly, when companies have common concerns, the existence of a social network facilitates joint action, reducing uncertainty by co-opting key external organisations with which the company is in some way interdependent.[17]

These are powerful arguments and they are well grounded in the substance of business life, as our interviewees have confirmed. UK directors see these kinds of 'deep interactions' with colleagues from other companies as entirely desirable and necessary, but they are also keen to point out that there is a line that must not be transgressed. It is the duty of all board members, executives and non-executives, to act at all times in the best interests of the company and its shareholders. Therefore, they must avoid conflicts of interest that might arise from having a role at another company, which in turn suggests limiting the number of roles and ensuring that roles are discrete. In this way, ethical dilemmas resulting from conflicts of interest might be avoided.

In France, where holding multiple directorships is endemic amongst the super-elite, the justifications offered for the practice inevitably are more elaborate than in Britain. Our interviewees, including well-known authorities on corporate governance like Senator Philippe Marini, certainly subscribe to the justifications for multiple directorships frequently voiced in the UK, and equally to the ethical requirement for independence and discretion in the exercise of roles. However, the fact remains that in France there is an entirely different corporate tradition, in which formal networking is so extreme that is smacks of oligarchy, and this requires more extensive explanation and justification. The explanation lies in the manner in which the state and business became entangled during the decades of reconstruction and 'directed' economic development that followed the Second World War. Unlike Britain, where top civil servants and company directors are separate tribes, France, in pursuit of commonly agreed objectives, forged an economic elite distinguished by its unity, coherence and sense of purpose. The elite determined to make France, through systematic application of state and private-sector resources, a leading economic power, characterised by technological sophistication, high levels of productivity, and command of international markets. This 'great national project' produced ideological unity across different sections of the economic elite, enabling individuals readily to cross boundaries and work equally comfortably within a government ministry or a large corporation.

The ideology and institutions that bind together the economic elite in France, seamlessly bridging the public-private divide, enable it to act in ways that would be impossible in the UK. When the giant engineering enterprise Alstom fell on hard times in 2002, confronted by huge debts and haemorrhaging cash, it was never in doubt that both the state and the private sector would rally to save the business, whatever complaints might be voiced within the European Union (EU). This shared reflex to preserve and invest in technologically advanced companies is lacking in Britain, where government ministries and large companies are incapable of a coherent joint response to an industrial crisis. The virtual elimination of entire indigenous industries in the UK – motor vehicles, shipbuilding, railway engineering – is not the product of anonymous market forces alone, but also of a series of feeble choices made over generations by a disjointed economic elite, in and beyond government. The British example serves to highlight to the French the virtues of their own system and the limits of neo-liberalism. In justification of multiple directorships and corporate alliances, therefore, the French can point to elite solidarity and coordinated action as delivering highly beneficial long-term results.

This is not to say that the French system is not without critics, inside as well as outside France. Elite solidarity and extensive interlocking directorships may encourage cronyism, heightening agency problems and reducing competition in the market for corporate control.[18] Alliances and power networks can be turned to work to the personal advantage of the PDG and other executives, rather than to the benefit of the company *per se*. Research in the US has shown that the more numerous are directorial interlocks, the lower the level of CEO turnover.[19] A study by of 84 PDG conducted by Bauer and Bertin-Mourot found that the 14 serving 25 years or more were in the most highly networked companies with 'hard cores' of stable shareholders.[20] Claude Bébéar's experience at AXA, where he served first as CEO (1985-2000) then, from July 2000, as non-executive chairman, is not atypical in this regard.[21]

A second major criticism of French-style interlocking directorships is that directors, because of their mutual dependency, lose their independence and ability to criticise the actions of the executive team.[22] The problem is exacerbated by the PDG fulfilling the roles of both Chairman and CEO. Recommendations made in the Viénot Report regarding independent board members have largely been met, but arguably not in such a way as to provide an adequate counterweight to PDG authority. As Clift reports, power relations within French company boards are such that so-called *administrateurs indépendents* may well be 'independent of the shareholders, but not of the PDG'.[23] Culturally, the French are 'anchored in long-standing personal relationships'.[24] Many directors are effectively the 'patsies' of the PDG, selected through friendship networks, or as the alumni of a particular *grands corps* or *grande école*. The sheer power wielded by Bébéar, for example, often regarded as the unofficial leader of the French business community, was on display in June 2002 when Vivendi was threatened by the prospect of bankruptcy. It was to Bébéar that the French business community turned. Asked by the Americans on the board if he would take Messier's place, he declined, but proposed Jean-René Fourtou, former vice-chairman of Aventis, instead; a few days later, on 3 July 2002, Fourtou was named as Vivendi's new CEO.[25]

A third frequently voiced criticism relates to the consequences of interlocking directorships for executive pay. The argument made is that the elite solidarity promoted by interlocks is intrinsically inflationary. Research conducted in the US confirms the point, Fich and White finding that interlocks add an average of 13 per cent to CEO salaries and bonuses.[26] In France, this is a difficult hypothesis to test because it is not mandatory, as in the UK, to publish CEO compensation in annual reports, the country's privacy laws working against transparency in this matter. The first company to publish the salaries of its top executives was Suez-Lyonnaise des Eaux in 1995, under the leadership of Jérôme Monod, a pace setter in the movement for corporate governance reform. One financial journalist wrote at the time, that this was 'akin to asking the top brass to walk naked down the Champs-Elysées'.[27] Claude Bébéar followed suit in 1996 when AXA was first listed on the New York Stock Exchange. More recently, the Nouvelles Régulations Economiques (NRE) and Bouton Report have brought about greater transparency of remuneration, although executive stock options are only revealed as a total for the top 10 senior executives.

The final point of criticism that can be made of business networking practices in France is that interlocks increase board size and reduce board effectiveness. Boards in France, as in the UK, typically operate on a consensual basis, what Hill refers to in the UK context as an ideology of board unity: 'collegiality is highly valued and a significant criterion in the choice of new directors'.[28] Directors are expected to be supportive of the executive team, and it is rare to rock the boat. As Pettigrew and McNulty highlight, 'within the context of the unitary board in the UK no board could effectively discharge its responsibilities to the shareholders or its employees if life was a constant contest between part-time [non-executive] and full-time [executive] board members'.[29] Non-executive directors lack the information of executive directors, and are at a further disadvantage in terms of their positional power and expertise. Their prospects for influence are thus constrained, dependent on their 'will and skill' in mobilising limited resources,[30] as illustrated by the case of Equitable Life, whose non-executive directors proved unwilling to challenge the charismatic CEO. However, collegiality leads to particular problems in France for two reasons. The first is that extensively interlocked boards tend to be larger than elsewhere, the average number of directors being 18 in France compared to 12 in the UK, making them 'unmanageable, and ... unable to act in a cohesive way'.[31] The second is that members of the business elite with numerous roles cannot keep abreast of the business. Claude Bébéar has condemned the holding of multiple directorships by PDG and CEOs, observing that 'a board membership should cost you a month of work a year. A chief executive doesn't have one month to sacrifice'.[32]

These are hard-hitting criticisms that draw attention to the perceived weaknesses of the French system of interlocking directorships. They are in effect part and parcel of an agenda for corporate governance reform that recognises the dangers of concentrating power in the hands of the elite without sufficient checks and balances. The British system, in contrast, has moved further down the road of reform, balancing the advantages of social networking against the dangers of cronyism. Yet, in certain respects, the French system retains in-built advantages over the more refined and uniform British model. These stem from the greater capacity for cohesive action in France on the part of the state and the business community. The champions of corporate governance reform will need to satisfy the French business elite that this systemic capability will not be lost in the clamour for transparency and accountability, leaving the business system rudderless, a victim of the vagaries of global economic forces.

The power of networks

There are, moreover, narrower and more personal reasons why corporate governance reforms might flounder in France. The power of the PDG to put together a prestigious, reputable board enhances, in turn, his personal attractiveness as a member of other companies' boards, boosting his own social capital. Social capital, according to Burt et al., is primarily about bridge building: building relationships that span what they term 'structural holes', connecting an individual with people outside their employment or immediate circle who might be valuable to them, and with whom they feel at ease. Successful French managers, they found, 'tend to have networks rich in structural holes'. This offers a distinct competitive advantage:

> The universal [principle] here is the brokerage principle in network theory, which says that there is a competitive advantage to building bridge relationships. Whether in the United States or France, resources flow disproportionately to people who provide indirect connections between otherwise disconnected groups.[33]

This quotation endorses Granovetter's view that the acquisition of information depends in part on the motivation of those with information to share it, but equally on the 'strategic location of a person's contacts in the overall flow of information'.[34] Granovetter highlights the paradoxical but nevertheless fundamental 'strength of weak ties', concerning the informal, interpersonal contacts through which individuals learned about job opportunities.[35] The fact that an individual's acquaintances are less likely to be socially involved with one another than his or her friends arguably makes such low-density networks more useful; as Granovetter succinctly put it, 'except under unlikely conditions, *no strong tie is a bridge*'.[36] Scott explains the significance of this insight:

> The importance of strong ties is well understood. Those to whom a person is closest (family and close friends, workmates, etc.) have many overlapping contacts. They all tend to know and to interact with one another in numerous situations and so there is a tendency for them to possess the *same* knowledge about job opportunities. … Conversely, they are less likely to be the sources of new information from more distant parts of the network. … It is through the relatively weak ties of less frequent contacts and of people in different work situations that new and different information is likely to become available.[37]

It was, Granovetter found, 'the short, weak chains of connection that were of greatest significance' in acquiring information about jobs.[38] Through such bridging relationships, he argued, small-scale interaction is translated into large-scale patterns, which then feed back into small groups. The cohesive power of weak ties is explained by the fact that such ties are more likely to link members of *different* small groups. As such they are 'indispensable to individuals' opportunities and to their integration into communities'.[39] Strong ties, on the other hand, are more concentrated in small groups, fostering local cohesion, and hence, in theory, greater fragmentation.

In the UK, research has shown that few directors are appointed following a formal interview process. Personal recommendation still matters most.[40] That said, over the past 20 years, Britain has exhibited some signs of becoming more meritocratic, as articulated by the Director General of the Confederation of British Industry (CBI), Sir Digby Jones:

> I am very proud of Britain in rising to the top. It has become less of a 'who you know' and more of a meritocracy. It matters not where you went to school, it really does not matter as long as you are good enough, nor who you know, in the way it used to. I think this is not just a post-war development, I think it is a development since the middle seventies, possibly after the early eighties' recession. I am thrilled to bits about that.[41]

Others, however, have had a different experience. One interviewee, a former grammar school boy who rose to be Vice President of a leading global bank (Citicorp), heading its international division, spoke of the 'closed shop' nature of British merchant banks to those without a public school background:

> I was a bit reserved about joining what seemed to me, and it has changed a lot in recent years, to be very much a 'closed shop' amongst the British merchant banks. I didn't have a public school background, I had a grammar school background, although I had all the degrees and many more than most I have met in the City. But nevertheless I felt the British merchant banks would not be interested in me.[42]

Sir Adrian Cadbury confirms the power of elite business networks in the UK, in which he detects a strong university link, dominated by the Oxford-Cambridge-London axis. Notably, though, he sees the French elite networks as more tightly knit and exclusive.

> When I was involved with the CBI, if you looked at them, the group of people who came together in those gatherings, even then, and this is going back to the 60s, there would have been a strong university domination. There were a lot of Oxford and Cambridge links and wider

London obviously, Imperial and so on, and there was a kind of net-work, I suspect, that ran across that. But I still wouldn't really call it an elite because there were chaps popping up ... In many ways it seems to me we [in Britain] actually have, curiously, a slightly more open society than the French. When you think King Edward VII was the best friend of a grocer, you know that couldn't happen in France.[43]

In fact, only 16 per cent of the top 100 FTSE directors identified by *The Times* in 2003 admitted to having an Oxbridge education (in fear, perhaps, of appearing to come from too privileged a background). Their elitism was nevertheless made manifest by the prevalence of titles. As many as six in the top 10, and 23 out of the 100, were endowed with elitist titles: Sir, Lord, Baroness and Dame, as opposed to the titles of 'Doctor' or 'Professor' which, being earned through academic achievement, are quintessentially meritocratic.[44] Our own research reveals as many as eight titled individuals in the top ten most powerful business leaders in the UK 1998, one earl and seven knights, four of whom were knighted in 1998 or soon afterwards.[45] Nevertheless, closer scrutiny reveals that of these ten, only two – Sir Mark Moody-Stuart and Lord Simon Cairns – can be said to have come from truly privileged backgrounds. Only four of the 10 attended Oxbridge (all, without exception, Cambridge colleges), and just four went to public or independent schools (one of them to Eton, Lord Cairns), the majority having been educated at grammar schools. Another, Bill Cockburn, had 'made it' the hard way, born into a family of eight children, joining the Post Office at the age of 18 and working his way up through the ranks of the business. Similarly, Sir William Purves left school at 16 to become an apprentice at the National Bank of Scotland, rising to become Chairman and Chief Executive of HSBC. John Bond, who joined the Midland Bank (now HSBC) at age 19, worked his way up to become Chairman. Yet another (Edmund Browne, who was knighted in 1998 and made a life peer in 2001) was the son of a Romanian survivor of Ausch-witz. Lord Browne enjoys an unrivalled reputation among the British business elite, arguably emerging as the superstar of UK business in the period under study.

This stands in stark contrast to our French super-elite. While half of the British top ten attended universities as far afield as Stirling in Scotland and University College Dublin in Ireland, only one of the French top ten did not attend one (or more) of the prestigious Parisian *grandes écoles*. As many as six of the top ten attended Polytechnique,[46] while four attended the French civil service school, the Ecole Nationale d'Administration (ENA),[47] and a further four attended Sciences-Po.[48] This confluence is noteworthy, suggestive of a much more concentrated grouping of elite members than in the UK. Testimony to the pre-eminence of Polytechnique and the networks it generates is to be found in Koscuisko-Morizet's *La Mafia polytechnicienne.*[49] Two of the top ten elite members, Jean-Marie Messier and Gérard Mestrallet, attended both Polytechnique and ENA; and a further pair, Michel Bon and Philippe Jaffré, attended Sciences-Po and ENA. Michel Bon, ranked second in the French super-elite, attended three *grandes écoles*, accumulating diplomas much as he has since accumulated directorships, obtained at the Ecole Supérieure des Sciences Economiques et Commerciales (ESSEC), in addition to Sciences-Po and ENA. The sole member of the top ten who did not attend an elitist institution is a self-made man: Edouard Leclerc, ranked in ninth position, founder of the retailer Leclerc, who has spent much of his life fighting the establishment. His son, Michel-Edouard, however, has a doctorate in economics from Sciences-Po, from which he also has a diploma – in the manner of the offspring of founder entrepreneurs, who, in the quest for legitimacy, wish to be seen to merit their boardroom positions.

Marceau points to the key role played by the informal networks based on common membership of alumni. The use of the familiar 'tu' (normally reserved for close friends, family members and children) in otherwise formal office surroundings underscores the special relationship between alumni, while the higher the posts held by powerful alumni, the greater their power to smooth the way for their younger *camerades*,[50] almost as a type of extended family. Jean-François Théodore, CEO of Euronext, spoke candidly in an interview of the power of networks, of useful relationships gleaned from his days at ENA, which subsequently revolved around the Ministry of Finance and the Treasury:

> To be frank, it is more a subset, because the classes at ENA consisted of around 140 people. Some people go to the Foreign Office and some to the Health Ministry. You may know them personally, but you don't have business directly with them. So the subset was more being able to go to the Treasury and meet people there ... At that time, people didn't stay in the Treasury for life. After civil service school you would stay in the Ministry of Finance for six or seven years, so repaying your debt for studies to the French state. Then people would stay in the Treasury for 10 to 15 years. The way it worked 25 years ago, you'd have lots of young people and only one director to control them, so it's a very sharp pyramid. People leave in around 10 to 15 years, depending on how close they are to the top, and then they enter business. Quite a sizeable number of people I knew are CEOs of big corporate companies. The

CEO of Suez was in the Treasury. The CEO of Renault was in the Budget and Ministry of Finance at the time. Ariane Obolensky, the head of the French Banking Federation, was at the French Treasury at the same time as me. This must have been around 1974 ... I suppose I have a kind of network in the world. Knowing people makes it easier to deal with people, because knowing them personally means I can call them.[51]

That several of Théodore's acquaintances at ENA and the Ministry of Finance subsequently rose to the level of CEO or Minister of State reveals the remarkable density of gifted individuals in a small number of key institutions. His comments throw into stark relief the capacity of such establishments to function as 'meeting places' for the French business and political elites, underlining the institutional nature of elite networking in France. The type of network described by Théodore arguably implies a less porous social boundary than that which marks out the British business elite.

While the French do not possess name-changing honours like the British, they do nevertheless award various categories of both the *Légion d'honneur* and the *Ordre national du Mérite*. The former, introduced in 1802 by Napoleon Bonaparte as a reward for military and civil endeavour, comprises five categories – in declining order of importance, the *grand-croix*, *grand officier*, *commandeur*, *officier* and *chevalier* – with the more recent *Ordre national du Mérite* introduced by General de Gaulle adopting the same categories. Six of the top ten French directors are endowed with various ranks of both of these honours (although none has been awarded either of the top two categories). Table 6.3 compares and contrasts the state honours of the super-elite members of France and the UK in 1998. For the purposes of comparison, state honours are divided into two categories, higher and lower. In the case of France, the former were signified by the ranks of *commandeur*, *grand officier* or *grand-croix* of either the *Légion d'honneur* or the *Ordre national du Mérite*. Lesser honours are the ranks of *chevalier* and *officier*. In the UK, the granting of a knighthood or barony signifies a higher state honour. There are many lesser honours, of which the CBE is by far the most prevalent in our sample. Ninety of the 100 members of the British super-elite of 1998 were endowed with a state honour, distributed equally amongst the higher and lower categories of distinction. In France, where a larger proportion of directors lacked any state honour, higher honours were awarded with greater parsimony, lower state honours being more than twice as prevalent as the higher honours.

Table 6.3 State honours of top 100 directors in France and the UK in 1998

	France	UK
Higher	25	46
Lower	52	44
None	23	10
Total	**100**	**100**

In both France and the UK, the honours system has the special function of legitimising the right of the elite to rule. Honours are a potent form of symbolic capital and, as such, function as a source of recognition and distinction. They are also a tool of social stratification and overt elitism. They are used to stratify and define membership of the elite by cutting out the majority and by grading the honours actually awarded. In the UK, some lesser honours are granted to worthy people from lower down in society, but the truly major honours are reserved for distinguished people at the top of their field. The award of a top honour symbolises arrival within the field of power, as an officially recognised member of the ruling elite. Here business stands shoulder to shoulder with the military, the judiciary, the medical profession, the civil service, the media, sporting and cultural heroes, and other pillars of the establishment.

The role of the family

While Granovetter's work mainly concerns relatively loose-knit acquaintances, the importance of family networks, especially in a French context, is fundamental. While managerially dominated companies displaced family firms at the core of the British economy in the early post-war period, as documented by Chandler, in France the family firm continues to matter.[52] Yvon Gattaz, the former head of the Conseil National du Patronat Français (CNPF), now the Mouvement des Entreprises de France (MEDEF), once remarked that there are two types of business leader in France: those who think that their child is capable of taking on the business, and those who have no children![53] Three of the top 20 members of the French super-elite are representatives of founding family dynasties (Edouard and Michel-Edouard Leclerc, and François Michelin). None of their British counterparts fulfils such a role. French family ownership and control is the highest in Europe, with the top five families controlling as much as 22 per cent of stock market capitalisation, and the top 10 families 29 per cent. This compares with just 4.1 per cent and 5.8 per cent respectively in the UK. Altogether, the top 15 families control more than one-third (35 per cent) of French stock market capitalisation.[54] The top 100 British companies contains just one family firm: the Bradford-based supermarket chain, William Morrison Supermarkets, which Sir Kenneth Morrison developed from his father's Yorkshire grocery stalls and shops which he took over in 1952.[55] Though David Sainsbury served as Executive Chairman of Sainsburys in 1998, the retailer has long since evolved from the family business it was in the late nineteenth century. In stark contrast, the French top 100 includes many which could be described as 'family firms', including Bouygues, Lagardère, L'Oréal, LVMH, Michelin, Peugeot, Pinault-Printemps-Redoute, Sodexho, Dassault Systèmes, Danone (founded by the Riboud family), Bolloré, Fromageries Bel, Galeries Lafayette, Leclerc, Pernod Ricard, Publicis and Yves Rocher.[56] Additionally, it is generally estimated that, despite the far-reaching internationalisation of French business in recent years, more than half of France's top 250 companies remain family-dominated.

There is in France an aristocracy of business that no longer exists in the UK. A battle for the control of Galeries Lafayette in spring 2005 was fundamentally a family affair, as the Moulin family, backed by BNP Paribas, battled it out with their cousins, the Meyers, for control of France's most famous retail chain. Whereas the Moulins and the Meyers previously owned stakes in the company of 31.7 per cent and 29.5 per cent respectively, the buyout saw the Moulin family emerge with 62.9 per cent of the company and BNP 37.1 per cent. The importance of continuing family ownership was emphasized following the battle by Philippe Houzé, co-chairman of the company: 'One of the key values of our group has always been its family rooting. At a decisive moment in its history, an optimal solution has been found with the full backing of the two families'.[57]

Marriage, of course, widens the family network to embrace a whole new family. One study of French bourgeois family networks has revealed that, on average, these may extend to 60-70 individuals.[58] Marceau draws attention to the role of the wife as 'co-gestionnaire de marque', manager of the 'brand image' of her husband, and to whom it falls to keep family contacts warm ('utilisables') through regular family gatherings. As such, the wife exercises a dual role, responsible at once for promoting the family as well as sustaining it, thus highlighting the economic function at the centre of the family, which is inseparable from its emotional, nurturing function. This concurs with Bourdieu's view that marriage is essentially a 'strategy' for protecting and enhancing the patrimony.[59] It is supported by our own research, which reveals a marriage rate of 98 per cent for the top 100 directors in France in 1998, and an average of 2.9 children per director. Perusal of the 2004 *Guide des Etats Majors* reveals that numerous French boards include family members – including leading firms, such as Michelin and Peugeot.[60] Edouard and Michel-Edouard Leclerc serve as joint PDG of the retailer Leclerc. A company board packed with relatives might well be less effective than other boards, selected primarily on the basis of their ability, albeit often through personal recommendation.[61] On the other hand, the stocking of boards with family members ensures continuity in management, allowing families such as Peugeot, which owns 26.5 per cent of the firm, to keep control of their 'birthright' in the event of an attempted takeover. The Supervisory Board of PSA Peugeot Citroën includes Thierry Peugeot as President, Jean-Philippe Peugeot as Vice-President, Bertrand Peugeot and Roland Peugeot, while Robert Peugeot serves on the *directoire*.

In family firms, the inner core of two or three long-serving executive directors, not related to the founding dynasty but promoted internally from within the company, may emerge as 'trusted lieutenants', on whom the owners rely. It is this role of 'general' that Lindsay Owen-Jones arguably fulfils at L'Oréal, trusted implicitly by the Bettencourt family, and rewarded handsomely for his achievements, which include a tenfold increase in the share price.[62] Hill reports that many senior non-family directors in family firms take a significant interest in the company share price – not because they are concerned about a possible takeover or the security of their positions, but rather because a high share price adds to their prestige and social capital among their peers.[63]

The French state elite

One of the most striking aspects of the French business, again absent in the UK, is the closeness of relations with the state. During the Chirac presidency, this has been described as 'l'Etat-Chirac', Jacques Chirac standing accused of filling key political and business appointments with individuals loyal to himself, on an unprecedented scale.[64] These include the heads of the National Assembly, Senate, Conseil d'Etat, Cour des Comptes, Conseil Constitutionnel, Commission Nationale de l'Informatique et des Libertés, Conseil Supérieur de l'Audiovisuel and even public-sector companies such as Electricité de France (EdF). The principle of 'keeping it in the family' applies at the highest levels. Chirac's daughter Claude was recently described by *Le Monde* as a 'daughter of influence': catching sight of her in the company of a Minister is sufficient, it seems, to spark rumours of an impending Cabinet reshuffle.[65]

The fact that so many of the top 100 elite members have studied at the main civil service school, ENA, or Sciences-Po, is illustrative of the interpenetration of business and politics at the highest levels. The fact that the business and political elite share a common *formation*, being educated in the same stables, fosters in turn a coherent worldview or 'pensée unique' on the part of the state elite. Many future business leaders serve in a ministerial cabinet prior to taking on their first major company role, often cementing relationships with powerful political figures. Political patronage may help to secure their first jobs outside the direct tutelage of the state, and may continue to serve them well in their subsequent career. While this helps to explain the cohesion and homogeneity of the French elite, at the same time it sheds light on its distance from the rest of society. As Bauer and Bertin-Mourot clarify: 'this common origin of business leaders, top civil servants and, increasingly, political leaders, implies an absence of debate or alternative project at the heart of the ruling class, and explains its divorce from the "ruled"'.[66]

The fact that two members of the business super-elite of 1998 are former Ministers of State illustrates the symbiotic relationship between business and the state. Edmond Alphandéry served as Minister of the Economy and Finance in the Balladur government (1993-95), in charge of privatisation, and Francis Mer as Minister of the Economy, Finance and Industry (2002-04) under Prime Minister Raffarin. One elite member, François Pinault, former PDG of Pinault-Printemps-Redoute (PPR), is a close personal friend of Chirac's. Many others, such as Philippe Jaffré and Jacques-Henri Friedmann, owe their careers to the state, by which they have been cosseted and promoted, most notably due to successive privatisation waves.

Both Jaffré and Friedmann made serious inroads into the field of power at the time the *noyaux durs* were put in place, the 'hard cores' of stable investors designed to provide newly privatised firms with an anchor following their change of status. The more important function of the *noyaux durs*, however, was to shore up company takeover defences against would-be predators, particularly foreign ones. In fact, they often built on existing, long-standing relationships, as, within each network, firms retained direct and indirect controlling holdings in each other. Effectively, state actors exploited elite networks to ensure that controlling stakes remained in safe hands.[67] In this way, the *noyaux durs* served to institutionalise coordinating networks, reinforcing the crossed shareholdings that had been the bedrock of French capitalism for several decades; these hard cores were peopled in many cases by close personal friends of Balladur, who masterminded the privatisation process, first as Finance Minister (1986-88) and later as Prime Minister (1993-95). The result, as Bauer points out, was a considerable bolstering of the privileges of the existing establishment.[68] Men with strong state backgrounds ended up running more than two-thirds of privatised firms.[69] The trajectory followed by Philippe Jaffré is not atypical of high-flying elite members, beginning his career at the Ministry of Finance, where he held several senior civil service positions, before graduating to take the helm at Crédit Agricole followed by Elf Aquitaine, later serving as Chief Financial Officer (CFO) at Alstom – all three formerly state-owned companies. Our own research reveals that eight of the top ten elite members have strong state backgrounds (all bar Edouard and Michel-Edouard Leclerc), and 14 of the top 20.

The role of the civil service *grands corps* is noteworthy in this respect too, acting as they do as funnels to channel the pick of the *grandes écoles* to the top jobs. Five of these – the engineering *corps*, the Corps des Mines and the Corps des Ponts et Chaussées, and the administrative *corps*, the Inspection des Finances, Conseil d'Etat and Cour des Comptes – co-opt just 50 25-year-olds of the 800,000 people in each generation. Co-option signifies a job with tenure, and the ability to take extended leave from the civil service without losing tenure, as well as the possibility of moving from administration to politics to business.[70] Almost half of top business leaders are members of a *grand corps*, and as many as three-quarters of those with strong state backgrounds.[71] Graduates of ENA, or 'énarques' as they are known, who are also members of a *grand corps* do significantly better in their subsequent careers than those who are not, particularly when that career contains a political element.[72] As Bauer et al. observe, the networks of the *grands corps* serve the establishment all the better for being able to obscure their elitism beneath a cloak of worthiness: 'these *grands corps* constitute the common well of the principal elites of the country, who are able to draw from the meritocratic ideal the reasons for their "merit"'.[73] Pierre Bilger explains how, following a two-year stint at the Inspection des Finances, his classification on graduation from ENA (fifth in the class) was reviewed, whereupon he found himself reclassified as second, behind Michel Pébereau, PDG of BNP.[74] This revaluation of his performance doubtless contributed to his eventual leadership of Alstom for a period of 12 years. While it is the case that *grands corps* membership among CAC-40 directors has declined in recent years, from 50 per cent in 1997 to 41 per cent by December 2002, this reflects the growing internationalisation of French boards, a quarter of which are now non-French, rather than any diminishing popularity on the part of *grands corps* membership. It is perhaps also for this reason that directors from ENA or Polytechnique have declined in number from 37 per cent of CAC-40 directors in 1998 to 31 per cent by December 2002.

Table 6.4 Equity participation of the French government in top 100 companies in 1998

Company	Top 100 Rank	% of Equity Held	Industry Group
Charbonnages de France	85	100.00	Oil and Gas, Mining and Materials
EdF	7	100.00	Utilities and Telecommunications
EMC	61	100.00	Oil and Gas, Mining and Materials
Gaz de France	32	100.00	Oil and Gas, Mining and Materials
La Poste	27	100.00	Utilities and Telecommunications
RATP	46	100.00	Transport and Distribution Services
SNCF	25	100.00	Transport and Distribution Services
Snecma	48	97.20	Manufacturing
Air France	28	94.57	Transport and Distribution Services
Cogema	52	81.50	Oil and Gas, Mining and Materials
France Télécom	2	75.00	Utilities and Telecommunications
Française des Jeux	74	72.00	Media, Consumer Services/Products
Aérospatiale	30	62.16	Manufacturing
Framatome	47	51.00	Utilities and Telecommunications
Renault	6	45.87	Manufacturing
Bull	54	17.40	Manufacturing
Seita	51	11.10	Media, Consumer Services/Products
Dassault Aviation	58	10.75	Manufacturing
Peugeot Citroën	24	5.77	Manufacturing
Total	9	1.70	Oil and Gas, Mining and Materials
Usinor	21	1.00	Oil and Gas, Mining and Materials
Airbus Industrie	66	* 0.00	Manufacturing
Elf Aquitaine	4	** 0.00	Oil and Gas, Mining and Materials

Notes: * Aérospatiale had a major shareholding in Airbus Industrie, giving the French government leverage over its direction.
** Following the privatisation of Elf Aquitaine in 1993, the French government retained an element of control through the possession of a 'golden share' which gave special powers to the Minister of Economic Affairs.

Of course, many of the hard cores, which peaked in 1996, have since unravelled, especially in non-financial firms, unable to withstand the new financial pressures associated with globalisation.[75] There have also been endogenous pressures for change, many of these coming from CEOs themselves (see Chapter 7).[76] It suffices to say at this stage that the erosion of the hard cores, though dramatic, is as yet incomplete. Table 6.4 reveals that the participation in 1998 of the French government in top 100 companies was sizeable, despite far-reaching privatisation. For example, while BT was the first of the UK's large state-owned utilities to be privatised in 1984, in 1998 the French state retained a 75 per cent stake in France Télécom, and still held a controlling interest of 51 per cent of equity in 2005. French capitalism is built on a presidential system, with the PDG continuing to wield enormous power despite corporate governance reform.[77] The sheer institutional strength of the state and the elite networks it promotes and sustains are such as to suggest that the French system of 'insider capitalism' may yet endure, as Loriaux explains:

> In the French case, it is not the institutions that funnel capital to investment that differ from those found, say, in the United States; rather, it is those that funnel talent to positions of power. It is the institutions that socialise elites. It is the institutions that produce culture rather than those that produce subsidies and credit that safeguard the tradition of developmentalism. It is the institutions that protect the supremacy of that culture in the firm that account for the difference in business behaviour.[78]

The influence of the institutions themselves, the elite schools and *grandes écoles*, or the Treasury, the sun around which the galaxy of state-dominated institutions revolves,[79] shows no sign yet of waning, as our own research demonstrates. By extension, the culture they promote is likely, too, to endure.

The importance of getting the 'right people' on board

One of the main recommendations of the Higgs Review was that the 'gene pool' of those who could serve on the boards of FTSE 100 companies should be expanded, such as to broaden the diversity and mix of experience of non-executive directors.[80] Much of the above discussion has focused on the accumulation of directorships on the part of both French and British company directors, which results in interlocking directorships between companies. While the Higgs Review did not specify a maximum number of directorships that could be held, nevertheless it did state that no additional directorship should be assumed without the prior approval of the chairman, and further that all non-executive directors should disclose their commitments and undertake to have sufficient time to devote to them. Yet it is clear that a concentration of directorships increases the 'power index' of the directors concerned, making them more experienced, more 'connected' with the business community at large, and in this sense more desirable and valuable to the companies concerned. The reputation of a company rests squarely on its board of directors, as well as on its performance.[81] There are few things more important to a company than getting the right people in place, as the Higgs Review makes clear: 'People are the key'.[82] The 'comfort factor' matters here too: board members understandably need to feel at ease with one another to perform at their best. At board level, personal qualities arguably count far more than systems, structures and procedures, and in a context where consensus is important, faces need to fit.[83] The fact that companies need experienced individuals on their boards inevitably limits the numbers of serving non-executive directors. The recommendations of the Higgs Review have heightened expectations of non-executive directors while increasing the demands of the role, so that experience is even more necessary.[84] At the same time, the greater demands of the role may reduce its appeal, causing the supply of potential directors to contract, especially since all directors, whether executive or non-executive, are ultimately liable to company shareholders, as the former board of the insurance company Equitable Life has learned to its cost.

In the UK, where business and politics do not benefit from the close relationship they have in France – as Sir Digby Jones puts it, 'business and the government don't pull the boat in the same direction in this country'[85] – non-executive directors with contacts are crucial, needed to provide access to the British political establishment, foreign governments and financial institutions. This leads to the appointment to company boards of former Cabinet members such as Lord Waldegrave, snapped up on leaving office by a financial institution, or former Chancellor of the Exchequer Kenneth Clarke, taken on by British American Tobacco for his connections with Brussels and his lobbying skills. Similarly, former diplomats are valued for their connections with foreign governments. Companies need their directors to function in a social and informational context that goes beyond company boundaries. Their 'boundary spanning activities' and associated interactions with external bodies are crucial to company performance and in reducing environmental uncertainty.[86] Non-executive directors have a vital role to play in acting as a bridge between the board and the outside establishment, with networks of personal contacts furnishing 'a two-way flow of communication',[87] hence serving as 'conduits for social influence'.[88]

Our own research has revealed that members of the super-elite in both France and the UK network within the field of power, not just in business but across a range of charitable institutions, public bodies, business associations and educational institutions as well as sports and arts charities. As Table 6.5 makes clear, serving on such boards and commissions is not a peripheral activity for business elites, but rather a mainstream medium for networking. Quangos and charities function as meeting places, where business elites come into contact with other elite groups – lawyers, medics and academics. The two nationalities nevertheless exhibit notable differences. Involvement in charities is significantly less widespread among the French super-elite than it is among their British counterparts, with a participation rate of just 10.3 per cent as against 44.9 per cent for UK directors. Similarly, UK directors are almost twice as likely to be involved with sports and arts institutions (displaying a participation rate of 28.1 per cent as against 15.4 per cent for the French group). On the other hand, French elite members are more likely to serve on the boards of business associations, such as industry bodies in motor vehicles or aerospace, than British elite members,[89] though business associations, like the Prince of Wales Business Leaders Forum of which Lord Browne is a member, are important too for the British business elite.

Table 6.5 Known board and commission memberships of top 100 directors of French and UK companies in 1998

	France % Participation Rate	UK % Participation Rate
Charitable Institution	10.26	44.94
Public Body	67.95	61.80
Business Association	84.62	69.66
Educational Institution	39.74	55.06
Arts/Sports Institution	15.38	28.09
	(n=78)	(n=89)

Headquarter proximity and the social bonds it encourages also play a key role, providing geographically-based interclass meeting places: in the Paris region, where the vast majority of listed French companies are located, and in the City of London, the hub of Britain's financial firms. Interdependence may influence headquarter proximity in the first place, and both may affect interlocking.[90] As Table 6.6 highlights, many of the British super-elite, 54 in all, are also members of private clubs, many located in and around Pall Mall, including the Athenaeum, Brooks's and the RAC. Such private members clubs, frequented by elites from a range of different fields, serve to foster the social bonds of friendship on which business connections thrive. Sporting clubs also function as mainstream meeting places, with golf clearly out in front as the most popular sporting club to join, one fifth of the super-elite being members of a golf club. (Bill Cockburn, former CEO of the Post Office, cites his failure to take golf lessons as the worst decision of his career.)[91] The popularity of these exclusive clubs among the super-elite underlines the social nature of many of the ties that enable the British super-elite to connect.

Table 6.6 Club memberships of top 100 directors of UK companies in 1998

Club	No. of Reports
Private Members'	
RAC	12
Athenaeum	7
Brooks's	7
Other	28
Total	**54**
Sporting	
Golf	20
Cricket	6
Tennis	6
Sailing	5
Other	5
Total	**42**
All Clubs	**96**

In short, there are powerful, logical economic reasons why individuals rich in contacts are appointed as directors, leading to the self-perpetuating cohesion of the business elite on both sides of the Channel. Members of interlocking directorates form the 'dominant segment' of the corporate elite; inevitably they are more sought-after than others.[92] As one commentator observes, 'the requirements of major PLCs will ensure that the same pool of talent, men, typically in their mid-to-late 50s, will continue to preside in the corridors of power'.[93]

Nevertheless, there are occasions when promoting friends and associates may prove problematic.[94] The experience of the former French Prime Minister and EU Commissioner Edith Cresson provides a warning of what may happen when patronage is taken too far. Cresson was taken to the European Court of Justice (ECJ) in July 2004 over allegations of nepotism during her period as EU commissioner (1995-99), despite criminal charges against her over the same issue having been dismissed by the Belgian court.[95] She stood accused of bringing almost her whole team with her from Paris, following the practice adopted by the majority of her French ministerial predecessors, and was strongly criticised in particular for hiring her dentist and close friend as a highly paid EU adviser on HIV/Aids, a subject about which he apparently knew nothing. As the *Guardian* reported, she became known in the UK and in Germany as 'the commissioner who employed her own dentist'.[96] Reproducing the strongly clientilistic social patterns of 'Latin', southern European member states was not an offence in Cresson's eyes. When questioned by a journalist, she allegedly retorted: 'Should we only work with people we have never seen before?'[97]

Conclusion

This chapter has sought to examine the 'field of power', the social space in which members of elite groups come together to discuss issues of mutual concern. Networks are created differently in France and the UK. In France, it is the *grandes écoles*, *grands corps*, business associations and the institutions of the state that forge the most enduring ties. In the UK, the clubs of Pall Mall, the arts, not-for-profit groups and particularly sporting interests play a key role, without which, as Jean-François Théodore explains, 'you've missed some connection'.[98] While the French business elite is tight-knit and institutionally embedded, the British arguably is more loosely affiliated, fostered by a complex of ties, some institutional and others ostensibly social in nature.

The cohesive power of weak ties, as articulated by Granovetter, which link members of different groups, is illustrated more accurately, arguably, by the British contingent, which displays greater variety of background and educational establishment than does the French. The French contingent, on the other hand, displays relatively strong ties, being more concentrated in terms of educational establishment and background. The elite solidarity and bonding exhibited by the French business elite is remarkable. Kadushin's study of friendship among the French financial elite highlights the importance of what he terms 'enforceable trust' among the elite.[99] Business, political and administrative elites share a common education, with the majority of the top 100 elite members owing the advancement of their career either to the state or to family relationships, fostering in turn local cohesion, but also potentially greater fragmentation with the wider social body. This concurs with the findings of Bauer and Bertin-Mourot, who contend that the French business elite, while extraordinarily homogenous, is nevertheless dominated by a single worldview which implies a 'lack of debate traversing this ruling class and its division from the "ruled".[100] The schism between rulers and ruled was nowhere more apparent than in the French rejection of the EU Constitution in May 2005. The French establishment was united in supporting the Constitution, which had been drawn up by the former President Valéry Giscard d'Estaing; but its concerns were patently not those of the people.[101] Chirac responded in Marie Antoinettesque fashion by replacing Prime Minister Raffarin, who had led the 'yes' campaign, with Dominique de Villepin, an unelected diplomat. As one radical socialist put it, 'The citizens asked to be heard. The President's reply is to appoint a man who ... has never bumped into a voter in his life'.[102]

To network with different kinds of individual and organisations is nevertheless vital to the genesis and flow of new ideas, as Jean-René Fourtou, who became PDG at Vivendi Universal in July 2002, explains:

> *Le vide* [void] has a huge function in organizations ... Shock comes when different things meet. It's the interface that's interesting ... If you don't leave *le vide*, you have no unexpected things, no creation. There are two types of management. You can try to design for everything, or you can leave *le vide* and say, 'I don't know either; what do you think?'[103]

Networks function as important 'enablers' for organisations.[104] Professional networks may reinforce existing ideas, contributing to 'group think', and leading in this way to 'the unification of outlook and policy'.[105] But networks may also, as Granovetter highlights, expose actors to new perspectives and opportunities, since 'the personal experience of individuals is closely bound up with larger-scale aspects of social structure, well beyond the purview or control of particular individuals'.[106]

French capitalism is above all a 'presidential' system, in which executives at the top wield enormous power, not easily held in check by so-called *administrateurs indépendents*.[107] The enduring influence of a powerful personality at the pinnacle of the French corporation – such as Bernard Arnault at LVMH, Claude Bébéar at AXA or Serge Kampf at Cap Gemini (renamed Capgemini in 2004) – is clearly less conducive to the creation of an independent-minded board of directors of the sort that Derek Higgs and others wish to promote in the UK. Claude Bébéar, indeed, argues that French company directors are never truly independent. This is the conclusion reached by the Institut Montaigne, a Paris-based free-market think-tank set up by Bébéar: 'It is always the same people on company boards, and many have amicable relations'.[108] But British firms can also be run by powerful personalities – such as Roy Ranson, former

CEO of Equitable Life, with whom the society's non-executive directors were allegedly too weak-willed to argue, or his successor Alan Nash, who likewise pursued a 'no surrender' policy over the withdrawal of bonuses for policyholders with guarantees. This blew a hole of £1.5 billion in the company's accounts and led to its having to close to new business.[109]

Individual directors in both countries may be appointed for a variety of reasons, but it is surely entirely appropriate that they should be persons seen as best able to assist the company in securing critical resources. Such resources may well include organisational prestige and legitimacy, access to capital markets, or access to external entities vital to organisational success.[110] The appointment of useful non-executive directors has been found to be positively associated with companies' share prices.[111] To appoint directors with due consideration given to their external contacts and networks, as well as to other criteria, such as knowledge, experience and independence, makes sound business sense, as Geletkanycz and Hambrick are at pains to emphasise: 'The external ties of senior executives are of great importance to the form and fate of their organizations'. So much so, indeed, that they consider it legitimate to assign them a market value.[112] The diploma awarded by *grandes écoles*, like the seal of approval offered by membership of a *grand corps*, is arguably inseparable from the persona that possession of it implies, going hand in hand with membership of a network or networks with key contacts.[113] Wisdom lies in recognising that 'resources flow disproportionately to people who provide indirect connections between otherwise disconnected groups'.[114] As Stanworth and Giddens put it, 'patterns of interlocking directorships indicate channels of communication. And channels which facilitate flows of information do also offer a *possible* means of using influence or power'.[115]

7
Corporate Governance and the New Global Economy

'In Anglo-Saxon countries, emphasis is placed for the most part on the objective of maximising share value, whereas in continental Europe, and particularly France, the emphasis is placed much more on the social interest of the company'.

Viénot Report, I [1]

In this chapter, we revisit the concept of corporate governance against the backdrop of the new global economy. The chapter considers the extraordinary reach of globalisation – *la mondialisation* as it is known in France – and the continuing internationalisation of French and UK business made possible by extensive inward and outward foreign direct investment (FDI). Companies in both countries have been driven by the logic of 'critical mass', of having sufficient power to enable them to play comfortably on the global stage, and this has led in turn to extensive corporate restructuring across national boundaries. Fresh corporate governance challenges have emerged as rival stakeholder groups – shareholders, directors, managers, employees and governments – located in different countries, jockey for position and local advantage. Are the old, national corporate governance regimes breaking down, and if so, are we witnessing the emergence of international standards of corporate governance, in tandem with the emergence of global business elites?

We do not share the view that living in an interdependent world necessarily will lead to homogeneity in corporate governance practices. Our position is that globalisation does not imply that all countries and companies will in time abandon their own distinctive identities, cultures and business practices. The logic of cultural reproduction, as we saw in Chapter 2, runs counter to any such proposition. A more accurate and realistic depiction of the new global economy is that it consists of a multitude of companies, each with a home base, competing across numerous national and pan-national jurisdictions, wherein local rules and practices are tempered by voluntary acceptance of international norms and regulations. In this conception, a correspondence of interests remains, and will continue to remain, between clusters of nationally based stakeholder groups, including companies, governments and business elites. These stakeholder groups are united by their history, institutions and culture; cooperating freely and competing together in what, somewhat paradoxically, given its hybrid nature, we call the 'new global economy'.

Globalisation and foreign direct investment

The notion that the raw forces of capitalism are bounded and directed according to different rules in different countries owes much to the work of Michel Albert, previously head of French planning and a former PDG of Assurances Générales de France (AGF), once France's second insurance company. In his seminal study *Capitalisme contre capitalisme*, Albert explores the notion of two vying capitalist systems: the neo-American model founded on individual achievement and short-term financial gain; and the Rhenish model, of German extraction but with strong Japanese connections, which prizes collective success and consensus.[2] While the former is market-oriented and dominated by 'the tyranny of the quarterly report',[3] the latter is network-oriented, and characterised by a close partnership between banking and industry. The national business system of France is generally perceived to be positioned towards the middle of the spectrum, somewhere between the US and Japanese systems, and is often typified as a variant of the continental European model of managed capitalism. The UK system, needless to say, is situated towards the US end of the spectrum.

Building on this analysis, Whitley and his colleagues speak of 'divergent capitalisms', different models of capitalism that can be identified by comparing and contrasting the main features of national business systems, implicitly challenging the view that systems are converging on the Anglo-American model.[4] They favour taking an institutional approach to the interpretation of global economic realities.[5] From this perspective, they argue that actors involved in rule making at international level remain embedded in national cultures and environments, from which they extend their behaviours and strategies into the global domain.[6] 'The question is not', Quack and Morgan point out, 'whether there is convergence or diversity, but how these contrasting tendencies become articulated in specific locations at specific times, and how their performance implications feed back into more long-term processes of institutional change at the national and international level'.[7]

In recent times, however, change has been inexorable at both the national and international levels. Powerful, all-pervasive agents – including technological advances, the emergence of newly industrialised countries (NICs), and the globalisation of markets – have combined to create a world in which competition is heightened, global, and increasingly uncertain.[8] There is considerable disagreement over where this is leading. Giddens points to the emergence of a 'global cosmopolitan society',[9] whereas Djelic and Quack see globalisation less radically, as 'contested and discontinuous processes' sharing 'quite a few similarities with earlier episodes of internationalization of economic activity'.[10] Beck, meanwhile, conceives of globalisation as dealing transnational corporations 'a quite unparalleled hand in the poker game over local ties and obligations'.[11] This new world, whose environmental hazards are enumerated by Monks in *The New Global Investors*,[12] is one where 'fixed assets are diminishing in importance and human assets are the opposite of fixed'.[13] 'Social dumping', where multinational companies move production sites to low-wage countries in pursuit of lower labour costs, is on the up. The problem was first highlighted in France in 1993 when Jean Arthuis warned of the inevitability of companies chasing hourly labour rates of one franc in China as against 50 at home.[14] Many European companies, particularly German manufacturing companies, such as VW, chose to relocate production to East European countries, such as Poland or the Czech Republic, where labour rates were lower and regulatory frameworks less exacting. With the enlargement of the European Union (EU) eastwards in 2004, however, wages in these countries are increasing. The favoured production site of German manufacturers is now the Ukraine. In the UK, the unattractive face of social dumping was amply revealed in 2004, when it emerged that one year after the British vacuum cleaner producer Dyson had moved production to Malaysia, purportedly to be nearer to suppliers, with a loss of 600 jobs in the South West, James Dyson and his wife had awarded themselves a £17 million bonus. Stung by widespread criticism in the UK, Dyson nevertheless retained its research facilities in the area.[15]

The brutal realities of the new global economy have proved challenging for the ruling elites of many countries, including the US, France and the UK, mainly because of job losses in areas of high unemployment. The population as a whole may benefit from the importation of low cost goods from the NICs, but this is little comfort to those suffering the effects of manufacturing plant closures. In the UK, the response of the ruling elite, at least of the axis between mandarins, politicians and corporate leaders, has been to accept almost completely the logic of global economic restructuring. The national strategy is to promote labour and capital market flexibility and to offer UK and overseas companies a free hand in making investment decisions. As can be seen from Table 7.1, FDI flows into the UK were very strong between 1998 and 2003, but outward FDI flows were even stronger, with a sharp peak in the year 2000. In other words, British companies, unconstrained by government, have responded very positively to investment opportunities in other countries. By the end of 2003, the accumulated stock of UK FDI was worth $1,129 billion, 13.8 per cent of the world total, placing the UK in second place behind the US with 25.2 per cent.[16]

Table 7.1 Inward and outward FDI flows for France and the UK, 1998-2003 ($ billion)

Year	France		UK	
	Inward	**Outward**	**Inward**	**Outward**
1998	31.0	48.6	74.3	122.8
1999	46.5	126.9	88.0	201.6
2000	43.3	177.4	118.8	233.4
2001	50.5	86.8	52.6	58.9
2002	48.9	49.4	27.8	35.2
2003	47.0	57.3	14.5	55.1

Source: United Nations (2005), *World Investment Report 2004*, New York: Tables B1 and B2.

The position in France differs subtly but significantly from that of the UK. Despite widespread hostility to globalisation among the population at large, there is a consensus amongst the ruling elite that it will bring extensive benefits, and that corporate sector participation is to be actively encouraged. However, there is not the same level of commitment to labour and capital market freedoms that prevails in the UK. In France, the approach taken is to combine selected market freedoms with instrumentalism. The political and business elites are willing to sacrifice certain (lesser) markets and certain (smaller) companies in the name of global competition, but they are unwilling, as yet, to expose what are perceived as core markets and core companies to the full force of global competition. Thus, for example, the state-owned Electricité de France (EdF) has been shielded by regulation of its domestic market while being encouraged to pursue a bold internationalisation strategy, effectively underwritten by the state. It is now the world's third largest electricity multinational just behind the German companies E.On and RWE.[17] Likewise, when core companies – Alstom, Vivendi and France Télécom most recently – have run into serious financial difficulties, the ruling elite invariable intervenes to provide a solution, however costly or problematic with respect to EU competition policy. The upshot is that France has emerged in recent years as a major international investor, as can be seen from Table 7.1, though not quite on the scale of the UK. By the end of 2003, the accumulated stock of French FDI totalled $643 billion, 7.8 per cent of the world total, just ahead of Germany with 7.6 per cent.[18]

The greater part of France's FDI stock is concentrated in the hands of companies deemed by the state and the business elite as core to the national interest, as can be seen in Table 7.2. In recent years, these companies have emerged as top-tier multinationals, ranked within the world's top 100 by the absolute value of their overseas holdings. This is significant because, for the first time in history, top French firms have pulled alongside their UK rivals in terms of the value of international assets. Between 1998 and 2003, for example, Carrefour became a world leader in retailing and Renault acquired a 44.4 per cent stake in the Japanese car giant Nissan, itself a major multinational company. UK companies, of course, still figure strongly in the league table, with the likes of Vodafone, BT and Shell amongst the very biggest companies in the world. However, British FDI is spread more widely than in France, the top ten UK non-financial multinationals accounting for 50.0 per cent of the nation's outward FDI stock in 2003, compared to 62.1 per cent in France.

FDI trends reveal a move away from manufacturing (down from 44 per cent of world stock in 1990 to 29 per cent in 2002) and towards services (up from 47 to 67 per cent over the same period).[19] Both French and UK companies are to the fore in numerous fields within the service sector.[20] In advertising, for example, France was home in 2003 to five of the world's 15 largest multinationals (led by Publicis) and the UK was home to a further four (led by WPP). France was strongly represented in construction, having three top 15 companies, including Bouygues and Eiffage. In hotels, Britain had four of the top 15 global companies in 2003, including the Intercontinental and Hilton groups, and France was home to the largest group of all, Accor. Two British companies (Pearson and Reed Elsevier) were amongst the top 15 media multinationals, as was France's Lagardère. The UK had three top 15 global catering businesses, including Compass and Whitbread, and France had two, including Sodhexo.

Table 7.2 Top ten non-financial transnational companies in France and the UK in 2002

	World Rank	Assets ($ billion) Foreign	Total
French Companies			
TotalFinaElf	8	79.0	89.6
France Télécom	9	73.5	111.7
Vivendi Universal	14	49.7	72.7
Electricité de France	18	47.4	151.8
Suez	23	38.7	44.8
Carrefour	33	28.6	40.8
Aventis *	39	23.8	32.6
Saint-Gobain	47	22.4	31.6
Pinault-Printemps-Redoute	55	19.2	31.5
Renault	63	17.4	55.8
UK Companies			
Vodafone	2	207.6	232.8
British Petroleum	4	126.1	159.1
Shell	6	94.4	145.3
Unilever	36	27.9	46.8
Anglo American **	46	22.5	33.6
GlaxoSmithKline	54	20.0	35.8
Diageo	57	18.5	26.7
National Grid Transco	68	16.5	35.6
BAT	71	15.6	26.1
Astra Zeneca	72	14.8	21.6

Notes: * Aventis was formed from the merger of Rhône-Poulenc and Hoechst Aktiengesellschaft of Germany.
** Anglo American was formed in May 1999 through the combination of Anglo American Corporation of South Africa (AACSA) and Minorco.

Source: United Nations (2005), *World Investment Report 2004*, New York: Tables B7 and B8.

France Télécom ranked number one in telecommunications in 2002 by scope of international operations, and by the same measure UK companies ranked fifth (Cable & Wireless), seventh (British Telecom), eleventh (Vodafone), and thirteenth (Colt). In insurance, AXA ranked second in the world by foreign income in 2002, with the UK's Aviva and Prudential placed eighth and tenth respectively. Six of the world's top 20 retailers in 2002, ranked by foreign sales, were French, headed by Carrefour and Pinault-Printemps-Redoute (PPR), and two more were British, Kingfisher and Tesco. Finally, in 2002, three British banks – HSBC, Barclays and

Royal Bank of Scotland (RBS) – were amongst the world's top 20 most internationalised banks, as were the French market leaders BNP-Paribas and Société Générale. While, in the EU, France and the UK are perceived as championing different philosophies, with the UK perceived as advocating free-market liberalism and France a competing social model, this formidable catalogue of French and UK companies with extensive global reach signals just how committed are the ruling elites of both countries, in their different ways, to exploiting the potentialities of the new global economy.

Corporate restructuring and the new global economy

French and UK companies are not alone in responding with alacrity to the opportunities and threats created by globalisation. US multinational companies remain dominant in many sectors and across Europe companies in numerous fields are looking to create global platforms to exploit global opportunities.[21] Likewise, the major Asian economies, notably Japan, are home to many of the world's largest multinational enterprises.

The most favoured means of quickly developing global presence is by taking over the operations of other companies. Mergers and acquisitions have occurred in a series of waves since the second half of the nineteenth century across the industrialised world, and many of today's largest companies originally became dominant in this way. In our own study period, 1998 to 2003, a cross-border merger and acquisitions wave surged strongly in 1999 and 2000 as companies pursued the logic of scale and scope economies on a transnational basis, as can be seen in Table 7.3.

Table 7.3 Cross-border mergers and acquisition sales and purchases by French and UK companies, 1998-2003 ($ billion)

| Year | France | | UK | |
	Sales	Purchases	Sales	Purchases
1998	16.9	30.9	91.1	95.1
1999	23.8	88.7	132.5	214.1
2000	35.1	168.7	180.0	382.4
2001	14.4	59.2	68.6	111.8
2002	30.1	33.9	53.0	69.2
2003	17.4	8.8	31.4	57.0

Source: United Nations (2005), *World Investment Report 2004*, New York: Tables B7 and B8.

In telecommunications, for example, the fashionable dogma was that for companies to survive in the long term, they needed control of integrated global networks. The most spectacular exponent of this philosophy was the UK's Vodafone, led by the visionary Sir Christopher Ghent. Vodafone took over Air Touch in the US in a $60.3 billion deal, and topped this when it acquired Mannesmann of Germany to create a company with a combined value of $202.8 billion. Other takeovers followed, including, in 2001 alone, the mobile telephony assets of Japan Telecom for $2.7 billion, Swisscom Mobile for $2.5 billion, and Airtel of Spain for $14.4 billion. The deals put together by Ghent had a combined value of $300 billion, and established Vodafone as the biggest mobile communications company in the world.

France Télécom, inspired by PDG Michel Bon, went down a similar route: in 2001-02 the company acquired Orange in the UK for $46 billion, Global One in the US for $4.3 billion, MobilCom in Germany for $4.3 billion, Equant in the Netherlands for $2.8 billion and Freeserve in the UK for $2.3 billion. Debts mounted to record levels, and in the first half of 2002 the company lost €12.2 billion, causing Bon to resign in September of that year. Meanwhile, a similar spending spree ensued at BT, beginning with the purchase of the worldwide telephony assets of AT&T in 1998 for $5.0 billion, and including Concert in the US in 1999 for $1.0 billion, and in 2000 Ireland's Esat Telecom and Telfort of the Netherlands for $1.8 billion. In 2001, Viag Interkom of Germany was acquired for $13.8 billion. As at France Télécom, shareholders began to count the costs of bold strategic moves, undermining confidence and prompting the resignation of CEO Peter Bonfield and Chairman Iain Vallance in 2002.

The appetite for mergers and acquisitions shown by French and UK companies at the beginning of the twenty-first century was not sector specific. Nor was it confined to cross-border activity. Table 7.4 summarises the results of our research into mergers and acquisitions involving top 100 French and UK companies between 1998 and 2003. Companies are classified as relatively stable if not involved in significant mergers or acquisitions. Many more French companies fell into this category – 60 compared to 45 – than did UK companies. In both countries, however, approximately one in ten top 100 companies lost their independence following takeover, including Castorama (taken over by Kingfisher), Promodès (taken over by Carrefour), Pechiney (taken over by Alcan of Canada), Lucas Varity (taken over by TRW of the US), Safeway (taken over by Morrisons), and Sun Life & Provincial (taken over by AXA). Some of these companies were relatively small and were acquired by a dominant rival. Interestingly, however, some once-dominant companies were taken over by smaller rivals with more dynamic management teams, as with the acquisition of the National Westminster Bank by the Royal Bank of Scotland.

Table 7.4 Mergers, acquisitions and takeovers involving top 100 companies in France and the UK, 1998-2003

Type of Activity	France	UK
Major Acquirer	23	32
Limited Merger and Acquisition Activity	60	45
Merged	6	13
Taken Over	11	10

Note: A major acquiring company is defined as one that made one or more acquisitions worth a minimum of $1 billion per deal in the period. Limited activity is ascribed to companies that made no acquisitions or one or more acquisitions with individual deal values under $1 billion. A company is seen to have merged when two companies of relatively even size came together, both changed name, and executive and non-executive directors from both sides made up the new board. A company was taken over when its identity was lost and very few members of its board were appointed to the board of the acquiring company.

Six French and 13 UK companies lost their independence by merging with a company of similar size. In these cases, the directors of both companies concluded that they could realise synergies and get more out of their collective assets by joining forces. In pharmaceuticals, for example, there was a spate of mergers motivated by the savings that might be made by spreading research and development costs. Rhône-Poulenc merged with Hoechst of Germany in 1999 to form Aventis in a deal worth $21.9 billion; also in 1999, Zeneca of the UK merged with Astra of Sweden to form AstraZeneca, valued at $34.6 billion; and in an all British affair, Glaxo Wellcome joined forces with SmithKline in 2000 to create GlaxoSmithKline, valued at $177 billion. In other cases, immediate cost savings were sought by rationalising plant and systems, as in the UK financial sector mergers in 2001 of the Halifax Building Society and the Bank of Scotland to form HBOS (valued at $45.5 billion), and the CGU and Norwich Union to form Aviva (valued at $28.8 billion). A similar logic underpinned the formation of the Anglo-Dutch steel company Corus in 1999, Air France-KLM in 2003, and the car components company Faurecia out of Bertrand Faure-ECIA and Sommer Allibert in 1999. Other mergers had the intention of boosting technological capabilities and market power, as in the case of EADS (the European Aeronautics, De-

204 Business Elites and Corporate Governance

fence & Space Company), combining Aérospatiale and DaimlerChrysler Aerospace in 2000, and Invensys, which brought together the British companies BTR and Siebe in a $15.2 billion deal in 1999.

The motivations behind mega-mergers such as these – cost savings, improved corporate capabilities, and increased market power – are similar to those that inspire companies to embark on the path of expansion through acquisition. Between 1998 and 2003, large numbers of French and UK top 100 companies (23 and 32 respectively) made one or more acquisitions in excess of $1 billion. There is no more elegant tribute to the ambitions of already dominant firms within the new global economy. Table 7.5 charts the number, size and geographical spread of deals, and reveals a number of interesting similarities and differences between French and UK companies. In both countries, the quest for 'critical mass' begins at home, as can be seen in major takeovers like RBS's takeover of National Westminster, and Total's of Elf Aquitaine. It is in the international arena, however, that big differences can be observed. The approach taken by French companies, most typically but not always, is to internationalise within the EU before expanding further afield, whereas UK companies look more naturally to the US and Commonwealth countries, as well as the EU, for major strategic opportunities.

Once again, history can be seen to have played an important part in shaping corporate strategies. France has for long been a key player in the EU, and its business leaders, no less than its politicians and civil servants, have seen the formation of pan-European companies and institutions, under French leadership whenever possible, as the best means of combating US domination of the global economy. The current success of Airbus, for example, is due in no small measure to French persistence over three decades in creating a company with the technological and managerial capabilities to rival Boeing. The formation of EADS in 2001, with an 80 per cent stake in Airbus, is indicative of the logic driving corporate restructuring in Europe. In 2003, EADS – a Franco-German-Spanish venture – had revenues of more than €30 billion and held significant positions in the global markets for civilian aircraft, military aircraft, helicopters, space launchers, satellite navigation, defence electronics, and missiles. Leadership roles within the business are allocated in recognition of national stakes in the business, initially with French and German co-chairmen and joint CEOs.[22] Pragmatically dividing power and positions in this way is something that members of the French business elite have learned through practical experience. The process could be seen at work, for example, in the formation of the Franco-German Aventis in 1999 and the subsequent merger, in April 2004, of Aventis with the French company

Sanofi Synthelabo to form Sanofi-Aventis, the third largest pharmaceuticals company in the world.

Table 7.5 Merger and acquisition deals worth $1.0 billion or more led by top 100 companies in France and the UK, 1998-2003

Location of Merged or Acquired Company	France		UK	
	No. of Deals	Total Value ($ billion)	No. of Deals	Total Value ($ billion)
Domestic	9	122.7	15	191.7
European Union	30	169.7	25	341.5
North America	21	115.0	32	376.6
Other International	3	11.4	10	32.5
Totals	**63**	**418.8**	**82**	**942.3**

Notes: North America comprises the US, Canada and Mexico.
Sources: The core source is the cross-border merger and acquisition tables contained in the annual volumes (1999 to 2004 inclusive) of the United Nations *World Investment Report*. However, these do not contain data relating to domestic mergers and acquisitions and there are occasional duplications, errors and omissions. We have therefore supplemented the United Nations data with other data drawn from individual company reports and accounts, reports of the *Datamonitor* company information service and other reliable sources.

Numerous other strategic thrusts in recent years have required considerable diplomatic finesse – given concerns about loss of national control over essential services, as French companies have extended their interests across Europe. In this category might be placed the acquisition of the Belgium energy company Tractabel by Suez in 1999 for $8.2 billion, making Suez a leading international supplier of electricity and electrical services, and the takeover by EdF between 1998 and 2002 of the UK electricity companies London Electricity, Seeboard and Eastern Electricity for a total of $7.2 billion. Other potentially sensitive acquisitions have included those of Petrofina of Belgium by Total in 1999 for $5.3 billion, Royale Belge by AXA in 1998 for $3.2 billion, Benelux Paribas by BNP in 2000 for $1.4 billion, Sun Life & Provincial by AXA in 2000 for $3.5 billion, and Gruppo GS of Italy by Carrefour in 1999 for $2.5 billion. In each case, local fears were allayed by the magnitude of the financial offer made to shareholders and reassurances given regarding continuity of employment and respect for local customs and practices. In Belgium, for example, the Electrabel subsidiary of Tractabel has 15,000 employees and a myriad of gas and electricity subsidiaries jointly owned with municipal authorities, which have two representatives on the Electrabel board.[23]

UK companies, like their French counterparts, have to some extent come to see Europe as a natural springboard for global expansion, as Table 7.5 confirms. The takeover of Mannesmann by Vodafone alone accounted for almost three-fifths by value of UK-led merger and acquisition deals in other EU countries between 1998 and 2003. However, while other deals may have been on a much lesser scale, they were transformational for the individual companies concerned; as with the $3.1 billion takeover of the Dutch company Benckiser by Reckitt & Coleman in 1999 to form the household cleaning products and medicines giant Reckitt Benckiser, and the acquisition in 2002 of the German company Reemtsma for $4.6 billion by Imperial Tobacco to consolidate its position as the fourth largest tobacco company in the world. HSBC likewise sought actively to develop its position in European banking through the takeover of Safra Holdings of Luxembourg for $2.6 billion and Crédit Commercial of France for $11.1 billion.

For HSBC, however, as for many other UK companies, the attractions of growth within Europe were matched, and often exceeded, by the lure of major takeover opportunities in North America, especially the US. Cultural affinity, shared language, the relative openness of the market for corporate control and the sheer size of the US economy are all powerful attractors for UK companies. Two of the most widely respected UK business leaders of modern times – Sir John Bond of HSBC and Lord Edmund Browne of BP – have built big positions for their companies in the US by making a series of major acquisitions. In the case of HSBC, the purchase of Republic New York in 1999 for $9.85 billion cemented the position of its Midland Marine subsidiary in the US market. The consumer credit business of Household International was acquired for $13.6 billion in 2003 to further extend the scope of HSBC operations and deepen its capabilities in forecasting risk in different markets and cultures.[24] These capabilities are of particular value in the emerging financial sector markets of China, Korea and the Middle East, where HSBC has grown rapidly under Bond's leadership, again through acquiring established companies and assimilating them rapidly into the HSBC group. BP likewise, under the leadership of Edmund Browne, made major US acquisitions in pursuit of rapid growth. The most transformational of these were AMOCO in 1998 for $56.0 billion and Atlantic Richfield (ARCO) in 2000 for $32.0 billion. These are huge figures, but the consensus amongst financial analysts is that Browne made sound bargains for BP in buying when oil prices were low – revenues and profits escalating when oil prices moved sharply upwards after 2002. As *Fortune* magazine has observed: 'through bold acquisitions and mergers, adept management and silky-smooth PR, he has put the once-stodgy BP at the forefront of the global energy industry. BP's $236.6 billion revenues vaulted it to the number 2 spot on the 2004 *Fortune* global 500'.[25] Browne, whose motto is 'no risk – no gain', went on to form TNK-BP in 2003, following the purchase by BP of a 50 per cent stake in the Russian oil conglomerate TNK for $6.8 billion. By 2004, BP had emerged as one of the powerful companies in the world, a genuine global enterprise, with just 17,500 of its 104,000 employees located in the UK, compared to 39,000 in the US.[26]

Enough has been said to demonstrate the scale and significance of mergers and acquisitions for the new global economy. The risks for both individual companies and members of the business elite are considerable. In some cases, when excessive prices are not paid and when projected synergies are achieved, the results – as at HSBC and BP – fully justify the pursuit of growth through acquisition. In other cases, when debts mount and operating losses ensue, as at France Télécom and BT, investors may lose confidence in the strategy and leadership of the company, resulting in asset sales and the dissolution of top executive teams. In our study period, both France and the UK witnessed tumultuous events at a small number of top 100 companies. Under the leadership of Jean-Marie Messier, Vivendi embarked on a spate of acquisitions in 1999 that lasted three years and involved numerous multi-billion dollar deals. The intention was to transform Vivendi from a nationally based utility company into a multinational media, services and communications empire deriving synergies from its capabilities in managing media and distribution networks. Big acquisitions were made in the US including US Filter in 1999 for $6.3 billion, Cendant Software in 1999 for $1 billion, the publisher Houghton Mifflin in 2001 for $2.3 billion, and USA Networks in 2002 for $10.7 billion. The largest of all acquisitions, in 2000 at a cost of $40.4 billion, was the drinks and media conglomerate Seagram, the Canadian owner of Universal Studios, to create Vivendi-Universal. In the event, the fall of Vivendi-Universal was just as rapid as its rise. Debts mounted to €37 billion and in March 2002 a loss of €13.6 billion was reported for 2001. By popular consensus, Messier was seen to have 'paid too much for too many acquisitions', leaving him with 'a pile of debt, a battered stock, and an iffy strategy'.[27] He resigned as PDG of Vivendi in July 2002.

The Vivendi story was paralleled in the UK by that of GEC, the electrical, electronics and defence equipment maker made famous by Lord Arnold Weinstock, CEO between 1963 and 1996, for its careful financial management and extensive cash reserves. George Simpson, a former executive at Rover, replaced Weinstock on his retirement, and the company embarked on a plan to transform itself from old-fashioned conglomerate to world leader in telecommunications equipment. GEC bought the US companies Reltec and Fore Systems for $2.1 and $4.2 billion respectively, and developed a new range of products to challenge the industry leaders, Cisco and Nortel. The defence electronics business was sold to British Aerospace, and the company changed its name to Marconi. When the telecommunications market turned downwards, Marconi found itself with weak sales, massive debts and mounting losses. By the time Simpson was forced to resign, in September 2001, the market capitalisation of the company had fallen by £30 billion, providing a dramatic illustration of the potential for a wrong-headed strategy to destroy shareholder value.[28]

Corporate disasters on the scale of those suffered by Vivendi and GEC-Marconi have raised the tempo of the debate on corporate governance and globalisation. Even before the fall of Messier, Vivendi had come under attack from shareholder activists, who in June 2001 petitioned the Paris Commercial Court to appoint an auditor to investigate the failure of the company to alert shareholders to the financial consequences of its strategy of growth through acquisitions.[29] At the same time, the fund management company Hermes wrote to the board criticising the company for its 'archaic voting structure' and lack of accountability to shareholders.[30] As Vivendi's share price plunged further, the disastrous consequences of the unbridled power wielded by Messier as PDG focused attention on the relative lack of checks and balances in the French system of corporate governance. In January 2003, the company responded by introducing new governance rules and structures, embodied in an Internal Charter and conforming to recommendations and regulations contained in the French Bouton Report and the US Sarbanes-Oxley Act (SOX).[31] At Marconi, the welter of criticism following the virtual collapse of the company was even more ferocious. Whereas Vivendi had valuable assets that could be sold to reduce its debts, shareholders at Marconi lost nearly the entire value of their investments, while company pensioners lost most of their pensions; both were further aggrieved by the issue of million pound payoffs to failed executives.[32] Incidents of this kind, though relatively few in number, have helped sustain the momentum for reform and the introduction of more robust international standards of corporate governance that might better protect investors from the dangers of reckless globalisation.

Corporate governance in an interdependent world

Pressure for corporate governance reform and the international harmonisation of standards has stemmed from two main sources: institutional investors concerned that dysfunctional boards might destroy shareholder value, and national and supra-national authorities troubled that further corporate scandals might discredit and ultimately destabilise the institutional foundations of the global economic order, portending a new age of economic nationalism. The sense of urgency driving both groups of reformers is indicative of the extent to which corporate ownership rights increasingly are distributed across national boundaries. In the US, for example, CalPERS, the California Public Employees' Retirement System, which had funds under management of $177 billion in December 2004, has championed the cause of investor rights and corporate governance reform around the world.[33] One tactic widely used by CalPERS has been to vote against the re-election of directors of companies in violation of its principles of good governance, such as employing an auditor to provide consultancy services.[34] Likewise, the US government has taken a more directive approach since the passing of the Sarbanes-Oxley Act in 2002 in the wake of the financial reporting *débâcles* at Enron, Adelphia, Tyco and WorldCom, granting the Security and Exchange Commission (SEC) extensive powers to deal with non-compliant companies, including foreign companies with 300 or more individual shareholders based in the US.[35]

The Sarbanes-Oxley Act, because of its reach and tough legal requirements, is a milestone in global corporate governance. Its core provisions relate to the introduction and reporting of internal financial controls, civil and criminal penalties for filing misleading financial reports, oversight of the accounting profession, and new rules for auditors and audit committees. The roles and duties of company officers and directors are specified in detail, and compliance is a requirement. There are regulations for the handling of complaints and expressions of concerns by employees; certification by officers of quarterly and annual operating and financial results; disclosure of off-balance sheet transactions and contractual obligations, reportable events such as write-offs, breaches of ethical codes and other major events; and the composition of audit committees, in particular that they should be composed entirely of independent directors, and that at least one member should be a financial expert.[36] If officers or directors fail to comply with the regulations, the SEC has powers to intervene and prosecute both companies and individuals who face criminal penalties for serious misdemeanours like destroying or falsifying documents or coercing independent auditors. While the Act has been criticised as ill-conceived, for mismatching ends and means, and benefiting precisely those groups who had been responsible for the collapse of Enron and WorldCom (auditors and accountants),[37] nevertheless it sets an exacting metric against which corporate standards may be judged.[38] It is no small matter, therefore, for a company like Vivendi-Universal to assert compliance with the provisions of Sarbanes-Oxley. The message to investors is one of reassurance, of adherence to the highest international standard of corporate governance, signalling that things have changed for the better since the cavalier days when Jean-Marie Messier seemingly lost sight of shareholder value in the quest for global expansion.

The assertiveness in recent years of US government and investor institutions has lent credence to the argument that globalisation is refashioning the institutions and behaviour of capitalist economies such as France on the Anglo-American model.[39] In *Runaway World*, Giddens points out the obvious parallels between globalisation and Americanisation:

> To many living outside Europe and North America, [globalisation] looks uncomfortably like Westernisation – or perhaps Americanisation, since the US is now the sole superpower, with a dominant economic, cultural and military position in the global order. Many of the most visible cultural expressions of globalisation are American – Coca-Cola, McDonalds, CNN.[40]

The Americanisation of French culture was apparently confirmed in December 2001, when Messier, while still PDG of Vivendi-Universal, tactlessly announced the death of the French 'cultural exception' at a press conference. This concerns the long-standing tradition of state support for the French film industry, perceived as struggling against the hegemony of Hollywood, which France had defended tooth and nail at the conclusion to the Uruguay Round of GATT (General Agreement on Tariffs and Trade) negotiations in 1993. This *faux pas* was not just a slight on the French national heritage. It offended the French political class, which believes in arming French cinema against the rampant Americanisation of the world film industry. The remark seems to have signalled, symbolically at least, the beginning of the end for Messier; as Péan and Cohen put it: 'Taken out of context, that sentence "killed" J2M.[41] Repeated by film professionals and relayed by numerous intellectuals and politicians, the polemic [surrounding Messier] became rapidly inflated'.[42]

In matters of corporate governance, however, Europe, and France in particular, looks not to the US but rather to the UK to set the standard.[43] This, as Aguilera points out, is due in part to British regulators, including the Financial Reporting Council (FRC), which enforces the UK corporate governance Combined Code, being first-movers in corporate governance innovation.[44] 'Corporate governance practices in this country', wrote Paul Myners in the foreword to his report on institutional investment in the UK, 'are unrecognizable from the pre-Cadbury world. On any reasonable analysis, these codes have done their job'.[45] His words are a ringing endorsement of the efforts of successive commissions to improve corporate governance practices in the UK. The Code of Best Practice to which the Cadbury Report gave rise, modified subsequently by the Greenbury and Hampel Committees, and which resulted in the Combined Code, has been widely influential outside the UK.[46] As the Hampel Report expressed it, the Cadbury Report 'struck a chord in many overseas countries: it has provided a yardstick against which standards of corporate governance in other markets are being measured'.[47] France, interestingly, was one of the first countries to respond, three years ahead of Germany, which, perhaps due to its existing two-tier system, exhibited much less sense of urgency. The first Viénot Report in particular was widely seen as the French equivalent of Britain's Cadbury Report, though in fact it was far less rigorous, lacking in particular disclosure obligations equivalent to those introduced by the London Stock Exchange (LSE) in June 1993 as a condition of continued listing.[48]

This observation apart, developments in recent years suggest that many corporate governance policies and practices have spread rapidly throughout the world. More than a decade ago, for example, the Cadbury Code recommended the adoption of independent audit and remuneration committees, and advocated the establishment of nomination committees to underpin good governance.[49] The UK is generally recognised as the European country where specialised governance committees – audit, remuneration and nomination – are most widespread.[50] As Table 7.6 demonstrates, committee coverage in top 100 companies in 1998 was as high as 94 per cent for audit committees and 95 per cent for remuneration committees, with nomination committees lagging some way behind at 74 per cent. As Conyon and Mallin point out, the relative reluctance of listed companies to put in place a nominations committee (the take-up of which had been just 51 per cent in 1995, according to their study of 298 British quoted companies), suggests a failure in corporate governance, 'since the absence of an independent nominations committee makes it unclear how directors are efficiently selected and recruited'.[51] By 2003, however, coverage of nomination committees had risen considerably to 93 per cent, while almost all top 100 companies had introduced an audit and a remunerations committee (98 and 97 per cent respectively).

Table 7.6 Frequency of specialised governance committees in top 100 companies in France and the UK, 1998-2003

Structure	France		UK	
	1998	2003	1998	2003
Audit Committee	33	67	94	98
Nominations Committee	14	37	74	93
Remuneration Committee	31	58	95	97

Note: In some cases, the data for 2003 refer to a successor company.

Meanwhile, in France, despite *le corporate governance* becoming something of a buzzword in the mid-1990s, initial implementation lagged behind the rhetoric. One year after the publication of the 1995 Viénot Report, a survey by Vuchet Ward Howell found that while three-quarters of CAC-40 companies had established committees to consider Viénot's recommendations, just over half showed any sign of implementation. By 1997, however, a KPMG survey found evidence of significant change.[52] Most CAC-40 companies had at least one specialist committee. A total of 32 CAC-40 companies were found to have a remuneration committee and 29 an audit committee. Just 12, however, had established a nominations committee, underlining the long-standing power of the PDG, who had traditionally selected members of the board, and often his own successor.[53] Our own research is consistent with that of earlier studies. The pattern revealed in Table 7.6 is one of gradually increasing coverage amongst top 100 companies with the largest of them, members of the CAC-40, leading the way. The number of audit committees doubled from 33 in 1998 to 67 in 2003, while remuneration committees almost doubled from 31 in 1998 to 58 five years later. Nomination committees, however, continued to lag behind, with just over a third of top 100 companies having established one by 2003, despite this being strongly recommended in the 2002 Bouton Report.[54] Carson explains this time lag in terms of developmental maturity, regarding nomination committees as a 'relatively immature' governance structure, compared to the 'highly developed and mature' governance mechanism of audit committees, and the 'developing and maturing' structure of remuneration committees.[55]

These findings, when taken together, suggest that convergence in corporate governance policies and practices is most likely to occur when organisational innovation is straightforward and unlikely to encounter resistance: hence the progress made in France in establishing audit and remuneration committees. Conversely, when innovation demands major institutional or cultural change, then gradual convergence or indeed continued divergence in practice is likely, even in the face of strong isomorphic pressures. The French business system, as we saw in Chapter 6, is highly networked and self-referencing, wherein the PDG of top companies play a pivotal coordinating role. Under this system, reciprocity and patronage are seen as natural to membership of the ruling elite, and devolving responsibility for the recruitment of directors to a nominations committee is seen by many as unnatural and potentially dangerous: hence the lesser rate of progress in this aspect of corporate governance reform.[56]

Enduring differences in governance regimes

In Chapter 1, we conceptualised a governance regime as existing on three related levels – practical, systemic and ideological – in which the rules, regulations and practices at the uppermost level are more visible and open to change than the systems and ideologies at the two lower, less visible levels (see Figure 1.1). The proposition that flows from this is that while corporate governance policies and practices may tend to converge as a result of isomorphic pressures, as between France and the UK since 1995, their actual implementation and consequences for action will continue to differ because of the lesser potentiality for change that exists in business systems, and yet more so in dominant ideologies. This can be seen most clearly with reference to two features that continue to differentiate the governance regimes of France and the UK: the extent of separation in the roles of CEO and Chairman, and the independence of non-executive directors from top management.

According to much of the latest thinking on the composition and conduct of corporate boards, the interests of shareholders are best safeguarded when the big strategic and tactical moves proposed by top executives are fully scrutinised, tested and approved by all members of the board; in direct consultation, in exceptional circumstances, with major investors. In order to avoid the destructive and sometimes catastrophic situations that have embroiled companies across the world, Vivendi, Alstom and Marconi included, governance systems are seen to be needed that might avoid situations from spiralling out of control, wherein risks are fully assessed and discussed before irreversible actions are taken. In this context, it is often recommended that power should be more evenly distributed throughout a board, and that all directors should be equally well informed and directly engaged in the decision making process. This is seen to require the separation of the roles of Chairman and CEO, and the appointment of non-executive directors who are genuinely independent of top management. Close cooperation is recommended between all parties, but not to the degree that executive and non-executive roles become blurred, or freedom of expression curbed. In other words, there must be an expectation that difficult issues can be raised and proposals challenged. To this end, formal but flexible decision-making processes are recommended, abandoning the comfortable informality that once characterised some boards. Widely approved refinements of this basic model include the adoption of semi-prescriptive board calendars to ensure that all major aspects of the business are scrutinised from time to time, and the appointment of a senior independent director to liaise with major investors over important matters.

Movement towards this 'ideal' has been most rapid in the UK in consequence of regular changes to the Combined Code. For example, following the Higgs Review of 2003, the criteria for qualification as a genuinely independent director were spelled out as not having been employed by the company in a five-year period prior to appointment to the board; having no close ties with the company's advisors, directors or senior employees; not serving on the board for longer than ten years; and not serving as the representative of a single large shareholder or group of shareholders. If a non-executive director is appointed to an LSE-listed company who does not satisfy these requirements, then the annual report must specify the reasons in accordance with the fundamental principle of the Combined Code, 'comply or explain'. UK companies have tended to opt for 'comply' rather than 'explain' with respect to most aspects of the Combined Code, such that by 1998 the functions of Chairman and CEO had been separated in 91 of our top 100 companies, rising to include all 100 by 2003-04.[57]

In France, the prevailing situation is very different because corporate governance regimes, in their reality and essential dynamics, are more the product of history, embraced in systems and mindsets, than conformance to a set of universally espoused principles. The option exists under French company law to separate the roles of Chairman and CEO, but in many quarters the belief persists that effective decision-making requires that power be concentrated in the hands of the PDG. In 1998, 23 of our top 100 French companies had separated the roles of Chairman and CEO and the figure remained at just 37 in 2003, highlighting the importance of cultural reproduction as a mechanism for moderating pressures for change. Likewise, while the first Viénot Report urged boards to resist reciprocal mandates and restrict the number of directorships an individual might hold, progress in this direction has been limited.[58] Only a handful of firms have been actively engaged in removing reciprocal mandates, and many of the most powerful PDG continue to hold multiple non-executive directorships. As discussed in Chapter 6, members of the French business elite continue to value corporate networking as a mechanism for coordinated action and fruitful engagement with the state. They are understandably reluctant to abandon the perceived benefits of long-standing institutional arrangements.

The natural affinities between the UK and the Anglo-American countries (Australia, Canada, New Zealand and the US) have ensured that these have borrowed significantly from the Combined Code, whereas French companies have clearly struggled with key governance concepts such as the independence of directors. This is hardly surprising. In the UK, there is a manifest divide between the owners and managers of companies, shareholdings are dispersed, and institutional investors control just over 70 per cent of equity. There is a standard corporate form that matches a standard governance code, whereas in France there is enduring diversity in relations between owners and managers. Some companies conform to the Anglo-American norm, but many others differ in remaining family owned or state owned or in having close relationships with other companies. In this situation, directors are often appointed to boards specifically to represent a family, institution or interest group, and for this reason alone cannot be classified as 'independent'. The logic of institutional arrangements thus runs counter to the ideals of the Combined Code. At interview, one director at MEDEF stressed the importance of competency over independence: 'a board of directors must be competent, irrespective of whether it is independent'.[59] Another, Senator Philippe Marini, prefers to speak of 'professional' directors rather than 'independent' directors, doubting whether non-executive directors in France would ever be fully independent, given the quintessential importance of their ties to one another:

The notion of the independent director is an empirical notion. I often prefer to speak of 'professional' directors rather than 'independent' directors. In French practice, to be a director, is a complement of activities. It is linked to the ties with capital, it is linked to the ties of friendship; it is linked to all kinds of things.[60]

The implications are considerable. In France, the prevalence of 'ties that bind' mean that members of the business elite exhibit considerable 'class solidarity', and consequently they are less exposed to challenge on the grounds of personal performance than their counterparts in the UK, as Table 7.7 confirms.

Table 7.7 Corporate governance interventions faced by the boards of the top 100 companies in France and the UK, 1998-2003

Type of Challenge	France	UK
No Major Intervention	77	64
Board Liquidated on Merger or Takeover	17	23
Performance of Director(s) Challenged	3	12
Conduct of Director(s) Challenged	3	1

Note: Boards of directors are open to intervention in their affairs in three main ways. First, a board may be liquidated or reconstituted when shareholders accept an offer of merger or takeover. Second, shareholders may require the departure of one or more directors, often the chief executive or chairman, on account of perceived under performance. Third, either shareholders or the authorities may take action with respect to conduct on the part of one or more directors that is perceived to have been inappropriate or unethical.

It can be seen that between 1998 and 2003, just three of the 100 most powerful directors of French companies suffered a career reversal as a result of alleged poor corporate performance. Jean-Marie Messier was forced to resign when Vivendi-Universal was weighed down by onerous debts, significant operating losses and reputational damage, and Michel Bon exited France Télécom for much the same reasons. These departures were acrimonious and atypical, requiring leading members of the elite to join forces and turn exceptionally against one of their own number. In these cases, as in that of Pierre Bilger, who left Alstom when financial crisis began to bite, corporate insiders were sacrificed, symbolically almost, to preserve the legitimacy of the majority. Both Messier and Bilger, stunned by the turn of events, have fought brave rearguard actions to defend their business reputations. Other business leaders were accused of personal misconduct. Two of them – Jean Peyrelevade and François Pinault – were caught up in the legal storm that raged for many years in the US concerning the purchase of the defunct insurance company Executive Life in 1991, led by Crédit Lyonnais, in contravention of US laws preventing the takeover of an insurance company by a bank, from which Pinault is said to have profited handsomely. He was finally cleared of fraud after a two-month trial in May 2005.[61]

The dramas surrounding the resignations of Messier, Bon and Bilger for alleged poor performance as PDG indicate the rarity of the event. In the UK, by contrast, there is a more sanguine attitude to the precariousness of life at the top, and a widespread understanding that loss of office is the price to be paid when the share price consistently falls below expectations, whether or not this can be attributed fairly to those in command. The 'bitter pill' of enforced resignation is almost invariably sweetened by a large payoff, and the prospect of taking up fresh assignments elsewhere. The system is paradoxical in that it is at once harsh and forgiving. Mounting shareholder criticism led to the resignations of Philip Watts as Chairman of Shell in March 2004, Peter Bonfield as CEO and Iain Vallance as Chairman of BT in 2002, Robert Ayling as CEO of British Airways in 2000, Peter Davis as CEO of Sainsbury's in 2004, George Simpson as CEO of Marconi in 2001 and Derek Wanless as CEO of National Westminster in 1999. The 'soft landing' typical of top executives' fall from grace is exemplified by Wanless, who between 2001 and 2004 was commissioned by the British government to produce a series of reports on healthcare funding and service provision. Only one member of the UK super-elite, Greg Hutchings of Tomkins, suffered serious adverse criticism on the grounds of personal conduct, an enquiry in 2000 suggesting that he had taken liberties in using the company jet for private purposes. Following his resignation in October 2000, Hutchings admitted that as a large shareholder he had run the company proprietarily, and that there had been some personal excesses for which he was apologetic, but insisted that the financial significance of these had been greatly exaggerated.[62]

Convergent tendencies and shareholder activism

France has been one of the success stories of the long era of economic growth that Western Europe has enjoyed since the end of the Second World War.[63] The ruling elite remains concerned with growth, with national economic strength and with the extension of the national business system. This does not mean maintaining the *status quo*. Rather, the French have done in the past whatever has been necessary in order to remain economically strong. In this respect, privatisation, mergers and acquisitions, network and alliance building, are all part of a single process of structural refinement in pursuit of national competitive advantage. All the while, the French have sought to avoid what are often perceived to be 'Anglo-Saxon' excesses, such as the readiness to liquidate once great companies in financial trouble rather than restructuring, with or without government support, in defence of established productive capabilities. Far from abandoning its distinctive business system, with its emphases on stability, strategy and the longer term, France has sought to adapt and strengthen it. As we have seen, far-reaching transformations are in train with respect to the internationalisation of production and ownership, and these changes have led to the introduction of corporate governance practices more in tune with shareholder-value oriented or financialised economic systems.[64] However, whilst these transformations are common in Western society, part-and-parcel of a general isomorphic tendency,[65] it is important to bear in mind that reform and restructuring have been long-standing objectives of French economic policy.

Indeed, the French appetite for economic reform predated the emergence of the global economy, to which arguably it has contributed. In the late 1980s, as Reaganism, which focused on the removal of rigidities in labour markets and the perceived need to roll back the state, gathered credence throughout the industrialised world, the French financial market was deregulated (the so-called 'little bang'). All price controls and most exchange controls were abolished; social legislation for 'hiring and firing' was relaxed; and, in 1986, France embarked on a vast privatisation programme that aimed within five years to return to private ownership the whole of the banking and insurance sectors and most of the industrial companies operating in competitive markets.[66] Privatisation continued under governments of both sides of the political divide. In 2003, the state reduced its stakes in a number of firms, including Renault-Nissan, Dassault Systèmes and Thomson. The National Assembly voted to reduce the state's share in Air France from 54.4 per cent to less than 20 per cent, but in the event the proposed sell-off was postponed due to the merger of the airline with KLM. A large stake in Air France-KLM was eventually put up for sale by the French government in December 2004.[67] June 2003 saw the expiry of agreements freezing the core shareholdings of EADS and the defence contractor Thales (previously Thomson CSF), including those of the state, opening the way for further change.[68] Divestments in 2004 included the aircraft-engine maker Snecma (Société nationale d'étude et de construction de moteurs d'aviation), the government's stake in which was reduced from 97 per cent to 62 per cent, raising €1.45 billion. Many observers were initially sceptical about privatisation.[69] However, it arguably has served to facilitate the internationalisation of French business and to open up France's former public sector to risk taking.[70] In creating employee-shareholders, mainly the salaried employees of large firms, who grew in number from 500,000 in 1988 to 1.5 million by the twenty-first century, it can be argued that privatisation encouraged the risk-taking mentality to spread more widely than the boards of top 100 companies.[71]

In reflecting on these changes, Morin argues that, in the late 1990s, France moved from being a 'financial network economy' to being a 'financial market economy'. He points to the increasingly significant role played by foreign institutional investors on the French stock market, making new demands on corporate management: 'Directly inspired by the American "shareholder value" model, the largest French groups are going through a managerial revolution, whose consequences are only now beginning to become apparent'.[72] The growth of the stock market in the 1990s is noteworthy in this regard. After a period of modernisation in the early 1990s by the Société des bourses françaises (SBF), the Paris Bourse became an increasingly significant vehicle for raising funds on the part of leading companies, as well as medium-sized businesses (the *second marché*, established in 1983), and young, potentially high-growth companies (the *nouveau marché*, founded in 1996). In 1998, stock market capitalisation as a percentage of GDP stood at 48.8 per cent in France, compared to 193.7 per cent in the UK.[73] The gap between the two countries was big but narrowing, the market capitalisation of the Bourse doubling between 1995 and 1998,[74] and in 2000 it merged with the Amsterdam and Brussels stock exchanges to form Euronext. The LSE remains the world's third largest stock exchange, after New York and Tokyo, but it now has a further significant rival. In 2002 and 2003, the volumes of equity trading on Euronext actually exceeded those of the LSE, although turnover remains much lower due to the preponderance of negotiated deals on the London exchange.[75]

Privatisation, cross-border mergers and increasing reliance of the stock market as a vehicle for raising capital have had important consequences for French business. One of the most significant of these has been the acquisition of extensive ownership rights in French companies by non-French nationals. Companies such as Sanofi-Aventis, created through large-scale mergers and acquisitions, may be headquartered in France, but their ownership is distributed and their boards are international, most often European, in outlook. Many others, whose shares are traded on Euronext, the LSE or the NYSE, have widely distributed patterns of ownership, often with US institutional shareholders strongly represented. The privatisation movement effectively opened up French companies to foreign investors hungry for equity stakes in politically stable countries, and by 1996 fully 25 per cent of listed corporate equity was held by foreigners.[76] In the period from March 1997 to December 1999, American institutional investors increased their holdings in French companies by 430 per cent to an average of €2,935 million. By 2000, foreign ownership of the equity of the top 40 companies had reached an average of more than 40 per cent, a record among the world's leading industrial nations, with institutional investors, many from the US, holding significant equity shares.[77] Foremost among these were (in order of size of investment) Capital Research (now the leading institutional investor in France), Fidelity (the world's leading institutional investor), Templeton, Wellington, TIAA Cref, Scudder, CalPERS, AIM, Morgan Stanley and Merrill Lynch.[78] More generally, France is the country in Europe where the level of employment by foreign companies is at its highest, about 25 per cent of the French workforce being employed by foreign-owned companies, more than in the US, UK or Germany.[79] An estimated 20,000 jobs are created annually through inward investment, double those lost in 2003-04 through company relocations to low-wage countries.[80]

As the ownership of French companies has become more distributed internationally, board membership has become more diversified by country of origin, although to a lesser degree than might be expected. Table 7.8 reveals that in 1998, the boards of France's top 100 companies remained overwhelmingly French in nationality (85 per cent). This is comparable to British boards, 83.7 per cent of which were composed of British nationals. French and British boards differ, however, in the 'hierarchy' of directors' nationalities that apply. While Britain's main source of foreign directors is the US (62 directors, amounting to 5.9 per cent), ahead of France in second place (20 directors, or 1.9 per cent), and the Netherlands in third (1.3 per cent), France's number one source for foreign directors in 1998 was Italy (45 directors, equal to 3.6 per cent), narrowly ahead of the UK (40 directors, or 3.2 per cent), with Germany in third position (2 per cent), and the US in fourth place, just 15 of a total of 1,260 directors coming from the US.

Many of the changes in corporate governance practice introduced in France in recent years, as many interviewees have confirmed, have followed from interventions made by foreign institutional investors or directors, as with the introduction of specialist board committees at Alstom under the guidance of Sir William Purves, Chairman of HSBC from 1987 to 1998. Developments such as these have been spurred on by the increasing presence in Europe of shareholder representative groups like Institutional Shareholder Services (ISS) which, in May 2005, just 20 years after its foundation, had 1,270 institutional clients controlling $23 trillion of the world's equity. ISS and similar organisations, because they cast votes on behalf of groups of institutional shareholders, have the power to ensure that companies whose equity is freely traded in significant volumes comply with recommended corporate governance standards.[81] They conduct research and take actions deemed necessary to keep the pursuit of shareholder value to the fore within companies. As Megginson confirms, the rise of capital market based finance, as opposed to bank finance, fuelled by wave after wave of privatisations and mergers, has promoted a spectacular growth in shareholding and share trading, highlighting 'the need to encourage the development of an effective system of corporate governance for publicly traded companies'.[82]

Table 7.8 Nationality profiles of the business elites of France and the UK in 1998

Country	Directors of French Companies		Directors of UK Companies	
	No.	%	No.	%
France	1,071	85.00	20	1.90
UK	40	3.17	877	83.52
Italy	45	3.57	1	0.10
Germany	25	1.98	10	0.95
USA	15	1.19	62	5.90
Spain	13	1.03	4	0.38
Netherlands	11	0.87	14	1.33
Belgium	9	0.71	4	0.48
Others	9	0.71	8	0.76
Switzerland	9	0.71	3	0.29
Japan	6	0.48	6	0.57
Canada	3	0.22	8	0.76
Brazil	2	0.16	0	0.00
Sweden	2	0.16	1	0.10
Australia	0	0.00	6	0.57
Austria	0	0.00	2	0.19
Denmark	0	0.00	3	0.29
Hong Kong	0	0.00	8	0.76
India	0	0.00	2	0.19
Ireland	0	0.00	2	0.19
New Zealand	0	0.00	2	0.19
South Africa	0	0.00	7	0.67
Total	**1,260**	**100.00**	**1,050**	**100.00**

Note: The data relate to 2,291 individuals, of whom 1,031 were directors of UK top 100 companies, 1,241 were involved in French top 100 companies and 19 were involved in both French and UK companies.

In the UK, the role of institutional investors has been under review since the Cadbury Report, with particular consideration being given to their 'voting on particular aspects of remuneration or … tabling advisory resolutions along lines now developing in the US'.[83] In short, should institutional investors take a more active role in the control – the strategy, direction and governance, the composition and quality of the board – of the companies of which they are part proprietors, thereby focusing the attention of management more sharply on the expectation and needs of shareholders? British (and American) financial institutions, often seen as being oriented towards short-term considerations, have traditionally displayed little interest in building and retaining controlling shareholdings, or using their influence with company boards.[84] As Myners highlights, their role in British economic life is central – UK institutional investors control more than £1,500 billion assets altogether, over half the value of UK equity markets – yet they remain low-key institutions.[85] Their overriding obligations lie with their clients on whose behalf they invest. To form close monitoring relationships with the companies in which they invest represents an expense that pension fund trustees would be reluctant to make on behalf of their clients. Nor are they able to commit themselves to individual companies in a way that might preclude them subsequently from selling out fast in the event of a collapse in the share price. They need to be free to handle risk as appropriate; understandably, the 'constellations of interest' identified by Scott need to be able to 'shift their relative positions as they buy and sell shares in the stock market'.[86]

Yet ownership arguably bestows responsibilities as well as benefits. As David Pitt-Watson of Hermes has explained, rising investor activism recognises the need for institutional investors to steward the shares that they own.[87] One empirical study of shareholder activism on the part of UK unit trusts has found that these are adopting an increasingly activist stance, with most having drawn up voting policies vis-à-vis their invested companies. Further, the study found that longer-term relationships with invested companies were actively being encouraged.[88] That said, just 40 per cent of UK institutional investors currently exercise their right to vote at annual and extraordinary general meetings.[89]

Many pension fund trustees, admittedly, lack business experience: 62 per cent of trustees lack any professional qualification in finance or investment, while more than 50 per cent received no more than three days' training on assuming their role as trustees.[90] Yet business acumen is increasingly necessary given the shift from state-funded to private pension provision. Trustees also lack the necessary degree of knowledge regarding their chosen investments that might allow them to compete with the information-gathering capacities of the stock exchange on which they rely for information on company performance. A deeper communication with the boards of companies in which they invest might bring them into contact with price-sensitive information, provoking a conflict of interest with investors. The majority of pension fund trustees (77 per cent) receive no support from in-house professional staff, and most are unpaid, yet increasingly 'wholly unrealistic demands' are being placed on them.[91] This explains the rise in Europe, following the US, of specialist intermediaries like ISS with the knowledge and capabilities to act on behalf of groups of institutional investors.

Rewarding business elites

One of the most burning issues facing institutional investors – fuelling much recent debate on corporate governance practice – is that of top executive remuneration, particularly the remuneration of CEOs. In recent years, in both France and the UK, the rewards attaching to membership of the business elite have escalated, rising much faster than for those lower down the corporate hierarchy. There is a growing perception that the elite is out of touch with the common man, ever willing to sacrifice the livelihoods of workers at home in pursuit of global ambitions and personal reward. The charge is that top executives have become ever more Americanised in their values and beliefs, embroiled in a 'culture of greed'.[92] The standard response is that European companies must compete in the global market for top executive talent and that while pay levels have risen rapidly, they are still far lower than in the US – hence the frequently expressed opinion that there is still considerable scope for further sharp rises in CEO remuneration in both France and the UK.

Whatever the merits of this argument, there is strong evidence to support the view that executive reward packages increasingly are being restructured along US lines. In the UK, where dispersed shareholdings are the norm, a contract of employment for a CEO will typically include three main elements: a basic salary; a bonus that depends on hitting short-term targets such as revenue growth; and a long-term incentive plan normally based upon the issue of stock options. Stock options are a defining feature of the US system and their use is intended as an incentive to improved performance, aligning the interests of shareholders and managers. The beneficiary of a stock option plan has the right to purchase company shares during a certain period at a price specified at the start of the period – in France, for example, this may be up to 20 per cent less than the market value of the shares. Effectively this is a one-way bet, since in the event of a falling share price, executives cannot lose anything (other than their jobs), unlike investors who have actually purchased their shares.[93] The advantage of these arrangements, from an investor perspective, is that the CEO is incentivised to perform at the highest level in both the short (bonus) and long (stock option) terms.[94] Indeed, the tendency since the early 1990s has been to shift the balance of reward away from basic salary in favour of bonus payments and stock options.[95] In this way, the interests of the CEO (personal wealth accumulation) and shareholders (corporate value creation) can be reconciled. The outcome can be seen in Table 7.9 with respect to the reward packages provided in 2003 to the CEOs of ten leading UK companies in 1998, as identified in Table A.2.2 of Appendix 2. The average salary paid was well over €3 million, of which one half was paid as a bonus. Share options were granted to nine out of ten CEOs, ranging widely in offer value, from €12.3 million for Lord Browne at BP to €0.5 million for Matthew Barrett at Barclays.

Reward packages are structured more variably in France than in the UK. For large international companies with relatively dispersed shareholdings that are open to challenge from institutional shareholders, the pattern, as might be expected, is quite similar, with a balance struck between basic salary, bonus and stock options (see Table 7.9). Annual salaries, calculated as basic pay plus bonus, are typically lower in France than in the UK. The average for a CAC-40 PDG was €1.83 million in 2002,[96] compared to €2.79 million for a CEO of one of the top 40 extant UK companies in Table A.2.2. Increasingly, however, French companies are granting stock options, as the business system becomes more financialised and shareholdings are dispersed. Moreover, there is considerable pressure to do so from investor groups based in the US and also from business leaders themselves. As Clift colourfully puts it with regard to the behaviour of French directors in recently privatised companies: 'their eyes lit up with dollar signs' as they saw just how much they stood to gain from US executive remuneration norms.[97]

It took but a short leap of the imagination for them to stop comparing reward differentials with others lower down the corporate hierarchy and to begin comparing themselves with their counterparts abroad. This tendency has increased, as Cheffins observes, as companies have expanded overseas, both through organic growth and mergers and acquisitions, legitimising the argument that the market for top executive talent is nowadays international, and that remuneration packages should be constructed to recruit and retain the very best people from around the world.[98] The implications were highlighted by the Daimler-Chrysler merger in 1997, when it was revealed that Chrysler's CEO, Robert Eaton, earned more than the entire Daimler management team put together![99]

Table 7.9 Reward packages of the CEOs of ten leading companies in France and the UK in 2003 (€000)

Company[1]	CEO	Cash Rewards					Offer Value of Stock Options[3]
		Basic Salary	Bonus	Other Benefits[2]	Total	Bonus as % Total	
France							
Suez Lyonnaise des Eaux	Gérard Mestrallet	1,028	746	0	1,774	42	0
France Télécom	Thierry Breton	900	447	10	1,357	33	0
Alcatel	Serge Tchuruk	1,524	0	10	1,534	0	3,350
Renault	Louis Schweitzer	928	1,050	4	1,982	53	5,336
Total	Thierry Desmarest	1,297	1,231	0	2,528	49	7,992
Danone	Franck Riboud	991	1,503	0	2,494	60	5,940
AXA	Henri de Castries	500	1,808	180	2,488	73	9,908
Alstom	Patrick Kron	880	660	61	1,601	41	0
Lafarge	Bertrand Collomb	875	733	25	1,633	45	5,936
Pinault-Printemps-Redoute	Serge Weinberg	1,500	300	69	1,869	16	3,960
Average		**1,042**	**848**	**36**	**1,926**	**41**	**4,242**
United Kingdom							
HSBC	Keith Whitson	1,150	2,231	76	3,458	65	1,313
Shell Transport & Trading	Philip Watts[4]	1,189	1,393	33	2,615	53	7,399
British Telecommunications	Ben Verwaayen	1,115	1,353	27	2,495	54	4,461
British Petroleum	Edmund Browne	2,046	2,701	83	4,830	56	12,312
Diageo	Paul Walsh	1,176	2,384	65	3,625	66	4,477

Table 7.9 (continued) Reward Packages of the CEOs of ten leading companies in France and the UK in 2003 (€000)

| Company [1] | CEO | Cash Rewards | | | Bonus as % Total | Offer Value of Stock Options [3] |
		Basic Salary	Bonus	Other Benefits [2]	Total	
United Kingdom (continued)							
Barclays	Matthew Barrett	1,753	822	129	2,704	30	506
Lloyds TSB	Peter Ellwood	717	717	578	2,012	36	3,794
Tesco	Terry Leahy	1,342	2,533	40	3,915	65	2,555
Sainsburys	Peter Davis	1,195	521	33	1,750	30	0
SmithKline Beecham	Jean-Pierre Garnier	1,460	2,366	615	4,441	53	4,935
Average		**1,314**	**1,702**	**168**	**3,184**	**51**	**4,175**

Notes: [1] The ten companies selected are drawn in descending order from Tables A.2.1 and A.2.2. Only those companies for which salary information is published in annual reports and accounts, and where the picture is not complicated by severance or retirement packages, have been included. In the UK, Unilever is also excluded because of its Anglo-Dutch board structure. For the UK, data are drawn from the top 14 companies. For France, data are drawn from the top 20 companies.
[2] Pension contributions have been excluded because the data are not available for French CEOs.
[3] Granting stock options enables the beneficiary to purchase (or not to purchase) a number of shares at a fixed price at specified date in the future. The offer value is the number of shares made available multiplied by the offer price. Stock options are usually exercised when the share price at the specified future date exceeds the offer price.
[4] Philip Watts was Executive Chairman and Managing Director.

Ten years after the publication in the UK of the Greenbury Report into directors' remuneration, executive pay continues to excite concern.[100] In a poll of more than 500 top executives conducted by the headhunter Russell Reynolds in 2004, 84 per cent of board members expressed concern over boardroom pay, with the hiatus between pay and performance viewed as the most pressing issue.[101] A typical illustration of 'reward for failure' is provided by Sir Peter Davis, former CEO of the supermarket chain Sainsburys, who left the business in June 2004 with the share price at an all time low, the dividend halved, one in five jobs axed, the company's credit rating lowered by Standard and Poor, and the company relegated to third place in the league table of British grocers behind Tesco and Asda, heading for the red for the first time in its 135-year history. Few could understand why Sir Peter deserved a payoff of £4 million.[102] The suspicion, voiced loudly following the publication of *The Independent Fat Cat List 2003*, is that US-style reward packages rarely improve CEO performance, and at times might actually create perverse incentives.[103] Academic research on the subject, although mixed, confirms the difficulty in proving a link between executive compensation and business performance. Conyon and Leech found only a weak association between the two variables.[104] In a later study by McKnight and Tomkins, a positive relationship was established between the award of stock options and firm performance.[105] The results of this study, however, might be due more to generally rising stock market prices during the period of investigation, than to actual management performance.

The public perception remains one of scepticism with regard to the behaviour of 'fat cat' members of the business elite. Remuneration committees, for example, are often dismissed as little more than a club in which one section grants large rewards to another on a reciprocal basis; a perception reinforced by Finkelstein's elaboration in *Why Smart Executives Fail* of the cultural roots and damaging consequences of out of control systems of executive reward.[106] The reforms introduced first in the UK by Sir Adrian Cadbury and complemented later by other contributors to the Combined Code are thus dismissed as largely ineffective, and Sir Adrian himself has acknowledged that remuneration committees are perhaps 'the least unsatisfactory means of dealing with an intractable problem'.[107] Yet the evidence available on the impact of corporate governance reform is more positive than is often suggested. There has been an extremely high level of compliance with the requirements of the Combined Code, strengthening the hand of more truly independent directors who sit on boards and remuneration committees, as Young has shown.[108] Members are of course subject to the inflationary pressures that stem from employing compensation consultants and from direct knowledge of levels of remuneration elsewhere. One of the unintended consequences of increased governance regulation has been that greater compulsory disclosure has effectively fuelled executive pay.[109] Indeed, as Main and Johnston discovered, the level of pay awarded to British CEOs whose companies were endowed with a remuneration committee were substantially higher than where there was none, almost as if senior executives were writing their own contracts with one hand and signing them with the other.[110]

This does not mean to say that high levels of remuneration are undesirable, or that non-executive directors are incapable of exerting their independence and authority. As Thompson suggests, the main impact of UK corporate governance reform has not been to make remuneration more sensitive to CEO performance, but rather – post-Greenbury – to limit the costs of CEO dismissal.[111] Greenbury suggested limiting the rolling contracts of CEOs to one year as a means of limiting the liquidated damages incurred on termination. This has largely happened. Moreover, poor performance does lead ultimately to dismissal, as Conyon and Florou demonstrated in their study of 460 listed companies between 1990 and 1998; although they found that only very poor levels of performance significantly affected turnover rates.[112] These results are supportive of the findings reported earlier in Table 7.7.

Unlike the UK, where payoffs for termination of contracts have dominated the public debate, perhaps the main cause for concern in France is the increasing use of stock options as a key component of CEO reward. Stock options were sanctioned by French law in 1970, although initially companies displayed little interest in them. This changed in 1987, when Finance Minister Balladur, keen to boost the Paris Bourse, introduced a favourable tax regime for stock options, enabling senior executives, often of newly privatised companies, to put in place schemes highly beneficial to themselves, entailing minimal risk.[113] A major public scandal broke when it emerged that Philippe Jaffré, the former PDG of Elf Aquitaine, had profited to the tune of between €23 million and €38 million, largely in stock options, on leaving Elf at the time of its takeover by Total in 1999. In 2000, Laurent Fabius reduced the holding period to qualify for reduced tax to four years (as compared to three years in the UK and US), for options granted from April 2000.[114] Selling the shares before this date would mean that the gain would be taxed as salary income, attracting tax of up to 52.8 per cent.[115]

While still relatively rare in Europe, with the exception of the UK, stock options are widely prevalent in France, both among listed and unlisted companies. Alcouffe and Alcouffe estimate that about 1,000 French companies were using stock options by 1997.[116] By the year 2000, the value of the stock options plans of large French companies was 40 times greater than in Germany, exceeding even the UK, 'the quintessential market economy in the EU'.[117] In 2001, taking into account the potential gains from stock options distributed by the top five most 'generous' companies in each economy, France was European leader, ahead of the UK in second place, followed by the Netherlands, and, some way behind, Italy, Germany and Spain. As *L'Expansion* remarked, 'With 22 billion francs [€3.35 billion], the French dominate the European landscape, including the United Kingdom, often considered to be the most American of European capitalisms ... The English are beaten!' When the top ten companies in both countries were taken into consideration, France was well ahead of the UK: €5.2 billion as against €3.6 billion in the UK, where just two companies, Glaxo Wellcome and BP, accounted for €2.6 billion.[118] French companies, in fact, accounted for seven of the top ten most 'generous' companies in 2001, these being, in order of potential gains to be made, Aventis, Total, BNP Paribas, Vivendi-Universal, Sanofi-Synthélabo, AXA and L'Oréal.[119]

Clearly, there is a need to avoid what the Organisation for Economic Cooperation and Development (OECD) Steering Group on Corporate Governance describes as 'camouflaged pay structures with sub-optimal incentives'.[120] Since 1993, US companies have been obliged by the SEC to publish evaluations of their stock option schemes. Interestingly, the perception of MEDEF is that stock options are less of a problem in France than in the UK. Agnès Lépinay, for example, insisted:

> There is much less of a problem in France than in the UK [with stock options]. There have been certain cases, but these have been relatively isolated, individual cases, such as the stock options attributed to Jaffré when he left Elf ... We are not at all the highest in the range. All the same, stock options have begun to reach the average of Anglo-Saxon countries.[121]

Yet, despite the sound and fury surrounding the notion of the 'social interest' of the firm, normally only top French executives and managers stand to benefit from stock options. In 2002, less than 3 per cent of employees of CAC-40 companies were eligible, 121,000 altogether (as against 2 per cent in 2000 and 1 per cent in 1999).[122] While this may appear to be a large number, representing a rise of 78 per cent in just one year, nevertheless 16 per cent of all options, approximately €400 million in total, were reserved for a small elite of just 10 individuals in each CAC-

40 company, 443 altogether, each one of whom stood to gain an average of €862,787 through stock options, admittedly less than the windfall of €3 million each had stood to gain the previous year.[123] In fact, total potential gains had shrunk considerably in the intervening period, from €8.9 billion in August 2001 to €2.5 billion one year on, due to a tumbling stock market. Nevertheless, gains realised in France remained higher in 2002 than in the UK, those of Aventis and BNP Paribas totalling €454 million and €428 million respectively, as against €283 million for HSBC and €264 million for GlaxoSmithKline.[124]

Moreover, while the tax advantages of share option schemes are considerable for both the company and the beneficiary, patently, 'the state and the social security system lose out'.[125] The use of stock options constitutes 'a real wealth transfer to the beneficiaries at the expense of other stockholders', which is uncosted and largely unrecognised.[126] Company share capital is diluted through such transfers.[127] It is odd that while the lucrative remuneration packages awarded to elite executives are justified by their contribution to the common weal, in fact the use of stock options detracts considerably from this goal, constituting a transfer of resources from the company to the occupants of certain executive positions.[128] Given the size of the transfers of ownership and wealth, it is difficult to see how this can continue. Options outstanding for CAC-40 companies amounted to 3.9 per cent of share capital in August 2002, although for some companies share capital has been diluted by more than 10 per cent, Vinci (16.5 per cent), Alcatel (12.8 per cent) and Dassault Systèmes (11.2 per cent) in particular.[129] In the US, where account is now taken of the real cost of stock options, the average company in the Standard and Poor 500 has options outstanding estimated to account for 15 per cent of share capital. An average of 2 per cent of share capital is being transferred each year to company executives through stock options – tantamount, it could be argued, to a legalised form of 'daylight robbery'.[130] Stock options have had a sizeable impact on the profitability of US companies: when stock options are taken into account, profits are shown to be declining since 1997; if they are ignored, the trend is shown to be rising.[131] This has led Paul Lee of Hermes to conclude that the widespread use of stock options is not conducive to the delivery of shareholder value, and that adverse consequences will follow as US pay structures are increasingly adopted around the world.[132]

Mindsets and the reflex of national sovereignty

It might be argued that the British vision of economic management, where the accent is on competition and relatively low taxes, has triumphed in the post-communist world. The UK has emerged as the unlikely 'pioneer of a looser, de-regulated, globalising, market-driven union'.[133] In Sir Digby Jones' view: 'it is not British arrogance or Little Englander to say this. Britain has taken some very hard decisions over the past 25 years ... these policies have delivered the most successful economy in Europe'.[134] The President of the European Commission, José Manuel Borroso, appointed in 2004, is notably pro-Atlantist, and the British Commissioner, Peter Mandelson, has been handed the portfolio for trade. The rejection of the EU constitutional treaty by the French in May 2005, followed by the Dutch in June, seemed to seal the 'victory' of Britain's free-market philosophy. Paradoxically, however, the triumph of the 'no' vote may have signified just the opposite: the rejection of 'Anglo-Saxon' liberalism which had become too threatening, and a longing for the lost comfort of protectionism – in other words, the democratic expression of cultural reproduction.

The UK's impressive performance during the EU downturn of 2002-03 was sustained mainly by private consumption, coupled by a relaxation in fiscal policy, which supported economic activity just as it began to flag. Much of the UK's rising influence in Europe has been to the detriment of the Franco-German alliance, which has dominated the EU for more than a decade. As Nicolas Bavarez, an *énarque* government adviser and the author of a recent book on French 'decline', *La France qui tombe* ('falling France'), expressed it: 'The French like to think that they are still the masters of Europe when they are no longer. The British refuse to believe that they are the new masters of Europe because they hate Europe so much'.[135] This notion of French decline has been reinforced by a spate of hard-hitting publications, which have shaken the French establishment, including *Adieu à la France qui s'en va* (*Goodbye to Disappearing France*) by Jean-Marie Rouart, *La France est-elle encore une grande puissance?* (*Does France still Count?*) by Pascal Boniface, and *L'Arrogance française* by Romain Gubert and Emmanuel Saint-Martin.[136] Bavarez claims that France is resting on the laurels of past successes, pointing out that government borrowing has risen from 23 per cent of GDP in 1980 to 62 per cent today, equal to €18,000 for each citizen.[137]

The UK owes much of its economic and cultural advance to its membership of the Anglo-American family of countries, and also to the penetration of the English language, now used as the corporate language of large European enterprises such as EADS and Siemens. As the former PDG of Alstom, Pierre Bilger, explained: 'Every time we speak between countries in Alstom we use English, bad English, but we speak in English'.[138] The use of English as a corporate language is all the more necessary given the sheer number of subsidiaries owned by French firms. In October 2004, the French Education Ministry announced that international English would henceforth be one of five essentials in a new national curriculum. An estimated 40 per cent of Europeans speak English as their mother tongue or second language, more than French, German, Spanish and Italian combined. A British Council study published in 2004 predicted that three billion people globally would be speaking English by the year 2015.[139]

However, as Loriaux observes, one institution which remains constant in France despite the fiercely blowing winds of change is that of the *grands corps de l'Etat*, which, as we saw in Chapter 6, play a pivotal role in the selection and education of the elite which leads France in the business, administrative, political and military domains:

> The *grands corps* 'house' the 'heads'. They are home to an elitist culture composed of language games and norms. That culture informs and constrains the way the French think about industrial development, both inside and outside the formal institutions of the state. Under the pressure of structural imperatives, the French liberalised their political economy, but did so within a framework of that culture. They liberalised the tools and institutions of financial and industrial policy. But the minds that conceived the liberalisation remained imbued with developmental prejudice.[140]

Recruitment at the highest echelons in France follows the 'high road' of the *grandes écoles* and *grands corps*, as opposed to a company-based path more likely to be followed in the UK. These are the key structuring structures that determine who gets to the top in France. But the elite character of French management, which in turn places business leaders at one remove from employees lower down the organisation, has also made them reluctant to dilute their own authority by decentralising decision-making in the firm.[141] Some organisational change has occurred, so that key decisions may now be taken in small executive boards comprising, perhaps, a CEO, a chief financial officer (CFO) and a chief executive vice-president.[142] As Senator Philippe Marini explained in a personal interview, the behaviour of the archetypal PDG is changing:

> Today things are more varied, and even a PDG of a traditional nature in a listed company depends to a greater extent than before on financial communication. He knows that the stakes of an AGM or 'hot show' that succeeds or fails are very important for him, and so his behaviour is evolving. So the French model is a model undergoing change. We are

keeping our tradition of a strong technostructure and management that regards itself as the repository of the true interests of the company.[143]

But the authority of the man at the helm remains 'Napoleonic' by British standards, while the lack of trust that pervades French life in general materialises as bureaucratic structures in France's business organisations and public institutions, resulting in a 'stalled society', a charge originally levelled by Crozier 40 years ago.[144] There are now 5.1 million civil servants in France, as against 4 million in 1980.[145] It is argued here that corporate governance reform in France is informed by, and intertwined with, the pervasive presence of the French state elite.

Moreover, while the rise of institutional investors in France is often presented as proof that the shareholder value paradigm is gaining ground, in fact there has been much evidence of share buy-backs on the part of top French companies, thanks to a law of 2 July 1998, which allows them to buy back up to 10 per cent of their capital, overturning that of 1966 which had prevented them from doing so. A good part of stock market activity since 1999, as O'Sullivan observes, has been more geared towards buying back shares than selling new ones. Within two years, more than 800 visas for stock buyback programmes had been issued by the Commission des Opérations de Bourse (COB). By September 2002, only two companies from among the CAC-40 had failed to request the approval of the COB for a buyback programme, these being ST Microelectronics and EADS.[146] Shares that have been repurchased in this way may be annulled, exchanged, used to finance an acquisition, or retained as a form of *autocontrôle*, to protect against takeover. The cancellation of shares increases the value of remaining shares, resulting in an increase (albeit short-term) in the company's share price. By early 2002, eight leading companies had cancelled their own shares: Air Liquide (amounting to 2.8 per cent of the company's share capital), Danone (6 per cent), Michelin (2.17 per cent), Peugeot (9.6 per cent), PPR (0.7 per cent), Saint-Gobain (10 per cent), TotalFinaElf (4.7 per cent) and Schneider (1.2 per cent).[147]

The voting dynamics of leading French companies are also noteworthy. These do not conform to Anglo-Saxon norms. In France, as in Sweden, dual shareholding structures comprising double or multiple voting rights are common, against generally accepted corporate governance best practice. Michelin, for example, awards double voting rights to investors who retain their shares for a period of four years. At the same time, many shares issued by companies do not carry any voting rights at all.[148] Multiple voting rights can be granted as part of clauses in articles of incorporation, or in by-laws. Since these are given up in the event of a share transfer, they constitute 'a particularly pernicious barrier to takeovers',[149] such that, as Lannoo points out, 'those countries that have multiple voting rights – Scandinavian countries, France and the Netherlands – are more often the bidder than the target of takeovers'.[150]

The rise of foreign ownership of French equity is sometimes interpreted as a sign that French politicians have somehow lost control, unable to intervene in an increasingly global economy in the traditional *dirigiste* fashion of previous years.[151] The Sanofi-Synthélabo-Aventis affair, however, shows that industrial patriotism *à la française* is alive and well. In January 2004, the French pharmaceuticals company Sanofi-Synthélabo launched a hostile bid for Aventis, the Franco-German company formed in 1999 by the merger of the mighty Hoechst and the more modest Rhône-Poulenc. The merger of Hoechst and Rhône-Poulenc had hardly been a marriage of equals: the agreed parity of 53 per cent and 47 per cent did not fully reflect the wider discrepancy in the respective size and turnover of the two partners.[152] Hoping to see the re-emergence of a French 'national champion' in the pharmaceuticals sector, Finance Minister Nicolas Sarkozy – a rising star in French politics – intervened to back the Sanofi-Synthélabo bid, while opposing a counter bid by the Swiss firm Novartis. In April 2004, an increased offer by the French pharmaceutical company (€53 billion) was accepted, much to the consternation of Chancellor Schröder, who accused Sarkozy of behaving in a 'nationalistic' manner.[153] On its foundation, Sanofi-Aventis became one of the world's largest pharmaceutical companies, present in more than 100 countries across five continents, with 99,700 employees and a market capitalisation of €80.3 billion.[154] While Aventis had had a two-tier system, with a management and supervisory board, Sanofi-Aventis, reverting to type, preferred to have one man in two roles, Jean-François Dehecq being appointed PDG of the new company. The company dropped its listing on the Frankfurt stock exchange and its headquarters moved from Strasbourg to Paris.

Not to be outdone by his political rival Sarkozy, President Chirac adopted a similar strategy of 'Frenchification' at EADS, seemingly determined to turn the Franco-German-Spanish aerospace joint venture into a French national company. Like Aventis, EADS had two CEOs, one from each major founding partner, Philippe Camus and Rainer Hertrich, and two co-chairmen, Jean-Luc Lagardère and Manfred Bischoff. Chirac's plan was to replace EADS' two CEOs with one French CEO, Noël Forgeard, a close personal associate; a move that took place in May 2005. There may be good reasons for moving to a simpler leadership structure. Two heads are not always better than one, as the Anglo-Dutch group Unilever was forced to admit in abandoning its long-standing dual chairman/CEO structure. But Chirac's plan at EADS was, allegedly, for EADS then to acquire Thales, the French defence electronics firm in which the state has a 31 per cent stake. German efforts to counter Chirac's plan included merging EADS with German naval shipyards and defence electronics to balance Thales and thus stop the French from assuming outright control.[155]

These cases provide striking examples of France seeking to reclaim to its advantage something it had previously ceded to, or shared with, Germany. Further illustrations of the state's continuing power to constrain the market place include the merger in May 2004 of Air France with the Dutch carrier KLM to form Air France-KLM, Europe's largest airline; and the four-year deadline successfully negotiated by Sarkozy with the European Commission in May 2004 for Alstom to enter into a partnership with a private-sector firm, as the price of its government bailout. As noted earlier, the French government favoured a partnership with the French nuclear group Areva, despite the Commission's preference for Siemens.[156] Such examples suggest that in the global economy, despite much talk recently of French decline,[157] heroic capitalism survives. The reflex of national sovereignty remains, and is capable of achieving results.

Conclusion

This comparison of corporate governance systems in France and the UK against the backdrop of the global economy throws into stark relief the battle currently being waged between the Anglo-American model of capitalism and the European social democratic model, as outlined by Albert. The picture is mixed, and the outcome is not a foregone conclusion.

Both models have arguably shown signs of change. On the one hand, what seemed in the UK to be a single-minded focus on the issue of shareholder value has widened to embrace corporate responsibilities to society. The objective of running companies in the long-term interests of shareholders is now increasingly coupled with a new concern for the common good. The term 'corporate social responsibility' (CSR) now features prominently on the websites of leading British companies, and usually occupies several pages of company annual reports, with some companies, such as Shell, British-American Tobacco (BAT) and BP, producing separate social and environmental reports.[158] This is partly in recognition of the fact that large companies have sizeable impacts on society, the economy and the environment, which have to be managed and minimised. Partly, too, it reflects society's preoccupations, championed by pop stars and politicians, such as fair trade for third world producers, the campaign to make poverty history, and relieving third world debt. At the same time, investors have begun to exercise more voice – in a significant, though not strident manner – on the policies of the companies in which they invest. Leading financial institutions are increasingly aware of the importance of social and environmental issues to investors, consumers and government. The erosion of public confidence in organisations as a result of corporate scandals has given licence for a new type of investment that is seen to be socially responsible.[159] A failure in trust arguably means reduced profits and business for everyone, whereas corporate social performance and corporate financial performance have been shown to be positively related.[160] Companies such as Tesco are proud to announce that they are highly placed in the UK-based FTSE4Good and Ethical Indices for ethical and socially responsible investment.[161]

At the same time, the strength of global competition has forced French companies to provide value for their shareholders, to become more transparent, and to focus more resolutely on financial issues and return on capital. The boards of directors of leading French companies are increasingly international, reflecting the changing composition of the shareholding body. Top companies are taking the issue of corporate governance much more seriously than hitherto, backed up by the legal muscle of the NRE and the *loi sur la sécurité financière*, which established the new Autorité des Marchés Financiers (AMF). They have also learned to recognise the importance of investor relations – this is something relatively new for many leading French companies. For example, investor relations at Euronext have risen dramatically in importance since 2001; as CEO Jean-François Théodore remarked in interview,:

> Two years ago we didn't have any investor relations. We were speaking to institutional investors, but in an institutional way. We were speaking about the market or trading, but not speaking about us. Now we have a small investors initiative, with four or five people, and we listen very, very carefully to what our shareholders are saying.[162]

Despite the enormous influence exercised by the British Combined Code internationally, and despite talk of the 'Americanisation' of both Britain and France, in different ways, the systems of governance obtaining in these two countries are rooted in each case in a distinct 'habitus', the origins of which go deep. As O'Sullivan writes, 'institutional and cultural factors continue to constrain the wholesale shift to an Anglo-Saxon system'.[163] Clift agrees, noting that 'there is a tendency to overemphasize evolutions ... at the international level, and to underplay continuities'.[164]

The argument that France is gradually embracing the shareholder value paradigm is not consistently borne out at this 'sedimentary' level. As the recent cases of Alstom, EADS and Sanofi-Aventis amply demonstrate, traditional *dirigisme* is alive and well in France, while the popularity of share buybacks casts growing stock market activity in a different light.

The very cohesion of the business elite, characterised by an 'enforceable trust' as articulated by Kadushin, underlines its fragmentation from employees lower down the organisational hierarchy. This, in itself, is nothing new. However, US-style remuneration, now making inroads in leading French companies, as Table 7.9 highlights, can only accentuate this division further. Though the salaries of leading CEOs are not as high in France as they are in the UK, leading French CEOs earning an average of €1.9 million in 2003 as against €3.2 million for leading British CEOs, nevertheless US executive remuneration norms are increasingly prevalent at the top. So, too, are bonuses for CEOs of under-performing companies, Patrick Kron receiving €733,000 in bonuses in 2003 despite Alstom's well-documented difficulties that year.

At the same time, it is increasingly clear, as Dawson argues, that corporate governance reform in itself is not enough.[165] Any regulatory measure, when introduced, may carry with it unforeseen consequences, an element of 'gamesmanship'. It is ironic that remuneration committees, designed initially as a means of monitoring executive pay, should have become one of the levers by which executive remuneration has continued its seemingly inexorable rise. Benchmarking, the perceived global nature of the market for executive talent, is another: the argument that remuneration packages should be designed to attract and retain the best talent around the world, has patently won the day. It is difficult to avoid the conclusion that efforts to induce restraint in this area may be ultimately doomed to failure, as large companies continue their rise to dominance, knocking out smaller players, with an increasing number of leading British companies, such as Tesco, BP and HSBC, breaking new profit records. Increasingly, this culture of high rewards is all around. In 2004-05, for example, football players in the English Premiership earned more than £1 billion between them; while, in June 2005, the Prime Minister's wife, Cherie Blair, thought nothing of collecting £30,000 for a single lecture in Washington on life at Number 10.[166]

Some commentators point to the contradiction between the globalisation of markets on the one hand, and the national nature of the governance polemic, and its apparent solutions, on the other.[167] In the global economy, so the argument goes, leading industrialised nations are required to re-examine their practices if they wish to succeed. Countries that exhibit leaner, more competitive practices are deemed to possess an inbuilt advantage, as illustrated by the UK. The 35-hour week, for example, introduced by the Jospin government in 1998, which became compulsory for companies with 20 employees or more in 2000, stood in stark contrast to the long working hours culture of the UK, which chose to opt out of the 1993 EU working hours directive.[168] In 2003, French workers worked an average of 1,431 hours, compared to 1,673 hours in the UK.[169] Thought to place a heavy burden on French business, and having failed singularly to reduce France's unemployment rate, which remained stubbornly stuck at 10 per cent, the 35-hour week was effectively abolished in March 2005, despite being perceived by many as an inalienable social gain. At the same time, a bank holiday was withdrawn on 16 May 2005, to public consternation, ostensibly to pay for the old, several thousand having perished in the heat wave of August 2003.

Yet to condemn the French social model is arguably to judge the French from a purely Anglo-American habitus and perspective. Concepts, like words, do not always translate easily from one worldview to another. Belief in France in the social interest of the firm remains – despite the abandonment of the 35-hour working week, the removal of production sites to low-wage countries, and the increasingly high remuneration packages awarded to senior executives. Similarly, the UK continues to resist tooth and nail any further move towards a European social democratic model, such as the removal of the British opt-out on the 48-hour working week, which MEPs sought to impose in May 2005. That said, as a fully-fledged member of the EU, and with the recent increase in majority voting, and the shift eastwards in its centre of gravity, the UK may ultimately have to accept further change in the area of company law, which may have the effect of moving it further away from the Anglo-American family of countries.

Nevertheless, it is the case that great strides have been made in corporate governance reform in both countries in little over a decade. What matters is structure, Sir Adrian Cadbury argues, not its particular form.[170] The cultural substrata that underlie both societies go deep, often acting as powerful impediments to, or facilitators of change. Like slow-moving glaciers, gradual, incremental change at this deeper level is much harder to observe. We do not notice the Earth's tectonic plates shifting; yet over time the results can be spectacular. Viewed in this light, over the long term, further convergence is likely. Our research over the period 1998 to 2003, however, has pointed overwhelmingly not to the convergence of the French and British business systems, but rather to the persistence of national distinctiveness, to the strength of cultural reproduction, despite globalisation and more than a decade of corporate governance reform.

8
Conclusion – Elites, Power and Governance

'Economics, management techniques, industrial psychology: all were frequently looked upon with grave suspicion, for they represented attempts to professionalize an activity long carried on jointly by "practical men" and gentlemanly amateurs'.

D.C. Coleman, 1973 [1]

This book has compared and contrasted corporate governance in two national business systems, seeking to delve beneath the surface to examine how power and authority are exercised by business elites in France and the UK. To this end it has explored key research themes concerning elites: their education, careers, lifestyles, networks, activities and reproduction, examining corporate governance in relation to the experience, mindsets and predilections of the directors who run global corporations. The aim has been to get to the bottom of how and why the French and UK business systems function in such different ways, drawing important conclusions with respect to the future of national business systems within the new global economy.

This concluding chapter reviews the main findings and arguments presented in earlier chapters. It brings together the key elements of our analysis and interpretation concerning elite cohesion, corporate and personal networking, the tendency towards cultural and social reproduction in both countries, and the importance of multiple 'structuring structures' in determining who rises to the top in business, winning admission to the circles of the ruling elite. The chapter underscores our findings on the relationship between corporate governance and business elites, which, it is argued, are inextricably meshed together. It considers to what extent corporate governance in the two countries is converging on a single model – more specifically, to what degree corporate governance in France is

239

assuming the governance characteristics of the UK business system. Finally, it reflects on the likely future development of corporate governance and business elites in both countries, in this way adding to the current debate on big issues of the day such as executive pay, business regulation, ethics and corporate social responsibility.

Elite cohesion and institutional solidarity

First, we have demonstrated that elite cohesion is achieved very differently in France and the UK. While the ties that bind the French business elite tend to be institutional and strong, those that unite the business elite in Britain are in part social in nature and relatively weak. In France, networking is an institutional feature, systemically embedded, whereas in the UK it is accepted that networking, though essential for companies and individual careers, should never compromise board members or prevent them from looking after the immediate interests of the business.

As Barsoux and Lawrence point out, 'Where America extols money ... Germany work and Great Britain blood, France has nailed its flag to the post of cleverness'.[2] The enormous value France places on intellect and educational achievement is apparent in the qualifications and career trajectories of its business elites. Whereas 28.4 per cent of the UK directors in our full sample had a higher degree, 80.6 per cent of the French could lay claim to five years or more in higher education, many attending more than one *grande école*. In France, elite coherence is fostered early in life by the likelihood of attending the same *lycées*, with more than one fifth of our sample (20.4 per cent) attending three Parisian *lycées* in particular, Louis-le-Grand, Janson-de-Sailly and Saint-Louis, as against 11.4 per cent attending the top three British schools, Eton, Winchester and Harrow. Elite coherence is boosted, more importantly, by the likelihood of attending the same *grandes écoles*. Foremost amongst these are Polytechnique, the Institut des Etudes Politiques de Paris (Sciences-Po), and the civil service school, the Ecole Nationale d'Administration (ENA), attended by 12.0 per cent, 11.8 per cent and 9.2 per cent of our sample respectively, with the most ambitious usually attending more than one of these establishments. This feature of the French system becomes yet more striking when the educational backgrounds of the super-elite, the 100 most powerful directors in France in 1998, are considered: 36 per cent attended one of three Parisian schools and 61 per cent attended either Polytechnique or Sciences-Po. This concentration on a handful of schools and institutions of higher education is itself illustrative of the fact that many high flyers embark on a career path that is well mapped out in advance, and, in this sense, secure. There is, of course, a parallel concentration in the UK on Oxbridge, attended by more than one-quarter of the British business elite (29.4 per cent of known attendances).

For those who do well in France, attendance at a *grande école* may be followed by the invitation to join one of the civil service *grand corps*, the 'clubbish' nature of which is exemplified by the characteristic *tutoiement* among members – the use of *tu*, the more familiar form of address. The *grands corps* serve as funnels to channel the cream of the *grandes écoles* to the top jobs, with the best students invited to spend time in a ministerial Cabinet under the tutelage of a leading politician – both indicative of, and preserving, the strong ties the French business elite enjoys with government, apparent too in the common pursuit of a qualification in political economy from Sciences-Po. The French business elite benefits also from the strong ties of company relationships, sometimes founded on cross shareholdings, but more especially on reciprocal directors' mandates. At the time of privatisation, elite solidarity was bolstered though the creation of the *noyaux durs*, peopled, naturally, by business elites.[3] These so-called 'hard cores' of stable shareholders were often built on long-standing relationships, as state actors exploited existing networks to ensure that controlling stakes remained in safe hands. While the *noyaux durs* may have unravelled substantially since the mid-1990s, the relationships on which they were founded often endure, cemented by interlocking directorships.

The use of *tu* among members of a particular *grands corps* is itself illustrative of the fact that elite solidarity in France is essentially institutional solidarity. Elite solidarity is institutionally embedded and served by the state – in the same way that two centuries previously Napoleon sought, through the creation of the *grandes écoles*, to institutionalise the recruitment of elites, thus promoting administrative efficiency. Similarly, in the aftermath of the Second World War, it was the strong belief of General de Gaulle that the Republic's elite had failed the country through its collaboration with the Germans, as a consequence of which he established ENA, the brainchild of Michel Debré, to bring in new blood, not drawing on the old families who were part of the former elite, now discredited.[4] The new school was conceived as providing future members of the administrative elite, rigorously selected and highly educated, who would direct and manage the apparatus of an expansive, modernising and transformatory state.

France's image is that of a nation of high taxes and bureaucracy, articulated most famously in Michel Crozier's seminal work, *Le Phénomène bureaucratique*, where bureaucracy is presented as a social tool that legitimises control of the many by the few.[5] Widespread criticism has been levelled against the *grandes écoles*, according to which their graduates, being relatively few in number, are inculcated in the view that they are an elite, omniscient, a superior caste set apart from the rest. As Crozier argues, 'At all levels of society the French, once they gain entry into an influential group, instinctively try to keep others out',[6] echoing Bourdieu's observation, 'Every real inquiry into the divisions of the social world has to analyse the interests associated with membership or non-membership'.[7] This theme of exclusion and inclusion is an important one, operating at all levels and in every arena in which elites come together. Pierre Bilger recounts his experience of both in his autobiography. Here, he explains how the award by the Minister of Industry of the prestigious *Légion d'honneur*, a sought-after emblem of elite membership, was followed six months later by the refusal of the Alstom remuneration committee to honour his stock options, which he interpreted as 'a desire for rupture and separation between the board of directors and the departing PDG'.[8]

At the same time, *grandes écoles* graduates have been criticised in the past as predominately risk-averse, their talents employed in scaling bureaucratic hierarchies rather than exploiting business opportunities. Nevertheless, France is highly efficient in its production and reproduction of business elites, institutionalised by the state to ensure that only its star pupils reach the higher echelons of business, politics and administration. The high level of training from which *grandes écoles* graduates benefit allows a rapid grasp of complex issues. This efficiency in producing and reproducing business elites is arguably a key source of French economic success in the post-war period. The mentality that characterises *grandes écoles* graduates is now far more ready to embrace risk than hitherto, as numerous examples in this book have shown.

Solidarity among the French elite is further reinforced by the extraordinary concentration of elite establishments, and individuals, in Paris and its surrounding area – home to the best schools, the best educational institutions, the key organs of government, the headquarters of most leading companies, as well as the *haute bourgeoisie* (in the stylish sixteenth *arrondissement*). Nine of the top ten schools most frequently attended by elite members are located in the Paris basin (eight in Paris proper and one in Versailles), as are nine of the top ten higher education institutions (the exception being Harvard), whereas the top British schools and universities are more evenly distributed throughout the UK, with none of the schools most frequently attended by British business elites, and just three institutions of higher education, located in London. While this formidable concentration on the Paris area has led in the past to accusations of a two-tier nation – most famously in *Paris et le désert français*[9] – there can be little doubt that the domination of the capital has played a key role in fostering strong ties among the French business elite. In stark contrast, elite cohesion in the UK is much weaker than in France. Large companies are much less densely networked, either by ties of ownership or by interlocking directorships. In consequence, elite solidarity is fostered indirectly through the involvement of members of the elite in 'third party' events and institutions, and in this sense elite solidarity is more assuredly based on social solidarity. Club membership is a powerful symbol of inclusion, signifying social acceptance while providing opportunities for interaction.[10] As Jean-François Théodore put it, 'People in the UK find a social life is very important to them. In France, people feel that private life is private life'.[11] This concurs with Donald Coleman's view that 'social ambition provided an immensely powerful motor of business activity', with profits offering 'a path to prestige, power, status, personal satisfaction, adventures made, purpose and achievements gained'.[12] Or as Harold Perkin put it, 'the pursuit of wealth *was* the pursuit of social status'.[13] Both Coleman and Perkin were describing Britain at the time of the industrial revolution; but their remarks still have currency today.

Elite cohesion in the UK is achieved through acquaintances rather than close friends and business associates – in other words predominately through weak ties, which paradoxically can be a source of great strength – an insight made famous by Granovetter. His thesis on 'the strength of weak ties' highlights how resources flow disproportionately to individuals who connect otherwise disparate groups. According to this view, 'weak ties, often denounced as generative of alienation ... are here seen as indispensable to individuals' opportunities and to their integration into communities'.[14] The indirect contacts that link members of the British business elite are often formed through cross-membership of elite non-business institutions, such as the boards of cultural, educational and charitable organisations. Private members' clubs likewise provide meeting places and bring together elite individuals from different fields. More that half of Britain's top 100 directors in 1998 belonged to a London club. Many more were members of elite sport clubs, and major sporting events such as racing at Ascot, the Henley regatta and sailing at Cowes provide symbolically-loaded opportunities for elite networking. One-fifth of the British super-elite regularly played golf, with tennis and cricket proving the next most popular sporting activities. Through his experience as a French Chief Executive Officer (CEO) in London, honoured by that City for his contribution, the perceptions of Jean-François Théodore are especially valid. He observes that if one declines to take part in sport – shooting, hunting and fishing in particular – an opportunity is lost, and 'you see very clearly that you've missed some connection'.[15] For Théodore, who has a fondness for opera, theatre and films, sport is an important cohesive force that binds the British business elite together. This said, the French too have recognised the value of corporate hospitality at elite sporting events. According to Messier, the plot to unseat him as PDG of Vivendi-Universal was hatched at a France-Wales rugby match held in Cardiff's Millennium Stadium.[16]

It is telling that elite cohesion is achieved in such different ways in two European countries just a few miles apart. In France, where ambitious individuals need above all to be institutionally bonded, possession of high-level qualifications is a prerequisite for entry into the elite, whereas this is not the case in Britain, where a surprising number of the super-elite of 1998 lacked a university degree. Even in the twenty-first century, Donald Coleman's thesis that British business is run largely by amateurs is, in some respects, apparently not too far off the mark. Coleman highlights the inbuilt British distrust of science and theoretically based knowledge, characterised by an 'admiration for well-bred ignorance and contempt for education'.[17] The remnants of this attitude are in evidence today, thrown into stark relief by comparison with the intellect-admiring and highly educated French business elite.

It is not uncommon for French chief executives to write books as a way of making their intellectual mark, recorded with pride in *Who's Who* entries, and often on the topic of governance. Jean Peyrelevade's *Pour un capitalisme intelligent* was written while PDG of Union des Assurances de Paris (UAP).[18] His follow-up to this book, written during his tenure at Crédit Lyonnais, was entitled, precisely, *Le Gouvernement d'entreprise* (1999).[19] Authoring such books permits ambitious members of the French business elite to stake out their claim as a potential leader of the business community. Whilst British academics have seen their social status and income eroded over the past quarter of a century, in France university professors have ascended on occasion to the uppermost echelons of politics and business. Professors of economics are especially valued. Notable examples include Raymond Barre, professor of economics at Sciences-Po and Paris I, who served as Prime Minister under Giscard d'Estaing (1976-81); Edmond Alphandéry, Professor of Economics at Paris II (1975-93) who served as Minister of the Economy (1993-95) and PDG of Electricité de France (EdF); and Lionel Jospin, Professor of Economics at the Institut Universitaire de Technologie de Paris-Sceaux (1970-81), and subsequently Prime Minister between 1997 and 2002. In the UK, meanwhile, just a handful of academics from the field of business have joined the boards of listed companies as non-executive directors (including Professors Sue Birley, Deanne Julius, and, more recently, Sandra Dawson); they form a tiny minority and none has held an executive role.

Transaction costs in a socially based system are arguably higher than in an institutionally based system. System-wide efficiency in the production and reproduction of business elites is not achieved in the UK. Whereas in France the system is geared towards providing future members of a highly selected, well-educated elite to run the state and its leading companies, in the UK the onus is not on institutions but individuals. The latter is more haphazard and more wasteful, depending primarily on the social ambition and networking skills of aspiring individuals.

Cultural reproduction

Secondly, it is clear that in both France and the UK, there is a strong tendency towards cultural reproduction, inducing continuity whilst not preventing change. In the course of this research, we have been struck continually by the salience of cultural reproduction, the reassertion of social and cultural patterns, often in the face of apparent change. This is in many ways consistent with the explanation offered by Bourdieu – namely that the ingrained and socially constituted dispositions of social classes lead actors to make choices and decisions which, in turn, reproduce existing social structures and status distinctions.[20] Newcomers, such as Peter Orton of HIT Entertainment, who succeed in advancing their fortunes and legitimacy, regularly adopt the social and cultural practices of the established elite, into which they become integrated.

Cultural reproduction manifests itself at board level in particular. The boardroom is a place of conformity, requiring a common mindset and pattern of behaviours to formulate and execute strategy. Efforts to increase the size of the 'gene pool' of British non-executive directors championed by the Higgs Review, or parallel attempts in France to limit the number of directors' mandates to no more than five, thus increasing, at least in theory, the requisite number of directors, are likely to find that existing boardroom cultures are resistant to change.[21] In the UK, where the former directors of Equitable Life have been sued by the successor board, the pool of directors is likely to remain restricted until issues of potential liability are clarified.[22] The fees for a non-executive director today are out of sync with the growing demands of the job and the risks that go with it. Similarly in France, the emphasis on directors' competence, presented in the Bouton Report as more important than independence, is likely to militate against any significant expansion in the numbers of potential directors, since only the experienced can arguably be competent. Lack of experience on the part of potential directors is an issue, too, in the UK. As Lord Waldegrave commented:

> The government thinks there's a huge pool of people who can be good non-execs just waiting to do it. The trouble is there are plenty of people who don't understand any of this, don't understand the liabilities involved, don't understand how serious it is being a director of a public company, who will put themselves on boards because they think that is the best thing to do, then get themselves into trouble and get the companies into trouble.[23]

Schools and institutions of higher education play a key part in the process of cultural reproduction in both countries, reinforcing, rather than lessening, social differences through establishing a system of dispositions, 'a present past that tends to perpetuate itself into the future'.[24] In the UK, public schools have endeavoured over decades and centuries to instil in their pupils a 'gentlemanly code' of behaviour where 'the ancient themes of chivalry, military prowess, and a code of honour [are] transmuted into a world in which cricket, moral virtue, and patriotism are identical'.[25] This equivalence between sporting and academic success was underlined by several of our interviewees. It was passage through such schools and the ancient universities which conferred, Coleman observes, 'membership of the right club', a notion which was 'an integral part of the gentlemanly ethos in practice', and which, illustrating the processes of cultural reproduction, has demonstrated a prodigious ability to survive.[26] The survival of the notion that sporting success and leadership are part and parcel of the same behavioural code was confirmed by a 2005 MORI survey of British captains of industry. Half of the 105 business leaders interviewed were found to have captained a school sports team, with 90 per cent having assumed at least two leadership roles at school, whether prefect, head boy or deputy head.[27] Clearly, it is still the same intrinsic type of natural leader and gifted sportsman who makes it to the top in British business, even if there are some small signs that both Britain and France are becoming more open, meritocratic societies. Sir Digby Jones, knighted in the January 2005 New Year Honours list, was a scholarship boy at Bromsgrove School, who has made it to the top by dint of hard work and natural talent. Lindsay Owen-Jones, sent by his parents to Uppingham School and Oxford, was the product of a family that invested in their son's education as a means of social advancement. (They intended their son to pursue a diplomatic career. At Oxford, however, he met Olivier Giscard d'Estaing, brother of the former president, who told him to go to INSEAD instead: 'Nothing ever gets done in chancelleries', he said, 'The real diplomacy gets done in business meetings'.[28]) Public school was expected above all, of course, to instil 'the habits of confident social superiority ... in a stratified society'.[29] Its continued ability to do so was illustrated by one business leader, who summed up his talents as follows: 'I was competitive and sporting and a natural leader and also quite clever and hardworking'.[30]

Sport is also emphasised in the French *grandes écoles*, at Polytechnique in particular, with its Napoleonic, military code and distinctive uniform. Jean-Louis Beffa, PDG at Saint-Gobain since 1986, extols the regime at Polytechnique, and explains how wearing the uniform in particular helped to diminish the sense of oddness he felt as a provincial boy from the south:

> The sportive training offered by the military staff at Ecole Polytechnique is one of great quality ... I remember that in my younger days, wearing the school's uniform meant a lot to me. For the young man coming from Nice (in the South of France) that I was, it was a way to erase all the differences that existed between students coming up from the provinces and those brought up in the prestigious Parisian preparatory courses, such as the Lycée Louis-le-Grand.[31]

The power of cultural reproduction also helps to explain the underrepresentation of women in the boardroom. While the relative absence of women from top management positions is often attributed to women's orientation towards home and family,[32] the failure of women to assimilate organisational cultures can be seen to be equally important. Ambitious female executives must assimilate the prevalent (male) culture sufficiently to be accepted by their colleagues. Driscoll and Goldberg note the particular importance for aspiring women managers of being able to play golf, enjoyed, as mentioned, by one fifth of British super-elite members.[33] This goes back to Bourdieu's concept of habitus. The executive class, in Britain and France, has practices and dispositions that women cannot easily follow. Women may struggle to satisfy cultural practices that include long working hours; a readiness to travel; never saying no; and the notion that the company always comes first. In failing to develop required cultural practices and mannerisms – such as the 'right' bearing, or a sense of self-assurance – women fail to qualify for membership of the top executive fraternity, from which they are effectively excluded. This partly explains why women succeed more easily in protected sub-cultures like personnel, removed from the front line of the company's commercial imperative, and more self-conscious about what is going on. Through failing to display internalised behaviours that define them as boardroom material, women suffer from what Bourdieu terms 'misrecognition' – the erroneous assumption that there are few women in the company at the right level worthy of promotion to the very highest positions.

Surface similarities and deeper structural differences

Thirdly, when comparing the governance regimes of two national business systems such as France and the UK, it is important to distinguish between ostensible, superficial similarities and deeper structural differences. In Figure 1.1, we present the dimensions of a national business system as a pyramid, existing on three interrelated levels.[34] Changes at the level of governance practices (the top layer), to recap, are only ever likely to prove stable and enduring if mirrored by parallel changes in the dominant ideology (the bottom layer).

Since the early 1990s, both France and the UK have experienced a plethora of governance reforms, such that the uppermost level depicted in Figure 1.1 has been subject to very strong isomorphic forces. Whether these reforms are likely to stick, however, depends ultimately on their being matched at level three; yet it is here that difference is most pronounced. To cite one small example, the uptake of the English language by French multinationals has been, as we have seen, dramatic in the past decade, widely used in meetings and emails despite the disapproval of the Académie Française, a staunch defender of the linguistic 'purity' of French. In January 2005, however, French trade unionists won an important victory over the imposed use of English at one company in particular, General Electric Medical Systems. The union claimed successfully that this breached the 1994 Toubon law, which requires all foreign expressions to be translated into French inside the workplace, as a result of which the company must now provide French translations of all vital documents.[35] This ruling was the first of its kind, running counter to the new trend for companies in France to use English as their first language, and providing a small but telling example of how the French may revert to type, even in the face of an apparent *fait accompli*.

This is not to say that there has been no change at this deeper, ideological level. The state machinery for the production of business elites provides an excellent training ground for the circumstances and conditions of globalisation. Informed by General de Gaulle's obsessive pursuit of grandeur, it engenders in its trainees an 'expansive mindset', an ability to think on a grand scale, such that the best students to emerge from elite establishments run by the state are not afraid of large numbers – the billions that, understandably, frighten many businessmen. Our research into the merger and acquisition (M & A) activities of the top 100 French companies from 1998 to 2003 reveals that 23 were major acquirers during the period, while many were engaged in limited M & A activity. This level of activity closely resembles that undertaken by top 100 UK companies, 32 of which were major acquirers during the period. However, the French deals tended to be lower in value, with M & A deals worth $1 billion or more led by top 100 French companies from 1998 to 2003 totalling $418.8 billion altogether, while those led by their British counterparts were worth more than twice as much, $942.3 billion.[36] The activities of major French acquirers such as AXA, France Télécom and Suez nevertheless suggest that the allegedly risk-averse mindset of *grandes écoles* graduates mentioned above now refers to a largely bygone era, having given way to an expansive mindset, which encourages bold moves. However, this does lead them, on occasion, to get it badly wrong. Individuals such as Jean-Marie Messier, who took Vivendi-Universal to the brink of bankruptcy following a spending spree costing billions of dollars, or Michel Bon of France Télécom, whose spate of acquisitions (including Wanadoo in 1998, Orange, Global One and Mobil-Com in 2000 followed by Equant and Freeserve in 2001) resulted in a debt mountain of €68 billion by 2002, do not necessarily think in marginal economic terms. Overly preoccupied with the grand scale perhaps, they tend to lack the 'shareholder value mindset' of seeking improvements at the margin, more typical of British businessmen. The French pursuit of glory and prestige represents a fundamental difference between the two business systems, highlighted by a British manager at Airbus UK: 'The French don't go in for the normal rate of return. The French go for glory over cost, whereas the British go for profit over cost!'[37]

The availability of information has also played a key role: 'instantaneous, free, and universal – [it] has brought the reality of change to everyone everywhere'.[38] Financial markets are increasingly demanding information that may impact on investment risk. The Nouvelles Régulations Economiques (NRE) have greatly expanded the scale and scope of information French firms are required to provide in annual reports, making it publicly available to investors and other interested parties.[39] The increasing internationalisation of French business at all levels – the composition of the board; ownership and investment; the listing of French companies on international stock exchanges, and so on – has already had profound consequences for corporate governance in France as well as for the French business elite. According to Pierre Bilger, the dramatic fall from grace experienced by Jean-Marie Messier in 2002 resulted from the rising tide of criticism from Vivendi's American directors and shareholders:

> A lot of French businessmen were thinking that the time had come to end the story ... The reputation of the country was at stake, and that of the French stock market, especially as a consequence of the involvement of Americans in the story.[40]

In Bilger's eyes, when the establishment ganged up on Messier to remove him from office, ultimately it acted in concert to safeguard the reputation of the French business model, which Messier was presumed guilty of bringing into disrepute. Messier bitterly resented the role of Claude Bébéar in his demise. In *Mon vrai journal*, he recounts a conversation between Bébéar and other business leaders which, he claims, took place at the aforementioned rugby match in Cardiff: '[Messier] represents a danger to the marketplace of Paris, and to France's image abroad', Bébéar is alleged to have said. 'We must act, we must have his scalp'.[41] In late spring 2002, the eight French directors on the board of Vivendi-Universal, who had backed Messier in the face of opposition from the five US directors, withdrew their support, one by one.

Such exemplary punishment of a member of the elite is not, of course, new in French history. From time to time, in a symbolic catharsis and confirmation of national identity and values, heads must roll. Examples of this include the Revolutions of 1789 and 1848, the seizure of power by Louis Bonaparte in 1851, the 1871 Commune, and the execution of alleged collaborators after the Liberation of 1944.[42] Such punishment arguably works to support the stability and cohesion of the group as a whole, 'cleansed' and absolved by the act of retribution. It is a sharp reminder, too, to any other elite member of the fate that may befall him should he – it is usually he – see himself as more important than the group. The ousting of Jean-Marie Messier thus fulfils a key function. It is a symbolic reaffirmation of the collective sentiments and ideas that together make up the unity and integrity of the French business model.

A second example of deeper, structural change is provided by the increasing press intrusion into the private lives of the elite, indicative of the fact that greater openness and transparency at the level of governance practices is making inroads into the dominant ideology, through a trickle-down effect. There has long been a reticence in France to expose the private lives of prominent individuals, backed up by draconian privacy laws. President

Mitterrand's illegitimate daughter, Mazarine Pingeot, was 20 before her existence was revealed in 1995 in the pages of *Paris Match*; prior to this, her father is said to have used an anti-terrorism unit to keep the fact of her existence a state secret. That the press turned a blind eye to their dalliances enabled Presidents Giscard, Mitterrand and Chirac to enjoy numerous relationships known about by those in the media but not reported on. There are signs, however, that the French press is increasingly willing to flout this taboo where a direct conflict of interest is perceived.[43] Mazarine Pingeot herself has now written an autobiography about her strange upbringing, entitled *Bouche Cousue* ('Not a Word'),[44] while the Chiracs have gone public on the pain they feel over the severe anorexia that afflicts their elder daughter, Laurence, who lives in care in Paris.[45]

Traditionally, French society has been extraordinarily tolerant of abuses of power, as its remarkable equanimity in the face of the widespread corruption and financial misdemeanours of its ruling elite amply demonstrates. Now, however, the sheer number of articles filling newspapers on the theme of petty corruption by elites suggests that the public is increasingly impatient for higher standards among those who rule over them. Business ethics are becoming a more pressing concern. Lindsay Owen-Jones sums up the importance of doing business honestly:

> Today, words are not enough. Only the facts – better performance – will do. But the facts have to be truthful. Business ethics are not a restraint that companies place on themselves for moral reasons. Doing business honestly is also the most efficient way to do business long-term … Short term, you can cheat and get away with it. Over time you can't.[46]

Yet the close links between business and politics, which gave rise, directly or indirectly, to many of the corporate scandals outlined in these pages, persist. Hervé Gaymard was replaced as Finance Minister in February 2005 not by a politician, as one might expect, but by the CEO of France Télécom, Thierry Breton.

Multiple structuring structures

Fourthly, the evidence we bring forth in this study confirms the hypothesis that multiple 'structuring structures' determine who rises to the top in both France and the UK. Bourdieu defines the enduring dispositions of 'habitus' as 'structured structures predisposed to function as structuring structures, that is, as principles which generate and organize practices and representations'.[47] The three main structures that determine who succeeds are family, education, and corporate and professional bodies. The benefit of a supportive, well-endowed, well-connected family, and the key role played by education in the process of selection, conferring membership of the 'right club' and creating opportunities for networking, are well understood. Both play an obvious role in the preservation and perpetuation of stratification, notwithstanding evidence of upward social mobility. It is interesting how often directors from less affluent backgrounds cite their families as a key reason for their success. Bill Cockburn, for example, attributes much of his career success to his mother: 'Despite the demands of managing a family of eight children she found time to coach me to aim high, work hard, have fun and develop a determination to succeed'.[48] Family ownership is of enduring significance in France, as indeed is the state, in stark contrast to the near complete corporatism of business life in the UK, which has evolved as the corporate economy *par excellence*, and in which ownership and control are profoundly separated.

It is clear from the careers data presented in this book, however, that companies and professional bodies equally are very important structures in their own right in determining who rises to the top. Organisations demonstrate the ability to structure careers by both inclusion and exclusion. Early career choices are critical. Mobility is generally frowned upon in France, implying that a candidate is disloyal, 'fly-by-night' and therefore suspect. The UK, influenced perhaps by American perceptions, is reputedly more favourable to the notion of mobility as a means of gaining experience.[49] In fact, at the pinnacle of the business elite in both countries, there is little evidence of frequent job moves. On the contrary, it is the people who remain in a company a long time, insiders who stay the course, who often do well. We might expect this of France, where CEOs, such as Owen-Jones at L'Oréal and Beffa at Saint-Gobain, regularly remain in post for 20 years and more. What is more surprising, perhaps, is that this is also true of the UK. Both Sir Mark Moody Stuart and Philip Watts, for example, who head our British super-elite, served their entire executive careers at Shell, while Lord Browne, in third position, has spent his working life at BP, which he joined in 1966 on leaving university. John Bond, Chairman of HSBC, joined the Midland Bank in 1961 (without a university education) and worked his way up. Bill Cockburn joined the Post Office in Glasgow in 1961 (also without a university education) and was appointed to its board in 1981, becoming CEO in 1992. Sir Terry Leahy's loyalty to Tesco, which he joined in 1979 as a marketing executive, becoming its CEO in 1997, has earned him the nickname 'Terry Tesco'.[50]

It is interesting that these three structuring structures of family, education and organisation should be equally important in both countries. France and the UK are endowed with very different institutions, though significantly we have found similar results. There is, of course, a notable exception to this generalisation. In France, unlike the UK, joining a government ministry immediately on completing an elite education, is considered a legitimate first career move, at least as desirable as joining the ranks of a large international company. There is a recognised equivalence of stature and experience between private and public organisations that enables high-flying state employees to move across to a private company at a high level in mid-career. For aspirants to the very top positions in society, seemingly, there is no significant public-private divide. In the UK, such moves are extremely rare and generally not welcomed: the mindsets, experiences and personal dispositions of business leaders and senior civil servants being seen as incompatible, if not entirely polarised.

Corporate governance and business elites

Corporate governance and business elites are linked inextricably together. In order to understand boards more fully, we need to turn the spotlight on the behaviour, mindsets and predilections of those who sit on boards. The study of corporate governance has all too seldom been concentrated on the very powerful, those at the summit of very large organisations.[51] It is companies, as legal entities, that have power, defined as command over resources, but it is through individuals – company directors – that power is exercised.

Our twin themes are linked, too, through the mechanisms of cultural reproduction, which generate social continuity while not entirely impeding reform. This helps to explain how business elites reproduce and regenerate themselves when their membership, at an individual level, is constantly changing. Power is shaped by the outcomes of earlier contests, allowing parvenus to gain admission into the inner circle. However, once admitted, one-time radicals most often fall in naturally with the existing rules, roles and worldview of the establishment, which they replenish and renew. The reassertion of old patterns even at a time of ostensible upheaval is noted by Coleman, who writes: 'And, as usual in partial revolutions, sooner or later the values of the revolutionaries succumb to those of the surviving elite who, in turn, modify their own standards to fit the new situation'.[52] Here Coleman joins hands with Bourdieu, whose conception of society is one of change and contestation within regulating, self-reproducing structures. Bourdieu contends that any challenge to the old guard and accompanying advance of new factions in society may lead, through the acquisition of symbolic capital by the latter, to the legitimisation and integration of the newcomers within the elite. In this way it leads, ultimately, to the reassertion of the *status quo*, albeit one that may have been modified slightly by the new elements incorporated and subsumed within it.

We have observed the importance of social reproduction in schools and institutions of higher education in both countries, ostensibly designed to promote the best, which they often do, of which there are many examples in this book. Yet, in many ways, schools and institutions of higher education, in looking for conformity rather than difference, promote the same, thus serving the establishment. Many of those who succeed in spite of their difference, or even because of their difference, seek through their success, by the logic of homologies, to conform, embracing elite practices and attitudes. This is well documented in Coleman's celebrated article, 'Gentleman and Players': successful players wanted their own sons to be gentlemen, to display the sought-after 'habits of confident social superiority' and follow the 'gentlemanly code' which, in Britain, only the public schools and ancient universities could instil, thus enabling 'the family crossing of the great social divide to be completed'.[53] The acquisition of symbolic capital and the material trappings of elitism may further reinforce the coherence of elite practices and attitudes. The self-made businessman François Pinault, for example, the son of a small farmer who left school at 16 and founded Pinault, now part of Pinault-Printemps-Redoute (PPR), owns a stylish château at Rambouillet at which President Chirac celebrated his victory in the 1995 presidential elections.

We have noted above the importance of cultural reproduction in the boardroom, which itself serves the *status quo*, despite calls for the gene pool of potential directors to be widened. The coherence of elite attitudes and practices in the boardroom works to exclude others from membership. Interestingly, the very features of corporate governance reform may also serve incumbent elites by legitimising them. The workings of remuneration committees are a case in point, demonstrating how elements of corporate governance reform can be subsumed and adapted to serve the *status quo* and promote the existing elite. Since the advent of remuneration committees in both countries, the remuneration packages of business executives, as we have seen, have been boosted rather than held in check. This is not to say that this could not, in future, be remedied – in particular by taking into consideration salary levels throughout the whole company.[54] Excessive pay awards to failed executives in particular give remuneration committees a bad name and diminish public confidence in their work, even when decisions on severance payments have been taken at a much earlier stage, at the time of appointment.

Competing capitalisms in an interdependent world

Much about the economies of France and the UK is strikingly similar, with populations near equal in size, and gross domestic product (GDP) and per capita GDP almost identical. Yet much that concerns these two national business systems is also sweepingly different – including annual hours worked; the continuing importance of family firms in France; and the value placed on qualifications in France, with the UK exhibiting signs of a long-standing anti-intellectualism. Even more fundamentally, the trajectories of the two economies have diverged since the 1960s as the UK progressively has abandoned manufacturing industry in favour of the service sector. A very different mindset has prevailed in France, where political and business elites have joined forces over decades to support large-scale manufacturing enterprises. One way or another, public resources have found their way into what are now private enterprises, building up manufacturing companies large enough and sufficiently capable to compete successfully in the global economy. The transport and power engineering sectors, for example, have flourished, creating a buoyant labour market for graduate engineers. In consequence, the status and rewards of engineers have remained high, elevating individual engineers to positions of power and authority within the ruling elite, from where they are well placed to promote the interests of the manufacturing sector – offering another potent illustration of how cultural reproduction works to further the interests of the established order.

The different economic paths taken by France and Britain are reflective of the profound differences in elite mindsets and institutional structures explored in this book. Yet for every difference between the two countries it is possible to point to a similarity, and accurately reflecting the balance between the two is one of the most demanding challenges of cross-national comparative research. Both French and British companies, with the support of their respective governments, have adopted a proactive stance towards globalisation. They are major international investors and, as we have seen, have rapidly embraced the potentialities of global restructuring in pursuit of lower costs and increased market share. The business systems of France and the UK may differ considerably in their *modus operandi*, but this should not mask their proven capacity to adapt pragmatically when gripped by the challenges of global competition. What we are witnessing, in effect, are the responses of two *competing capitalisms* to globalisation, rather than the struggle between two 'divergent capitalisms' perceived by Whitley.[55] Perhaps this is nit-picking, but our essential point remains: while French and British companies and business leaders will continue to think and do many things differently, they will simultaneously think and do many other things that are very similar. Cultural reproduction should neither be confused with a lack of change nor with the triumph of difference over similarity.

This stands out in our comparison of corporate governance and business elites in France and the UK, which throws into salient relief the battle currently being fought between the so-called Anglo-American model of capitalism and the European social democratic model. In each case there is evidence of continuity and change, similarity and difference. In the UK, the once single-minded preoccupation with issues of shareholder value has given way to a broader concern for the social responsibilities of the corporation. There is a greater focus on social and environmental matters, sustainability, and ethical investment. Following the recommendations of the Turnbull Report on internal control, the London Stock Exchange (LSE) requires listed companies to provide in annual reports a statement on the management of risks that are considered to be 'significant to the fulfilment of its business objectives',[56] including social, environmental and reputational risks.[57] There is a greater understanding that cultural differences impact on performance, and a growing recognition worldwide of the importance to business success of speaking other languages – even if in the UK we so often lack the competence, or inclination, to do so.[58] As Peter Orton expressed it to us, 'the thing I most regret is that I was never given a French lesson: if I could speak four or five languages ... the opportunities would have been so great'.[59] In France, far-reaching internationalisation has forced listed companies to provide greater value for shareholders, to acknowledge the importance of investor relations, to focus more resolutely on financial issues and return on capital, and, to be more transparent through greater compulsory disclosure. There are signs, too, that the French public wishes to see higher ethical standards amongst its business and political elites, that petty corruption will no longer be tolerated as extensively as hitherto – though it remains part of the cultural fabric of the nation, as the resignation of Hervé Gaymard in 2005 confirms.

Yet, despite the increasing espousal on both sides of the Channel of many of the principles of sound corporate governance discussed in this book, our research points not to rapid convergence between the French and British business systems, but rather to the persistence and preservation of distinctive national traditions. Outward expressions of convergence, depicted at the uppermost level of Figure 1.1, are regularly challenged by the more deep-rooted structural continuities expressed in legal, institutional, political and intellectual practices. When we consider the key issue of convergence, it is often very difficult to discern precisely what is actually happening due, at times, to the blur created by the sheer number of signs and symbols of change on display, from the widespread adoption of governance committees to the increasingly sophisticated interventions of institutional investors. However, when we look deeper, we find incontrovertible evidence of inner structural continuity. In the course of the past 20 years, the French have privatised, engaged in mega-mergers, ceded the franc for the euro, and, since 1995, adopted many of the tenets of good corporate governance as recommended by a succession of French governance committees, following the British lead. This has led to new laws, the NRE and the *loi sur la sécurité financière* in particular. Yet their inner structures remain, in essence, remarkably similar to hitherto. There is, for example, little prospect of the French abandoning the dense corporate networks, bound together by multiple director interlocks, that are deemed by the British to compromise the independence of non-executive directors. Likewise, the strategy of overt expansion pursued by many large French companies in recent years, including Carrefour, EdF and Michelin, is also, paradoxically, a strategy of control, continuity and maintaining 'Frenchness'. Increasingly, French CEOs see themselves as international, while fundamentally French. As Daniel Bernard, PDG of Carrefour has expressed it: 'I consider myself, really, as international, but of French culture'.[60]

Jean-Louis Beffa, who refuses to 'play chameleon' with the notion of company identity, stresses the importance for companies operating on an international scale of retaining a distinctive national identity:

> At Saint-Gobain, we make it very clear that we are a French company and at the same time, we seek to be a company where non-French personnel can flourish. Playing chameleon would imply that we were trying to hide our French identity. Most companies who adopt a chameleon approach hold a strong position in one area and try to reassure the national environment in which they are active. But these companies remain indelibly marked by their national origin. At Saint-Gobain, we tell our managers that our system works on three levels: we have a French core, a European base and a worldwide strategy.[61]

As one of France's longest-standing companies, with a history stretching back almost 350 years, the glassmaker Saint-Gobain is itself an exemplar of change within continuity, or continuity within change. Its history mirrors, to a degree, the history of France. Established in 1665 as part of the economic reflation plan instigated by Colbert, one of France's greatest public administrators, its creations include the Hall of Mirrors at Versailles, and the futuristic, glass-fronted buildings of La Défense, the business sector situated outside Paris. Nationalised in 1982 under the Left, Saint-Gobain was the first company to be privatised four years later under the Right.

Final thoughts

The cultural substrata that underlie French and British society are deep rooted and enduring; we ignore them at our peril. In his most recent book, *Understanding the Process of Economic Change*, D.C. North emphasises the importance of structural and institutional continuity in determining the performance of present-day economies.[62] He is concerned with the underlying determinants of how economies evolve and rules change, finding that 'adaptive efficiency' depends very much on a society's ability to create and preserve institutions that are stable, broadly accepted and productive. French and British companies, in playing the global economic game, superficially may look the same, but when we dig deeper, much of what we find is distinctively French or British, giving rise to paradox and contradiction – as exemplified by the persistent attitude of British business leaders to government interference, urging politicians to keep their distance, while at the same time envying French business for the support it receives from the state.

Real change, Bourdieu suggests, can only ever be achieved through small, incremental changes; as DiMaggio observes: 'Bourdieu's is a world not of revolutions, or even of social change, but of endless transformations'.[63] Grand, sweeping reforms, of the sort in which France engages from time to time, should be eschewed, he argues, since sweeping changes lead to sweeping backlashes. Change, he claims, can only come from doing a lot of small things systematically, 'because those little things generate changes that generate changes'.[64] Thus, in Bourdieu's eyes, it is not the revolutionary or the social engineer who brings lasting change, but the gardener. Ultimately, his view is akin to that of Voltaire, as expressed in *Candide ou l'Optimisme*: 'il faut cultiver notre jardin'.[65]

This perspective on institutional and cultural change is one that we share. The UK, since the publication of the Cadbury Report, has come a long way in matters of corporate governance. Incremental rather than revolutionary change has been the order of the day. Widespread acceptance of the strictures of the Combined Code has put British companies in the vanguard of a process of reform now sweeping the world. Yet, even in the UK, the impact cannot be described as transformational. It will take many years yet before regulatory and procedural reforms percolate downwards to modify permanently the behaviour of members of the business elite. Compliance with a corporate governance code, as Roberts et al. point out, should never be taken as a proxy for board effectiveness. Their research into the roles of non-executive directors suggests instead that 'the key to board effectiveness lies in the degree to which non-executives acting individually and collectively are able to create accountability within the board in relation to *both* strategy *and* performance'.[66] In other words, what counts most are not the technical or legal aspects of a governance regime, but rather the quality of the performances of individual actors and the interactions between them – conditioned, of course, by the framework within which they operate.[67] Our own research has led to a very similar conclusion. A boardroom is more than a place where the agents of shareholders take decisions within a carefully specified set of rules and regulations. They are in essence small, elite communities that function in accordance with established cultural norms and standards. It follows that differences in the governance of French and British companies cannot be expunged simply by insisting on compliance with a universal code of best practice. Nor would it be desirable to do so. Convergence, in our view, does not mean that the corporate governance regimes of different countries should closely resemble one another, but rather that each should set the same exacting business and ethical standards. For, as Rousseau reminds us in *The Social Contract*, it is not form, but substance, which matters most – it is not so much the number, or timbre, of the different voices of the general will which should concern us, but on the contrary 'the common interest which unites them all'.[68]

Appendix 1 – Sources and Methods

This note provides a guide to the data sources and procedures underpinning the research for this book.

Research design

An elite group is defined by the selectivity of its membership and the rights and privileges that group membership confer. In the business world, the most exclusive groups are the boards of large companies, and, as a general rule, the bigger the company, the greater the status and rewards of board membership. We pragmatically define 'elite companies' as the one hundred largest enterprises in France and Britain respectively on 1 January 1998, and the 'business elites' of the two countries as consisting of the directors at the apex of those companies. The time period selected for the study was 1998 to 2003 inclusive. This was felt to be long enough to reveal patterns and trends but short enough to constitute a distinct historical period.

The research divided into four related sub-projects. First, a study of corporate governance within top 100 companies focusing on structures and events; secondly, a study of the education, qualifications, careers, roles and responsibilities of the full set of directors of top 100 companies; thirdly, an in-depth study of the social backgrounds, accomplishments and career trajectories of the 100 most powerful directors in France and the UK respectively; fourthly, an experiential study of the social reality of business elites and corporate governance based upon a set of semi-structured interviews with French and British elite members and governance experts.

Definition of top 100 companies

Selection through application of a single measure of corporate size was deemed inappropriate: turnover would favour retail companies and total capital employed natural resource companies, whilst using the number of employees would preference service sector companies. A composite measure was therefore developed, based on total capital employed, turnover, profit before tax, and number of employees. A number of sources were used to identify companies that might be considered for inclusion, such as listings published in *The Financial Times* and *Le Guide des Etats Majors des*

Grandes Entreprises (1998 and 1999 editions). Relevant data were gathered from a range of sources, including annual reports and accounts, for each of 500 (250 for each country) contender companies. These were then ranked for each individual measure and a composite ranking, weighting each measure equally, was generated to determine the rank order of top 100 companies presented in Tables A.2.1 and A.2.2 of Appendix 2.

Definition of business elite membership

For each company, annual reports and accounts were consulted to identify individuals holding the most senior posts in 1998. The resulting lists were confirmed through reference to various published works. For the UK, the main sources were *Who's Who* (1998-2004 editions) and the *PWC Corporate Register* (1999 edition). For France, the main sources were *Who's Who in France* (1998-2004 editions) and *Le Guide des Etats Majors des Grandes Entreprises* (1998-2004 editions).

In the case of UK companies, which all had a single-tier unitary board composed of executive and non-executive directors, all board members were included other than those holding purely honorary positions. In France, however, companies can choose between one of a number of governance models available under the law. Here the convention is to separate executive from non-executive directors. Non-executive directors sit in the 'upper house' and perform a range of strategic and control functions on behalf of different stakeholder groups. Executive directors sit in the 'lower house' and have operational responsibility for the business. There is limited overlap in membership between the two groups, most often confined to a single person, the Président-Directeur Général (PDG), who performs the combined role of Chairman and Chief Executive Officer (CEO). Most often there is a *conseil d'administration* (Board of Directors) and a *comité exécutif* (Executive Committee or Board) or alternatively a *conseil de surveillance* (Supervisory Board) and a *directoire* (Executive Board). Although there are important legal differences, the *comité exécutif* and the *directoire* essentially comprise a small number of top executives, charged with the day-to-day running of the enterprise, who report to the *conseil d'administration* or *conseil de surveillance*. The decision was taken to select directors from both 'upper' and 'lower' houses as members of the French business elite. However, only executive directors designated as belonging to a company's 'inner circle', as revealed in annual reports, were admitted to the database as direct equivalents to UK executive members of a main board.

The concept of power and its application

We define power as 'command over resources'. The resources in question may be economic, cultural, social or symbolic, and 'command' may be exercised either by organisations or individuals. Corporate power is the sum of all power available to the organisation, and equates the total value of its economic, cultural, social and symbolic capital. In order to derive a proxy measure for 'power', we first calculated mean values for total capital employed, turnover, profit before tax, and number of employees for the top 100 companies in each country. The next step was to divide the individual company scores for each measure by the mean values for that measure and multiply by 100, yielding a maximum of four scores per company (values were missing for some). The individual scores were then summed and the mean calculated to give a corporate power score for each company.

These scores proved valuable in measuring differences and similarities in the concentration and distribution of corporate power between the two countries. Possession of the scores also enabled an analysis of the distribution of power at the level of the individual director. Different types of directors have more or less command over resources. CEOs, for instance, possess greater power within their organisation than others, and those combining the CEO role with that of Chairman have greater power still. Likewise, non-executive directors, by virtue of their limited connection with the business, have less power than their executive counterparts. This led to the decision to attach weights to the different director roles identified during the course of the research, as shown in Table A.1.1.

The next step in the procedure was to sum the weights attributable to individual director roles in a company, and on that basis calculate the value of each defined share of corporate power. Those with more heavily weighted roles were thus attributed larger percentage shares of corporate power. It follows that the percentage shares distributed were smaller for companies with many directors and larger for those with fewer directors.

In both France and the UK, it is possible for individuals to be a director of more than one company. By combining person-by-person their shares of corporate power, it is possible to generate top director 'power indices' for the two countries. Our procedure was to rank individuals by total power score and then apply a filter to exclude individuals active in only one top 100 company, with the exception of individuals of high role status such as chairmen, joint chairmen, chief executives, joint chief executives and managing directors. The results are presented in Tables A.2.3 and A.2.4 of Appendix 2.

Table A.1.1 Relative power weightings for elite directors

Type of Board	Role	Weight
France Type 1		
Conseil	Président-Directeur Général	3.00
d'Administration	Joint Président-Directeur Général	1.50
	Président	1.00
	Joint Président	0.75
	Administrateur (non-executive)	0.25
Comité Exécutif	Directeur Général	2.00
	Membre	1.00
France Type 2		
Conseil de Surveillance	Président (executive)	1.50
	Vice-Président (executive)	1.25
	Président (non-executive)	1.00
	Vice-Président (non-executive)	0.50
	Membre	0.25
Directoire	Président	2.00
	Directeur Général	1.50
	Membre	1.00
UK		
Board of Directors	Chairman and CEO	3.00
	Chairman and Joint CEO/MD	1.75
	Chairman (executive)	1.50
	Chairman (non-executive)	1.00
	Deputy or Vice Chairman (executive)	1.25
	Deputy or Vice Chairman (non-executive)	0.50
	CEO	2.00
	Joint CEO	1.50
	Executive Director	1.00
	Non-Executive Director	0.25

The project database

The focal point of the research was the project database. This consists of 14 linked data tables and 12 secondary tables managed by a relational database management system. The user can take either a company or an elite director view of the data. Data on companies are held relating to size, activities, ownership, shareholders, and governance structures. The cluster of tables relating to elite directors contains personal details, career records, current roles, committee memberships, relationships, education, and qualifications. The information retrieval and reporting tools of the system enable the conduct of complex searches and analytical procedures, as required, for instance, in the analysis of director networks. Data were collected for the top

100 French and British companies and a total of 2,291 company directors, of which 1,241 sat on French boards, 1,031 on UK boards, and 19 on boards in both France and the UK. The approach taken was to collect publicly available data from multiple sources, as detailed in Table A.1.2.

Table A.1.2 Main publicly available sources of data for the project

Source Category	Method of Access	Value of Sources
Annual reports and accounts of French and UK companies, 1997-2004 inclusive	Printed copies supplied by companies and electronic copies sourced from company websites	Financial, activity, employment, event, shareholder, governance and director data
Datamonitor company reports	Datamonitor Business Information Centre electronic data service	Activity, event and director data
Datastream	Datastream electronic data service	Financial and other company data
Le Guide des Etats Majors des Grandes Entreprises	Published annual editions for 1998-2004 inclusive	Data on turnover, employment and profit before tax of French companies. Data on type and composition of boards and directors
Financial Times	Published annual rankings of UK companies by market capitalisation for 1998 and 1999	Financial and other company data
PWC Corporate Register	Edition for March 1999	Data on directors
Hemscott Company Guru Academic	Hemmington Scott electronic data service	Director profiles providing data on career, education, qualifications, activities, interests, honours and clubs
Who's Who in France and *Who's Who in the UK*	Published volumes for 1998-2003 inclusive	Data relating to families, education, career, interests and honours of directors
Numerous academic and business publications	Business Source Premier search engine	Company and director data relating mainly but not exclusively to events
Websites of companies and other organisations	Google and Highbeam Research search engines	As above

Beyond the database

The database informed all aspects of the research. However, the data were not sufficient to support three of the four sub-projects undertaken. First, our research on corporate governance structures and events required more intensive research on various top 100 companies. The approach taken was to build up case files containing articles and other documents. Secondly, our more intensive study of the top 100 directors in France and the UK required additional data to be gathered on such matters as social origins. A targeted search conducted by e-mail and telephone led to numerous gaps being filled. Thirdly, our socially grounded qualitative study of business elites was based upon in-depth semi-structured interviews. These covered education, family, lifestyle, career, networks, governance, and the exercise of power by business elites. Of the 32 elite informants, 19 gave permission to be named and quoted, while 13 wished to remain anonymous.

Coding and classification

Numerous decisions were made during the course of the research relating to coding and systems of classification. The strategy adopted was one of 'post-coding', which demands the retention of the original data values and the creation of additional database fields to hold the coded values needed for classification.

Classifying occupations, careers, social origins or any other facet of the social order is invariably fraught with difficulty. It may be that many subjects conform neatly to type, but there are always others whose situation is more complex or 'fuzzy' and therefore less amenable to classification. This problem is compounded in cross-national comparative studies because social institutions in different countries, in education and politics for example, have unique aspects, and this renders problematic direct comparison of some aspects of social reality. We took the decision therefore to make all systems of classification as transparent as possible, and this criterion has informed the design and wording of many of the statistical tables presented in the book.

In examining social origins, we were mainly interested in the type of family that a person came from rather than the broader social milieu in which they grew up. We decided to 'keep it simple' and work within a classification system based on four well-recognised classes: upper, upper-middle, lower-middle, and lower, as described in Table A.1.3.

Table A.1.3 Classification of social origins

Social Class of Parental Family	Evidence Needed for Inclusion of Subject in Class
Upper	Born into a family with substantial wealth and a large income based on inheritance or a parent occupying a leading position in society. Strong evidence of advantages resulting from family possession of very high levels of economic, cultural, social and symbolic capital.
Upper-Middle	Born into a family with one or more parent with a prestigious job and high earnings. Strong evidence of advantages resulting from family possession of high levels of economic, cultural and social capital.
Lower-Middle	Born into a family with a middling income and comfortable lifestyle. Some evidence of advantages resulting from family possession of economic and cultural capital.
Lower	Born into a family with a modest or low income. Little evidence of advantages resulting from family possession of significant amounts of capital of any kind.

We trawled widely for evidence, including the testimony of subjects themselves, in order to classify individuals with a reasonable degree of confidence. The search was confined to the top 100 most powerful members of the French and British business elites, yet even then we failed to gather sufficient evidence to classify 15 individuals, six French and nine British.

The simplest part of educational classification was higher education discipline, for which the categories adopted are largely self-explanatory other than in borderline cases. Medicine, for instance, could have been classified alongside law as a professional subject, but we opted to classify it together with science and engineering subjects, including mathematics. Likewise, economics might have been classified with the humanities and social sciences, but we considered it to be more cognate with business and administrative sciences. Executive management education was deemed a special class of postgraduate experience requiring significant work experience as well as academic qualifications for admission. In practice, this meant taking an MBA or an intensive short programme like the Harvard Advanced Management Programme or the Tuck Executive Programme.

It is more difficult in a cross-national study to establish classes for the types of educational institution attended by members of the business elite. Decisions were made on which institutions to include in this category and which to exclude after pulling together many of the available lists of top rank institutions of higher education. The results are displayed in Table A.1.4.

Table A.1.4 High status higher education institutions in France and the UK, 1945-85

Institution	Most Highly Regarded Institutions, 1945-85
French *Grandes Ecoles*	Ecole Centrale Paris, Ecole de Management de Lyon, Ecole des Hautes Etudes Commerciales Paris, Ecole des Hautes Etudes Commerciales du Nord, Ecole des Mines de Paris, Institut d'Etudes Politiques de Paris – Sciences-Po, Ecole Nationale des Ponts et Chaussées, Ecole Nationale Supérieure de l'Aéronautique et de l'Espace, Ecole Nationale Supérieure des Postes et Télécommunications, Ecole Nationale Supérieure du Pétrole et des Moteurs, Ecole Normale Supérieure de Paris, Ecole Normale Supérieure des Arts et Métiers, Ecole Polytechnique, Ecole Supérieure d'Electricité, Ecole Supérieure de Commerce de Paris, Ecole Supérieure des Sciences Economiques et Commerciales, INSEAD.
French Universities	Bordeaux I, Lyon I, Paris I-Panthéon Sorbonne, Paris II-Panthéon Assas, Paris IV-Sorbonne, Paris V-René Descartes, Paris VI-Pierre et Marie Curie, Paris VII-Jussieu, Paris IX-Dauphine, Paris X-Nanterre, Paris XI-Paris Sud, Montpellier I, Strasbourg I, Toulouse I.
UK Universities	Birmingham, Bristol, Cambridge, Durham, Edinburgh, Exeter, Glasgow, Imperial College London, King's College London, Leeds, Liverpool, London Business School, London School of Economics, Manchester, Nottingham, Oxford, Sheffield, Southampton, St Andrews, University College London, Warwick.

At school level, given the generation of directors under consideration, it was judged reasonable to consider French *lycées* as comparable to UK grammar schools. Likewise, while acknowledging that 'independent' schools in France have for long been more 'dependent' on state funds that their counterparts in the UK, and that many are Catholic establishments, it was decided that 'independent' was a legitimate class of institution. In terms of higher education, the institutional differences between France and the UK are even starker because of the high standing of the *grandes écoles* in comparison with many universities, notwithstanding the small size and specialised character of many of these institutions. In order to provide a reasonable basis for comparison, the decision was taken to include more French than UK institutions in the class 'top tier institutions 1945-85'.

The most problematic of all the classification systems we adopted relates to higher qualifications. A UK first degree was taken to be a Bachelor's degree, or an MA from Oxford, Cambridge or one of the Scottish universities for which there was no separate lower degree. The *licence* was taken as the equivalent award from a French university. Likewise, a UK taught Master's degree and a French *maîtrise* were both designated as higher degrees. The MBA was considered as equivalent. A *diplôme* awarded by one of the French *grandes écoles* was also considered a higher degree on the basis that two years of advanced preparatory study are required before embarking on a *diplôme* course. This is controversial and it can be argued that these are more akin to a first degree than a master's. At doctoral level, the PhD and DPhil were taken as UK qualifying awards and the *doctorat du troisième cycle* and *doctorat d'Etat* as French qualifying awards. Awards from other countries were compared to French and UK awards and classified appropriately.

Data analysis and presentation

In analysing data and presenting results, the research team kept three main principles to the fore. First, the purpose of comparative data analysis is to help in answering questions relating to the extent of similarities and differences between systems and entities. Secondly, we decided at an early stage to address the needs of a broad general audience rather than a narrow specialist audience. This meant placing a premium on systematic and clear presentation of tables and figures. Thirdly, we adopted the principle of transparency in spelling out our procedures and working methods. Much of the data manipulation required was carried out using SQL queries to interrogate multiple tables simultaneously. Data were exported into spreadsheets and statistical packages for statistical analysis and the preparation of tables for publication.

Appendix 2 – Reference Data

Table A.2.1 Top 100 French companies in 1998

Company	Rank	Total Capital Employed (M€)	Turnover (M€)	Profit (M€)	Employees (No.)
Suez Lyonnaise des Eaux	1	72,145	29,029	612	175,000
France Télécom	2	30,060	23,893	2,266	165,042
Vivendi	3	19,948	25,474	823	220,000
Elf Aquitaine	4	26,484	38,768	854	83,700
Alcatel	5	18,336	28,340	701	189,549
Renault	6	15,522	25,274	827	140,905
Electricité de France (EdF)	7	113,104	29,118	290	116,919
Saint-Gobain	8	22,182	16,324	858	107,968
Total	9	15,809	29,131	1,160	54,381
Auchan	10	13,750	22,425	na	107,000
Intermarché	11	na	21,599	na	75,000
Carrefour	12	5,958	25,805	546	109,300
Leclerc	13	na	21,343	na	65,000
Michelin	14	8,087	12,149	592	123,254
Danone	15	11,547	13,488	559	80,631
AXA	16	26,420	54,673	2,010	11,700
Alstom	17	5,771	14,239	327	110,000
Lafarge	18	11,493	9,377	559	64,656
Pinault-Printemps-Redoute	19	5,893	13,595	401	64,078
Promodès	20	7,627	16,871	247	55,000
Usinor	21	10,543	10,976	313	51,394
L'Oréal	22	6,280	10,537	641	47,242
LVMH	23	9,545	7,323	742	32,348
Bouygues	24	5,054	13,884	115	100,000
PSA Peugeot Citroën	25	12,709	28,475	-422	140,200
SNCF	26	40,777	11,318	-146	175,000
La Poste	27	11,745	13,702	9	317,214
Air France	28	7,734	9,256	286	46,385
Thomson-CSF	29	9,138	5,869	323	44,800
Aérospatiale	30	11,022	8,583	216	37,087

Company	Rank	Total Capital Employed (M€)	Turnover (M€)	Profit (M€)	Employees (No.)
Accor	31	5,522	4,845	230	121,000
Gaz de France	32	14,989	8,415	229	25,038
Schneider Electric	33	4,494	7,226	335	61,500
Casino	34	2,888	13,593	170	56,352
Air Liquide	35	7,080	5,851	471	27,600
Rhône-Poulenc	36	24,348	13,713	-761	68,400
Pechiney	37	4,901	10,633	277	34,000
Lagardère	38	4,980	10,047	210	46,230
Eridania Beghin-Say	39	8,091	9,703	290	20,653
ST Microelectronics	40	5,618	3,669	371	28,000
Sodexho	41	3,165	4,497	82	140,000
Valeo	42	2,967	5,179	226	36,100
Système U	43	na	7,714	na	24,000
Eiffage	44	1,880	5,000	92	42,501
Framatome	45	6,610	2,790	149	19,097
RATP	46	12,531	2,877	13	39,461
Cora	47	na	7,318	na	19,000
Snecma	48	4,562	3,515	114	22,000
Galeries Lafayette	49	1,426	4,627	99	29,200
Cap Gemini	50	2,060	3,076	116	28,059
Seita	51	19,601	2,804	126	8,146
Cogema	52	2,087	4,979	159	18,856
Legrand	53	2,181	1,985	162	22,100
Bull	54	1,457	3,752	92	21,267
Pernod Ricard	55	2,199	2,904	206	12,650
Bertrand Faure - ECIA	56	1,393	3,537	65	26,000
Comptoirs Modernes	57	276	4,992	96	24,647
Dassault Aviation	58	1,434	3,209	201	12,583
Castorama	59	1,784	3,215	71	17,046
EMC	60	2,209	2,970	87	11,829
Besnier	61	na	4,269	na	14,000
Bolloré Technologies	62	1,145	3,565	52	22,000
Sonepar Distribution	63	na	4,269	na	14,000
Labinal	64	1,897	1,951	63	23,044
Sagem	65	1,226	2,555	106	14,000
Airbus Industrie	66	na	10,589	na	2,500

Company	Rank	Total Capital Employed (M€)	Turnover (M€)	Profit (M€)	Employees (No.)
Ciments Français	67	2,834	1,986	94	9,390
Sommer Allibert	68	na	2,584	48	19,151
Technip	69	4,768	1,809	96	5,600
Imetal	70	2,172	1,685	101	9,933
Esso	71	689	5,563	79	2,430
Spie	72	601	2,456	14	26,000
BNP	73	18,185	1,334	13	5,138
Française des Jeux	74	1,010	5,204	54	730
SEB	75	633	1,806	79	14,356
Decathlon	76	na	1,738	na	19,000
Sema	77	363	1,708	66	16,300
Vallourec	78	1,095	1,540	44	14,410
Publicis	79	490	4,011	35	7,363
PMU	80	549	5,270	na	1,998
Primagaz	81	1,616	1,516	53	7,152
Club Méditerranée	82	1,077	1,254	-197	25,000
Fimalac	83	2,308	1,334	58	4,004
Bongrain	84	783	1,758	48	9,905
Charbonnages de France	85	4,050	1,171	-924	13,615
André	86	925	1,508	30	13,000
Strafor Facom	87	1,342	1,346	34	10,336
Bel	88	987	1,415	62	7,807
Soufflet	89	980	2,936	na	2,379
3 Suisses International	90	na	2,211	na	8,000
Moulinex	91	831	1,224	31	11,066
Chargeurs	92	791	1,379	46	6,600
Sodiaal	93	na	2,677	4	6,296
Plastic Omnium	94	400	1,246	21	8,822
Socopa	95	na	1,951	na	5,300
Pomona	96	312	1,334	13	5,138
La Cana	97	na	1,403	8	4,516
Carat France	98	na	2,287	na	410
Yves Rocher	99	na	1,216	na	9,215
Coopagri Bretagne	100	na	1,326	6	3,805

Table A.2.2 Top 100 UK companies in 1998

Company	Rank	Total Capital Employed (M€)	Turnover (M€)	Profit (M€)	Employees (No.)
Shell	1	28,473	61,891	5,311	102,000
HSBC	2	34,077	17,736	7,341	132,969
British Telecom	3	24,106	22,831	4,754	129,200
Unilever	4	12,002	49,024	3,906	265,000
British Petroleum	5	43,834	64,182	5,384	55,650
Diageo	6	12,483	26,136	3,524	70,122
Barclays	7	22,387	12,553	2,534	84,300
Lloyds TSB	8	20,417	10,677	4,670	92,655
Tesco	9	6,975	24,296	1,075	124,172
Sainsburys	10	7,458	21,414	1,062	107,226
BTR	11	5,373	11,949	1,910	110,498
Cable & Wireless	12	14,995	10,339	3,225	46,550
Glaxo Wellcome	13	7,102	11,785	3,967	53,068
SmithKline Beecham	14	8,226	11,512	2,437	55,400
Royal & Sun Alliance	15	12,492	14,450	1,300	43,485
British Airways	16	12,439	12,763	857	60,675
Hanson plc	17	4,772	18,436	2,667	56,000
Marks & Spencer	18	7,789	12,174	1,725	48,200
Abbey National	19	17,547	13,502	1,889	23,498
British Steel	20	8,912	10,408	1,627	50,100
ICI	21	6,821	16,336	765	69,500
Rio Tinto	22	10,100	6,957	1,787	51,016
Prudential	23	12,092	16,667	1,726	22,120
CGU	24	20,876	24,787	839	26,175
General Electric	25	5,122	9,258	1,558	71,963
NatWest	26	19,286	3,859	1,493	77,000
British Gas	27	22,985	7,902	1,847	21,891
Bass	28	7,888	7,759	704	83,461
P&O	29	9,505	8,739	641	69,533
BAT	30	4,639	10,562	1,337	57,884
Granada	31	7,239	6,042	976	66,037
Halifax	32	10,656	4,664	2,408	32,097
Post Office	33	3,937	8,681	697	191,315

Company	Rank	Total Capital Employed (M€)	Turnover (M€)	Profit (M€)	Employees (No.)
Asda Stores	34	4,148	11,252	598	78,450
Associated British Foods	35	4,856	7,684	1,255	40,371
Zeneca	36	4,924	7,670	1,596	31,400
Cadbury Schweppes	37	4,153	6,232	1,458	41,320
Kingfisher	38	3,078	9,465	769	49,225
Boots	39	2,799	7,416	638	85,349
Norwich Union	40	12,950	8,452	597	16,325
Billiton	41	6,761	4,802	739	36,748
British Aerospace	42	5,771	10,732	340	43,000
Safeway	43	4,201	10,306	502	50,969
Allied Domecq	44	4,388	6,570	889	37,448
Great Universal Stores	45	4,931	4,966	921	34,664
Royal Bank of Scotland	46	12,699	2,360	1,122	26,699
Tomkins	47	1,765	7,454	739	65,300
BOC	48	4,974	5,431	657	40,755
Siebe	49	3,760	5,420	718	49,799
Whitbread	50	4,817	4,723	563	63,407
National Power	51	8,100	4,953	1,080	4,348
Scottish & Newcastle	52	4,095	4,951	623	44,559
Standard Chartered	53	6,877	2,251	1,285	24,760
LucasVarity	54	2,440	6,913	467	55,946
Bank of Scotland	55	6,554	2,608	1,096	20,793
Rentokil Initial	56	1,183	4,153	616	138,635
Rolls Royce	57	3,844	6,400	408	42,600
Scottish Power	58	4,584	4,620	945	14,356
Nationwide	59	6,323	4,487	678	11,784
Sun Life & Provincial	60	11,875	4,774	428	7,415
BAA	61	8,054	2,480	709	12,535
Inchcape	62	2,329	9,249	158	46,112
Legal & General	63	4,696	4,647	901	7,203
RMC	64	3,759	6,028	437	30,799
Compass	65	352	5,469	204	130,543
Ladbroke	66	3,541	5,636	300	42,878
Railtrack	67	6,745	3,643	573	10,700

Company	Rank	Total Capital Employed (M€)	Turnover (M€)	Profit (M€)	Employees (No.)
United Utilities	68	5,887	3,175	690	9,902
Tate & Lyle	69	2,101	4,651	220	25,401
GKN	70	1,865	4,185	600	32,678
Centrica	71	3,341	11,581	-920	15,423
Pilkington	72	3,388	4,250	224	39,100
Coats Viyella	73	1,831	3,626	139	69,488
Reuters	74	558	4,256	924	16,005
Thames Water	75	5,198	2,051	618	10,995
Pearson	76	5,811	3,386	190	18,306
EMI	77	1,924	4,887	539	17,869
Rank Group	78	4,097	3,078	96	43,478
Vodafone	79	1,533	3,649	960	9,640
Alliance & Leicester	80	5,368	1,651	583	8,387
Imperial Tobacco	81	2,818	5,727	453	3,296
Severn Trent	82	5,014	1,848	552	10,413
British Energy	83	5,346	2,886	408	5,692
National Grid	84	3,202	2,377	849	4,218
Reckitt & Colman	85	2,602	3,244	447	16,500
Williams	86	1,460	3,291	375	31,228
United News & Media	87	1,205	3,346	551	18,150
Dixons	88	1,655	4,096	323	21,519
Unigate	89	1,061	3,151	442	30,175
Somerfield	90	1,114	4,668	136	23,211
Stagecoach Holdings	91	2,587	2,040	234	32,640
PowerGen	92	3,527	4,330	312	3,456
ICL/Fujitsu	93	2,184	3,654	72	20,708
Morrisons Supermarkets	94	1,069	3,214	200	26,985
Woolwich	95	2,784	1,263	594	6,760
Anglian Water	96	4,398	1,255	405	5,131
Reed International	97	2,296	2,670	270	14,600
Hays	98	1,416	2,274	291	17,499
Schroders	99	3,055	1,564	362	5,603
Southern Electric	100	1,567	2,620	367	6,499

Table A.2.3 Top 100 French business elite members in 1998

Name	Rank	Company	Position
Jaffré, Philippe	1	Elf Aquitaine	Chairman and CEO
		BNP	NE Director
		Gaz de France	NE Director
		Suez Lyonnaise des Eaux	NE Director
Bon, Michel	2	France Télécom	Chairman and CEO
		Air Liquide	NE Director
		Bull	NE Director
		Lafarge	NE Director
		Sonepar Distribution	NE Director
Tchuruk, Serge	3	Alcatel	Chairman and CEO
		Aérospatiale	NE Director
		Alstom	NE Director
		Thomson-CSF	NE Director
		Total	NE Director
		Vivendi	NE Director
Mestrallet, Gérard	4	Suez Lyonnaise des Eaux	CEO
		Fimalac	NE Director
		Sagem	NE Director
		Saint-Gobain	NE Director
		AXA	NE Director
		Casino	NE Director
Bébéar, Claude	5	AXA	CEO
		Saint-Gobain	NE Director
		Schneider Electric	NE Director
Beffa, Jean-Louis	6	Saint-Gobain	Chairman and CEO
		BNP	NE Director
		Vivendi	NE Director
		AXA	NE Director
Messier, Jean-Marie	7	Vivendi	Chairman and CEO
		LVMH	NE Director
		Saint-Gobain	NE Director
		Strafor Facom	NE Director
Desmarest, Thierry	8	Total	Chairman and CEO
		Cogema	NE Director
Leclerc, Edouard	9	Leclerc	Joint Chairman and CEO
Leclerc, Michel-Edouard	10	Leclerc	Joint Chairman and CEO
Gallois, Louis	11	SNCF	Chairman and CEO
		Air France	NE Director
		Thomson-CSF	NE Director

Name	Rank	Company	Position
Gourgeon, Pierre	12	Intermarché	Chairman and CEO
Schweitzer, Louis	13	Renault	Chairman and CEO
		BNP	NE Director
		Pechiney	NE Director
Friedmann, Jacques-Henri	14	AXA	NE Chairman
		Alcatel	NE Director
		BNP	NE Director
		Elf Aquitaine	NE Director
		Vivendi	NE Director
Owen-Jones, Lindsay	15	L'Oréal	Chairman and CEO
		Air Liquide	NE Director
		BNP	NE Director
		Lafarge	NE Director
de la Martinière, Gérard	16	AXA	Managing Director
		Schneider Electric	NE Director
Michelin, François	17	Michelin	CEO
		PSA Peugeot Citroën	NE Director
Daurès, Pierre	18	Electricité de France	CEO
		Cogema	NE Director
		Framatome	NE Director
Bernard, Daniel	19	Carrefour	Chairman and CEO
		Alcatel	NE Director
		Comptoirs Modernes	NE Director
Folz, Jean-Martin	20	PSA Peugeot Citroën	CEO
Halbron, Jean-Pierre	21	Alcatel	Managing Director
		Alstom	NE Director
		Framatome	NE Director
Monod, Jérôme	22	Suez Lyonnaise des Eaux	NE Chairman
		Total	NE Director
Bourmaud, Claude	23	La Poste	Chairman and CEO
Collomb, Bertrand	24	Lafarge	Chairman and CEO
		Elf Aquitaine	NE Director
		Unilever PLC	NE Director
Fourtou, Jean-René	25	Rhône-Poulenc	Chairman and CEO
		Pernod Ricard	NE Director
		Schneider Electric	NE Director
		AXA	NE Director
Pébereau, Michel	26	BNP	Chairman and CEO
		Elf Aquitaine	NE Director
		Galeries Lafayette	NE Director
		Lafarge	NE Director
		Renault	NE Director
		Saint-Gobain	NE Director
		AXA	NE Director

Name	Rank	Company	Position
Bilger, Pierre	27	Alstom	Chairman and CEO
		Elf Aquitaine	NE Director
Mulliez, Gérard	28	Auchan	NE Chairman
		Decathlon	NE Director
Lauvergeon, Anne	29	Alcatel	Executive Director
		Pechiney	NE Director
		Suez Lyonnaise des Eaux	NE Director
Jaclot, François	30	Suez Lyonnaise des Eaux	Managing Director
Peugeot, Pierre	31	PSA Peugeot Citroën	Executive Chairman
Saint-Geours, Frédéric	32	PSA Peugeot Citroën	Managing Director
Satinet, Claude	33	PSA Peugeot Citroën	Managing Director
Bouriez, Philippe	34	Cora	Chairman and CEO
Dehecq, Jean-François	35	Elf Aquitaine	Executive Director
		Air France	NE Director
		Pechiney	NE Director
		Yves Rocher (Group)	NE Director
Alphandéry, Edmond	36	Electricité de France	NE Chairman
		Usinor	NE Director
Bouygues, Martin	37	Bouygues	Chairman and CEO
Mer, Francis	38	Usinor	Chairman and CEO
		Air France	NE Director
		Electricité de France	NE Director
Syrota, Jean	39	Cogema	Chairman and CEO
		Framatome	NE Director
		Sagem	NE Director
		Total	NE Director
		Usinor	NE Director
		Suez Lyonnaise des Eaux	NE Director
Damlamian, Jean-Jacques	40	France Télécom	Executive Director
		Bull	NE Director
Joly, Alain	41	Air Liquide	Chairman and CEO
		BNP	NE Director
		Lafarge	NE Director
Champeaux, Jacques	42	France Télécom	Executive Director
		Sema	NE Director
Barth, Jean-Paul	43	Alcatel	Executive Director
		Framatome	NE Director
		Thomson-CSF	NE Director
Michot, Yves	44	Aérospatiale	Chairman and CEO
		Dassault Aviation	NE Director

Name	Rank	Company	Position
		Thomson-CSF	NE Director
		Airbus Industrie	NE Director
Halley, Paul-Louis	45	Promodès	Chairman and CEO
Arnault, Bernard	46	LVMH	Chairman and CEO
		Vivendi	NE Director
		Diageo	NE Director
d'Hautefeuille, Eric	47	Saint-Gobain	Managing Director
		Gaz de France	NE Director
Ranque, Denis	48	Thomson-CSF	Chairman and CEO
Pineau-Valencienne,	49	Schneider Electric	Chairman and CEO
Didier		Rhône-Poulenc	NE Director
		Sema	NE Director
		AXA	NE Director
Riboud, Franck	50	Danone	Chairman and CEO
Defforey, Hervé	51	Carrefour	Managing Director
		Comptoirs Modernes	NE Director
Dejouany, Guy	52	Alcatel	NE Director
		Saint-Gobain	NE Director
		Vivendi	NE Director
		AXA	NE Director
Bellon, Pierre	53	Sodexho	Chairman and CEO
		Air Liquide	NE Director
Peyrelevade, Jean	54	Air Liquide	NE Director
		Bouygues	NE Director
		Lagardère	NE Director
		LVMH	NE Director
		Renault	NE Director
		Club Méditerranée	NE Director
		Suez Lyonnaise des Eaux	NE Director
Couvreux, Christian	55	Casino	CEO
Valot, Daniel	56	Total	Executive Director
		Technip Groupe	NE Director
Blanchard-Dignac,	57	Air France	NE Director
Christophe		Electricité de France	NE Director
		France Télécom	NE Director
		SNCF	NE Director
Comolli, Jean-	58	Seita	Chairman and CEO
Dominique		Pernod Ricard	NE Director
Girardot, Paul-Louis	59	Vivendi	Executive Director
		Eiffage	NE Director
Lagardère, Jean-Luc	60	Lagardère	CEO
		Renault	NE Director
Forgeard, Noël	61	Airbus Industrie	CEO
Gadonneix, Pierre	62	Gaz de France	Chairman and CEO

Name	Rank	Company	Position
Ladreit de Lachar-rière, Marc	63	Fimalac	Chairman and CEO
		France Télécom	NE Director
		L'Oréal	NE Director
		André	NE Director
		Casino	NE Director
François-Poncet, Michel	64	Eridania Béghin-Say	NE Director
		LVMH	NE Director
		Schneider Electric	NE Director
		Total	NE Director
		AXA	NE Director
Gandois, Jean	65	BNP	NE Director
		Danone	NE Director
		Schneider Electric	NE Director
		PSA Peugeot Citroën	NE Director
		Suez Lyonnaise des Eaux	NE Director
		Vallourec	NE Director
Meloni, Stefano	66	Eridania Béghin-Say	Chairman and CEO
Espalioux, Jean-Marc	67	Accor	CEO
Kasriel, Bernard	68	Lafarge	Managing Director
Grappotte, François	69	Legrand	Chairman and CEO
		France Télécom	NE Director
Lachmann, Henri	70	Strafor Facom	Chairman and CEO
		Bertrand Faure – ECIA	NE Director
		Schneider Electric	NE Director
		Vivendi	NE Director
		AXA	NE Director
Roger, Bruno	71	Saint-Gobain	NE Director
		Thomson-CSF	NE Director
		AXA	NE Director
		Cap Gemini	NE Director
		Pinault-Printemps-Redoute	NE Director
Faurre, Pierre	72	Sagem	Chairman and CEO
		Pernod Ricard	NE Director
		Saint-Gobain	NE Director
		Suez Lyonnaise des Eaux	NE Director
Goutard, Noël	73	Valeo	Chairman and CEO
		Alcatel	NE Director
Weinberg, Serge	74	Pinault-Printemps-Redoute	CEO
d'Escatha, Yannick	75	Cogema	NE Director
		Electricité de France	NE Director

Name	Rank	Company	Position
		Framatome	NE Director
		France Télécom	NE Director
Roverato, Jean-François	76	Eiffage	Chairman and CEO
Rodier, Jean-Pierre	77	Pechiney	Chairman and CEO
Bernheim, Antoine	78	Bolloré Technologies	NE Director
		Bouygues	NE Director
		Ciments Français	NE Director
		Eridania Béghin-Say	NE Director
		LVMH	NE Director
		André	NE Director
		AXA	NE Director
Ricard, Patrick	79	Pernod Ricard	Chairman and CEO
		Eridania Béghin-Say	NE Director
de Royère, Edouard	80	Air Liquide	NE Director
		Danone	NE Director
		L'Oréal	NE Director
		Sodexho	NE Director
		Michelin	NE Director
Vincent, Jacques	81	Danone	Managing Director
Desmarescaux, Philippe	82	Rhône-Poulenc	Managing Director
		SEB	NE Director
Dubrule, Paul	83	Auchan	CEO
		Accor	NE Chairman
Dassault, Serge	84	Dassault Aviation	Chairman and CEO
		Aérospatiale	NE Director
		Thomson-CSF	NE Director
Calvet, Jacques	85	Galeries Lafayette	NE Director
		Vivendi	NE Director
		André	NE Director
		AXA	NE Director
Le Lorier, Anne	86	Aérospatiale	NE Director
		France Télécom	NE Director
		Renault	NE Director
Viénot, Marc	87	Alcatel	NE Director
		Rhône-Poulenc	NE Director
		Vivendi	NE Director
Potier, Benoît	88	Air Liquide	Managing Director
Spinetta, Jean-Cyril	89	Air France	Chairman and CEO
Jachiet, Nicolas	90	Dassault Aviation	NE Director
		Electricité de France	NE Director
		SNCF	NE Director
Dromer, Jean	91	Air Liquide	NE Director
		LVMH	NE Director

Name	Rank	Company	Position
		Suez Lyonnaise des Eaux	NE Director
Parayre, Jean-Paul	92	Bolloré Technologies	Managing Director
		Bouygues	NE Director
		PSA Peugeot Citroën	NE Director
		Vallourec	NE Director
Prot, Baudouin	93	BNP	Managing Director
		Pechiney	NE Director
		Rhône-Poulenc	NE Director
		Accor	NE Director
		Pinault-Printemps-Redoute	NE Director
Davignon, Etienne	94	Pechiney	NE Director
		Accor	NE Director
		ICL/Fujitsu	NE Director
		Suez Lyonnaise des Eaux	NE Director
Pachura, Edmond	95	Usinor	Executive Director
		SNCF	NE Director
Seillière de Laborde, Ernest-Antoine	96	Cap Gemini	NE Chairman
		Eridania Béghin-Say	NE Director
		Valeo	NE Director
		PSA Peugeot Citroën	NE Director
Randaxhe, Jean-Luc	97	Esso	Chairman and CEO
Bolloré, Vincent	98	Bolloré Technologies	Chairman and CEO
		Bouygues	NE Director
		Seita	NE Director
Kron, Patrick	99	Imetal	CEO
Pinault, François	100	Pinault-Printemps-Redoute	Executive Vice Chairman

Table A.2.4 Top 100 UK business elite members in 1998

Name	Rank	Company	Position
Moody-Stuart, Mark	1	Shell	Chairman, Joint CEO
Watts, Philip	2	Shell	Joint CEO
Browne, Edmund	3	British Petroleum	CEO
		SmithKline Beecham	NE Director
Bonfield, Peter	4	British Telecom	CEO
		ICL/Fujitsu	NE Vice Chairman
		Zeneca	NE Director
Cockburn, Bill	5	British Telecom	CEO
		Centrica	NE Director
FitzGerald, Niall	6	Unilever	Executive Chairman
		Prudential	NE Director
Bond, John	7	HSBC	CEO
		British Steel	NE Director
Purves, William	8	HSBC	Executive Chairman
		Alstom	NE Director
		Shell	NE Director
Vallance, Iain	9	British Telecom	Executive Chairman
		Royal Bank of Scotland	NE Director
Roberts, John	10	Post Office	CEO
Marshall, Colin	11	British Airways	NE Chairman
		Inchcape	NE Chairman
		British Telecom	NE Vice Chairman
		HSBC	NE Director
Anderson, Iain	12	Unilever	Executive Director
		British Telecom	NE Director
		Scottish & Newcastle	NE Director
Sanderson, Bryan	13	British Petroleum	Executive Director
		British Steel	NE Director
Buchanan, John	14	British Petroleum	Executive Director
		Boots	NE Director
Taylor, Martin	15	Barclays	CEO
Chase, Rodney	16	British Petroleum	Executive Director
		BOC	NE Director
Olver, Richard	17	British Petroleum	Executive Director
		Reuters	NE Director
Sutherland, Peter	18	British Petroleum	NE Chairman
Prosser, Ian	19	Bass	Chairman and CEO
		British Petroleum	NE Director
		Lloyds TSB	NE Director
Peelen, Jan	20	Unilever	Executive Director
		Barclays	NE Director
Thompson, Peter	21	Rentokil Initial	CEO

Name	Rank	Company	Position
		BAT	NE Director
		Sainsburys	NE Director
Butler, Clive	22	Unilever	Exccutive Director
		Lloyds TSB	NE Director
Buxton, Andrew	23	Barclays	Executive Chairman
		SmithKline Beecham	NE Director
Brown, Richard	24	Cable & Wireless	CEO
Moffat, Brian	25	British Steel	Chairman and CEO
		HSBC	NE Director
Strachan, Ian	26	BTR	CEO
Ayling, Robert	27	British Airways	CEO
		Royal & Sun Alliance	NE Director
McGrath, John	28	Diageo	CEO
		Boots	NE Director
Miller Smith, Charles	29	ICI	CEO
		HSBC	NE Director
Scott, Robert	30	CGU	CEO
Davis, Peter	31	Prudential	CEO
		Boots	NE Director
Keenan, Jack	32	Diageo	CEO
Dougal, Andrew	33	Hanson	CEO
Middleton, Peter	34	Barclays	Executive Vice Chairman
		Bass	NE Director
		United Utilities	NE Director
Varney, David	35	British Gas	CEO
Leahy, Terry	36	Tesco	CEO
Walters, Peter	37	SmithKline Beecham	NE Chairman
		EMI	NE Vice Chairman
		HSBC	NE Vice Chairman
Hutchings, Gregory	38	Tomkins	Chairman and CEO
Simpson, George	39	General Electric	CEO
		Alstom	NE Director
		ICI	NE Director
		Pilkington	NE Director
Ellwood, Peter	40	Lloyds TSB	CEO
Bain, Neville	41	Post Office	NE Chairman
		Safeway	NE Director
		Scottish & Newcastle	NE Director
Angus, Michael	42	Boots	NE Chairman
		Whitbread	NE Chairman
		British Airways	NE Vice Chairman
		NatWest	NE Director
Leschly, Jan	43	SmithKline Beecham	CEO
Greener, Anthony	44	Diageo	Executive Chairman

Name	Rank	Company	Position
		Reed International	NE Director
Wanless, Derek	45	NatWest	CEO
Broughton, Martin	46	BAT	CEO
		Whitbread	NE Director
Mendelsohn, Robert	47	Royal & Sun Alliance	CEO
Stocken, Oliver	48	Barclays	Executive Director
		Pilkington	NE Director
		Rank Group	NE Director
Lipworth, Sydney	49	NatWest	Executive Vice Chairman
		Zeneca	NE Chairman
Collins, Christopher	50	Hanson	Executive Chairman
Allen, Charles	51	Granada	CEO
Smith, Brian	52	BAA	NE Chairman
		Cable & Wireless	NE Chairman
Hampel, Ronald	53	ICI	Executive Chairman
		British Aerospace	NE Director
Adriano, Dino	54	Sainsburys	CEO
Eilledge, Elwyn	55	BTR	NE Chairman
		British Gas	NE Director
Pitman, Brian	56	Lloyds TSB	Executive Chairman
Wilson, Robert	57	Rio Tinto	Executive Chairman
		Boots	NE Director
		Diageo	NE Director
Oates, John	58	Marks & Spencer	Joint CEO
		British Telecom	NE Director
		Diageo	NE Director
Wright, Patrick	59	BAA	NE Director
		British Petroleum	NE Director
		Unilever	NE Director
Stevens, Derek	60	British Airways	Executive Director
		CGU	NE Director
Harding, Christopher	61	Legal & General	NE Chairman
		United Utilities	NE Chairman
		General Electric	NE Director
		Post Office	NE Director
Gilbertson, Brian	62	Billiton	Chairman and CEO
Harvey, Richard	63	Norwich Union	CEO
Davis, Leonard	64	Rio Tinto	CEO
Jacomb, Martin	65	Prudential	NE Chairman
		Marks & Spencer	NE Director
		Rio Tinto	NE Director
Gillam, Patrick	66	Standard Chartered	Executive Chairman
		Royal & Sun Alliance	NE Chairman
Olsen, Rodney	67	Cable & Wireless	Executive Director

Name	Rank	Company	Position
		Standard Chartered	NE Director
Ingram, Robert	68	Glaxo Wellcome	CEO
Smith, Colin	69	Safeway	CEO
Reid, David	70	Tesco	Executive Vice Chairman
Mulcahy, Geoffrey	71	Kingfisher	CEO
		Bass	NE Director
Davies, John	72	Lloyds TSB	Executive Vice Chairman
Gyllenhammar, Pehr	73	CGU	NE Chairman
		Pearson	NE Director
Foster, Peter	74	CGU	Executive Director
		Railtrack	NE Director
Giordano, Richard	75	British Gas	NE Chairman
		Rio Tinto	NE Director
Leighton, Allan	76	Asda	CEO
Flower, Martin	77	Coats Viyella	CEO
		Severn Trent	NE Director
Weston, Garry	78	Associated British Foods	Executive Chairman
King, Henry	79	Rentokil Initial	NE Chairman
MacKay, Francis	80	Compass	CEO
Robinson, Gerrard	81	Granada	Executive Chairman
Sunderland, John	82	Cadbury Schweppes	CEO
		Rank Group	NE Director
Sainsbury, David	83	Sainsburys	Executive Chairman
Sykes, Richard	84	Glaxo Wellcome	Executive Chairman
		Rio Tinto	NE Director
Blackburn, Michael	85	Halifax	CEO
Barnes, David	86	Zeneca	CEO
Dunn, Lydia	87	HSBC	NE Vice Chairman
		General Electric	NE Director
Bauman, Robert	88	British Aerospace	NE Chairman
		BTR	NE Vice Chairman
		Reuters	NE Director
Robinson, Ian	89	Scottish Power	CEO
		Asda	NE Director
Collum, Hugh	90	SmithKline Beecham	Executive Director
		Safeway	NE Director
Rice, Victor	91	LucasVarity	CEO
Wood, Mark	92	Sun Life & Provincial	CEO
Henry, Keith	93	National Power	CEO
Rudd, Nigel	94	Williams	Executive Chairman
		Pilkington	NE Chairman
		Barclays	NE Director

Name	Rank	Company	Position
Hogg, Christopher	95	Reuters	Executive Chairman
		Allied Domecq	NE Chairman
		SmithKline Beecham	NE Director
Margetts, Robert	96	ICI	Executive Director
		Legal & General	NE Director
Robins, Ralph	97	Rolls Royce	Executive Chairman
		Cable & Wireless	NE Director
		Marks & Spencer	NE Director
		Schroders	NE Director
		Standard Chartered	NE Director
Gardiner, John	98	Tesco	NE Chairman
Thompson, David	99	Boots	Joint CEO
		Cadbury Schweppes	NE Director
Tugendhat, Christo-pher	100	Abbey National	Executive Chairman
		BOC	NE Director
		Rio Tinto	NE Director

Notes

Chapter 1. Business Elites and Corporate Governance

[1] As Dr George Cox, Director General of the Institute of Directors, put it: 'I do believe the standard of corporate governance here [in Britain] is higher than anywhere else in the world. I've no doubt about that at all. And that's internationally recognised, but not recognised at home.' Interview with George Cox, Institute of Directors, London, 24 April 2003.

[2] Charkham, J. (1994), *Keeping Good Company: a Study of Corporate Governance in Five Countries*, Oxford: Clarendon Press.

[3] Peck, S. and Ruigrok, W. (2000) 'Hiding Behind the Flag? Prospects for Change in German Corporate Governance', *European Management Journal*, 18, 4, 420-30.

[4] Schleifer, A. and Vishny, R.W. (1997) 'A Survey of Corporate Governance', *Journal of Finance*, 52, 2, June, 737-83 (p.737).

[5] Maclean, M. (1999) 'Corporate Governance in France and the UK: Long-Term Perspectives on Contemporary Institutional Arrangements', *Business History*, 41, 1, 88-116.

[6] See www.ecgi.org/codes.

[7] Bottomore, T.B. (1966) *Elites and Society*, Harmondsworth: Penguin, p.14.

[8] *Report of the Committee on the Financial Aspects of Corporate Governance* (1992), London: Gee (the Cadbury Report).

[9] Association Française des Entreprises Privées/Conseil National du Patronat Français, *Le Conseil d'Administration des sociétés cotées* (1995), Paris: ETP (Viénot I).

[10] The Cadbury Committee was not asked to examine the relationship between good corporate governance and company performance, for example, nor the role of market control and product market competition, which in turn raises questions regarding the complementarity and substitutability of the elements of different corporate governance systems. Maclean, M. (1999) 'Corporate Governance in France and the UK'. See also Dedman, E. (2000) 'An Investigation into the Determinants of UK Board Structure Before and After Cadbury', *Corporate Governance: an International Review*, 8, 2, April, 133-53.

[11] George Cox underlined this point in a personal interview: 'Corporate governance here [in Britain] is very different to the States and Europe.'

[12] Dr Stefan Kirsten, ThyssenKrupp AG, 'Principles of Good Corporate Governance', Conference on 'Good Profits: Re-building Trust in Corporations', the Royal Institute of International Affairs, Chatham House, London, 11 February 2003.

[13] Interview with Pierre Bilger, former PDG Alstom, Paris, 3 January 2003.

[14] Maclean, M. (2002) *Economic Management and French Business from de Gaulle to Chirac*, Basingstoke: Palgrave Macmillan, pp.6-7.

[15] Hofstede, G. (1980) *Culture's Consequences*, London: Sage.

[16] Bourdieu sees society as a complex web of interweaving fields, which he describes in terms of struggles for power (see Chapter 2).

[17] Mayeur, J.-M. (1981) 'Towards a Prosopography of Elites in Modern and Contemporary France', in Howorth, J. and Cerny, P., eds., *Elites in France: Origins, Reproduction and Power*, London: Pinter, 240-50 (p.242).

[18] Ibid.

[19] Basani, B. (1998) 'Patronat: les parrains ne sont plus ce qu'ils étaient', *Le Nouvel Économiste*, 11 December 1998, 48-53 (p.49).

[20] Dr John Mellor, Chairman of the Foundation for Independent Directors (FID), shares this view. Interview with Dr Mellor, Bristol, 26 November 2002.

[21] Pierre Bilger agreed that independence was not a concept that could be validated according to any sort of objective criteria. Interviews with George Cox and Pierre Bilger.

[22] N.K. Denzin, cited in Silvermann, D. (2000) *Doing Qualitative Research: a Practical Handbook*, London: Sage, p.95.

[23] Marini, P. (1996) *La Modernisation du droit des sociétés*, Paris: La Documentation Française.

[24] Formerly the Conseil National du Patronat Français (CNPF), renamed MEDEF in 1998. The new name was prompted partly by the negative connotations of the word 'patronat' in France.

[25] Burgess, R. (1984) *In the Field: an Introduction to Field Research*, London: Allen and Unwin, cited in Mason, J. (1996) *Qualitative Researching*, London: Sage, p.38.

[26] Bourdieu, P. (1999) *The Weight of the World: Social Suffering in Contemporary Society*, London: Polity Press, p.615.

[27] Bourdieu, P. (1996) 'Understanding', *Theory, Culture and Society*, 13, 2, 17-37 (p.28).

[28] Ibid.

[29] Kadushin, Charles (1995) 'Friendship among the French Financial Elite', *American Sociological Review*, 60, April, 202-21 (p.206).

[30] Economist Intelligence Unit (2004) *Country Profile: 2004*, London: EIU, p.37.

[31] O'Sullivan, M. (2002) 'The Stock Market and the Corporate Economy in France', paper given at International Conference on European Financial Systems and the Corporate Sector', 4-5 October, Maastricht.

[32] Ricketts, M. (1994) *The Economics of Business Enterprise*, Brighton, p.218.

[33] The results of this seminal study by A.A. Berle and G.C. Means (1932) *The Modern Corporation and Private Property*, New York, are discussed in Scott, J. (1985) *Corporations, Classes and Capitalism*, 2nd edition, London: Hutchison, pp.59-64.

[34] Hill, S. (1995) 'The Social Organization of Boards of Directors', *British Journal of Sociology*, 46, 2, 245-78 (pp.246-7).

[35] Fama, E.F. and Jensen, M. (1983) 'Separation of Ownership and Control', *Journal of Law and Economics*, 26, 301-25.

[36] Hendry, J. (2005) 'Beyond Self-interest: Agency Theory and the Board in a

Satisficing World', *British Journal of Management*, 16, S55-S63.
[37] Hamel, G. (2000) *Leading the Revolution*, cited in 'Bosses gather for audience with Enron admirer' (2003) *Independent*, 29 March, p.17.
[38] 'Wal-Mart judged top US company for second year running' (2003), *The Times*, 1 April, p.26.
[39] Rayner, A. (2003) 'Sentence Plea in WorldCom Case', *The Times*, 14 August, p.25.
[40] Collins, J.C. and Porras, J. (1994) *Built to Last: Successful Habits of Visionary Companies*, New York: Harper Collins.
[41] Messier bought Houghton Mifflin for $2.2 billion, and USA Networks for $10.3 billion. For each new purchase the price tag seemed to increase. 'Rise and Fall of a French Master of the Universe' (2002), *The Times*, 2 July, p.23.
[42] 'Dismay as Vivendi puts modern art collection up for sale' (2003), *The Times*, 11 February, p.23.
[43] EIU (2003), *Country Report: United Kingdom*, January, p.29.
[44] DataMonitor Report, Alstom, March 2003.
[45] BBC World Business Report, 27 August 2003.
[46] Sabbagh, D. (2003) 'Marconi jobs at risk as £3.1bn rescue unveiled', *The Times*, 19 March, p.27.
[47] Styles, P. and Taylor, B. (1993) 'Maxwell – the Failure of Corporate Governance', *Corporate Governance: an International Review*, 1, 1, 34-45.
[48] 'French chief who quit got £780,000' (2003), *The Times*, 7 May, p.21.
[49] Cruver, B. (2002) *Anatomy of Greed: the Unshredded Truth from an Enron Insider*, London: Hutchinson, p.14.
[50] Sabbagh, D. (2003) 'Marconi jobs at risk as £3.1bn rescue unveiled'.
[51] O'Sullivan, M. (2002) 'The Stock Market and the Corporate Economy in France'.
[52] See, for example, Buckley, C. (2003) 'Angry investors attack Corus board's pay policy', *The Times*, 30 April, p.25.
[53] Glaxo took control of Wellcome through a hostile takeover in 1995. The merger with SmithKline Beecham followed in 2000.
[54] Garnier's salary for 2002 was $1.45 million. His share options for the year amounted to 11.6 times his salary. His performance bonus for the year was 1.4 times his salary. Performance criteria were not disclosed. Further benefits included £132,000 spent on personal and family travel. Court, M. (2003) 'Feeding the cats', *The Times*, 20 May, p.21.
[55] BBC World Business Report, 27 August 2003.
[56] Kemeny, L. (2003) 'Glaxo acts to prevent revolt', *Sunday Times*, 20 April, p.3.1.
[57] Court, M. (2003) 'City shareholders take a swipe at the corporate fat cats', *The Times*, 20 May, p. 1.
[58] Court, M. (2003) 'Investors face ban on corporate pay votes', *The Times*, 20 May, p.21.
[59] DiMaggio, P.J. and Powell, W.W. (1991) 'The Iron Cage Revisited: Institutional Isomorphism and Collective Rationality in Organizational Fields', in Powell, W.W. and DiMaggio, P.J., *The New Institutionalism in Organizational Analysis*, Chicago and London: University of Chicago Press, 41-62.

60 Djelic, M-L. (1998) *Exporting the American Model: the Postwar Transformation of European Business*, Oxford: OUP; Whitley, R. (1999) *Divergent Capitalisms*, Oxford: OUP; and Calori, R. and De Woot, P. (1994) *A European Management Model – Beyond Diversity*, New Jersey: Prentice Hall.

Chapter 2. Theoretical Perspectives on Business Elites and Corporate Governance

1 Bourdieu, P. (1984) *Distinction: a Social Critique of the Judgement of Taste*, translated by R. Nice, London: Routledge and Kegan Paul, p.476.

2 Foucault, M. (1978) *The History of Sexuality: Volume I, Introduction*, translated by R. Hurley, Harmondsworth: Penguin, p.11.

3 Lemert, C. (2000) 'The Clothes Have no Emperor: Bourdieu on American Imperialism', *Theory, Culture and Society*, 17, 1, 97-106 (p.102).

4 A point explored in Clegg, S.R. (1988) *Frameworks of Power*, London: Sage.

5 Foucault, M. (1979) *Discipline and Punish: the Birth of the Prison*, translated by A.M. Sheridan, Harmondsworth: Penguin.

6 Lemert, C. (2000) 'The Clothes Have no Emperor', p.103.

7 Bourdieu, P. (1995) *Passport to Duke*, Paris: Mimeo.

8 Tournier, M. (1975) *Les Météores*, Paris: Gallimard (Folio), p. 549.

9 Eick, D. (2001) 'Discourse of Language and Symbolic Power', in Grenfell, M. and Kelly, M., eds., *Pierre Bourdieu: Language, Culture and Education – Theory into Practice*, 2nd edition, Bern: Peter Lang, 85-96 (pp.88-89).

10 Scott, J. (1991) 'Networks of Corporate Power: a Comparative Assessment', *Annual Review of Sociology*, 17, pp. 181-203 (p.189).

11 Foucault regards human sexuality, for example, as 'placed by power in a binary system, licit and illicit, permitted and forbidden'. Foucault, M. (1978) *The History of Sexuality: Volume I*, p.83.

12 Bourdieu, P. (1984) *Distinction*, p.172.

13 Bourdieu, P. (1999) 'Scattered Remarks', *European Journal of Social Theory*, 2, 3, 334-40 (p.336).

14 Swartz, D. (1997) *Culture and Power: the Sociology of Pierre Bourdieu*, Chicago: Chicago University Press, p.107.

15 Bourdieu, P. (1999) 'Scattered Remarks', p.336; Foucault, M. (1978) *The History of Sexuality: Volume I*, p. 94.

16 Bourdieu, P. (1991) *Language and Symbolic Power*, translated by G. Raymond and M. Adamson, edited by J.B. Thomson, Cambridge: Polity Press, pp.163-64.

17 Calhoun, C. and Wacquant, L. (2002) 'Social Science with a conscience: Remembering Pierre Bourdieu (1930-2002)', *Thesis Eleven*, 70, 1-14. Swartz, D. (1997) *Culture and Power*, pp.16-28.

18 Sirinelli, J-F. (1988) *Génération intellectuelle*, Paris: Fayard, cited in Swartz, D. (1997) *Culture and Power*, p.17. On the ENS, see Sirinelli, J-F. (1981) 'The Ecole Normale Supérieure and Elite Formation and Selection during the Third Republic', in Howorth, J. and Cerny, P., eds., *Elites in France*, London: Pinter, pp.66-77.

[19] Calhoun, C. and Wacquant, L. (2002) 'Social Science with a conscience', p.2.

[20] Bourdieu, Pierre (1988) *Homo Academicus*, Stanford, CA: Stanford University Press, p.xxvi, cited in Swartz, D. (1997) *Culture and Power*, p.18. The term 'oblate' comes from the Latin 'oblatus' – a child donated to God, who joined a monastery as a child and spent his life there, demonstrating acute loyalty to the institution that took him from lowly origins.

[21] Bourdieu, P. (1994) *The State Nobility: Elite Schools in the Field of Power*, translated by L.C. Clough, Cambridge: Polity Press.

[22] Bourdieu, P. (1970) *La Reproduction: éléments pour une théorie du système d'enseignement*, Paris: Minuit; Bourdieu, P. (1979) *The Inheritors: French Students and their Relation to Culture*, Chicago: University of Chicago Press. See also Vaughan, M. (1981) 'The grandes écoles: selection, legitimation, perpetuation', in Howorth, J. and Cerny, P., eds., *Elites in France*, 93-103.

[23] Bourdieu, P. (1984) *Homo Academicus*, Paris: Minuit, p.100; MacAllester Jones, M. (1993) 'Masters of Science? On Subject and Object in *Homo academicus*', *French Cultural Studies*, 4, 3, 253-62 (p.258).

[24] Swartz, D. (1997) *Culture and Power*, p.18.

[25] Bourdieu, P. (1962) *The Algerians*, Boston, MA: Beacon Press; Bourdieu, P. (1979) *Algeria 1960*, Cambridge: CUP.

[26] *Actes de la Recherche en Sciences Sociales*.

[27] Foucault's sense of alienation in the ENS is underlined by his attempted suicide while studying there. See Calhoun, C. and Wacquant, L. (2002) 'Social Science with a conscience', p.2.

[28] Bourdieu, P. (1999) 'Scattered Remarks', p.337.

[29] Bourdieu, P. and Wacquant, L. (1992) *An Invitation to Reflexive Sociology*, Cambridge: Polity Press.

[30] Though the patterns of social class formation may be looser in present times than in the past, economic class divisions continue to exercise a substantial impact on life chances, a point stressed by John Scott in 'Social Class and Stratification in Late Modernity', *Acta Sociologica*, 45, 1, 23-35.

[31] Calhoun, C. and Wacquant, L. (2002) 'Social Science with a conscience', p.6.

[32] Bourdieu, P. (1984) *Distinction*; Bourdieu, P. (1992) *Les Règles de l'art: genère et structure du champ artistique*, Paris: Seuil.

[33] According to Zukin, modern urban lifestyles are now dominated by 'an aggressive pursuit of cultural capital'. Zukin, S. (1998) 'Urban Lifestyles: Diversity and Standardisation in Spaces of Consumption', *Urban Studies*, 35, 5-6, 825-39 (p.825).

[34] Bourdieu, P. (1999) 'Scattered Remarks', p.337.

[35] Pettigrew, A. and McNulty, T. (1998) 'Sources and Uses of Power in the Boardroom', *European Journal of Work and Organizational Psychology*, 7, 2, 197-214 (p.202).

[36] Created as a small family business in 1966, with funds of just £10,000, Sodexho has been run according to strict financial principles: as founder Pierre Bellon put it, 'You don't spend more than you have in the cash-box'. It now has 286,000 employees and more than 25,000,000 customers daily. Henisse, P. (2001) 'Sodexho:

Comment gérer l'héritage du chef ?', *L'Expansion*, 654, 11-24 October, 81-82.

[37]   'Vodafone more than a match for Mannesmann' (1999) *Corporate Finance*, March, 184, p.22.

[38]   As Scott explains, 'Status relations originate in the distribution of prestige or social honour within a community when people judge one another as superior or inferior in relation to their values, and so give or withhold reputation and accord a particular standing to a person's way of life'. 'Social Class and Stratification in Late Modernity', p.45.

[39]   Thompson, J.B. (1991) 'Editor's Introduction', in Bourdieu, P., *Language and Symbolic Capital*, Cambridge, MA: Harvard University Press, p.13.

[40]   Bourdieu, P. (1984) *Distinction*, p.170.

[41]   Bourdieu, P. (1996) 'On the Family as a Realized Category', *Theory, Culture and Society*, 13, 3, 19-26 (p.26).

[42]   Bourdieu, P. (1984) *Distinction*, p.171.

[43]   Solomon, M.R. (1983) 'The Role of Products as Social Stimuli: a Symbolic Interaction Perspective', *Journal of Consumer Research*, 10, December, 319-29.

[44]   Bourdieu, P. (1986) *Distinction*, p.313.

[45]   Le Wita, B. (1994) *French Bourgeois Culture*, translated by J.A. Underwood, Cambridge: Cambridge University Press, p.141.

[46]   Hyman *et al.* nevertheless note the tendency of heads of affluent households, influenced by habitus, to behave and think affluently. Hyman, M.R. *et al.* (2002) 'Augmenting the Household Affluence Construct', *Journal of Marketing*, Summer, 13-32.

[47]   Bourdieu, P. (1984) *Distinction*, pp.232-44.

[48]   Bourdieu, P. (2001) 'Television', pp.249-50.

[49]   Bubolz, M.M. (2001) 'Family as Source, User and Builder of Social Capital', *Journal of Socio-Economics*, 30, 129-31 (p.131). Bubolz adds that 'through its nurturance, care-giving, and socialization function [the family] develops (or fails to develop) values, attitudes, expectations and habitual patterns of behaviour on which social capital ... depend[s]' (p.131).

[50]   Bourdieu, P. (1996) 'On the Family', p.19.

[51]   Ibid., p.21.

[52]   Ibid., p.24.

[53]   Ibid.

[54]   Bourdieu, P. (1972) 'Les stratégies matrimoniales dans le système de reproduction', *Annales Econ. Soc. Civil.*, 4-5, 1105-27 (p.1107) ; Bourdieu, P. (1962) 'Célibat et condition paysanne', *Etudes rurales*, 5-6, 32-136.

[55]   Leppard, D. (2003) 'Golden Dynasties to Merge Down Aisle', *Sunday Times*, 20 July, p.7.

[56]   Bourdieu, P. (1984) *Distinction*, p.241.

[57]   Foucault, M. (1978) *The History of Sexuality: Volume I*, p.107.

[58]   Ibid., p.111.

[59]   Ibid., p.5.

[60]   Ibid., p.106.

[61]   One interviewee, Jean-Claude Le Grand, Director of Corporate Strategic Recruit-

ment at L'Oréal, played both one of the most elitist sports, polo, and one of the most popular, football, whilst recognising that these were at either end of the class spectrum. Bonnie Erickson describes this as 'cultural variety', which displays a 'hierarchy of knowledge' rather than a 'hierarchy of tastes', enabling the individual to relate both to his peers and superiors (through polo) and employees (through football). Erickson, B.H. (1996) 'Culture, Class and Connections', *American Journal of Sociology*, 102, 1, July, 217-51 (p.219).

62 Bourdieu, P. (1984) *Distinction*, pp.53-56.
63 Ibid., p.55.
64 Weisz, G. (1983) *The Emergence of Modern Universities in France, 1863-1914*, Princeton: Princeton University Press, p.369.
65 Barsoux and Lawrence assert that this is the only *baccalauréat* option that counts, referring to 'the dictatorship of the bac C'. Barsoux, J-L. and Lawrence, P. (1990) *Management in France*, London: Cassell, p.32.
66 Ouchi, W. and Johnson, J. (1978) 'Types of Organizational Control and Their Relationship to Emotional Well Being', *Administrative Science Quarterly*, 23, June, 293-317; Schein, E. (1985) *Organisational Culture and Leadership*, London: Jossey Bass, p.6.
67 Scott, J. (1985) *Corporations, Classes and Capitalism*, 2nd edition, London: Hutchinson, 59-60.
68 Chandler, A.D. Jr. (1962) *Strategy and Structure: Chapters in the History of the Amnerican Industrial Enterprise*, Cambridge, MA: MIT Press; Chandler, A.D. Jr. (1977) *The Visible Hand: the Managerial Revolution in American Business*, Cambridge, MA: Belknap; Chandler, A.D. Jr. (1990) *Scale and Scope: the Dynamics of Industrial Capitalism*, Cambridge, MA: Belknap. The best overview of Chandler's work and its application within the context of France and the UK is by Whittington, R. and Mayer, M. (2000) *The European Corporation: Strategy, Structure, and Social Science*, Oxford: OUP.
69 Berle, A.A. and Means, G.C. (1932) *The Modern Corporation and Private Property*, New York: Macmillan.
70 Scott, J. (1985) *Corporations, Classes and Capitalism*, pp. 64-67. Scott asserts that holdings of between 5 and 10 per cent may be regarded as instances of family control, albeit limited in nature.
71 Ibid., p.68.
72 In 1980 these included the Harriman, Rothschild, Kirby, Kemper and Dupont families. See Scott, J. (1985) *Corporations, Classes and Capitalism*, p.71.
73 Ibid., p.74.
74 Scott, J. (1986) *Capitalist Property and Financial Power*, Brighton: Wheatsheaf, p.87.
75 Scott, J. (1982) *The Upper Classes: Property and Privilege in Britain*, London: Macmillan.
76 Mills, C. Wright (1959) *The Power Elite*, Oxford: OUP, p. 122, cited in Scott, J. and Griff, C. (1984) *Directors of Industry: the British Corporate Network 1904-76*, Oxford: Polity Press, p.132.
77 Scott, J. (1991) 'Networks of Corporate Power: a Comparative Assessment', p.184.

294 Business Elites and Corporate Governance

[78] Scott, J. and Griff, C. (1984) *Directors of Industry*, pp. 132-33; Useem, M. (1984) *The Inner Circle: Large Corporations and the Rise of Business Political Activity in the US and UK*, Oxford: OUP.

[79] Scott, J. (1991) 'Networks of Corporate Power: a Comparative Assessment', p. 182.

[80] Scott, J. and Griff, C. (1984) *Directors of Industry*, p.181.

[81] Scott, J. (1986) *Capitalist Property and Financial Power*, p.78.

[82] Scott, J. and Griff, C. (1984) *Directors of Industry*, p.134.

[83] Hamdouch, A. (1989) *Etat d'influence*, Paris: Presses du CNRS.

[84] Kadushin, C. (1995) 'Friendship among the French Financial Elite', *American Sociological Review*, 60, April, 202-21 (p.203). Key restaurants play a similar role.

[85] Higgs, D. (2003) *Review of the Role and Effectiveness of Non-Executive Directors*, Department of Trade and Industry, London, January (the Higgs Review).

[86] Granovetter, M. (1973) 'The Strength of Weak Ties', *American Journal of Sociology*, 78, 1360-80 (p.1378).

[87] Scott, J. (2000) *Social Network Analysis*, 2nd edition, London: Sage, p.35.

Chapter 3. Governance Regimes in Comparative Perspective

[1] Zola, E. (1895) *Germinal*: Paris: Fasquelle.

[2] By December 2003, country codes of corporate governance had been adopted in Australia, Austria, Belgium, Brazil, Canada, Cyprus, the Czech Republic, Denmark, France, Germany, Greece, Hong Kong, India, Indonesia, Ireland, Italy, Japan, Kenya, Korea, Malaysia, Macedonia, Malta, Mexico, the Netherlands, Pakistan, Peru, Poland, Portugal, Romania, Russia, Singapore, Slovakia, South Africa, Spain, Sweden, Switzerland, Turkey, the UK and the US.

[3] These included the European Shareholders Association or the European Association of Securities Dealers.

[4] For an international index of corporate governance codes, see www.ecgi.org/codes_codes.htm.

[5] Committee on the Financial Aspects of Corporate Governance (1992) *The Financial Aspects of Corporate Governance*, London: Gee (the Cadbury Report).

[6] *Directors' Remuneration: the Report of a Study Group Chaired by Sir Richard Greenbury* (1995), London: Gee (the Greenbury Report); Hampel, R (1998) *Committee on Corporate Governance: Final Report*, London: Gee; Higgs, D. (2003) *Review of the Role and Effectiveness of Non-Executive Directors*, Department of Trade and Industry (DTI), January (the Higgs Review).

[7] Cadbury, Sir A. (2002) *Corporate Governance and Chairmanship: a Personal View*, Oxford: OUP, p.31.

[8] The Cadbury Report, p.15.

[9] Cadbury, Sir A. (2002) *Corporate Governance and Chairmanship*, p.1.

[10] Berle, A.A. and Means, G.C. (1932) *The Modern Corporation and Private Property*, New York: Macmillan. See also Daily, C.M. *et al.* (2003) 'Corporate Governance: Decades of Dialogue and Data', *Academy of Management Review*, 28, 3, 371-82; Daily, C.M. *et al.* (2003) 'Governance Through Ownership: Centuries of Practice,

Decades of Research', *Academy of Management Journal*, 46, 2, 151-58.
[11] Cadbury, Sir A. (2002) *Corporate Governance and Chairmanship*, p.7.
[12] Toms, S. and Wright, M. (2004) 'Divergence and Convergence within Anglo-American Corporate Governance Systems: Evidence from the US and UK, 1950-2000', *Business History*, 47, 2, April, 267-91.
[13] Treadway Commission (1987) *Report of the National Commission on Fraudulent Financial Reporting*, Washington. Toms, S. and Wright, M. (2004) 'Divergence and Convergence within Anglo-American Corporate Governance Systems'; Cheffins, B.R. (2001) 'Corporate Governance Reform: Britain as an Exporter', *Hume Papers on Public Policy*, 8, 1, 10-28 (p.12).
[14] Cadbury, Sir A. (2002) *Corporate Governance and Chairmanship*, pp.57-58.
[15] Maclean, M. (1999) 'Corporate Governance in France and the UK: Long-term Perspectives on Contemporary Institutional Arrangements', *Business History*, 41, 1, 88-116.
[16] The Higgs Review.
[17] Association Française des Entreprises Privée/Conseil National du Patronat Français (1995) *Le Conseil d'administration des sociétés cotées*, Paris: IEP (Viénot I); Marini, P. (1996) *La Modernisation du droit des sociétés*, Paris: La Documentation Française; AFEP/Mouvement des Entreprises de France (1999) *Rapport du Comité sur le gouvernement d'entreprise présidé par M. Marc Viénot* (Viénot II); MEDEF/AFEP (2002) *Pour un meilleur gouvernement des entreprises cotées* (the Bouton Report).
[18] Law no. 2001-420, 15 May 2001.
[19] AFG-ASFFI (1998) *Recommandations sur le gouvernement d'entreprise*, p.1.
[20] For a comparative study of privatisation in Britain and France, see Wright, V. (1995) 'The Industrial Privatization Programmes of Britain and France: the Impact of Political and Institutional Factors', in Jones, P., ed., *Party, Parliament and Personality: Essays Presented to Hugh Berrington*, Routledge: London, 99-120. On privatisation in France, see Maclean, M. (1997) 'Privatisation, *dirigisme* and the Global Economy: an End to French Exceptionalism?', *Modern and Contemporary France*, 5, 2, 215-28.
[21] Maclean, M. (2002) *Economic Management and French Business from de Gaulle to Chirac*, Basingstoke: Palgrave Macmillan, pp.194-98.
[22] We owe this information to David Love of British Energy.
[23] Conyon, M.J. and Gregg, P. (1994) 'Pay at the Top: a Study of the Sensitivity of Top Director Remuneration to Company Specific Shocks', *National Institute Economic Review*, 3, 83-92.
[24] 'Directors' Remuneration – Control and Common Sense' (1995) *Corporate Governance: an International Review*, 3, 1, p.2.
[25] Bruce, A. and Buck, T. (1997) 'Executive Reward and Corporate Governance, in Keasey. K. *et al.*, eds., *Corporate Governance: Economic, Management and Financial Issues*, Oxford: OUP, 80-102.
[26] Korn/Ferry International (2002) *Gouvernement d'entreprise en France en 2002*, Paris, December, p.14.
[27] This was the title of a 1988 novel by Tom Wolfe, which captured the *Zeitgeist* of

the heady, greedy 1980s.

28 American National Can, acquired by Pechiney in 1988, was sold in 1995 to put the company on a sound financial footing in preparation for privatisation.

29 Waters, R. (1991) 'The French Edge Ahead', *Financial Times*, 18 November, p.16.

30 Franks, J. and Mayer, C. (1990) 'Capital Markets and Corporate Control: a Study of France, Germany and the UK', *Economic Policy*, 191-231.

31 Gugler, K., ed. (2001) *Corporate Governance and Economic Performance*, Oxford: OUP, p.7.

32 Ibid., p.8.

33 Korn/Ferry International (2002) *Gouvernement d'entreprise en France*, p.60.

34 Charkham, J. (1994) *Keeping Good Company: a Study of Corporate Governance in Five Countries*, Oxford: Clarendon Press, p.132.

35 Morin, F. (1998) *Le Modèle français de détention et de gestion du capital*, Paris : Editions de Bercy.

36 Useem, M. (1996) *Investor Capitalism*, New York: Basic Books.

37 Interview with Xavier Barrière, Human Resource Director (Europe), Air Liquide, Paris, 26 May 2003.

38 Maclean, M. (2002) *Economic Management and French Business*, p.203.

39 At the parliamentary enquiry into the collapse of Crédit Lyonnais in 1994, ex-PDG Jean-Yves Haberer admitted that the heads of large state-owned banks regularly colluded to agree their results. Having selected, on one occasion, the date of the death of Henri IV as an interim figure (1610, or a figure of FF1,610 million), Haberer was amused to observe that one of FF1,611 million was announced by the BNP the following week. Séguin, P. and d'Aubert, F. (1994) *Crédit Lyonnais*, 2, Paris: Assemblée Nationale, p.66.

40 Styles, P. and Taylor, B. (1993) 'Maxwell – the Failure of Corporate Governance', *Corporate Governance: an International Review*, 1, 1, January, 34-45.

41 Warner, J. (2004) 'Outlook: banking on compensation as BCCI marathon reaches court', *Independent*, 13 January.

42 Kay, M.J. and Silberston, A. (1995) 'Corporate Governance', *National Institute Economic Review*, 153, p.84.

43 Mansell, I. (2003) 'Polly Peck fugitive targets presidential post in Cyprus', *The Times*, 11 November, p.21.

44 Cadbury, Sir A. (2002) *Corporate Governance and Chairmanship*, p.11.

45 HMSO (1995) *Report of the Board of Banking Supervision Inquiry into the Circumstances of the Collapse of Barings*, London.

46 Gapper, J. and Denton, N. (1995) 'The Barings Report: Singapore Suggests Cover-ups from the Top', *Financial Times*, 18 October.

47 'France' (1997) Corporate Governance: an International Review, 5, 1, January, p.46.

48 Hayward, J. (1998) *'Moins d'Etat* or *Mieux d'Etat*: the French Response to the Neo-liberal Challenge', in Maclean, M., ed., *The Mitterrand Years: Legacy and Evaluation*, Basingstoke: Macmillan, 23-35 (p.28).

49 Routier, A. (1989) *La République des loups*, Paris: Calmann-Lévy.

50 Bremner, C. (2003) 'Elf Bosses were "victims of a corrupt system"', *The Times*, 9 June.

51 This was his second trial: Le Floch-Prigent was already serving a three-year sentence for a previous corruption conviction in the Elf-Bidermann affair.

52 Bremner, C. (2003) 'Elf Bosses were "victims of a corrupt system"'.

53 BBC News, 24 April 2003.

54 Ibid.

55 Bremner, C. (2003) '13 jailed in £200m French oil scandal', *The Times*, 13 November, p.18.

56 *L'Humanité*, 6 January 2001; *Le Monde*, 12 January 2001.

57 Lichfield, J. (2001) 'French VIPs at risk if "Mr Chips" talks', *Independent on Sunday*, 11 February, p.19; Bremner, C. (2001) 'The French Revolution', *The Times*, 16 January, 2-3.

58 On a personal note, having met and interviewed Pierre Bilger two months prior to his resignation as Chairman of the Board of Alstom, it is difficult to avoid the conclusion that he has been made a scapegoat. He spoke openly for an hour and a half. We do not believe that he would have done so, nor agreed to be interviewed in the first place, had he had an inkling of what lay just around the corner. This unfortunate case exemplifies the total responsibility that must be assumed by the PDG.

59 Personal statement by Pierre Bilger, 18 August 2003.

60 'Alstom, chronique d'un sauvetage d'Etat' (2003) *L'Expansion*, 27 August.

61 Sage, A. (2003) 'French face trial in US over Crédit Lyonnais', *The Times*, 4 December, p.36.

62 Personal statement by Jean Peyrelevade, 2 October 2003.

63 Ibid.

64 'The Godfather of corporate governance' (2003), *The Times*, 25 April, p.35.

65 Dyckhoff, N. (1995) *Pay at the Top: a Practical Guide to Getting It Right*, London: Spencer Stuart, p.18.

66 Cadbury, Sir A. (2002) *Corporate Governance and Chairmanship*, p.98.

67 ICMG (1995) *Who Holds the Reins?* London: ICMG, p.7.

68 Le Wita, B. (1994) *French Bourgeois Culture*, translated by J.A. Underwood, Cambridge: CUP, p.8.

69 The second Viénot Report discussed the financial disclosure of estimated (provisional) consolidated annual accounts, final consolidated accounts and final consolidated half-yearly accounts, but not individual remuneration.

70 Marc Viénot, 22 July 1999, cited in *Business Week*.

71 Interview with Madame Agnès Lépinay, Director of Economic, Financial and Fiscal Affairs, MEDEF, 26 May 2003, Paris.

72 Five in companies with fewer than 200 employees.

73 For a full list of the remuneration of French PDG, see Korn/Ferry International (2002) *Gouvernement d'entreprise en France*, p.39.

74 The Bouton Report, p.14.

75 Korn/Ferry International (2002) *Gouvernement d'entreprise en France*, p.13.

76 Ibid., p.17.

77 Hopkins, N. (2003) 'New inquiry into Vivendi', *The Times*, 16 September, p.23.

78 Korn/Ferry International (2002) *Gouvernement d'entreprise en France*, p.39.

298   *Business Elites and Corporate Governance*

[79] Interview with Jean-Claude Le Grand, Director of Corporate Recruitment, L'Oréal, Clichy, Paris, 10 March 2003.

[80] MEDEF Comité d'Ethique (2003) *La Rémunération des dirigeants d'entreprise, mantataires sociaux*, May, p.2.

[81] Ibid., p.3.

[82] Interview with Agnès Lépinay.

[83] O'Connell, D. (2003) 'Storm over £13m for MG Rover chiefs', *Sunday Times*, 9 November, p.3.8.

[84] Buckley, C. (2003) 'Angry investors attack Corus board's pay policy', *The Times*, 30 April, p.25.

[85] Butler, S. (2003) 'Boots chairman under fire over chief's pay deal', *The Times*, 2 May, p.29.

[86] Hart, J. (2003) 'C & W chief's payoff cut', *The Times*, 19 June, p.23.

[87] Reported in the *Guardian*, 7 July 2003.

[88] Daily, C.M. et al. (2003) 'Corporate Governance: Decades of Dialogue and Data', p.375.

[89] Leppard, D. and Winnett, R. (2003) 'Taxpayers to plug £25 million hole in MPs' pensions', *Sunday Times*, 25 May, p.28.

[90] Rose points elsewhere to the difficulties of using 'the family firm' as a generic term, since family firms, in which ownership and control are united in some respect, vary widely in structure, scale, scope, boundaries and legal status. Rose, M.B. (1994) 'The Family Firm in British Business', in Kirby, M.W. and Rose, M.B., eds., *Business Enterprise in Modern Britain: from the Eighteenth to the Twentieth Century*, London: Cass, 61-87 (pp.61-62).

[91] Jones, G. and Rose, M.B. (1993) 'Family Capitalism', in Jones, G. and Rose, M.B., eds., *Family Capitalism*, London: Cass, pp. 1-16 (p.1).

[92] European Commission (1995) *Small and Medium-sized Enterprises: a Dynamic Source of Employment, Growth and Competitiveness in the European Union*, Brussels, p.3.

[93] Bloch and Kremp's dataset of 280,000 firms revealed that in 2000, individuals or families remained the primary category of owners in France, holding on average half the capital. See Kremp, E. and Sevestre, P. (2001) 'France', in Gugler, K., ed., *Corporate Governance and Economic Performance*, 121-29 (p.122).

[94] Goergen, M. and Renneboog, L. (2001) 'United Kingdom', in Gugler, K., ed., *Corporate Governance and Economic Performance*, 184-200 (p.184).

[95] Cadbury, Sir A. (2002) *Corporate Governance and Chairmanship*, p.5.

[96] Liliane Bettencourt is linked, through Gesparal, to Nestlé, which owns 49 per cent of L'Oréal.

[97] Interview with Jean-Claude Le Grand.

[98] Hoar, R. (2003) 'Seven over 70', *Management Today*, October, p.60.

[99] Landes, D.S. (1949) 'French Entrepreneurship and Industrial Growth in the Nineteenth Century', *Journal of Economic History*, 9, 44-61.

[100] Chandler, A.D. Jr. (1990) *Scale and Scope: the Dynamics of Industrial Capitalism*, Cambridge MA: Belknap, pp.236-94.

[101] There is an obvious danger in rushing to generalisations about the competitive

nature of British capitalism. Church, for instance, draws attention to the narrow empirical base of Chandler's research, and supports Payne's conclusion, which differentiates between small and large family firms: 'whereas the *small* family business positively promotes growth the *large* public company which retains elements of family control probably retards growth'. Church, R. (1993) 'The Family Firm in Industrial Capitalism: International Perspectives on Hypotheses and History', in Jones, G. and Rose, M.B., eds., *Family Capitalism*, p.20. Church endorses Florence's suggestion that family business leaders may have been as keen on profit retention and long-term growth as salaried managers, but were more likely to be put under pressure by their relatives, greedy for generous dividends.

[102] Chandler, Jr, A.D. (1990) *Scale and Scope*, p.294.

[103] Chadeau, E. (1993) 'The Large Family Firm in Twentieth-Century France', in Jones, G. and Rose, M.B., eds., *Family Capitalism*, 184-205, p.191.

[104] Rahman, B. (2003) 'L'Oréal boosts its Shu Uemura stake', *Financial Times*, 20 November 2003, p.17.

[105] Interview with Jean-Claude Le Grand.

[106] Le Foll, A. and de Pirey, E. (2003) 'L'heureuse alliance de l'héritier et du manager', *La Gazette de la société et des techniques*, 23, November, 1-4 (p.1).

[107] French inheritance law divides estates equally among surviving offspring, according to the Napoleonic Code, which may cause difficulties regarding succession.

[108] Scott, J. (1985) *Corporations, Classes and Capitalism*, 2nd edition, London: Hutchinson, pp.131-42.

[109] Plessis, A. (1985) *La Politique de la Banque de France de 1851 à 1870*, Geneva: Droz, p.154. Though Plessis is describing the bank a century earlier, the description still resonates today.

[110] Fabius, L. (1994) 'Privatisations: attention danger', *Le Nouvel Observateur*, 14 April.

[111] Scott, J.P. and Griff, C. (1984) *Directors of Industry: the British Corporate Network 1904-76*, Oxford: Polity Press, p.102.

[112] Based on Stock Exchange data (1983), cited in Scott, *Corporations, Classes and Capitalism*, p.78.

[113] Bloch, L. and Kremp, E. (2001) 'Ownership and Voting Power in France, in Barca, F. and Becht, M., eds., *The Control of Corporate Europe*, Oxford: OUP, 106-27 (p.122).

[114] Myners, P. (2001) *Institutional Investment in the UK: a Review*, HM Treasury, March, p.27 (the Myners Report).

[115] Ann Robinson, Director General of NAPF, seminar hosted at Bank of England, 12 May 1997.

[116] Davis, E.P. (1997) *Can Pension Systems Cope? Population Ageing and Retirement Income Provision in the European Union*, London: RIIA, p.43.

[117] Ibid., p.42.

[118] Between 1950 and 1990, life expectancy rose from 68 to 81 years for French women and from 63 to 73 for men, while in the UK it rose from 71 to 79 for women and from 66 to 73 for men. Dependency ratios are expected to increase

from 22 per cent to 39 per cent in France over the period 1990 to 2040, and from 24 per cent to 39 per cent in the UK. Taverne, D. (1995) *The Pension Time Bomb in Europe*, London: Federal Trust, p.3.

[119] The Balladur pension reforms of 1993, which affected private sector pensions, increased the number of years of contribution (from 2003) from 37.5 to 40 years. Salaries were henceforth linked to prices rather than earnings, and pensions calculated on the best 25 years rather than the best 10. Guélaud, C. (2003) 'M. Balladur a ouvert la voie de la réforme en 1993', *Le Monde*, 25-26 May, p.9.

[120] Carati, G. and Tourani Rad, A. (2000) 'Convergence of Corporate Governance Systems', *Managerial Finance*, 26, 10, 66-83.

[121] Maréchal, A. (1998) 'Les critères d'investissement des grands gestionnaires de fond internationaux dans les entreprises françaises', *Bulletin de la COB*, 322, March.

[122] Morin, F. (2000) 'Transformation in the French Model of Shareholding and Management', *Economy and Society*, 29, 1, February, 31-53.

[123] De Tricornot, A. (2001) 'Qui possède les entreprises européennes?', *L'Expansion*, 21 December-3 January, p.140.

[124] Cadbury, Sir A. (2002) *Corporate Governance and Chairmanship*, p.10.

[125] Doran, J. (2003) 'Calpers sues NYSE over trading scam', *The Times*, 17 December, p.21.

[126] Snoddy, R. (2003) 'Investors square up for fight with board of BSkyB', *The Times*, 5 November, p.23.

[127] Equitable's former auditors Ernst & Young are also under fire, being sued by the insurer's current management for £2.05 billion. Senior A. and Seib, C. (2005) '£3.75 billion Equitable lawsuit is make or break for savers', *The Times*, 11 April, p.11.

[128] Senior, A. (2003) 'Ex-directors fight Equitable's £3.2bn claim', *The Times*, 22 September, p.23.

[129] Penrose, Rt. Hon. Lord (2004), *Report of the Equitable Life Inquiry*, London: HMSO, March, pp.703, 723-724, 741. See also Senior A. and Seib, C. (2005) '£3.75 billion Equitable lawsuit is make or break for savers', p.11.

[130] The Cadbury Report, p.22, para. 4.12.

[131] Wheatcroft, P. (2003) 'Life, but not as we know it', *The Times*, 23 September, p.25.

[132] Hall, P.A. (1987) 'The Evolution of Economic Policy Under Mitterrand', in Ross, G, Hoffmann, S. and Malzacher, S. eds., *The Mitterrand Experiment*, New York: OUP, p.59.

[133] Bloch, L. and Kremp, E. (2001) 'Ownership and Control in France', p.122.

[134] The seven *entreprises publiques* were Charbonnages de France, EdF, EMC, Gaz de France, La Poste, RATP and SNCF.

[135] Weber, H. (1986), *Le Parti des patrons: le CNPF (1946-1986)*, Paris: Seuil, pp.113-115.

[136] Maclean, M. (2005) 'The Interventionist State: Demise or Transformation?', in Raymond, G and Cole, A., eds., *Redefining the French Republic*, Manchester: MUP.

137 Sage, A. (2003) 'Europe set to approve E3bn rescue for Alstom', *The Times*, 22 September, p.25; 'Alstom rescue approval' (2003) *The Times*, 23 September, p.23.
138 Charkham, J. (1994) *Keeping Good Company*, p.120.
139 Jameson, A. and Sage, A. (2003) 'UK unions attack ministers over Alstom', *The Times*, 23 September, p.27.
140 Interview with Per Staehr, Chairman and Chief Country Representative of all Bombardier Transportation rail companies in the UK, Milton Keynes, 28 April 2003.
141 Buckley, C. *et al.* (2005) 'Rover finally stalls', *The Times*, 8 April, 1-2.
142 Sage, A. (2004) 'French minister pledges State sell-offs', *The Times*, 5 May, p.23.
143 Ibid.
144 EIU, *Country Report: France*, July, p.19.
145 Tricker, B. (1996) 'Whose Company is It Anyway?', *Corporate Governance: an International Review*, 4, 1, January, p.2.
146 Cited in Kremp, E. and Sevestre, P. (2001) 'France', p.121.
147 Charkham, J. (1994) *Keeping Good Company*.
148 Pierre Bilger, former PDG of Alstom, explained that his predecessor at what was then Alcatel Alsthom had proposed his nomination in March 1991. Interview with Pierre Bilger, Chairman of the Board, Alstom, January 2003, Paris.
149 Peyrelevade, J. (1993) *Pour un capitalisme intelligent*, Paris: Grasset & Fasquelle, p.55.
150 Ibid., p.52.
151 Letreguilly, H. (1997) 'France', *International Financial Law Review*, Supplement on Corporate Governance, April, 18-22.
152 Moutet, A. (1997) *Les Logiques de l'entreprise: la rationalisation dans l'industrie française de l'entre-deux-guerres*, Paris: Editions de l'Ecole des Hautes Etudes en Sciences Sociales, pp.449-50.
153 Ibid., p.125.
154 Korn/Ferry International (2002) *Gouvernement d'entreprise en France*, pp.18-19. Note, however, that Michelin and Lagardère have a different legal structure, being *sociétés en commandite par actions*, not *sociétés anonymes*.
155 Ibid., p.9.
156 Ibid., p.36. By 2004, Peyrelevade and Messier held just one relatively minor role apiece, and their biographical data had been erased from the *Guide des Etats Majors*. This however was indicative of their fall from grace rather than a fundamental change in what was deemed acceptable.
157 Sabbagh, D. (2003) 'Messier called to top-pay enquiry', *The Times*, 2 October, p.32.
158 The Bouton Report, p.9.
159 Ibid.
160 Korn/Ferry International (2002) *Gouvernement d'entreprise en France*, p.36.
161 Ibid., p.26.
162 Interview with Pierre Bilger.
163 IoD, *Entreprise with Integrity*, London.
164 The Cadbury Report, p.21, para. 4.9.

302 *Business Elites and Corporate Governance*

[165] Plautus, cited in Cadbury, Sir A. (2002) *Corporate Governance and Chairmanship*, p.34.
[166] The Higgs Review, p.3.
[167] Ibid., paras. 9.10-9.14, pp.36-7.
[168] Ibid., para 8.8, p.34.
[169] Ibid., paras 15.16, 15.18, p.69.
[170] Ibid., para. 10.9, p.40.
[171] Hotton, R. (2003) 'Top chairmen condemn Higgs', *The Times*, 10 March, p.21.
[172] The Higgs Review, para. 5.7, p.24.
[173] Ibid., para. 12.9, p.55.
[174] Ibid., para. 12.5, p.53.
[175] Ibid., paras. 11.1 and 11.6, p.47.
[176] Interview with Sir Adrian Cadbury, Solihull, 12 June 2003.
[177] The Bouton Report, p.8.
[178] Senior, A. (2003) 'Non-execs spurn Higgs', *The Times*, 17 April, p.27.
[179] Interview with Lord William Waldegrave, Director, UBS, and former Cabinet minister, London, 23 June 2003.
[180] Merrell, C. (2003) 'Higgs plans to be watered down', *The Times*, 10 May, p.52.
[181] Interview with Sir Adrian Cadbury.
[182] Hosking, P. (2005) 'Sir Ken agrees influx of non-execs', *The Times*, 19 May, 48-49.
[183] Rigby, E. and Goff, S. (2005) 'Morrison's chief loosens grip', *Financial Times*, 27 May, p.1.
[184] Korn/Ferry International (2002) *Gouvernement d'entreprise en France*, p.5.
[185] Interview with Pierre Bilger.
[186] Cadbury, Sir A. (2002) *Corporate Governance and Chairmanship*, p.52.
[187] Johnson, J.L. *et al.* (1996), 'Boards of Directors: a Review and Research Agenda', *Journal of Management*, 22, 409-38 (p.433), cited in Heracleous, L. (2001) 'What is the Impact of Corporate Governance on Organisational Performance?', *Corporate Governance: an International Journal*, 9, 3, July, 165-73 (p.168).
[188] Gillies, J. and Morra, D. (1997) 'Does Corporate Governance Matter?', *Business Quarterly*, Spring, 71-77 (p.77), cited in Heracleous, L. (2001) 'What is the Impact of Corporate Governance on Organisational Performance?', p.170.
[189] Hosking, P. (2005) 'Governance league table deals blow to blue chips', *The Times*, 15 April, p.55.
[190] Interview with Lord Waldegrave.
[191] Lerougetel, A. (2004) 'Alain Juppé condamné pour corruption: le Président Chirac directement exposé', *Politis*, 3 February.
[192] Scott, C. (2005) 'Finance Minister Resigns', *Australasian Business Intelligence*, 15 March 2005.

Chapter 4. Social Origins and the Education of Business Elites

[1] Simon, J. (1865) *L'Ecole*, Paris, cited in Harrigan, P.J. (1980) *Mobility, Elites and Education in French Society of the Second Empire*, Waterloo, Ontario: Wilfred

Laurier University Press, p.127.

2   Cappelli, P. and Hamori, M. (2005) 'The New Road to the Top', *Harvard Business Review*, 83, 1, 25-32.

3   Wacquant, L.J.D. (1996) 'Foreword', in Bourdieu, P., *The State Nobility: Elite Schools in the Field of Power*, translated by L.C. Clough, Cambridge: Polity Press, p.xii.

4   Bourdieu, P. (1994) *The State Nobility*, p.133; Swartz, D. (1997) *Culture and Power: the Sociology of Pierre Bourdieu*, Chicago: Chicago University Press, p.196.

5   Marceau, J. (1981) '*Plus ça change plus c'est la même chose*: Access to Elite Careers in French Business', in Howorth, J. and Cerny, P., eds., *Elites in France*, London: Pinter, 104-33.

6   Swartz, D. (1997) *Culture and Power*, p.196.

7   The ESC of Lyon, Rouen and Le Havre were established in 1871.

8   For Bourdieu's complete list of 84 French institutions of higher education, major and minor, see Bourdieu, P. (1994) *The State Nobility*, pp.133-35. Bourdieu examines the socio-academic background of 21 *grandes écoles*, exploring 15 in greater depth.

9   Wacquant, L.J.D. (1996) 'Foreword', *The State Nobility*, p.xii.

10 Giddens, A. (1974) 'Elites in the British Class Structure', in Stanworth, P. and Giddens, A., eds., *Elites and Power in British Society*, Cambridge: CUP, 1-21 (p.17).

11 Stanworth, P. and Giddens, A. (1974) 'An Economic Elite: a Demographic Profile of Company Chairmen', in Stanworth, P. and Giddens, A., eds., *Elites and Power in British Society*, 81-101 (p.81).

12 Mills, C.W. (1959) *The Power Elite*, Oxford: OUP, p.4.

13 Interview with Lord Waldegrave, Director, UBS, London, 23 June 2003.

14 Interview with Jean-François Théodore, Euronext, London, 7 November 2003.

15 Halsey, A.H. (1995) *Change in British Society*, 4th edition, Oxford: OUP, p.35.

16 Ibid.

17 Ibid., p.136.

18 Reported in the *Guardian*, 20 April 2002.

19 Midgley, C. (2005) 'Follow the customer, not the competition', *The Times*, T2, 19 May, 4-5.

20 Halsey, A.H. (1995) *Change in British Society*, p.152.

21 Ibid., pp.152-55.

22 See also Bourdieu, P. (1988) *Homo Academicus*, Stanford: Stanford University Press; Bourdieu, P. and Passeron, J-C. (1979) *The Inheritors*, Chicago: University of Chicago Press; Bourdieu, P. and Passeron, J-C. (1990) *Reproduction in Education, Society and Culture*, 2nd edition, translated by R. Nice, London: Sage; Bourdieu, P. *et al.* (1992) *Academic Discourse: Linguistic Misunderstanding and Professorial Power*, Cambridge: Polity Press.

23 Wacquant, L.J.D. (1996) 'Foreword', *The State Nobility*, p.ix.

24 Bourdieu, P. (1984) *Distinction: a Social Critique of the Judgement of Taste*, translated by R. Nice, London: Routledge and Kegan Paul.

25 Bourdieu, P. (1996), *The State Nobility*, pp.35-36.

304 *Business Elites and Corporate Governance*

26 Bourdieu, P. (1991) *Language and Symbolic Power*, translated by G. Raymond and M. Adamson, edited by J.B. Thomson, Cambridge: Polity Press, pp 43-65.
27 Bourdieu, P. (1996), *The State Nobility*, p.83.
28 Ibid., p 42.
29 Bourdieu, P. (1991) *Language and Symbolic Power*, p.57.
30 Ibid., pp.73-74.
31 Bourdieu, P. *et al.* (1973) 'Les stratégies de reconversion: les classes sociales et le système d'enseignement', *Information sur les Sciences Sociales*, 12, 5, 61-113.
32 Bourdieu, P. (1990) 'Academic Order and Social Order', Preface to the 1990 edition, Bourdieu, P. and Passeron, J-C., *Reproduction in Education, Society and Culture*, p.xi.
33 Bourdieu, P. (1996), 'Prologue', *The State Nobility*, p.5.
34 Bourdieu, P. (1990) 'Academic Order and Social Order', p. x; Swartz, D. (1997) *Culture and Power*, p.201.
35 Bourdieu, P. (1990) 'Academic Order and Social Order', p.ix.
36 Bourdieu, P. (1996), *The State Nobility*, p.40.
37 Ibid., p.6.
38 Ibid., p.37.
39 Ibid., p.45.
40 Ibid., p.5.
41 Charting the social origins of prizewinners in the 'Concours Général' from 1966 to 1986, as determined by their father's or mother's occupation, Bourdieu discovered that these remained largely stable. Ibid., p.54.
42 Swartz, D. (1997) *Culture and Power*, p.191.
43 Bourdieu, P. and Saint Martin, M. (1973) 'Le Patronat', *Actes de la Recherche en Sciences Sociales*, 20-21, 3-82 (p.23). (All translations by M. Maclean unless stated otherwise.)
44 Swartz, D. (1997) *Culture and Power*, p.203.
45 Harrigan, P.J. (1980) *Mobility, Elites and Education*, p.117.
46 Day, C.R. (1978) 'The Making of Mechanical Engineers in France: the Ecoles d'Arts et Métiers, 1803-1914', *French Historical Studies*, 10, Spring, 439-60 (p.440).
47 Harrigan, P.J. (1980) *Mobility, Elites and Education*, pp.158-59.
48 Ibid., p.140.
49 Bourdieu, P. and Saint Martin, M. (1973) 'Le Patronat', p.24.
50 Vaughan, M. (1981) 'The Grandes Ecoles: Selection, Legitimation, Perpetuation', in Howorth, J. and Cerny, P., eds., *Elites in France*, 93-103 (p.94).
51 Moody, J.N. (1978) *French Education Since Napoleon*, Syracuse: Syracuse University Press, pp.157-58.
52 Majault, J. (1967) *La Révolution de l'enseignement*, Paris: Laffont, p.11, quoted in Moody, J.N. (1978) *French Education Since Napoleon*, p.157.
53 Ibid., p.159.
54 Ponteil, F. (1966) *Histoire de l'enseignement en France: les grandes étapes 1789-1964*, Paris: Sirey, pp.401-2.
55 Moody, J.N. (1978) *French Education Since Napoleon*, p.157.

56 Weisz, G. (1983) *The Emergence of Modern Universities in France*, p.376.
57 Fougère, L., ed. (1974) Le Conseil d'Etat 1799-1974, Paris, cited in Stevens, A. (1981) 'The Contribution of the Ecole Nationale d'Administration to French Political Life', in Howorth, J. and Cerny, P., eds., Elites in France, 134-53 (p.135).
58 Vaughan, M. (1981) 'The Grandes Ecoles', pp.93-94.
59 Daumard, A. (1958) 'Les élèves de l'Ecole Polytechnique de 1815 à 1848', *Revue d'histoire moderne et contemporaine*, 5, 226-34 (pp.230-31).
60 Vaughan, M. (1981) 'The Grandes Ecoles', p.99.
61 Suleiman, E.N. (1978) *Elites in French Society: the Politics of Survival*, Princeton: Princeton University Press, pp.4, 277.
62 Granick, D. (1962) *The European Executive*, New York: Doubleday, p. 149, cited in Hall, D. and de Bettignies, H-C. (1968) 'The French Business Elite', *European Business*, 19, October, 52-61 (p.57).
63 Two earlier attempts to establish an Ecole Nationale d'Aministration (in 1848 and 1936) had failed.
64 *Journal Officiel* (1945), 238, 10 October. Interestingly, ENA's website describes the school as 'the melting-pot of a great diversity of recruitment'. See www.ena.fr.
65 According to this survey, PDG were least likely to hail from the southwest region. Hall, D. and de Bettignies, H-C. (1968) 'The French Business Elite', p.54.
66 Moody, J.N. (1978) *French Education Since Napoleon*, p.193.
67 Suleiman, E. (1997) 'Les élites de l'administration et de la politique dans la France de la Ve République: Homogénéité, puissance, permanence', in Suleiman, E. and Mendras, H., eds., *Le Recrutement des élites en Europe*, Paris: La Découverte, p.33
68 1.4 per cent workers and 1.0 per cent employees. Suleiman, E. (1997) 'Les élites de l'administration et de la politique', p.35.
69 Hall, D. and de Bettignies, H-C. (1968) 'The French Business Elite', p.55.
70 Marceau, J. (1981) *'Plus ça change plus c'est la même chose'*, p.118.
71 Suleiman, E. (1997) 'Les élites d l'administration et de la politique', p.21.
72 Ibid., p.26.
73 Suleiman, E.N. (1978) *Elites in French Society*, p.197.
74 Kosciusko-Morizet, J.A. (1973) *La « Mafia » Polytechnicienne*, Paris: Seuil, pp.125-26.
75 Ibid., p.125.
76 Suleiman, E.N. (1978) *Elites in French Society*, p.179.
77 Granick, D. (1972) Managerial Comparisons of Four Developed Countries: France, Britain, United States and Russia, Cambridge, MA: MIT Press; Whitley, R. et al. (1981) Masters of Business: the Making of a New Elite? New York: Tavistock.
78 Suleiman, E.N. (1978) *Elites in French Society*, pp.196-219.
79 Mills, C.W. (1959) *The Power Elite*, Oxford: OUP, pp.83-88.
80 Hall, D. and de Bettignies, H-C. (1968) 'The French Business Elite', p.55.
81 Bourdieu, P. (1996), *The State Nobility*, p.292.
82 Ibid.

[83] Ibid., p.293. See also Bourdieu, P. and Saint Martin, M. (1973) 'Le Patronat', pp.27-28.

[84] Weisz, G. (1983) *The Emergence of Modern Universities in France*, p.369.

[85] Barsoux and Lawrence suggest that this is the only *baccalauréat* option that counts, referring to 'the dictatorship of the bac C'. Barsoux, J-L. and Lawrence, P. (1990) *Management in France*, London: Cassell, p.32.

[86] Suleiman, E.N. (1978) *Elites in French Society*, p.188.

[87] Stanworth, P. and Giddens, A. (1974) 'An Economic Elite', p.88.

[88] Halsey, A.H. *et al.* (1980) *Origins and Destinations: Family, Class and Education in Modern Britain*, Oxford: Clarendon.

[89] Rubinstein, W.D. (1987) *Elites and the Wealthy in Modern British History: Essays in Social and Economic History*, Brighton: Harvester Press, p.181.

[90] Whitley, R. (1973) 'Commonalities and Connections Among Directors of Large Financial Institutions', *Sociological Review*, 21, 4, 613-32 (p.618).

[91] Whitley, R. (1974) 'The City and Industry', p.67.

[92] Cappelli, P. and Hamori, M. (2005) 'The New Road to the Top'.

[93] Wakeford, F. and J. (1974) 'Universities and the Study of Elites', in Stanworth, Philip and Giddens, Anthony, eds. (1974) *Elites and Power in British Society*, 185-97.

[94] Whitley, R. (1974) 'The City and Industry', p.67.

[95] Perkin, H. (1978) 'The Recruitment of Elites in British Society Since 1800', *The Journal of Social History*, 12, 2, Winter, 222-34 (p.229).

[96] Vaughan, M. and Archer, M.S. (1971) *Social Conflict and Educational Change in England and France 1789-1848*, Cambridge: CUP, pp.51-52.

[97] Ibid., p.55.

[98] Ibid.

[99] Briggs, A. (1969) 'Developments in Higher Education in the United Kingdom: Nineteenth and Twentieth Centuries' in Niblett, W.R., ed., *Higher Education: Demand and Response,* London: Tavistock Publications, p.97.

[100] Sizer, J. (1987) 'An Analysis of the Trends Impacting on the UGC and British Universities', *Financial Accountability and Management*, 3, 1, p.9.

[101] Shattock, M. (1996) 'The Creation of the British University System' in Shattock, M., ed., *The Creation of a University System*, Oxford: Blackwell, 1-30.

[102] UK Higher Education Statistics Agency, www.hesa.ac.uk.

[103] Perkin, H. (1978) 'The Recruitment of Elites', p.229.

[104] Davis, C. (2005) 'UK sees endowments rise', *THES*, 20 May, p.10.

[105] Wakeford, F. and J. (1974) 'Universities and the Study of Elites', p.196.

[106] Ibid., p.197.

[107] Nicholas, T. (1999) 'The Myth of Meritocracy: an Inquiry into the Social Origins of Britain's Business Leaders Since 1850', Working Paper No. 53/99, Department of Economic History, London School of Economics, pp.1-2.

[108] Scott, J. (1982) *The Upper Classes: Property and Privilege in Britain*, London: Macmillan.

[109] Perkin, H. (1978) 'The Recruitment of Elites', p.230.

[110] Stanworth, P. and Giddens, A. (1974) 'An Economic Elite', p.83.

[111] Crouzet, F. (1985) *The First Industrialists*, Cambridge: CUP.
[112] Rubinstein, W.D. (1987) *Elites and the Wealthy*, p.173.
[113] Ibid., p.172.
[114] Ibid., p.175.
[115] Ibid.
[116] Nicholas, T. (1999) 'The Myth of Meritocracy', pp. 26, 4.
[117] Rubinstein, W.D. (1987) *Elites and the Wealthy*, p.182.
[118] Hannah, L. (1993) 'Cultural Determinants of Economic Performance', *Historical Analysis in Economics*, London, p.170, cited in Nicholas, T. (1999) 'The Myth of Meritocracy', p.2.
[119] Ibid., p.3.
[120] Stanworth, P. and Giddens, A. (1974) 'An Economic Elite', p.99.
[121] Snow, J. (2003) 'Secrecy and Sorcery Wreck the Gong Show', *Sunday Times*, 5 January, News Review, p.4.
[122] Stanworth, P. and Giddens, A. (1974) 'An Economic Elite', pp.88, 101.
[123] Ouchi, W. and Johnson, J. (1978) 'Types of Organizational Control and Their Relationship to Emotional Well Being', *Administrative Science Quarterly*, 23, June, 293-317 (p.297).
[124] Locke, R. (1988) 'Educational Traditions and the Development of Business Studies after 1945 (an Anglo-French-German Comparison)', *Business History*, 30, 1, 84-103.
[125] Windolf, P. (2002) *Corporate Networks in Europe and the United States*, Oxford: OUP, p.136.
[126] Giddens, A. (1974) 'Elites in the British Class Structure', p.14.
[127] Ibid., p.16.
[128] Whitley, R. (1974) 'The City and Industry: the Directors of Large Companies, their Characteristics and Connections', in Stanworth, P. and Giddens, A., eds., *Elites and Power in British Society*, 65-80 (p.65).
[129] Rubinstein observes that the value system and attitudes engendered by establishments of privilege, specifically English public schools, 'emphasized conformity, rote learning, the cult of the "gentleman" and of athleticism'. Rubinstein, W.D. (1987) *Elites and the Wealthy*, p.209.
[130] Nicholas, T. (1999) 'The Myth of Meritocracy', p.4.
[131] Vaughan, M. (1981) 'The Grandes Ecoles', p.101.
[132] Rubinstein, W.D. (1987) *Elites and the Wealthy*, p.193.
[133] Coleman, D.C. (1973) 'Gentlemen and Players', *Economic History Review*, 2nd series, 26, 92-116 (p.103), reproduced in Cassis, Y., ed. (1994) *Business Elites*, Aldershot, Hants: Edward Elgar, 125-49.
[134] Interview with George Cox, Institute of Directors, London, 24 April 2003.
[135] Interview with Jean-Claude Le Grand, Director of Corporate Recruitment, L'Oréal, Clichy, Paris, 10 March 2003.
[136] Giddens, A. (1974) Preface, p.xii.
[137] Bourdieu, P. (1977) *Outline of a Theory of Practice*, Cambridge: CUP, cited in Swartz, D. (1997) *Culture and Power*, p.70.
[138] Halpin, T. (2004) 'Richer Students still have Edge', *The Times*, 29 March, p.4.

139 Marceau, J. (1981) '*Plus ça change plus c'est la même chose*', p.129.
140 Mosca, G. (1939) *The Ruling Class*, edited by A. Livingston, translated by H.D. Kahn, New York: McGraw-Hill, p.58.

Chapter 5. Elite Careers and Lifestyles

1 Bourdieu, P. (1986) *Distinction: a Social Critique of the Judgement of Taste*, translated by R. Nice, London: Routledge and Kegan Paul, p.6.
2 Windolf, P. (2002) *Corporate Networks in Europe and the United States*, Oxford: OUP, p.148.
3 Datamonitor (2004) *Sodexho Alliance Company Report*, http://dbic.datamonitor.com.
4 Reier, S. (1995) 'You think fighting takeovers is tough? Look at what big Lyonnaise des Eaux had to do in Paris', *Financial World*, 24 October, 164, 22, p.40.
5 Interview with Iain Gray, Managing Director and General Manager, Airbus UK, Bristol, 4 February 2003.
6 Bourdieu, P. (1986) *Distinction*, pp.295-97.
7 Interview with George Cox, Director General, IoD, London, 24 April 2003.
8 Ibid.
9 Cappelli, P. and Hamori, M. (2005) 'The New Road to the Top', *Harvard Business Review*, 83, 1, January, 25-32.
10 Simpson, P., French, R. and Harvey, C. (2005) 'Leadership and Negative Capability', *Human Relations*, 55, 10, 1209-26.
11 Zweigenhaft, R.L. and Domhoff, G. W. (1998) *Diversity in the Power Elite: Have Women and Minorities Reached the Top?*, New Haven: Yale University Press, pp.41-42.
12 Higgs, D. (2003) *Review of the Role and Effectiveness of Non-Executive Directors*, Department of Trade and Industry (DTI), January, p.18 (the Higgs Review).
13 Interview with Sir Adrian Cadbury, Solihull, 12 June 2003.
14 Singh, V. and Vinnicombe, S. (2003) *Women Pass a Milestone: 101 Directorships on the FTSE 100 Boards: the Female FTSE Report 2003*, Cranfield School of Management, p.23.
15 As Sir Adrian Cadbury asserts, 'it is not possible seriously to suggest that there is a shortage of potential outside directors when so few women are board members … The responsibilities which many women carry in voluntary organisations and in public life will have given them a different type of experience from that of executives; as a result they can bring a particular kind of value added to a board.' Cadbury, Sir A. (2002) *Corporate Governance and Chairmanship: a Personal View*, Oxford: OUP, p.61.
16 Tyson, L. (2003) The Tyson Report on the Recruitment and Development of Non-Executive Directors, London Business School, June, p.5.
17 Zeïtoun, T.A. (2003) 'Les conseils d'administration: 5,08% de femmes', *Les Echos*, 7 March, p.16.
18 Zweigenhaft, R.L. and Domhoff, G.W. (1998) *Diversity in the Power Elite*.

[19] The Higgs Review, p.18.

[20] Organisation for Economic Cooperation and Development (OECD) Steering Group on Corporate Governance (2003) *Survey of Corporate Governance Developments in OECD Countries*, November, p.65.

[21] Huffmann, M.L. (1999) 'Who's In Charge? Organizational Influences on Women's Representation in Managerial Positions', *Social Science Quarterly*, 80, 4, December, 738-76; Wellington, S. *et al.* (2003) 'What's Holding Women Back?', *Harvard Business Review*, June, 18-19.

[22] Interview with Jean-Claude Le Grand, Director of Corporate Recruitment, L'Oréal, Paris, 10 March 2003.

[23] Ibid.

[24] Zweigenhaft, R.L. and Domhoff, G.W. (1998) *Diversity in the Power Elite*, p.69.

[25] Singh, V. and Vinnicombe, S. (2003) *Women Pass a Milestone*, p.19.

[26] Bourdieu, P. (2001) *Masculine Domination*, translated by R. Nice, Cambridge: Polity; Hartmann, M. (2000) 'Class-specific Habitus and the Social Reproduction of the Business Elite in Germany and France', *Sociological Review*, 241-61.

[27] Singh and Vinnicombe note that, by 2003, one-third of female directors of the top 100 British companies were titled, as against one-fifth of male directors, this discrepancy implying that women are still having to work harder to prove themselves than men. Singh, V. and Vinnicombe, S. (2003) *Women Pass a Milestone*, p.2.

[28] Kanter, R.M. (1977) *Men and Women of the Corporation*, New York: Basic Books.

[29] Zweigenhaft, R.L. and Domhoff, G. W. (1998) *Diversity in the Power Elite*, p.53.

[30] Bourdieu, P. (1986) *Distinction*, pp.232-33.

[31] Le Wita, B. (1994) *French Bourgeois Culture*, p.69.

[32] Bourdieu, P. (1986) *Distinction*, p.311.

[33] Garnham, N. (1986) 'Bourdieu's Distinction', *Sociological Review*, 34, May, 423-33 (p.427).

[34] Bourdieu, P. (1986) *Distinction*, p.466.

[35] Ibid., p.483.

[36] Le Wita, B. (1994) *French Bourgeois Culture*, p.21.

[37] Ibid., p.13.

[38] Garnham, N. (1986) 'Bourdieu's Distinction', p.425.

[39] Bourdieu, P. (1986) *Distinction*, p.7. See also the Introduction by R. Johnson to Bourdieu, P. (1993) *The Field of Cultural Production*, Cambridge: Polity Press, p.2; Berger, B.M. (1986) 'Review Essay: Taste and Domination', *American Journal of Sociology*, 91, 6, 1445-53 (p.1448).

[40] Bourdieu, P. (1986) *Distinction*, p.231.

[41] Deleuze, G. (1972) *Différence et répétition*, 2nd edition, Paris: PUF, pp.1, 7.

[42] Bourdieu, P. (1986) *Distinction*, p.315.

[43] Ibid., p.467.

44 Bourdieu, P. (1990) *The Logic of Practice*, translated by R. Nice, Stanford: Stanford University Press, p.54.

45 Bourdieu, P. (1986) *Distinction*, p.471.

46 Foucault, M. (1979) *Discipline and Punish: the Birth of the Prison*, translated by A.M. Sheridan, Harmondsworth: Penguin; Le Wita, B. (1994*) French Bourgeois Culture*, p.2.

47 Le Wita, B. (1994) *French Bourgeois Culture*, p.141.

48 Laura Thompson describes the class-ridden, yet seemingly class-less race-goers at Epsom in 1995 as follows: 'There seemed to be something almost dangerous about the role-playing ... It wasn't funny, it was meaningless. And, if it was meaningless, it was therefore extremely meaningful: if there was no reason at all for prancing around a course, dressed as something out of the Great Exhibition, the fact that it was still being done gave to those class-ridden stereotypes in the structure of the racecourse an embittered significance.' Thompson, L. (1996) *Quest for Greatness*, London: Michael Joseph, p.101, cited in Adonis, A. and Pollard, S. (1997) *A Class Act*, p.236.

49 Maclean's (2003), 116, 9, p.32.

50 Adonis, A. and Pollard, S. (1997) *A Class Act*, p.229.

51 Holt, R. (1989) *A History of British Sport*, Oxford: OUP, p.3.

52 Interview with George Cox.

53 Interview with Sir Adrian Cadbury.

54 Adonis, A. and Pollard, S. (1997) *A Class Act*, p.239.

55 Interview with Jean-Claude Le Grand.

56 Hennig, M. and Jardim, A. (1977) *The Managerial Woman*, New York: Anchor Press/Doubleday, p.45.

57 Zweigenhaft, R.L. and Domhoff, G.W. (1998) *Diversity in the Power Elite*, pp.52-53.

58 Interview with Sir Digby Jones, Director General, CBI, Bristol, 5 March 2004.

59 Interview with Larry Hirst, CEO IBM UK, London, 22 September 2003.

60 Adonis, A. and Pollard, S. (1997) *A Class Act*, p.228.

61 Among the most noteworthy are Messier, J-M. (2002) *Mon vrai journal*, Paris: Balland; Bilger, P. (2004) *Quatre millions d'euros: le prix de ma liberté*, Paris: Bourin; and Bébéar, C. and Manière, P. (2003) *Ils vont tuer le capitalisme*, Paris: Plon, this last-mentioned condemning corporate excess.

62 Alphandéry, E. (2000) *La Réforme obligée*, Paris: Grasset.

63 Dassault, S. (2001) *Un Projet pour la France*, Paris: Editions du Layeur.

64 Interview with Pierre Bilger, former PDG Alstom, 3 January 2003, Paris.

65 At one event to which the interviewers were invited in the course of this study, held in the Mediterranean, the host exhibited a small collection of original paintings by celebrated artists, including Claude Monet and Vincent Van Gogh.

66 Interview with Pierre Bilger.

67 Interview with Sir Adrian Cadbury.

68 Interview with Xavier Barrière, HRM Director (Europe), L'Air Liquide, Paris, 26 May 2003.

69 D.R. Hoffmann, cited in Wakeford, F. and J. (1974) 'Universities and the Study

of Elites', in Stanworth, P. and Giddens, A., eds., *Elites and Power in British Society*, London: CUP, 185-97 (p.192).

[70] Sir Mark Moody-Stuart is also Chairman of Business Action for Sustainable Development, although in this instance a premium of disinterestedness is not reaped, since this role is open to interpretation as a PR campaign to appear socially and environmentally responsible. (In fact, Sir Mark has been accused of this by 'Greenwash Guerrillas'. See the *Guardian*, 11 January 2003.)

[71] Interview with Louis Sherwood, Director, HBOS, Bristol, 5 November 2003.

[72] Interview with Sir Adrian Cadbury.

[73] Cox, G. (2003) 'Unsung Heroes of War', *IoD News*, April, p.3.

[74] Le Wita, B. (1994) *French Bourgeois Culture*, pp.126-28.

[75] Interview with Xavier Barrière.

[76] Interview with Iain Gray.

[77] Scott, J. (2002) 'Social Class and Stratification in Late Modernity', *Acta Sociologica*, 45, 1, 23-35 (p.30).

[78] Bourdieu, P. (1986) *Distinction*, p.466.

[79] Perkin, H. (1989) *The Rise of Professional Society: England Since 1880*, London: Routledge, p. 420, cited in Adonis, A. and Pollard, S. (1997) *A Class Act*, p.223.

[80] Scott, J. (2002) 'Social Class and Stratification in Late Modernity', p.34.

[81] Cadbury, Sir A. (2002) *Corporate Governance and Chairmanship*, pp.222-3.

[82] Dawson, S. (2004) 'Balancing Self-Interest and Altruism: Corporate Governance alone is not enough', *Corporate Governance: an International Review*, 12, 2, April, 130-33 (p.131).

[83] Monks, R. (2001) *The Global Investors: How Shareowners can Unlock Sustainable Prosperity Worldwide*, Oxford: Capstone, p.5.

[84] The 100 richest professionals in the City of London enjoyed estimated combined personal wealth of £9 billion in 2004, the majority being owners of hedge funds or running private-equity firms. Koenig, P. and Beresford, P. (2004) 'Revealed: the City's top 100 who are worth £9 bn', *Sunday Times*, 13 June, p.3.1, and Koenig, P. (2004) 'Inside the Hidden City', *Sunday Times*, 13 June, p.3.5-8.

Chapter 6: Networks, Power and Influence

[1] Russell, B. (1938) *Power: a Social Analysis*, New York: Norton, p.12, cited in Pettigrew, A. and McNulty, T. (1995) 'Power and Influence in and around the Boardroom', *Human Relations*, 48, 8, 845-73 (p.851).

[2] Weber, M. (1968) *Economy and Society*, I, New York: Bedminster Press, p.53, cited in Giddens, A. (1974) 'Elites in the British Class Structure', in Stanworth, P. and Giddens, A., eds., *Elites and Power in British Society*, Cambridge: CUP, p.17.

[3] Dahl, R. (1957) 'The Concept of Power', *Behavioural Science*, 2, 201-15; Yeo, H-J. *et al.* (2003) 'CEO Reciprocal Interlocks in French Corporations', *Journal of Management and Governance*, 7, 1, 87-108 (p.91).

[4] Higley, J. *et al.* (1976) *Elite Structure and Ideology*, Oslo: Universitetsforlget,

pp.17, 135-6, cited in Thomas, A.B. (1978) 'The British Business Elite: the Case of the Retail Sector', *Sociological Review*, 26, 2, 305-26 (p.324).

5   Scott, J. (1985) *Corporations, Classes and Capitalism*, 2nd edition, London: Hutchinson, p.68.

6   Hamdouch, A. (1989) *L'Etat d'influence*, Paris: Presses du CNRS, p.11.

7   Useem, M. (1984) *The Inner Circle: Large Corporations and the Rise of Business Political Activity in the US and UK*, Oxford: OUP.

8   Pettigrew, A. (1992) 'On Studying Managerial Elites', *Strategic Management Journal*, 13, Winter Special Edition, 163-82.

9   Hill, S. (1995) 'The Social Organization of Boards of Directors', *British Journal of Sociology*, 46, 2, 245-78.

10   Fich, E. and White, L. (2003) 'CEO Compensation and Turnover: the Effects of Mutually Interlocked Boards', *Wake Forest Law Review*, 38, 935-59 (p.941).

11   Vicknair, D. *et al.* (1993) 'A Note on Audit Committee Independence: Evidence from the NYSE on "Grey" Area Directors', *Accounting Horizons*, 7, 1, March, 53-57.

12   Yeo, H-J. *et al.* (2003) 'CEO Reciprocal Interlocks in French Corporations', p.88.

13   Windolf, P. (2002) *Corporate Networks in Europe and the United States*, Oxford: OUP.

14   Higgs, D. (2003) *Review of the Role and Effectiveness of Non-Executive Directors*, Department of Trade and Industry (DTI), January, p.18 (the Higgs Review).

15   Korn/Ferry International (2002) *Gouvernement d'entreprise en France en 2002*, Paris, December, pp.53-60.

16   Maclean, M. (2002) *Economic Management and French Business from de Gaulle to Chirac*, Basingstoke: Palgrave Macmillan.

17   Pfeffer, J. (1972) 'Size and Composition of Corporate Boards of Directors: the Organization and Environment', *Administrative Science Quarterly*, 17, 218-28.

18   Yeo, H-J. *et al.* (2003) 'CEO Reciprocal Interlocks in French Corporations', p.89.

19   Fich, E. and White, L. (2003) 'CEO Compensation and Turnover', pp.948, 953. This point is confirmed by Kevin Hallock in his 1997 article 'Reciprocally Interlocking Boards of Directors and Executive Compensation', *Journal of Financial and Quantitative Analysis*, September, 32, 3, 331-44.

20   Bauer, M. and Bertin-Mourot, B. (1997) *Radiographie des grands patrons français: les conditions d'accès au pouvoir 1985-1994*, Paris: l'Harmattan.

21   Such incestuousness was frowned upon in the UK by the Higgs Review, which recommended that no chief executive should become chairman of same company. In particular, chairmen should be independent of the company at the time of appointment. Higgs Review, p.24, paras. 5.7, 5.8.

22   Hermalin, B.E. and Weisbach, M.S. (1998) 'Endogenously Chosen Boards of Directors and their Monitoring of the CEO', *The American Economic Review*, 88, 1, March, 96-118.

23   Clift, B. (2004) 'The French Model of Capitalism: Exceptionalism under Threat?', Paper presented at Political Studies Association, April, University of Lincoln.

24   Burt, R.S. *et al.* (2000) 'The Social Capital of French and American Managers', *Organization Science*, 11, 2, March-April, 123-47 (p.136).

[25] Rossant, J. and Matlack, C. (2002) 'A Talk with the Godfather', *Business Week*, 29 July, 3793, p.58.

[26] Fich, E. and White, L. (2003) 'CEO Compensation and Turnover', pp.948, 953.

[27] Reier, S. (1995) 'You think fighting takeovers is tough? Look at what big Lyonnaise des Eaux had to do in Paris', *Financial World*, 24 October, 164, 22, p.40.

[28] Hill, S. (1995) 'The Social Organization of Boards of Directors', p.256.

[29] Pettigrew, A. and McNulty, T. (1998) 'Sources and Uses of Power in the Boardroom', *European Journal of Work and Organizational Psychology*, 7, 2, 197-214 (p.212).

[30] Ibid., p.202.

[31] Yeo, H-J. *et al.* (2003) 'CEO Reciprocal Interlocks in French Corporations', p.101.

[32] Tagliabue, J. (2003) 'When Bébéar speaks, French Companies Listen', *New York Times*, 18 November.

[33] Burt, R.S. *et al.* (2000) 'The Social Capital of French and American Managers', p.141.

[34] Granovetter, M. (1974) *Getting a Job*, Cambridge, MA: Harvard University Press, p.52, cited in Scott, J. (2000) *Social Network Analysis*, 2nd edition, London: Sage, p.35.

[35] Granovetter, M. (1973) 'The Strength of Weak Ties', *American Journal of Sociology*, 78, 1360-80. See also Granovetter, M. (1983) 'The Strength of Weak Ties: a Network Theory Revisited', *Sociological Theory*, 1, 201-33.

[36] Granovetter, M. (1973) 'The Strength of Weak Ties', p.1364.

[37] Scott, J. (2000) *Social Network Analysis*, p.35.

[38] Ibid.

[39] Granovetter, M. (1973) 'The Strength of Weak Ties', p.1378.

[40] Cole, R. (2003) 'Word of mouth is acclaimed as the best form of recommendation', *The Times*, Supplement on *The Power 100*, 15 October, p.3. The Higgs Review recommends 'an open, fair and rigorous appointment process' which it considers 'essential to a successful board'. The Higgs Review, p.13, para. 1.20.

[41] Interview with Sir Digby Jones, Director General of the CBI, Bristol, 5 March 2004.

[42] Interview with Dr John Mellor, Chairman, Foundation for Independent Directors, Bristol, 26 November 2002.

[43] Interview with Sir Adrian Cadbury, Solihull, 12 June 2003.

[44] *The Times* (2003) Supplement on *The Power 100*, 15 October, 1-16.

[45] This includes Niall Jennings, ranked seventh in the super-elite, who was knighted in 2002, but who, as an Irish citizen, cannot use the title 'Sir' – his title is essentially honorary.

[46] Bébéar, Beffa, Desmarest, Messier, Mestrallet and Tchuruk.

[47] Bon, Jaffré, Messier and Mestrallet.

[48] Beffa, Bon, Jaffré and Michel-Edouard Leclerc.

[49] Kosciusko-Morizet, J.A. (1973) *La « Mafia » Polytechnicienne*, Paris: Seuil.

[50] Marceau, J. (1981) '*Plus ça change plus c'est la même chose*: Access to Elite Careers in French Business', in Howorth, J. and Cerny, P., eds., *Elites in France*,

London: Pinter, 104-33 (pp.118-19).

51   Interview with Jean-François Théodore, CEO, Euronext, London, 7 November 2003.

52   This is confirmed by Bauer and Bertin-Mourot, who, in their 1996 comparative study of French, German and British business leaders, found that 'it is ... in Great Britain that the relationship between the managers of large enterprises and founding families is the least pronounced, and in France where it is the most'. Bauer, M. and Bertin-Mourot, B. (1996) *Vers un modèle européen des dirigeants?* *Comparaison Allemagne/France/Grande-Bretagne*, Paris: CNRS/Boyden, p.134.

53   Bauer, M. and Bertin-Mourot, B. (1997) *Radiographie des grands patrons français*, p.50.

54   Lemaître, F. (2003) 'La France, championne du capitalisme familial', *Le Monde*, 18 April, cited in Clift, B. (2004) 'The French Model of Capitalism'.

55   Hoar, R. (2003) 'Seven over 70', *Management Today*, October, p.60.

56   Dassault Systèmes differs from the others, in that it was previously nationalised under the Socialists in 1982. Nevertheless, family members continue to serve on the board: Laurent Dassault on the *conseil d'administration*, and Serge Dassault as honorary president of the Dassault Aviation group.

57   Butler, S. (2005) 'Buyout of Galeries Lafayette ends feud', *The Times*, 30 March, p.49.

58   Marceau, J. (1978) 'Le rôle des femmes dans les familles du monde des affaires', in Michel, A., ed., *Les Femmes dans la société marchande*, Paris: PUF, 113-24 (p.121).

59   Bourdieu, P. (1972) 'Les stratégies matrimoniales dans le système de reproduction', *Annales Econ. Soc. Civil.*, 4-5, 1105-27 (p.1107).

60   In 2004, the supervisory board of PSA Peugeot Citroën included four members of the Peugeot family: Thierry, Jean-Philippe, Bertrand and Roland Peugeot. Edouard Michelin acted as General Manager (*gérant*) of Michelin, while Pierre Michelin served as a member of the supervisory board.

61   Hermalin, B.E. and Weisbach, M.S. (1998) 'Endogenously Chosen Boards of Directors', p.96.

62   Interview with Jean-Claude Le Grand, Director of Corporate Recruitment, Paris, 10 March 1003.

63   Hill, S. (1995) 'The Social Organization of Boards of Directors', p.272.

64   Gattegno, H. and Le Cœur, P. (2004) 'L'"Etat-Chirac" impose les siens au sommet du pouvoir', *Le Monde*, 13 July, p.6. Tony Blair, of course, is not immune to such patronage. His holiday venues alone (including in 2004 Silvio Berlusconi's mansion in Sardinia and Cliff Richard's luxury holiday home on Barbados) illustrate his skilful manoeuvring through a seamless web of power and influence. Milmo, C. (2004) 'Around the world with Tony Blair (courtesy, as usual, of his many friends in high places)', *Independent*, 10 August, p.14.

65   Campbell, M. (2004) 'Daughter steals the Chirac spotlight', *Sunday Times*, 6 June, p.1.29.

66   Bauer, M. and Bertin-Mourot, B. (1996) *Vers un modèle européen des dirigeants?*, p.138.

67 Loriaux, M. (2003) 'France: a New Capitalism of Voice?', in Weiss, L., ed., *States in the Global Economy*, Cambridge: CUP, 101-20 (p.113).

68 Bauer, M. (1988) 'The Politics of State-Directed Privatisation: the Case of France, *West European Politics*, 11, 4, October, 49-60.

69 Bauer, M. and Bertin-Mourot, B. (1996) *Vers un modèle européen des dirigeants?*

70 Loriaux, M. (2003) 'France: a New Capitalism of Voice?', p.107.

71 Bauer, M. and Bertin-Mourot, B. (1997) *Radiographie des grands patrons français*, p.49.

72 Stevens, A. (1981) 'The Contribution of the Ecole Nationale d'Administration to French political life', in Howorth, J. and Cerny, P., eds., *Elites in France*, 134-53 (p.144).

73 Bauer, M. *et al.* (1995) *Les No 1 des 200 plus grandes entreprises en France et en Grande-Bretagne: deux modèles contrastés de fabrication du « mérite »*, Paris: CNRS/Boyden, p.99.

74 Bilger, P. (2004) *Quatre millions d'euros: le prix de ma liberté*, Paris: Bourin, p.107.

75 Loriaux, M. (2003) 'France: a New Capitalism of Voice?', p.116.

76 Clift, B. (2004) 'The French Model of Capitalism'.

77 The megalomaniac potential of this power was satirised in the case of Jean-Marie Messier, whose nickname, 'J2M', was ridiculed in the French press as 'J6M', meaning 'Jean-Marie Messier, moi-même, maître du monde' ('Jean-Marie Messier, myself, master of the world').

78 Loriaux, M. (2003) 'France: a New Capitalism of Voice?', p.120.

79 An observation made by Professor Elie Cohen at the annual conference of the Association for the Study of Modern and Contemporary France (ASMCF), held at Royal Holloway, University of London, September 1996.

80 In January 2003, there were 5,172 executive, 4,610 non-executive and 1,689 chairmen posts in total held by directors in British listed companies. The Higgs Review, p.18.

81 As Useem insists, 'In considering an executive for promotion to the uppermost positions in a firm, the manager's reputation within the firm remains of paramount importance, but it is not the only reputation that has to count. The executive's standing within the broader corporate community – as cultivated through successful service on the boards of several other large companies, leadership in major business associations, and the assumption of civic and public responsibilities – is increasingly a factor'. Useem, M. (1984) *The Inner Circle*, p.5.

82 The Higgs Review, p.13, para. 1.20.

83 Hill, S. (1995) 'The Social Organization of Boards of Directors', pp.251, 268.

84 The Higgs Review, p.11, para. 1.6.

85 Interview with Sir Digby Jones.

86 Geletkanycz, M.A. and Hambrick, D.C. (1999) 'The External Ties of Top Executives', *Administrative Science Quarterly*, 42, 654-81 (p.654).

87 Hill, S. (1995) 'The Social Organization of Boards of Directors', p.270.

88 Geletkanycz, M.A. and Hambrick, D.C. (1999) 'The External Ties of Top Executives', p.657.

316 Business Elites and Corporate Governance

[89] Michel-Edouard Leclerc, for example, has served since 1985 as co-president of the Association des Centres Distributeurs.

[90] Palmer, D. *et al.* (1986) 'The Ties that Bind: Organizational and Class Bases of Stability in a Corporate Interlock Network', *American Sociological Review*, 51, December, 781-96 (p.795).

[91] Cockburn, B. (1995) 'A pillar of the post', *Director*, 49, 1, August, p.66.

[92] Useem and McCormack stress that 'members of the interlocking directorate can be expected to far more often serve as business representatives to government and non-profit organizations than the remainder of the corporate elite'. Useem, M. and McCormack, A. (1981) 'The Dominant Segment of the British Business Elite', *Sociology*, 15, 3, 381-406 (p.385).

[93] Ashworth, J. (2003) 'Changing the image: new cliques in charge as gentlemen's club closes its doors', *The Times*, Supplement on *The Power 100*, 15 October, p.16.

[94] Hill, however, does not regard patronage as a problem. Hill, S. (1995) 'The Social Organization of Boards of Directors', p.268.

[95] 'Cresson to face court in nepotism case' (2004) *Independent*, 20 July, p.21.

[96] Osborn, A. (2004) 'Back to her prime', *Guardian*, 30 January.

[97] *The Economist*, 6 March 1999, cited in Stevens, A. with Stevens, H. (2001) *Brussels Bureaucrats? The Administration of the European Union*, Basingstoke: Palgrave, p.70.

[98] Interview with Jean-François Théodore.

[99] Kadushin, C. (1995) 'Friendship among the French Financial Elite', *American Sociological Review*, 60, April, 202-21 (p.219).

[100] Bauer, M. and Bertin-Mourot, B. (1997) *Radiographie des grands patrons français*, p.150.

[101] Jenkins, S. (2005) 'The peasants' revolt', *Sunday Times*, 5 June, p.4.1.

[102] Bremner, C. (2005) 'Chirac gives writer-diplomat task of picking up the pieces', *The Times*, 1 June, 6-7.

[103] Jean-René Fourtou, *Fortune*, 25 November 1996, p.165, quoted in Burt, R.S. *et al.* (2000) 'The Social Capital of French and American Managers', p.129.

[104] Interview with Iain Gray.

[105] Mills, C.W. (1959) *The Power Elite*, Oxford: OUP, 122-3.

[106] Granovetter, M. (1973) 'The Strength of Weak Ties', p.1377.

[107] O'Sullivan, M. (2002) 'The Stock Market and the Corporate Economy in France'.

[108] 'Independent? Moi?' (2003) *The Economist*, 366, 8315, 15 March, p.63.

[109] Senior, A. (2003) 'Society gambled with its future, High Court told', *The Times*, 26 September, p.31.

[110] Johnson, R.B. (1997) 'The Board of Directors Over Time: Composition and the Organizational Life Cycle', *International Journal of Management*, 14, 3, 1, September, 339-44 (p.342).

[111] Johnson, J.L. *et al.* (1996) 'Boards of Directors: a Review and Research Agenda', *Journal of Management*, 22, 3, 409-38 (p.420).

[112] Geletkanycz, M.A. and Hambrick, D.C. (1999) 'The External Ties of Top Executives', p.677.

113 Marceau, J. (1981) '*Plus ça change plus c'est la même chose*', p.119.
114 Burt, R.S., *et al.* (2000) 'The Social Capital of French and American Managers', p.141.
115 Stanworth, P. and Giddens, A. (1975) 'The Modern Corporate Economy: Interlocking Directorships in Britain 1906-70', *Sociological Review*, 23, 1, 5-28 (p.22).

Chapter 7: Corporate Governance and the New Global Economy

1 AFEP/CNPF (1995) *Le Conseil d'administration des sociétés cotées*, Paris: IEP, p.8. (Viénot I.)
2 Albert, M. (1991) *Capitalisme contre capitalisme*, Paris: Seuil.
3 Ibid., p.87.
4 Whitley, R. (1999) *Divergent Capitalisms*, Oxford: OUP.
5 Quack, S. *et al.*, eds. (2000) *National Capitalisms, Global Competition and Economic Performance*, Amsterdam: John Benjamins.
6 Djelic, M-L. and Quack, S. (2003) 'Introduction', in Djelic, M-L. and Quack, S., eds., *Globalization and Institutions: Redefining the Rules of the Economic Game*, Cheltenham: Edward Elgar, p.11.
7 Quack, S. and Morgan, G. (2000) 'National Capitalisms, Global Competition and Economic Performance', in Quack, S. *et al.*, eds. (2000) *National Capitalisms*, p.22.
8 Cadbury, Sir A. (2002) *Corporate Governance and Chairmanship: a Personal View*, Oxford: OUP, p.198.
9 Giddens, A. (1999) *Runaway World: How Globalisation is Shaping Our Lives*, London: Profile, pp.16, 19.
10 Djelic, M-L. and Quack, S. (2003) 'Conclusion', in Djelic, M-L. and Quack, S., eds., *Globalization and Institutions*, p.302.
11 Beck, U. (2000) *What is Globalization?* Cambridge: Polity Press, p.7.
12 Monks, R. (2001) *The Global Investors: How Shareowners can unlock Sustainable Prosperity Worldwide*, Oxford: Capstone, 153-57.
13 Cited in Cadbury, Sir A. (2002) *Corporate Governance and Chairmanship*, p.216.
14 Arthuis, J. (1993) *L'Incidence économique et fiscale des délocalisations hors du territoire national des activités industrielles et de services*, Commission des Finances au Sénat, Paris, 337, 4 June.
15 BBC News, 12 November 2004.
16 UN (2005) *World Investment Report 2004*, New York and Geneva: UN Table B.4, p.382.
17 Ibid., Table A.III.8, p.328.
18 Ibid., Table B.4, p.382.
19 Ibid., Figure A.I.1, p.263.
20 The figures and details given in this paragraph are taken from Tables A.III.5 to A.III.10 inclusive of the United Nations (2005) *World Investment Report 2004*, pp.322-31.
21 Castells, M. (1996) *The Rise of Network Society*, Cambridge, MA: Blackwell.

22 The German company Daimler-Chrysler owns 30 per cent of EADS and the French government and Lagardère jointly own 30 per cent. The recent promotion of Noël Forgeard from PDG of Airbus to CEO of EADS in May 2005 led to a further round of negotiations regarding the division of control within Airbus, the most profitable part of EADS. Hollinger, P. (2005) 'Investors still divided over Airbus successor', *Financial Times*, 10 May, p.28.

23 Tucker, S. (2005) 'Knight Vinke steps up Suez fight' *Financial Times*, 10 May, p.28.

24 Ringshaw, G. (2004) 'Sir John Bond: Lifetime Achievement Award', *Sunday Telegraph*, 14 November.

25 Schwartz, N.D. (2004) 'Inside the Head of BP', *Fortune*, 26 July.

26 Sylvester, R. (2005) 'Lord Browne: BP chief with a noble cause to make big profits', *Daily Telegraph*, 12 February.

27 Guyon, J. (2002) 'Getting Messier', *Fortune*, 10 June.

28 Birkinshaw, J. (2004), 'The Destruction of Marconi', *Business Strategy Review*, 15, 1, 74-75.

29 Garrity, W. (2002) 'Vivendi governance under fire', *Billboard*, 29 June.

30 Gilbert, N. (2002) 'Hermes criticises governance at Vivendi', *Financial News*, 4 June.

31 CCN (2003) 'Vivendi-Universal Board Meeting', *Canadian Corporate News*, 29 January.

32 Fletcher, R. and Fagan, M. (2001) 'The shareholders' revolt', *Sunday Telegraph*, 22 July.

33 Palmeri, C. and Lacy, S. (2004), 'CalPERS: getting back to business', *Business Week*, 13 December.

34 Tucker, S. (2004) 'Calpers likely to tone down hardline tactics', *Financial Times*, 23 July.

35 Andrews, D. (2005) 'Non-US Corporations take Buyback Action over Sarbanes-Oxley', *International Law Review*, 24, 1, February.

36 Shein, J.B. (2005) 'Trying to Match SOX: Dealing with New Challenges and Risks Facing Directors', *Journal of Private Equity*, 8, 2, Spring, 20-27.

37 A point noted by Tony Blair. See Blitz, J. (2005) 'Attack by Blair on US-style red tape', *Financial Times*, 27 May, p.1. One of the architects of the Act has criticised its reforms as 'excessive'. Tucker, S. and Parker, A. (2005) 'Sarbanes Oxley law goes too far, says its author', *Financial Times*, 8 July, p.11.

38 Romano, R. (2004) 'The Sarbanes-Oxley Act and the Making of Quack Corporate Governance', ECGI Working Paper Series in Finance, 52, 1-216.

39 Mauduit, L. (2003) 'Du capitalisme rhénan au capitalisme américain, la mutation de l'économie s'accélère', *Le Monde*, 29 July. See also 'A Survey of France: the Grand Illusion: France is Changing but cannot face up to it. Blame its exaggerated suspicion on the American Way' (1999) *The Economist*, 5 June. Loriaux, however, disputes this claim: Loriaux, M. (2003) 'France: a New Capitalism of Voice?', in Weiss, L., ed., *States in the Global Economy*, Cambridge: CUP, 101-20 (p.108).

40 Giddens, A. (1999) *Runaway World*, p.15.

41 'J2M' is an acronym for Jean-Marie Messier.

42 Péan, P. and Cohen, P. (2003) *La Face cachée du Monde: du contre-pouvoir aux abus de pouvoir*, Paris: Mille et Une Nuits, p.425.
43 Cadbury, Sir A. (2002) *Corporate Governance and Chairmanship*, p.199.
44 Aguilera, R.V. (2005) 'Corporate Governance and Director Accountability: an Institutional Comparative Perspective', *British Journal of Management*, 16 supplementary edition, 39-53.
45 Myners, P. (2001) *Institutional Investment in the UK: a Review*, HM Treasury, March, p.3. (The Myners Report.)
46 *The Combined Code: Principles of Good Governance and Code of Best Practice* (2000).
47 *Hampel Report on Corporate Governance* (1998), para. 1.5, cited in Cheffins, B.R. (2001) 'Corporate Governance Reform', p.13.
48 Tunc, A. (1997), 'Corporate Governance *à la Française*: the Viénot Report', in Patfield, F.M., ed., *Perspectives in Company Law*, 2, London: Kluwer International, p.128, cited in Cheffins, B.R. (2001) 'Corporate Governance Reform', p.14.
49 For the recommendations regarding audit committees, see The Cadbury Report, p.28, para. 4.35, point 4.3 in the Code of Best Practice. For remuneration committees, see p.31, para. 4.42, point 3.3 in the Code of Best Practice.
50 Frontezak, S. (1999) 'Gouvernement d'entreprise: évolutions récentes en France et à l'étranger', *Bulletin COB*, 338, September, 1-24 (p.6).
51 Conyon, M. and Mallin, C. (1997) 'A Review of Compliance with Cadbury', *Journal of General Management*, 2, 3, Spring, 24-37 (p.27). The Cadbury Report also confirmed the overriding popularity of audit and remuneration committees *vis-à-vis* nominations committees.
52 KPMG (1997) *Gouvernement d'entreprise: évolution de la pratique deux ans après le rapport Viénot*, Paris: KPMG.
53 Peyrelevade, J. (1993) *Pour un capitalisme intelligent*, Paris: Grasset & Fasquelle, p.55.
54 The Bouton Report, section VI, p.17.
55 Carson, E. (2002) 'Factors Associated with the Development of Board Subcommittees', *Corporate Governance*, 10, 1, January, 4-18. Here, Carson is discussing the Australian corporate context.
56 Claude Bébéar's desire to control his own succession at AXA extended to his committing the name of his chosen heir to a sealed envelope, addressed to the company's supervisory board, to be opened in the event of his death. See 'The difficulty of being a dauphin' (1999) *The Economist*, 9 April, 352, 8135, p.64.
57 The last company of our top 100 to separate the functions of Chairman and CEO was Shell, Philip Watts serving as Executive Chairman and Managing Director until his resignation early in 2004.
58 'Vive le gouvernance' (1997) *The Economist*, 11 January, p.84.
59 Interview with Agnès Lépinay.
60 Interview with Senator Philippe Marini, French Senate, 14 January 2004, Paris.
61 Litterick, D. (2005) 'Jury clears Pinault of fraud', *Daily Telegraph*, 12 May.
62 Bennett, N. (2000) 'Tumbril at Tomkins', *Sunday Telegraph*, 15 October.

63   Maclean, M. (2002) *Economic Management and French Business from de Gaulle to Chirac*, Basingstoke: Palgrave Macmillan.

64   Williams, K. (2000) 'From Shareholder Value to Present-day Capitalism', *Economy and Society*, 29, 1, 1-12; Froud, J. *et al.* (2000) 'Shareholder Value and Financialization: Consultancy Promises, Management Moves', *Economy and Society*, 29, 1, 80-110.

65   DiMaggio, P. and Powell, W.W. (1991) 'The Iron Cage Revisited: Institutional Isomorphism and Collective Rationality in Organisational Fields', in Powell, W.W. and DiMaggio, P., eds., *The New Institutionalism in Organisational Analysis*, Chicago: University of Chicago Press, 63-82.

66   Maclean, M. (2002) *Economic Management and French Business*.

67   Sage, A. (2004) 'France to sell E700m holding in airline', *The Times*, 10 December, p.60.

68   EIU (2004) *Country Report: France*, April, p.38.

69   Bauer, M. (1988) 'The Politics of State-Directed Privatisation: the Case of France', *West European Politics*, 11, 4, October, 49-60 (p.57).

70   Timmins, N. (2001) 'Europe adopts UK approach to spreading the risk', *Financial Times Supplement*, 2, Europe Reinvented, February, p.7.

71   Dedieu, F. and Hénisse, P. (2001) 'Les salariés actionnaires voient s'envoler leurs rêves de fortune', *L'Expansion*, 4-17 January, p.90.

72   Morin, F. (2000) 'A Transformation in the French Model of Shareholding and Management', *Economy and Society*, 29, 1, February, 36-53 (p.37). See also Hancké, B. (2001) 'Revisiting the French Model: Coordination and Restructuring in French Industry', in Soskice, D. and Hall, P., eds., *Varieties of Capitalism: the Institutional Foundations of Comparative Advantage*, Oxford: OUP, 307-34.

73   Lannoo, K. (1999) 'A European Perspective on Corporate Governance', p.274; Wymeersch, E. (1998) 'A Status Report on Corporate Governance Rules and Practices in Some Continental European States', in Hopt, K.J. *et al.*, eds., *Comparative Corporate Governance: the State of the Art and Emerging Research*, Oxford: Clarendon Press, 1045-1199 (p.1057).

74   In 1995, the market capitalisation of the Paris Stock Exchange stood at FF2,445,199. By 1998 it had grown to FF5,538,627. Figures according to the FIBV. We owe this information to Jean-François Théodore, CEO, Euronext.

75   Statistics according to FESE, year to date, December 2003. Data provided by Jean-François Théodore.

76   Aguilera, R.V. (2005) 'Corporate Governance and Director Accountability', Table 1, p.45.

77   De Tricornot, A. (2001) 'Qui possède les entreprises européennes ?', *L'Expansion*, 21 December-3 January, p.140.

78   Kechidi, M. (2003) 'Fusions et acquisitions: la financiarisation des logiques de concentration', Working Paper, Lereps, University of Toulouse.

79   Interview with Xavier Barrière, Human Resource Director (Europe), Air Liquide, 26 May 2003, Paris.

80   Basani, B. and Lechypre, E. (2004) 'Délocalisations: la grande peur française', *L'Expansion*, 691, November, 36-39 (p.38).

81   PR Newswire (2005) 'Institutional Shareholder Services acquired Deminor International's corporate governance unit', 25 May.
82   Megginson, W.L. (2000) 'Privatization and the Rise of Global Capital Markets', *Financial Management*, 22 December.
83   The Cadbury Report, p.32, para. 4.46.
84   Scott, J. (1990) 'Corporate Control and Corporate Rule', p.362.
85   The Myners Report, pp.1, 4.
86   Scott, J. (1990) 'Corporate Control and Corporate Rule', p.357.
87   Rutter, J. (2000) 'Investor Activism on the Rise', *Global Investor*, 135, September, 17-21.
88   Solomon, A. and Solomon, J.F. (1999) 'Empirical Evidence of Long-Termism and Shareholder Activism in UK Unit Trusts', *Corporate Governance*, 7, 3, 288-300.
89   Steele, M. (2005) 'Time for investors to come in from the cold', *Financial Times*, Supplement on Mastering Corporate Governance, 1, 20 May, pp.6, 8.
90   The Myners Report, p.5.
91   Ibid., pp.1, 5. Pension fund trustees are themselves increasingly reliant on investment consultants for advice, described by Myners as 'a tiny group of providers, mainly actuarial firms, [which] dominate this small and not particularly profitable market', and on whom, in turn, a heavy burden is placed (p.1).
92   Dawson S. (2004) 'Balancing Self-Interest and Altruism: Corporate Governance Alone is Not Enough', *Corporate Governance*, 12, 2, April, 130-33.
93   A point made by Ruth Bender (2005) 'Just rewards for a new approach to pay', *Financial Times*, Supplement on Mastering Corporate Governance, 3, 3 June, 4-5 (p.5).
94   Lee, P. (2002) 'Not Badly Paid but Paid Badly', *Corporate Governance*, 10, 2, April, 69-74.
95   McKnight, P.J. and Tomkins, C. (1999) 'Top Executive Pay in the United Kingdom: a Corporate Governance Dilemma', *International Journal of Business Economics*, 6, 2, 223-43 (p.225).
96   Korn/Ferry International (2002) *Gouvernement d'entreprise en France en 2002*, Paris, December, p.39.
97   Clift, B. (2004) 'Debating the Restructuring of French Capitalism and Anglo-Saxon Institutional Investors: Trojan Horses or Sleeping Partners?', *French Politics*, 2, 2, 333-46 (p.341).
98   Cheffins, B.R. (2003) 'Will Executive Pay Globalise Along American Lines?', *Corporate Governance*, 11, 1, January, 8-24.
99   Monks, R.A.G. (2001) *The New Global Investors*, p.72.
100 *Directors' Remuneration: the Report of a Study Group Chaired by Sir Richard Greenbury* (1995), 17 July, London: Gee. (The Greenbury Report.)
101 Ashworth, J. (2004) 'Fat stomachs and fat cats prey on the minds of Britain's bosses', *The Times*, 6 December, 36-37.
102 Butler, S. (2004) 'Sainsbury heads for red as Davis legacy costs £550m', *The Times*, 20 October, p.21.
103 Warner, J. (2003) 'The Independent fat cat list 2003', *Independent*, 20 May.
104 Conyon, M. and Leech, D. (1994) 'Top Pay, Company Performance and Corpo-

[105]   rate Governance', *Oxford Bulletin of Economics and Statistics*, 56, 3, 229-47.
McKnight, P.J. and Tomkins, C. (1999) 'Top Executive Pay in the United Kingdom', 233-39.

[106]   Finkelstein, S. (2003) *Why Smart Executives Fail*, New York: Portfolio.

[107]   Cadbury, Sir A. (2002) *Corporate Governance and Chairmanship*, p.222.

[108]   Young, S. (2000) 'The Increasing Use of Non-executive Directors: its Impact on UK Board Structure and Governance Arrangements', *Journal of Business, Finance & Accounting*, 27, 9-10.

[109]   Bender, R. (2005) 'Just rewards for a new approach to pay', p.5.

[110]   Main, B, and Johnston, J. (1993) 'Remuneration Committees and Corporate Governance', *Accounting and Business Research*, 23, 91A, 351-62.

[111]   Thompson, S. (2005) 'The Impact of Corporate Governance Reforms on the Remuneration of Executives in the UK', *Corporate Governance*, 13, 1, January, 19-25.

[112]   Conyon, M.J. and Florou, A. (2002) 'Top Executive Dismissal, Ownership and Corporate Performance', *Accounting and Business Research*, 32, 4, 209-25.

[113]   O'Sullivan, M. (2002) 'The Stock Market and the Corporate Economy in France', Paper presented at conference on European Financial Systems and the Corporate Sector, 4-5 October, Maastricht.

[114]   MEDEF/AFEP (2002) *Pour un meilleur gouvernement des entreprises cotées*, section V, p.15. (The Bouton Report.)

[115]   O'Sullivan, M. (2002) 'The Stock Market and the Corporate Economy in France'.

[116]   Alcouffe, A. and Alcouffe, C. (1997) 'Control and Executive Compensation in Large French Companies', p.96.

[117]   Goyer, M. (2001) 'Corporate Governance and the Innovation System in France 1985-2000', p.143.

[118]   Jacquin, J-B. (2001) 'Stock-options, la France championne d'Europe', 92-93.

[119]   Ibid., p.94.

[120]   OECD Steering Group on Corporate Governance (2003) *Survey of Corporate Governance Developments in OECD Countries*, November, p.66.

[121]   Interview with Agnès Lépinay.

[122]   Dedieu, F. (2002) 'Stock-options 2002: palmarès de crise', p.51; Dedieu, F. (2001) 'Stock-options: l'hiver meurtrier', *L'Expansion*, 648, 21 June-4 July, 88-89.

[123]   Dedieu, F. (2002) 'Stock-options 2002: palmarès de crise', p.52.

[124]   Ibid., p.51.

[125]   Arthuis Report on Stock Options.

[126]   OECD Steering Group on Corporate Governance (2003) *Survey of Corporate Governance Developments in OECD Countries*, p.54; Bliss, R. (2003) 'Common sense about executive stock options', *Chicago Fed Letter*, 188, April.

[127]   Alcouffe, A. and Alcouffe, C. (1997) 'Control and Executive Compensation in Large French Companies', p.97.

[128]   The Bouton Report distinguishes between two classes of stock options, 'options de *souscription* d'actions', which entail a new share issue, which Bouton regards as a dilution of company share capital, and 'options d'*achat* d'actions' involving the purchase of existing shares, which, in his view, does not. (The Bouton Report,

section 5, p.15.) Both, however, regardless of type, constitute a clear transfer of resources.

[129] Dedieu, F. (2002) 'Stock options 2002: palmarès de crise', p.50.

[130] Stock options were condemned as 'theft' by Michelle Edkins, Director of Corporate Governance at Hermes Investment Management (HIM), in 2001. O'Sullivan, M. (2002) 'The Stock Market and the Corporate Economy in France'.

[131] Cadbury, Sir A. (2002) *Corporate Governance and Chairmanship*, pp.224-25.

[132] Lee, P. (2002) 'Not Badly Paid but Paid Badly'.

[133] Bremner, C. (2004) 'How Britain rose from its sickbed and became the envy of Europe', *The Times*, 15 October, 32-33 (p.32).

[134] Ibid.

[135] Ibid.

[136] Rouart, J-M. (2003) *Adieu à la France qui s'en va*, Paris: Grasset; Boniface, P. (1998) *La France est-elle encore une grande puissance?*, Paris: Editions des Sciences-Po; Gubert, R. and Saint-Martin, E. (2003) *L'Arrogance française*, Paris: Balland.

[137] Bavarez, N. (2003) *La France qui tombe*, Paris: Perrin, p.17.

[138] Interview with Pierre Bilger.

[139] BBC News, 9 December 2004.

[140] Cited in Loriaux, M. (2003) 'France: a New Capitalism of Voice?', p.112.

[141] Amable, B. and Hancké, B. (2001) 'Innovation and Industrial Renewal in Comparative Perspective', p.123.

[142] Interview with Pierre Bilger.

[143] Interview with Senator Philippe Marini.

[144] Crozier, M. (1963) *Le Phénomène bureaucratique*, Paris: Seuil; Crozier, M. (1970) *L Société bloquée*, Paris: Seuil.

[145] Bavarez, N. (2003) *La France qui tombe*, p.17.

[146] O'Sullivan, M. (2002) 'The Stock Market and the Corporate Economy in France'.

[147] Kechidi, M. (2003) 'Fusions et acquisitions: la financiarisation des logiques de concentration'.

[148] Interestingly, while seeking to promote Vivendi's merger with Seagram in 2000, Jean-Marie Messier had promised that the new company would be a model of good governance. Once agreement was reached on the merger, he restricted shareholders' voting rights to ensure that Vivendi-Universal remained insulated from unwanted takeover, such that shareholders with two per cent of company shares or more would forego their voting rights if turnout at the AGM were significantly less than 100 per cent. Far from listening to the voices of major investors, this measure effectively removed their voting rights, since turnout at annual meetings is normally low. 'French corporate governance – ambivalent' (2000) *The Economist*, 7 October, p.73.

[149] OECD Steering Group on Corporate Governance (2003) *Survey of Corporate Governance Developments in OECD Countries*, p.43.

[150] Lannoo, K. (1999) 'A European Perspective on Corporate Governance', p.276.

[151] ICMG (1995) *International Corporate Governance: Who Holds the Reins?*, London: ICGM, p.44.

152   Trouille, J-M. (2001) 'The Franco-German Industrial Partnership', in Maclean, M. and Trouille, J-M., eds., *France, Germany and Britain: Partners in a Changing World*, Basingstoke: Palgrave Macmillan, p.80.
153   EIU (2004), *Country Report: France*, July, p.19.
154   See www.sanofi-aventis.com.
155   Sage, A. (2004) 'Airbus boss tipped for EADS job as Chirac schemes', *The Times*, 9 December, p.64.
156   EIU (2004), *Country Report: France*, July, p.19.
157   Basini, B. *et al.* (2002) 'Déclin? Quel déclin?', *L'Expansion*, 661, March, 10-11.
158   See www.shell.com, www.bat.com and www.bp.com.
159   Guthrie, J. (2004) 'The misguided moral code of corporate responsibility', *Financial Times*, 20 April.
160   Study by Joshua Margolis and JP Walsh, cited in Donaldson, T. (2005) 'Defining the value of doing good business', *Financial Times*, Supplement on Mastering Corporate Governance, 3, 3 June, 2-3 (p.2).
161   See www.tesco.com.
162   Interview with Jean-François Théodore.
163   O'Sullivan, M. (2005) 'Analysing Change in Corporate Governance: the Example of France', in Keasey, K. *et al.*, eds. (2005) *Corporate Governance: Accountability, Enterprise and International Comparisons*, London: John Wiley, 351-87.
164   Clift, B. (2004) 'Debating the Restructuring of French Capitalism and Anglo-Saxon Institutional Investors', p.343.
165   Dawson, S. (2004) 'Balancing Self-Interest and Altruism'.
166   O'Connor, A. (2005) 'The billion-pound game', *The Times*, 8 June, p.80.
167   Lannoo, K. (1999) 'A European Perspective on Corporate Governance', p.269.
168   1993 Working Time Directive (93/104/EC).
169   2003 OECD survey of 25 industrialised countries, cited in 'French bid *au revoir* to 35-hour workweek' (2005) *International Business*, 22 March.
170   Cadbury, Sir A. (2002) *Corporate Governance and Chairmanship*, p.230.

Chapter 8. Conclusion – Elites, Power and Governance

1   Coleman, D.C. (1973) 'Gentlemen and Players', in Coleman, D.C. (1992) *Myth, History and the Industrial Revolution*, London: Hambledon and London, 123-52.
2   Barsoux, J-L. and Lawrence, P. (1990) *Management in France*, London: Cassell, p.30.
3   Bauer, M. (1988) 'The Politics of State-Directed Privatisation: the Case of France, *West European Politics*, 11, 4, October, 49-60.
4   Interview with Jean-François Théodore, CEO, Euronext, 7 November 2003, London.
5   Crozier, M. (1963) *Le Phénomène bureaucratique*, Paris: Seuil.
6   Crozier, M., cited in Barsoux, J-L. and Lawrence, P. (1990) *Management in France*, p.83.
7   Bourdieu, P. (1984) *Distinction: a Social Critique of the Judgement of Taste*, translated by R. Nice, London: Routledge and Kegan Paul, p.476.

[8] Bilger, P. (2004) *Quatre millions d'euros: le prix de ma liberté*, Paris: Bourin, pp.16, 329.

[9] Gravier, J-F. (1958) *Paris et le désert français*, 2nd edition, Paris: Flammarion.

[10] Whitley, R. (1973) 'Commonalities and Connections Among Directors of Large Financial Institutions', *Sociological Review*, 21, 4, 613-32 (p.615).

[11] Interview with Jean-François Théodore.

[12] Coleman, D.C. (1992) *Myth, History and the Industrial Revolution*, pp.127-28.

[13] Perkin, H. (1969) *The Origins of Modern English Society, 1780-1880*, London: Routledge, p.63.

[14] Granovetter, M. (1973) 'The Strength of Weak Ties', *American Journal of Sociology*, 78, 1360-80 (p.1378).

[15] Interview with Jean-François Théodore.

[16] Messier, J-M., with Messarovitch, Y. (2002), *Mon vrai journal*, Paris: Balland, p.59.

[17] Coleman, D.C. (1992) *Myth, History and the Industrial Revolution*, p.130.

[18] Albert, M. (1991) *Capitalisme contre capitalisme*, Paris: Seuil; Peyrelevade, J. (1993) *Pour un capitalisme intelligent*, Paris: Grasset & Fasquelle.

[19] Peyrelevade, J. (1999) *Le Gouvernement d'entreprise*, Paris: Economica.

[20] Bourdieu, P. (1984) *Distinction*, pp.170-71.

[21] Pye, A. (2001) 'A Study in Studying Corporate Boards Over Time: Looking Backwards to Move Forwards', *British Journal of Management*, 12, 33-45.

[22] Seib, C. (2005) 'Equitable Life "aimed for deep pockets"', *The Times*, 12 April, p.47.

[23] Interview with Lord William Waldegrave, investment banker, UBS, 23 June 2003, London.

[24] Bourdieu, P. (1990) *The Logic of Practice*, translated by R. Nice, Stanford: Stanford University Press, p.54.

[25] Coleman, D.C. (1992) *Myth, History and the Industrial Revolution*, p.142.

[26] Coleman, D.C. (1992) *Myth, History and the Industrial Revolution*, p.133.

[27] Ashworth, J. (2005) 'The school sports team skippers who graduated as captains of industry', *The Times*, 5 January, p.15.

[28] 'Englishman who inspired L'Oréal with je ne sais quoi' (2003) *The Times*, 20 September.

[29] Coleman, D.C. (1992) *Myth, History and the Industrial Revolution*, p.141.

[30] Ashworth, J. (2005) 'The school sports team skippers who graduated as captains of industry', p.15.

[31] *McKinsey Quarterly* (1989) 3, Autumn, p.6.

[32] Davidson, M.J. and Cooper, C.L., eds. (1993) *European Women in Business and Management*, London: Paul Chapman.

[33] Driscoll, D-M. and Goldberg, C. (1993) *Members of the Club: the Coming of Age of Executive Women*, New York: Free Press.

[34] Maclean, M. (2002) *Economic Management and French Business from de Gaulle to Chirac*, Basingstoke: Palgrave Macmillan, p.7.

[35] Bremner, C. (2005) 'French hail victory over English', *The Times*, 12 January, p.37.

[36] United Nations (1999, 2000, 2001, 2002, 2003, 2004) *World Investment Report*, New York and Geneva: UN.

[37] Personal interview, Airbus UK, Filton, Bristol, 10 July 2004.

[38] Monks, R. (2001) *The Global Investors: How Shareowners can unlock Sustainable Prosperity Worldwide*, Oxford: Capstone, p.9.

[39] Egan, M.L. *et al.* (2003) 'France's *Nouvelles Régulations Economiques*: Using Government Mandates for Corporate Reporting to Promote Environmentally Sustainable Economic Development', Paper presented at Annual Conference of Association for Public Policy and Management, Washington DC, November.

[40] Interview with Pierre Bilger, former PDG, Alstom, Paris, 3 January 2003.

[41] Messier, J-M., with Messarovitch, Y. (2002), *Mon vrai journal*, p.61.

[42] Turkle, S.R. (1975) 'Symbol and Festival in the French Student Uprising (May-June 1968)', in Falk Moore, S. and Myeroff, B., eds., *Symbol and Politics in Communal Ideology*, Ithaca: Cornell University Press, 68-100.

[43] Bremner, C. (2004) 'Whistle is blown on manager's TV lover', *The Times*, 12 October, p.14.

[44] Follain, J. (2005) 'My life in the shadow of the Sphinx', *Sunday Times*, 27 February, p.4.3; Pingeot, M. (2005) *Bouche Cousue*, Paris: Julliard.

[45] Bremner, C. (2004) 'Chiracs break taboo by going public on daughter's anorexia', *The Times*, 7 December, p.8.

[46] Lindsay Owen-Jones, cited in *McKinsey Quarterly* (1989) Autumn, 3, p.40.

[47] Bourdieu, P. (1990) *The Logic of Practice*, p.53.

[48] Cockburn, B. (1995) 'A pillar of the post', *Director*, 49, 1, August, p.66.

[49] Barsoux, J-L. and Lawrence, P. (1990) *Management in France*, p.64.

[50] Midgley, C. (2005) 'Follow the customer, not the competition', *The Times*, T2, 19 May, pp.4-5.

[51] Pye, A. and Pettigrew, A. (2005) 'Studying Board Context, Process and Dynamics: Some Challenges for the Future', *British Journal of Management*, 16, S27-S38.

[52] Coleman, D.C. (1992) *Myth, History and the Industrial Revolution*, p.129.

[53] Ibid., p.131.

[54] Cadbury, Sir A. (2002) *Corporate Governance and Chairmanship: a Personal View*, Oxford: OUP, p.222; MEDEF Comité d'Ethique (2003) *La Rémunération des dirigeants d'entreprise, mandataires sociaux*, May.

[55] Whitley, R. (1999) *Divergent Capitalisms*, Oxford: OUP.

[56] Institute of Chartered Accountants in England and Wales (1999) *Internal Control: Guidance for Directors on the Combined Code*, London, September, p.4, para. 10.

[57] Egan, M.L. *et al.* (2003) 'France's *Nouvelles Régulations Economiques*'.

[58] Korn/Ferry (2005) 'Increased demand for multi-languages among senior executives', *Executive Recruiter Index*, 6th edition.

[59] Interview with Peter Orton, Chairman, HIT Entertainment, London, 2 September 2003.

[60] *Fortune (Europe)* (2000) 142, 1, 26 June, p.79.

[61] Beffa, J-L. (1992) 'How to Maintain a French Identity while Pursuing Worldwide Leadership', Conference on 'Business Life: Theory and Practice', Paris, March.

62 North, D.C. (2005) *Understanding the Process of Economic Change*, Princeton: Princeton University Press.

63 DiMaggio, P. (1979) 'Review Essay: On Pierre Bourdieu', *American Journal of Sociology*, 84, 1460-74 (p.1470).

64 Bourdieu, cited in Swain, H. (2000), 'Move over, shrinks', *THES*, 14 April, p.19.

65 Voltaire (1966) *Candide ou l'Optimisme, Romans et contes*, Paris: Garnier-Flammarion, p.259.

66 Roberts, R. *et al.* (2005) 'Beyond Agency Conceptions of the Work of the Non-executive Director: Creating Accountability in the Boardroom', *British Journal of Management*, 16, p.S6.

67 Huse, M. (2005), 'Accountability and Creating Accountability: a Framework for Exploring Behavioural Perspectives on Corporate Governance', *British Journal of Management*, 16, S65-S79.

68 Rousseau, J-J. (1966) *Du Contrat social*, Paris: Garnier-Flammarion, p.69.

Bibliography

Books

Adonis, A. and Pollard, S. (1997) *A Class Act: the Myth of Britain's Classless Society*, London: Hamish Hamilton.

Albert, M. (1991) *Capitalisme contre capitalisme*, Paris: Seuil.

Barsoux, J-L. and Lawrence, P. (1990) *Management in France*, London: Cassell.

Bauer, M. with Bertin-Mourot., B. (1987) *Les 200: Comment devient-on un grand patron?* Paris: Seuil.

Bauer, M. and Bertin-Mourot, B. (1996) *Vers un modèle européen des dirigeants? Comparaison Allemagne/France/Grande-Bretagne*, Paris: CNRS/Boyden.

Bauer, M. and Bertin-Mourot, B. (1997) *Radiographie des grands patrons français: les conditions d'accès au pouvoir 1985-1994*, Paris: l'Harmattan.

Bauer, M., Bertin-Mourot, B., Thobois, P. (1995) *Les No 1 des 200 plus grandes entreprises en France et en Grande-Bretagne*, Paris: CNRS/Boyden.

Bavarez, N. (2003) *La France qui tombe*, Paris: Perrin.

Beck, U. (2000) *What is Globalization?*, Cambridge: Polity Press.

Berle, A.A. and Means, G.C. (1932) *The Modern Corporation and Private Property*, New York: Macmillan.

Bilger, P. (2004) *Quatre millions d'euros: le prix de ma liberté*, Paris: Bourin.

Birnbaum, P. (1994) *Les Sommets de l'Etat: essai sur l'élite du pouvoir en France*, Paris: Seuil.

Bottomore, T.B. (1966) *Elites and Society*, Harmondsworth: Penguin.

Bourdieu, P. (1970) *La Reproduction: éléments pour une théorie du système d'enseignement*, Paris: Minuit.

Bourdieu, P. (1977) *Outline of a Theory of Practice*, translated by R. Nice, Cambridge: CUP.

Bourdieu, P. (1979) *The Inheritors: French Students and their Relation to Culture*, Chicago: University of Chicago Press.

Bourdieu, P. (1982) *Ce que parler veut dire*, Paris: Fayard.

Bourdieu, P. (1986) *Distinction: a Social Critique of the Judgement of Taste*, translated by R. Nice, London: Routledge and Kegan Paul.

Bourdieu, P. (1988) *Homo Academicus*, Stanford: Stanford University Press.

Bourdieu, P. (1990) *In Other Words: Essay Toward a Reflexive Sociology*, Stanford: Stanford University Press.

Bourdieu, P. (1990) *The Logic of Practice*, translated by R. Nice, Stanford: Stanford University Press.

Bourdieu, P. (1991) *Language and Symbolic Power*, translated by G. Raymond and M. Adamson, edited and introduced by J.B. Thomson, Cambridge: Polity Press.

Bourdieu, P. (1992) *Les Règles de l'art: genère et structure du champ artistique*, Paris: Seuil.

Bourdieu, P. (1993) *The Field of Cultural Production*, edited and introduced by R. Johnson, Cambridge: Polity Press.

Bourdieu, P. (1994) *The State Nobility: Elite Schools in the Field of Power*, translated by L.C. Clough, Cambridge: Polity Press.

Bourdieu, P. (1998) *Acts of Resistance: Against the Tyranny of the Market*, New York: New Press.

Bourdieu, P. (2001) *Masculine Domination*, translated by R. Nice, Cambridge: Polity Press.

Bourdieu, P. *et al.* (1993) *La Misère du monde*, Paris: Seuil.

Bourdieu, P. and Haacke, H. (1994) *Libre échange*, Paris: Seuil.

Bourdieu, P. and Passeron, J-C. (1979) *The Inheritors*, Chicago: University of Chicago Press.

Bourdieu, P. and Passeron, J-C. (1990) *Reproduction in Education, Society and Culture*, 2nd edition, translated by R. Nice, London: Sage.

Bourdieu, P. et al. (1992) *Academic Discourse: Linguistic Misunderstanding and Professorial Power*, Cambridge: Polity Press.

Bourdieu, P. and Wacquant, L. (1992) *An Invitation to Reflexive Sociology*, Cambridge: Polity Press.

Bunting, M. (2004) *Willing Slaves*, London: Harper Collins.

Cadbury, Sir A. (2002) *Corporate Governance and Chairmanship: a Personal View*, Oxford: OUP.

Cassis, Y., ed. (1994) *Business Elites*, Aldershot: Edward Elgar.

Castells, M. (1996) *The Rise of the Network Society*, Cambridge, MA: Blackwell.

Chandler, A.D. Jr. (1962) *Strategy and Structure: Chapters in the History of the American Industrial Enterprise*, Cambridge, MA: MIT Press.

Chandler, A.D. Jr. (1977) *The Visible Hand: the Managerial Revolution in American Business*, Cambridge, MA: Belknap.

Chandler, A.D. Jr. (1990) *Scale and Scope: the Dynamics of Industrial Capitalism*, Cambridge MA: Belknap.

Charkham, J. (1994) *Keeping Good Company: a Study of Corporate Governance in Five Countries*, Oxford: Clarendon Press.

Charkham, J. and Simpson, A. (1999) *Fair Shares: the Future of Shareholder Power and Responsibility*, Oxford: OUP.

Clegg, S.R. (1988) *Frameworks of Power*, London: Sage.

Collins, J.C. and Porras, J. (1994) *Built to Last: Successful Habits of Visionary Companies*, New York: Harper Collins.

Crozier, M. (1963) *Le Phénomène bureaucratique*, Paris: Seuil.

Cruver, B. (2002) *Anatomy of Greed: the Unshredded Truth from an Enron Insider*, London: Hutchinson.

Davis, E.P. (1997) *Can Pension Systems Cope? Population Ageing and Retirement Income Provision in the European Union*, London: RIIA.

Deleuze, G. (1972) *Différence et répétition*, 2nd edition, Paris: PUF.

Djelic, M-L. (1998) *Exporting the American Model: the Postwar Transformation of European Business*, Oxford: OUP.

Djelic, M-L. and Quack, S., eds. (2003) *Globalization and Institutions: Redefining the Rules of the Economic Game*, Cheltenham: Edward Elgar.

Driscoll, D-M. and Goldberg, C. (1993) *Members of the Club: the Coming of Age of Executive Women*, New York: Free Press.

Finkelstein, S. (2003) *Why Smart Executives Fail: And What You Can Learn from Their Mistakes,* New York: Portfolio.

Foucault, M. (1972) *The Discourse on Language*, translated by A.M. Sheridan, New York: Vintage.

Foucault, M. (1978) *The History of Sexuality: Volume I, Introduction*, translated by R. Hurley, Harmondsworth: Penguin.

Foucault, M. (1979) *Discipline and Punish: the Birth of the Prison*, translated by A.M. Sheridan, Harmondsworth: Penguin.

Foucault, M. (1980) *Power/Knowledge: Selected Interviews and Other Writings, 1972-1977*, edited by C. Gordon, New York: Pantheon.

Gattaz, Y. and Simmonot, P. (1999) *Mitterrand et les patrons 1981-1986*, Paris: Fayard.

Giddens, A. (1973) The Class Structure of the Advanced Societies, London: Hutchinson.

Giddens, A. (1999) *Runaway World: How Globalisation is Shaping Our Lives*, London: Profile.

Glass, D.V. (1954) *Social Mobility in Britain*, London: Routledge and Paul.

Granick, D. (1972) *Managerial Comparisons of Four Developed Countries: France, Britain, United States and Russia*, Cambridge, MA: MIT Press.

Grenfell, M. and Kelly, M., eds. (2001) *Pierre Bourdieu: Language, Culture and Education – Theory into Practice*, 2nd edition, Bern: Peter Lang.

Gubert, R. and Saint-Martin, E. (2003) *L'Arrogance française*, Paris: Balland.

Gugler, K., ed. (2001) *Corporate Governance and Economic Performance*, Oxford: OUP.

Guttsman, W.L. (1968) *The British Political Elite*, London: Macgibbon and Kee.

Halsey, A.H. (1995) *Change in British Society*, 4th ed., Oxford: OUP.

Hamdouch, A. (1989) *L'Etat d'influence*, Paris: Presses du CNRS.

Harrigan, P.J. (1980) *Mobility, Elites and Education in French Society of the Second Empire*, Waterloo, Ontario: Wilfred Laurier University Press.

Hennig, M. and Jardim, A. (1977) *The Managerial Woman*, New York: Anchor Press/Doubleday.

Holt, R. (1989) *A History of British Sport*, Oxford: OUP

Jeanneney, J-N. (1981) *L'Argent caché: milieux d'affaires et pouvoirs politiques dans la France du XXe siècle*, Paris: Fayard.

Keasey, K. *et al.*, eds (1997) *Corporate Governance: Economic, Management and Financial Issues*, Oxford: OUP.

Keasey, K. *et al.*, eds (2005) *Corporate Governance: Accountability, Enterprise and International Comparisons*, London: John Wiley.

Kosciusko-Morizet, J.A. (1973) *La « Mafia » Polytechnicienne*, Paris: Seuil.

Le Wita, B. (1994) *French Bourgeois Culture*, translated by J.A. Underwood, Cambridge: CUP.

Maclean, M., ed. (1998) *The Mitterrand Years: Legacy and Evaluation*, Basingstoke: Macmillan.

Maclean, M. (2002) *Economic Management and French Business from de Gaulle to Chirac*, Basingstoke: Palgrave Macmillan.

Mallin, C.A. (2004) *Corporate Governance*, Oxford: OUP.

Messier, J-M. with Messarovitch, Y. (2002), *Mon vrai journal*, Paris: Balland.

Mills, C.W. (1959) *The Power Elite*, Oxford: OUP.

Mills, C.W. and Horowitz, I.L. (1967) *Power, Politics and People: the Collected Essays*, Oxford: OUP.

Monks, R. and Minow, N. (1995) *Corporate Governance*, Oxford: Blackwell.

Monks, R. (2001) *The Global Investors: How Shareowners can unlock Sustainable Prosperity Worldwide*, Oxford: Capstone.

Moody, J.N. (1978) *French Education Since Napoleon*, Syracuse: Syracuse University Press.

Mooney, B. and Simpson, B. (2003) *Breaking News: How the Wheels Came Off at Reuters*, Chichester: Capstone.

Morin, F. (1998) *Le Modèle français de détention et de gestion du capital*, Paris: Editions de Bercy.

Mosca, G. (1939) *The Ruling Class*, translated by H.D. Kahn, New York: McGraw-Hill.

Moutet, A. (1997) *Les Logiques de l'entreprise: la rationalisation dans l'industrie française de l'entre-deux-guerres*, Paris: Editions de l'Ecole des Hautes Etudes en Sciences Sociales.

North, D.C. (2005) *Understanding the Process of Economic Change*, Princeton: Princeton University Press.

Pareto, V. (1935) *The Mind and Society*, New York: Harcourt, Brace.

Pareto, V. (1968) *The Rise and Fall of the Elites: an Application of Theoretical Sociology*, New Jersey: Bedminster Press.

Peyrelevade, J. (1993) *Pour un capitalisme intelligent*, Paris: Grasset & Fasquelle.

Ploix, H. (2003) *Le Dirigeant et le gouvernement d'entreprise*, Paris: Pearson Education France.

Ponteil, F. (1966) *Histoire de l'enseignement en France: les grandes étapes 1789-1964*, Paris: Sirey.

Quack, S. *et al.*, eds. (2000) *National Capitalisms, Global Competition and Economic Performance*, Amsterdam: John Benjamins.

Ricketts, M. (1994) *The Economics of Business Enterprise*, Brighton: Harvester Wheatsheaf.

Roe, M.J. (2003) *Political Determinants of Corporate Governance: Political Context, Corporate Impact*, Oxford: OUP.

Rouart, J-M. (2003) *Adieu à la France qui s'en va*, Paris: Grasset.

Routier, A. (1989) *La République des loups*, Paris.

Rubinstein, W.D. (1981) *Men of Property: the Very Wealthy in Britain Since the Industrial Revolution*, London: Croom Helm.

Rubinstein, W.D. (1987) *Elites and the Wealthy in Modern British History: Essays in Social and Economic History*, Brighton: Harvester Press.

Scott, J. (1982) *The Upper Classes: Property and Privilege in Britain*, London: Macmillan.

Scott, J. (1985) *Corporations, Classes and Capitalism*, 2nd edition, London: Hutchinson.

Scott, J. (1986) *Capitalist Property and Financial Power*, Brighton: Wheatsheaf.

Scott, J., ed. (1990) *The Sociology of Elites*, Cheltenham: Edward Elgar.

Scott, J. (2000) *Social Network Analysis*, 2nd edition, London: Sage.

Scott, J., ed. (1994) *Power*, 3 vols, London: Routledge.

Scott, J. (1996) *Stratification and Power: Structures of Class, Status and Command*, Cambridge: Polity Press.

Scott, J. (1997) *Corporate Business and Capitalist Classes*, Oxford: OUP.

Scott, J. *et al.*, eds. (1985) *Networks of Corporate Power*, Cambridge: Polity Press.
Scott, J. and Griff, C. (1984) *Directors of Industry: the British Corporate Network 1904-76*, Oxford: Polity Press.
Stanworth, P. and Giddens, A., eds. (1974) *Elites and Power in British Society*, Cambridge: CUP.
Stevens, A. with Stevens, H. (2001) *Brussels Bureaucrats? The Administration of the European Union*, Basingstoke: Palgrave.
Stone, L., ed. (1975) *The University in Society, I, Oxford and Cambridge from the 14th to the Early 19th Century*, Princeton: Princeton University Press.
Suleiman, E. (1978) *Elites in French Society: the Politics of Survival*, Princeton: Princeton University Press.
Suleiman, E. (1979) *Les Elites en France: grands corps et grandes écoles*, translated by M. Meusy, Paris: Seuil.
Suleiman, E. (1974) *Politics, Power and Democracy in France: the Administrative Elite*, New York: Tavistock.
Suleiman, E. and Mendras, H., eds. (1997) *Le Recrutement des élites en Europe*, Paris: La Découverte.
Swartz, D. (1997) *Culture and Power: the Sociology of Pierre Bourdieu*, Chicago: Chicago University Press.
Taverne, D. (1995) *The Pension Time Bomb in Europe*, London: Federal Trust
Tricker, R.I., ed. (2000) *Corporate Governance*, Dartmouth: Ashgate.
Useem, M. (1984) *The Inner Circle: Large Corporations and the Rise of Business Political Activity in the US and UK*, Oxford: OUP.
Useem, M. (1996) *Investor Capitalism*, New York: Basic Books.
Vaughan, M. and Archer, M.S. (1971) *Social Conflict and Educational Change in England and France 1789-1848*, Cambridge: CUP.
Weber, H. (1986), *Le Parti des patrons: le CNPF (1946-1986)*, Paris: Seuil.
Weisz, G. (1983) *The Emergence of Modern Universities in France, 1863-1914*, Princeton: Princeton University Press.
Whitley, R. (1999) *Divergent Capitalisms*, Oxford: OUP.
Whitley, R. *et al.*, (1981) *Masters of Business: the Making of a New Elite?* New York: Tavistock.
Whittington, R. and Mayer, M. (2000) *The European Corporation: Strategy, Structure, and Social Science*, Oxford: OUP.
Windolf, P. (2002) Corporate Networks in Europe and the United States, Oxford: OUP.
Zweigenhaft, R.L. and Domhoff, G.W. (1998) *Diversity in the Power Elite*, New Haven: Yale University Press.

Articles

Aguilera, R.V. (2005) 'Corporate Governance and Director Accountability: an Institutional Comparative Perspective', *British Journal of Management*, 16, supplementary edition, 39-53.
Aguilera, R.V. and Jackson, G. (2003) 'The Cross-National Diversity of Corporate Governance: Dimensions and Determinants', *Academy of Management Review*, 28, 3, 447-65.

Alcouffe, A. and Alcouffe, C. (1997) 'Control and Executive Compensation in Large French Companies', *Journal of Law and Society*, 24, 1, March, 85-103.

Amable, B. and Hancké, B. (2001) 'Innovation and Industrial Renewal in Comparative Perspective', *Industry and Innovation*, 8, 2, 113-33.

Andrews, D. (2005) 'Non-US Corporations take Buyback Action over Sarbanes-Oxley', *International Law Review*, 24, 1, February.

Anheier, H.K. *et al.* (1995) 'Forms of Capital and Social Structure in Cultural Fields: Examining Bourdieu's Topography', *American Journal of Sociology*, 100, 4, January, 859-903.

Basini, B. (1998) 'Patronat: les parrains ne sont plus ce qu'ils étaient', *Le Nouvel Économiste*, 11 December 1998, 48-53.

Bauer, M. (1988) 'The Politics of State-Directed Privatisation: the Case of France', *West European Politics*, 11, 4, October, 49-60.

Berger, B.M. (1986) 'Review Essay: Taste and Domination', *American Journal of Sociology*, 91, 6, 1445-53.

Bourdieu, P. (1972) 'Les stratégies matrimoniales dans le système de reproduction', *Annales Econ. Soc. Civil.*, 4-5, 1105-27.

Bourdieu, P. (1993) 'Introduction', *French Cultural Studies*, 4, 3, 1-4.

Bourdieu, P. (1996) 'Understanding', *Theory, Culture and Society*, 13, 2, 17-37.

Bourdieu, P. (1996) 'On the Family as a Realized Category', *Theory, Culture and Society*, 13, 3, 19-26.

Bourdieu, P. (1999) 'Scattered Remarks', *European Journal of Social Theory*, 2, 3, 334-40.

Bourdieu, P. (2001) 'Television', *European Review*, 9, 3, 245-56.

Bourdieu, P. *et al.* (1973) 'L'Evolution des chances d'accès à l'enseignement supérieur en France (1962-1966)', *Higher Education*, 2, November, 407-22.

Bourdieu, P. *et al.* (1973) 'Les stratégies de reconversion: les classes sociales et le système d'enseignement', *Information sur les Sciences Sociales*, 12, 5, 61-113.

Bourdieu, P. and St. Martin, M. (1973) 'Le Patronat', *Actes de la Recherche en Sciences Sociales*, 20-21, 3-82.

Bourdieu, P. and Wacquant, L. (1999) 'On the Cunning of Imperialist Reason', *Theory, Culture and Society*, 16, 1, 41-58.

Bubolz, M.M. (2001) 'Family as Source, User and Builder of Social Capital', *Journal of Socio-Economics*, 30, 129-31.

Burt, R.S. *et al* (2000) 'The Social Capital of French and American Managers', *Organization Science*, 11, 2, March-April, 123-47.

Calhoun, C. and Wacquant, L. (2002) 'Social Science with a Conscience: Remembering Pierre Bourdieu (1930-2002)', *Thesis Eleven*, 70, 1-14.

Cappelli, P. and Hamori, M. (2005) 'The New Road to the Top', *Harvard Business Review*, 83, 1, 25-32.

Carati, G. and Tourani Rad, A. (2000) 'Convergence of Corporate Governance Systems', *Managerial Finance*, 26, 10, 66-83.

Carson, E. (2002) 'Factors Associated with the Development of Board Sub-committees', *Corporate Governance*, 10, 1, January, 4-18.

Cheffins, B.R. (2001) 'Corporate Governance Reform: Britain as an Exporter', *Hume Papers on Public Policy*, 8, 1, 10-28.

Cheffins, B.R. (2001) 'History and the Global Corporate Governance Revolution: the

UK Perspective', *Business History*, 43, 4, October, 87-118.

Cheffins, B.R. (2003) 'Will Executive Pay Globalise Along American Lines?', *Corporate Governance*, 11, 1, January, 8-24.

Clift, B. (2004) 'Debating the Restructuring of French Capitalism and Anglo-Saxon Institutional Investors: Trojan Horses or Sleeping Partners?', *French Politics*, 2, 2, 333-46.

Clift, B. (2004) 'The French Model of Capitalism: Exceptionalism under Threat?', Paper presented at Political Studies Association, April, University of Lincoln.

Coleman, D.C. (1973) 'Gentlemen and Players', in Coleman, D.C. (1992) *Myth, History and the Industrial Revolution*, London: Hambledon and London, 123-52.

Conyon, M.J. (1998) 'Directors' Pay and Turnover: an Application to a Sample of Large UK Firms', *Oxford Bulletin of Economics and Statistics*, 60, 4, 485-507.

Conyon, M.J. and Florou, A. (2002) 'Top Executive Dismissal, Ownership and Corporate Performance', *Accounting and Business Research*, 32, 4, 209-25.

Conyon, M.J. and Gregg, P. (1994) 'Pay at the Top: a Study of the Sensitivity of Top Director Remuneration to Company Specific Shocks', *National Institute Economic Review*, 3, 83-92.

Conyon, M. and Leech, D. (1994) 'Top Pay, Company Performance and Corporate Governance', *Oxford Bulletin of Economics and Statistics*, 56, 3, 229-47.

Conyon, M.J. and Mallin, C. (1997) 'A Review of Compliance with Cadbury', *Journal of General Management*, 2, 3, Spring, 24-37.

Daily, C.M. *et al.* (2003) 'Corporate Governance: Decades of Dialogue and Data', *Academy of Management Review*, 28, 3, 371-82.

Daily, C.M. *et al.* (2003) 'Governance Through Ownership: Centuries of Practice, Decades of Research', *Academy of Management Journal*, 46, 2, 151-58.

Daumard, A. (1958) 'Les élèves de l'Ecole Polytechnique de 1815 à 1848', *Revue d'histoire moderne et contemporaine*, 5, 226-34.

Dawson, S. (2004) 'Balancing Self-Interest and Altruism: Corporate Governance Alone is Not Enough', *Corporate Governance*, 12, 2, April, 130-33.

Day, C.R. (1978) 'The Making of Mechanical Engineers in France: the Ecoles d'Arts et Métiers, 1803-1914', *French Historical Studies*, 10, Spring, 439-60.

Dedman, E. (2000) 'An Investigation into the Determinants of UK Board Structure Before and After Cadbury', *Corporate Governance: an International Review*, 8, 2, April, 133-53.

De Tricornot, A. (2001) 'Qui possède les entreprises européennes ?', *L'Expansion*, 21 21 December-3 January, 140.

DiMaggio, P. (1979) 'Review Essay: On Pierre Bourdieu', *American Journal of Sociology*, 84, 1460-74.

Egan, M.L. *et al.* (2003) 'France's *Nouvelles Régulations Economiques*: Using Government Mandates for Corporate Reporting to Promote Environmentally Sustainable Economic Development', Paper presented at 25th Annual Conference of Association for Public Policy and Management, Washington DC, November.

Erickson, B.H. (1996) 'Culture, Class and Connections', *American Journal of Sociology*, 102, 1, July, 217-51.

Fama, E.F. and Jensen, M. (1983) 'Separation of Ownership and Control', *Journal of Law and Economics*, 26, 301-25.

Fich, E. and White, L. (2003) 'CEO Compensation and Turnover: the Effects of

Mutually Interlocked Boards', *Wake Forest Law Review*, 38, 935-59.

Fich, E. and White, L. (2004) 'Ties that Bind', *Stern Business*, Spring-Summer.

Forbes, W. and Watson, R. (1993) 'Managerial Remuneration and Corporate Governance: a Review of the Issues, Evidence and Cadbury Committee Proposals', *Accounting and Business Research*, 23, 91A, 331-38.

Franks, J. and Mayer, C. (1990) 'Capital Markets and Corporate Control: a Study of France, Germany and the UK', *Economic Policy*, 191-231.

Frontezak, S. (1999) 'Gouvernement d'entreprise: évolutions récentes en France et à l'étranger', *Bulletin COB*, 338, September, 1-24.

Garnham, N. (1986) 'Bourdieu's *Distinction*', *Sociological Review*, 34, May, 423-33.

Gay, K. (2001) 'A Boardroom Revolution? The Impact of the Cadbury Nexus on the Work on Non-Executive Directors of FTSE 350 Companies', *Corporate Governance: an International Journal*, 9, 3, July, 152-64.

Geletkanycz, M.A. and Hambrick, D.C. (1999) 'The External Ties of Top Executives', *Administrative Science Quarterly*, 42, 654-81.

Goyer, M. (2001) 'Corporate Governance and the Innovation System in France 1985-2000', *Industry and Innovation*, 8, 2, August, 135-58.

Granovetter, M. (1973) 'The Strength of Weak Ties', *American Journal of Sociology*, 78, 1360-80.

Granovetter, M. (1983) 'The Strength of Weak Ties: a Network Theory Revisited', *Sociological Theory*, 1, 201-33.

Hall, D. and de Bettignies, H-C. (1968) 'The French Business Elite', *European Business*, 19, October, 52-61.

Hallock, K. (1997) 'Reciprocally Interlocking Boards of Directors and Executive Compensation', *Journal of Financial and Quantitative Analysis*, September, 32, 3, 331-44.

Hartmann, M. (2000) 'Class-specific Habitus and the Social Reproduction of the Business Elite in Germany and France', *The Sociological Review*, 241-61.

Hendry, J. (2005) 'Beyond Self-Interest: Agency Theory and the Board in a Satisficing World', *British Journal of Management*, 16, S55-S63.

Heracleous, L. (2001) 'What is the Impact of Corporate Governance on Organisational Performance?', *Corporate Governance: an International Journal*, 9, 3, July, 165-73.

Hermalin, B.E. and Wesibach, Michael S. (1998) 'Endogenously Chosen Boards of Directors and Their Monitoring of the CEO', *The American Economic Review*, 88, 1, March, 96-118.

Hesketh, A.J. (2000) 'Recruiting an Elite? Employers' Perceptions of Graduate Education and Training', *Journal of Education and Work*, 13, 3, 245-71.

Hill, S. (1995) 'The Social Organization of Boards of Directors', *British Journal of Sociology*, 46, 2, 245-78.

Hoar, R. (2003) 'Seven over 70', *Management Today*, October, 60.

Huse, M. (2005) 'Accountability and Creating Accountability: a Framework for Exploring Behavioural Perspectives of Corporate Governance', *British Journal of Management*, 16, S65-S79.

Hyman, M.R. *et al.* (2002) 'Augmenting the Household Affluence Construct', *Journal of Marketing*, Summer, 13-32.

Ishida, H. *et al.* (1995) 'Class Origin, Class Destination and Education: a Cross-National Study of Ten Industrial Nations', *American Journal of Sociology*, 101, 1,

July, 145-93.

Jacquemin, A. and de Ghellinck, E. (1980) 'Familial Control, Size and Performance in the Largest French Firms', *European Economic Review*, 13, 81-91.

Johnson, J.L. *et al.* (1996) 'Boards of Directors: a Review and Research Agenda', *Journal of Management*, 22, 3, 409-38.

Johnson, R.B. (1997) 'The Board of Directors Over Time: Composition and the Organizational Life Cycle', *International Journal of Management*, 14, 3, 1, September, 339-44.

Kadushin, C. (1995) 'Friendship among the French Financial Elite', *American Sociological Review*, 60, April, 202-21.

Kay, M.J. and Silberston, A. (1995) 'Corporate Governance', *National Institute Economic Review*, 153.

Kechidi, M. (2003) 'Fusions et acquisitions: la financiarisation des logiques de concentration', Working Paper, Lereps, University of Toulouse.

Kochan, T.A. (2002) 'Addressing the Crisis in Confidence in Corporations: Root Causes, Victims, and Strategies for Reform', *Academy of Management Executive*, 2002, 16, 3, 139-41.

König, T. and Gogel, R. (1981) 'Interlocking Corporate Directorships as a Social Network', *American Journal of Economic Sociology*, 40, 37-50.

Korn/Ferry International (2002) *What Directors Think, Corporate Board Member*, Special issue, 5, 6, November-December.

Landes, D.S. (1949) 'French Entrepreneurship and Industrial Growth in the Nineteenth Century', *Journal of Economic History*, 9, 44-61.

Lannoo, K. (1999) 'A European Perspective on Corporate Governance', *Journal of Common Market Studies*, 37, 2, 269-94.

Lee, P. (2002) 'Not Badly Paid but Paid Badly', *Corporate Governance*, 10, 2, April, 69-74.

Le Foll, A. and de Pirey, E. (2003) 'L'heureuse alliance de l'héritier et du manager', *La Gazette de la société et des techniques*, 23, November, 1-4.

Lemert, C. (2000) 'The Clothes Have No Emperor: Bourdieu on American Imperialism', *Theory, Culture and Society*, 17, 1, February, 97-106.

Letreguilly, H. (1997) 'France', *International Financial Law Review*, Supplement on Corporate Governance, April, 18-22.

Locke, R. (1988) 'Educational Traditions and the Development of Business Studies after 1945 (an Anglo-French-German Comparison)', *Business History*, 30, 1, 84-103.

Maclean, I. (1993) 'Bourdieu's Field of Cultural Production', *French Cultural Studies*, 4, 3, 283-89.

Maclean, M. (1997) 'Privatisation, *dirigisme* and the Global Economy: an End to French Exceptionalism?', *Modern and Contemporary France*, 5, 2, 215-28.

Maclean, M. (1999) 'Corporate Governance in France and the UK: Long-term Perspectives on Contemporary Institutional Arrangements', *Business History*, 41, 1, 88-116.

Maclean, M. (1999) 'Towards a European Model? A Comparative Evaluation of Recent Corporate Governance Initiatives in France and the UK', *Journal of European Area Studies*, 7, 2, 227-45.

Maclean, M., Harvey, C. and Press, J. (2001) 'Elites, Ownership and the Internationalisation of French Business', *Modern and Contemporary France*, 9, 3, August, 313-25.

Main, B, and Johnston, J. (1993) 'Remuneration Committees and Corporate Governance', *Accounting and Business Research*, 23, 91A, 351-62.

Maréchal, A. (1998) 'Les critères d'investissement des grands gestionnaires de fond internationaux dans les entreprises françaises', *Bulletin de la COB*, 322, March.

Mayer, M.C.J. and Whittington, R. (1999) 'Strategy, Structure and "Systemness": National Institutions and Corporate Change in France, Germany and the UK, 1950-1993', *Organization Studies*, 20, 6, 933-59.

McKnight, P.J. and Tomkins, C. (1999) 'Top Executive Pay in the United Kingdom: a Corporate Governance Dilemma', *International Journal of Business Economics*, 6, 2, 223-43.

Megginson, W.L. (2000) 'Privatization and the Rise of Global Capital Markets', *Financial Management*, 22 December.

Melewar, T. C. and Mott, A. (2003) 'Is the French Model of Capitalism Becoming More Like the Anglo-Saxon Model?', *Journal of General Management*, 28, 4, Summer, 47-63.

Mintz, B. and Schwartz, M. (1981) 'Interlocking Directorates and Interest Group Formation', *American Sociological Review*, 46, 851-69.

Mizruchi, M.S. and Stearns, L.B. (1988) 'A Longitudinal Study of the Formation of Interlocking Directorates', *Administrative Science Quarterly*, 33, 194-210.

Morin, F. (2000) 'A Transformation in the French Model of Shareholding and Management', *Economy and Society*, 29, 1, February, 36-53.

Nicholas, T. (1999) 'The Myth of Meritocracy: an Inquiry into the Social Origins of Britain's Business Leaders Since 1850', Working Paper No. 53/99, Department of Economic History, LSE.

Oliver, A.L. and Ebers, M. (1998) 'Networking Network Studies: an Analysis of Conceptual Configurations in the Study of Inter-organizational Relationships', *Organization Studies*, 19, 4, 549-83.

O'Sullivan, M. (2002) 'The Stock Market and the Corporate Economy in France', Paper presented at International Conference on European Financial Systems and the Corporate Sector, 4-5 October, Maastricht.

O'Sullivan, M. (2003) 'The Political Economy of Comparative Corporate Governance', *Review of International Political Economy*, 10, 1, February, 23-72.

Palmer, D. *et al.* (1986) 'The Ties that Bind: Organizational and Class Bases of Stability in a Corporate Interlock Network', *American Sociological Review*, 51, December, 781-96.

Payne, G. (1989) 'Social Mobility', *The British Journal of Sociology*, 40, 3, 471-92.

Peck, S. and Ruigrok, W. (2000) 'Hiding Behind the Flag? Prospects for Change in German Corporate Governance', *European Management Journal*, 18, 4, 420-30.

Pedersen, T. and Thomsen, S. (1997) 'European Patterns of Corporate Ownership: a Twelve-Country Study', *Journal of International Business Studies*, 4, 759-78.

Perel, M. (2003) 'An Ethical Perspective on CEO Compensation', *Journal of Business Ethics*, 48, 381-91.

Perkin, H. (1978) 'The Recruitment of Elites in British Society Since 1800', *The Journal of Social History*, 12, 2, Winter, 222-34.

Pettigrew, A. (1992) 'On Studying Managerial Elites', *Strategic Management Journal*, 13, 163-82.

Pettigrew, A. and McNulty, T. (1995) 'Power and Influence in and around the Boardroom', *Human Relations*, 48, 8, 845-73.

Pettigrew, A. and McNulty, T. (1998) 'Sources and Uses of Power in the Boardroom', *European Journal of Work and Organizational Psychology*, 7, 2, 197-214.

Pfeffer, J. (1972) 'Size and Composition of Corporate Boards of Directors: the Organization and Environment', *Administrative Science Quarterly*, 17, 218-28.

Prandy, K. (1998) 'Class and Continuity in Social Reproduction: an Empirical Investigation', *The Sociological Review*, 46, 2, 340-64.

Pye, A. (2001) 'A Study in Studying Corporate Boards Over Time: Looking Backwards to Move Forwards', *British Journal of Management*, 12, 33-45.

Pye, A. and Pettigrew, A. (2005) 'Studying Board Context, Process and Dynamics: Some Challenges for the Future', *British Journal of Management*, 16, S27-S38.

Roberts, R. *et al.* (2005) 'Beyond Agency Conceptions of the Work of the Non-executive director: Creating Accountability in the Boardroom', *British Journal of Management*, 16, S6.

Rogerson, P. (1999) 'Open Season', *The Accountant*, April, 16.

Romano, R. (2004) 'The Sarbanes-Oxley Act and the Making of Quack Corporate Governance', ECGI Working Paper Series in Finance, 52, 1-216.

Rubenstein, W.D. (1986) 'Education and the Social Origins of British Elites, 1880-1970', *Past and Present*, 112, 163-207.

Ruderman, M.N. *et al.* (2002) 'Benefits of Multiple Roles for Managerial Women', *Academy of Management Journal*, 45, 2, 369-86.

Rutter, J. (2000) 'Investor Activism on the Rise', *Global Investor*, 135, September, 17-21.

Schleifer, A. and Vishny, R.W. (1997) 'A Survey of Corporate Governance', *Journal of Finance*, 52, 2, June, 737-83.

Scott, J. (1990) 'Corporate Control and Corporate Rule: Britain in an International Perspective', *British Journal of Sociology*, 41, 3, September, 351-73.

Scott, J. (1991) 'Networks of Corporate Power: a Comparative Assessment', *Annual Review of Sociology*, 17, 181-203.

Scott, J. (1996) 'A Tool Kit for Social Network Analysis', *Acta Sociologica*, 39, 2, 211-16.

Scott, J. (2002) 'Social Class and Stratification in Late Modernity', *Acta Sociologica*, 45, 1, 23-35.

Shein, J.B. (2005) 'Trying to Match SOX: Dealing with New Challenges and Risks Facing Directors', *The Journal of Private Equity*, 8, 2, Spring, 20-27.

Short, H. and Keasey, K. (1997) 'Institutional Voting in the UK: is Mandatory Voting the Answer?', *Corporate Governance: an International Review*, 5, 1, January, 37-44.

Singh, V., Vinnicombe, S. and Johnson, P. (2001) 'Women Directors on Top UK Boards', *Corporate Governance: an International Journal*, 9, 3, July, 206-16.

Sizer, J. (1987) 'An Analysis of the Trends Impacting on the UGC and British Universities', *Financial Accountability and Management*, 3, 1, 9.

Solomon, M.R. (1983) 'The Role of Products as Social Stimuli: a Symbolic Interaction Perspective', *Journal of Consumer Research*, 10, December, 319-29.

Stanworth, P. and Giddens, A. (1975) 'The Modern Corporate Economy: Interlocking Directorships in Britain 1906-70', *Sociological Review*, 23, 1, 5-28.

Stearns, L.B. and Mizruchi, M.S. (1986) 'Broken Tie Reconstitution and the Functions of Interorganizational Interlocks', *Administrative Science Quarterly*, 31, 522-38.

Solomon, A. and Solomon, J.F. (1999) 'Empirical Evidence of Long-Termism and Shareholder Activism in UK Unit Trusts', *Corporate Governance*, 7, 3, 288-300.

Thompson, S. (2005) 'The Impact of Corporate Governance Reforms on the Remuneration of Executives in the UK', *Corporate Governance*, 13, 1, January, 19-25.

Toms, S. and Wright, M. (2002) 'Corporate Governance, Strategy and Structure in British Business History, 1950-2000', *Business History*, 44, 3, July, 91-124.

Toms, S. and Wright, M. (2005) 'Divergence and Convergence within Anglo-American Corporate Governance Systems: Evidence from the US and UK, 1950-2000', *Business History*, 47, 2, April, 267-91.

Tricker, B. (1996) 'Whose Company is it Anyway?', *Corporate Governance: an International Review*, 4, 1, January, 2.

Useem, M. (1982) 'Classwise Rationality in the Politics of Managers and Directors of Large Corporations in the United States and Great Britain', *Administrative Science Quarterly*, 27, 199-226.

Useem, M. and McCormack, A. (1981) 'The Dominant Segment of the British Business Elite', *Sociology*, 15, 3, 381-406.

Vicknair, D. *et al.* (1993) 'A Note on Audit Committee Independence: Evidence from the NYSE on "Grey" Area Directors', *Accounting Horizons*, 7, 1, March, 53-57.

Whitley, R. (1973) 'Commonalities and Connections Among Directors of Large Financial Institutions', *Sociological Review*, 21, 4, 613-32.

Whitley, R. (1980) 'The Impact of Changing Industrial Structures on Business Elites, Managerial Careers, and the Roles of Business Schools', *International Studies of Management and Organisation*, 10, 1-2, 110-36.

Yeo, H-J. *et al.* (2003) 'CEO Reciprocal Interlocks in French Corporations', *Journal of Management and Governance*, 7, 1, 87-108.

Young, S. (2000) 'The Increasing Use of Non-executive Directors: its Impact on UK Board Structure and Governance Arrangements', *Journal of Business, Finance & Accounting*, 27, 9-10.

Ziegler, N. (1995) 'Institutions, Elites and Technological Change in France and Germany', *World Politics*, 47, April, 341-72.

Book Chapters

Bloch, L. and Kremp, E. (2001) 'Ownership and Voting Power in France, in Barca, F. and Becht, M., eds., *The Control of Corporate Europe*, Oxford: OUP, 106-27.

Briggs, A. (1969) 'Developments in Higher Education in the United Kingdom: Nineteenth and Twentieth Centuries' in Niblett, W.R., ed., *Higher Education: Demand and Response*, London: Tavistock Publications, 95-116.

Bruce, A. and Buck, T. (1997) 'Executive Reward and Corporate Governance, in Keasey. K. *et al.*, eds., *Corporate Governance: Economic, Management and Financial Issues*, Oxford: OUP, 80-102.

Chadeau, E. (1993) 'The Large Family Firm in Twentieth-Century France', in Jones, G. and Rose, M.B., eds., *Family Capitalism*, London: Cass, 184-205.

Dimaggio, P.J. (1992) 'Nadel's Paradox Revisited: Relational and Cultural Aspects of Organizational Structure', in Nhoria, N. and Eccles, R.G, eds., *Organizations and*

Networks: Structure, Form and Action, Boston, MA: Harvard Business School Press, 118-42.

DiMaggio, P.J. and Powell, W.W. (1991) 'The Iron Cage Revisited: Institutional Isomorphism and Collective Rationality in Organizational Fields', in Powell, W.W. and DiMaggio, P.J., eds., *The New Institutionalism in Organizational Analysis*, Chicago: University of Chicago Press, 63-82.

Eick, D. (2001) 'Discourses on Language and Symbolic Power', in Grenfell, M. and Kelly, M., eds., *Pierre Bourdieu: Language, Culture and Education*, Bern: Peter Lang, 85-96.

Ezzamel, M. and Watson, R. (1997) 'Wearing Two Hats: the Conflicting Control and Management Roles of Non-Executive Directors', in Keasey, K. *et al.*, eds., *Corporate Governance: Economic, Management and Financial Issues*, Oxford: OUP, 54-79.

Gerbod, P. (1981) 'The Baccalaureate and its Role in the Recruitment and Formation of French Elites in the Nineteenth Century', in Howorth, J. and Cerny, P., eds., *Elites in France*, London: Pinter, 46-56.

Giddens, A. (1974) 'Elites in the British Class Structure', in Stanworth, P. and Giddens, A., eds., *Elites and Power in British Society*, Cambridge: CUP, 1-21.

Goergen, M. and Renneboog, L. (2001) 'United Kingdom', in Gugler, K., ed., *Corporate Governance and Economic Performance*, Oxford: OUP, 184-200.

Hall, P.A. (1987) 'The Evolution of Economic Policy Under Mitterrand', in Ross, G., Hoffmann, S. and Malzacher, S. eds., *The Mitterrand Experiment*, New York: OUP, 54-73.

Hancké, B. (2001) 'Revisiting the French Model: Coordination and Restructuring in French Industry', in Soskice, D. and Hall, Peter, eds., *Varieties of Capitalism: the Institutional Foundations of Comparative Advantage*, Oxford: OUP, 307-34.

Hayward, J. (1998) '*Moins d'Etat* or *Mieux d'Etat*: the French Response to the Neo-liberal Challenge', in Maclean, M., ed., *The Mitterrand Years: Legacy and Evaluation*, Basingstoke: Macmillan, 23-35.

Kremp, E. and Sevestre, P. (2001) 'France', in Gugler, K., ed., *Corporate Governance and Economic Performance*, Oxford: OUP, 121-29.

Johnson, D. (1981) 'Introduction', in Howorth, J. and Cerny, P., eds., *Elites in France*, London: Pinter, 1-4.

Jones, G. and Rose, M.B. (1993) 'Family Capitalism', in Jones, G. and Rose, M.B., eds., *Family Capitalism*, London: Cass, 1-16.

Jones, T. (2001) 'Language Change and Social Change: Temptations of the Populist Fallacy', in Grenfell, M. and Kelly, M., eds., *Pierre Bourdieu: Language, Culture and Education*, Bern: Peter Lang, 41-49.

Loriaux, M. (2003) 'France: a New Capitalism of Voice?', in Weiss, L., ed., *States in the Global Economy*, Cambridge: CUP, 101-20.

Maclean, M. (2001) 'Corporate Governance and Business Cultures in France, Germany and Britain: Convergence or Conflict?', in Maclean, M. and Trouille, J-M., eds., *France, Germany and Britain: Partners in a Changing World*, Basingstoke: Palgrave Macmillan, 53-69.

Marceau, J. (1978) 'Le rôle des femmes dans les familles du monde des affaires', in Michel, A., ed., *Les Femmes dans la société marchande*, Paris: PUF, 113-24.

Marceau, J. (1981) '*Plus ça change plus c'est la même chose*: Access to Elite Careers in French Business', in Howorth, J. and Cerny, P., eds., *Elites in France*, London: Pinter, 104-33.

Marceau, J. (1989) 'France', in Bottomore, T. and Brym, R.J., eds., *The Capitalist Class: an International Study*, London: Harvester Wheatsheaf, 47-72.

Mayeur, F. (1981) 'Women and Elites from the Nineteenth to the Twentieth Century', in Howorth, J. and Cerny, P., eds., *Elites in France*, London: Pinter, 57-65.

Mayeur, J-M. (1981) 'Analytical Afterword: Towards a Prosopography of Elites in Modern and Contemporary France', in Howorth, J. and Cerny, P., eds., *Elites in France*, London: Pinter, 240-50.

O'Sullivan, M. (2005) 'Analysing Change in Corporate Governance: the Example of France', in Keasey, K. *et al.*, eds (2005) *Corporate Governance: Accountability, Enterprise and International Comparisons*, London: John Wiley, 351-87.

Pahl, R.E. and Winkler, J.T. (1974) 'The Economic Elite: Theory and Practice', in Stanworth, P. and Giddens, A., eds., *Elites and Power in British Society*, Cambridge: CUP, 102-22.

Reynolds, S. (1998) 'Women and Political Representation during the Mitterrand Presidency – or the Family Romance of the Fifth Republic', in Maclean, M., ed., *The Mitterrand Years: Legacy and Evaluation*, Basingstoke: Macmillan, 185-97.

Rose, M.B. (1994) 'The Family Firm in British Business', in Kirby, M.W. and Rose, M.B., eds., *Business Enterprise in Modern Britain: from the Eighteenth to the Twentieth Century*, London: Cass, 61-87.

Rubinstein, W.D. (1974) 'Men of Property: Some Aspects of Occupation, Inheritance and Power Among Top British Wealthholders', in Stanworth, P., and Giddens, A., eds., *Elites and Power in British Society*, Cambridge: CUP, 144-69.

Schubert, J.D. (2001) 'Schizophrenia and Symbolic Violence', in Grenfell, M. and Kelly, M., eds., *Pierre Bourdieu: Language, Culture and Education*, Bern: Peter Lang, 97-107.

Scott, J. and Griff, C. (1985) 'Bank Spheres of Influence in the British Corporate Network', in Stokman, F.N. *et al.*, eds., *Networks of Corporate Power: a Comparative Analysis of Ten Countries*, Oxford: Polity, 214-33.

Shattock, M. (1996) 'The Creation of the British University System' in Shattock, M., ed., *The Creation of a University System*, Oxford: Blackwell, 1-30.

Short, H. and Keasey, K. (1997) 'Institutional Shareholders and Corporate Governance', in Keasey, K. *et al.*, eds., *Corporate Governance: Economic, Management and Financial Issues*, Oxford: OUP, 18-53.

Sirinelli, J-F. (1981) 'The Ecole Normale Supérieure and elite formation and selection during the Third Republic', in Howorth, J. and Cerny, P., eds., *Elites in France*, London: Pinter, 66-77.

Stanworth, P. and Giddens, A. (1974) 'An Economic Elite: a Demographic Profile of Company Chairmen', in Stanworth, P. and Giddens, A., eds., *Elites and Power in British Society*, Cambridge: CUP, 81-101.

Stevens, A. (1981) 'The Contribution of the Ecole Nationale d'Administration to French Political Life', in Howorth, J. and Cerny, P., eds., *Elites in France*, London: Pinter, 134-53.

Swartz, D. (1985) 'French Interlocking Directorships: Financial and Industrial Groups', in Stokman, F.N. *et al.*, eds., *Networks of Corporate Power*, Oxford: Polity, 184-98.

342 *Business Elites and Corporate Governance*

Thompson, J.B. (1991) 'Editor's Introduction', in Bourdieu, P., *Language and Symbolic Power*, Cambridge, MA: Harvard University Press, 1-31.

Turkle, S.R. (1975) 'Symbol and Festival in the French Student Uprising (May-June 1968)', in Falk Moore, S. and Myeroff, B., eds., *Symbol and Politics in Communal Ideology*, Ithaca: Cornell University Press, 68-100.

Vaughan, M. (1981) 'The grandes écoles: Selection, Legitimation, Perpetuation', in Howorth, J. and Cerny, P., eds., *Elites in France*, London: Pinter, 93-103.

Wacquant, L.J.D. (1996) 'Foreword', in Bourdieu, P., *The State Nobility: Elite Schools in the Field of Power*, translated by L.C. Clough, Cambridge: Polity Press, ix-xxii.

Wakeford, F. and J. (1974) 'Universities and the Study of Elites', in Stanworth, P. and Giddens, A., eds., *Elites and Power in British Society*, Cambridge: CUP, 185-97.

Weber, M. (1968) 'Status Groups and Classes', in Roth, G. and Wittich, C., eds., *Economy and Society*, Vol. 1, New York: Bedminster Press, 302-7.

Whitley, R. (1974) 'The City and Industry: the Directors of Large Companies, their Characteristics and Connections', in Stanworth, P. and Giddens, A., eds., *Elites and Power in British Society*, Cambridge: CUP, 65-80.

Wymeersch, E. (1998) 'A Status Report on Corporate Governance Rules and Practices in Some Continental European States', in Hopt, K.J. et al., eds., *Comparative Corporate Governance: the State of the Art and Emerging Research*, Oxford: Clarendon Press, 1045-1199.

Reports

Association Française des Entreprises Privée/Conseil National du Patronat Français (1995) *Le Conseil d'administration des sociétés cotées*, Paris: IEP.

Association Française des Entreprises Privée/Mouvement des Entreprises de France (1999) *Rapport du Comité sur le gouvernement d'entreprise présidé par M. Marc Viénot*.

Association Française de la Gestion Financière/ Association des Sociétés et Fonds Français d'Investissement (1998) *Recommendations sur le gouvernement d'entreprise*.

The Combined Code: Principles of Good Governance and Code of Best Practice (2000).

Committee on the Financial Aspects of Corporate Governance (1992) *The Financial Aspects of Corporate Governance*, London: Gee.

Directors' Remuneration: the Report of a Study Group Chaired by Sir Richard Greenbury (1995), 17 July, London: Gee.

Economist Intelligence Unit (1998, 1999, 2000, 2001, 2002, 2003, 2004), *Country Profile: France*, London: EIU.

Economist Intelligence Unit (1998, 1999, 2000, 2001, 2002, 2003, 2004), *Country Profile: United Kingdom*, London: EIU.

European Commission (1995) Small and Medium-sized Enterprises: a Dynamic Source of Employment, Growth and Competitiveness in the European Union, Brussels.

Hampel, R. (1998) Committee on Corporate Governance: Final Report, London: Gee.

Higgs, D. (2003) *Review of the Role and Effectiveness of Non-Executive Directors*, Department of Trade and Industry, London, January.

HMSO (1995) Report of the Board of Banking Supervision Inquiry into the Circumstances of the Collapse of Barings, London.

Institute of Chartered Accountants in England and Wales (1999) *Internal Control: Guidance for Directors on the Combined Code*, London, September.

International Capital Markets Group (1995) *International Corporate Governance: Who Holds the Reins?*, London: ICMG

Korn/Ferry International (2002) *Gouvernement d'entreprise en France en 2002*, Paris, December.

KPMG (1997) Gouvernement d'entreprise: évolution de la pratique deux ans après le rapport Viénot, Paris : KPMG

Marini, P. (1996) *La Modernisation du droit des sociétés*, Paris: La Documentation Française.

Mouvement des Entreprises de France/Association Française des Entreprises Privée (2002) *Pour un meilleur gouvernement des entreprises cotées.*

Mouvement des Entreprises de France Comité d'Ethique (2003) *La Rémunération des dirigeants d'entreprise, mandataires sociaux*, May.

Myners, P. (2001) Institutional Investment in the UK: a Review, HM Treasury, March.

Organisation for Economic Cooperation and Development Steering Group on Corporate Governance (2003) *Survey of Corporate Governance Developments in OECD Countries*, November.

Penrose, Rt. Hon. Lord (2004), *Report of the Equitable Life Inquiry*, London: HMSO, March.

Singh, V. and Vinnicombe, S. (2003) Women Pass a Milestone: 101 Directorships on the FTSE 100 Boards: the Female FTSE Report 2003, Cranfield School of Management.

Smith, Sir R. (2003) *Audit Committees Combined Code Guidance*, Financial Reporting Council, London, January.

Treadway Commission (1987) Report of the National Commission on Fraudulent Financial Reporting, Washington

Tyson, L. (2003) The Tyson Report on the Recruitment and Development of Non-Executive Directors, London Business School, June.

United Nations (1999, 2000, 2001, 2002, 2003, 2004) *World Investment Report*, New York and Geneva: UN.

Index

on taste and culture 37-8, 150, 156, 245
see also 'structuring structures'
Bouton Report 295n.17
  on directorial appointments 79, 81, 165, 212, 245-6
  on executive remuneration 65, 322n.128
  Vivendi responds to 208
Bouygues 58, 166, 183, 199, 269
Bouygues, Martin 128, 277
Breton, Thierry 225, 251
Bristol University 88, 108, 110
British Aerospace 167, 273
British Airways 46, 166, 272
British American Tobacco (BAT) 189, 200, 235, 272
British Gas 19, 272
British Petroleum/TNK-BP (BP) 272
  executive remuneration 225, 229
  interlocking directorships 167, 169
  multinational company 200, 206-7
  social responsibility 235
British Telecom (BT) 272
  CEO remuneration at 225
  interlocking directorships 167, 169
  multinational business 200, 202
  privatisation 188
Bronfman family 17
Brown, Cedric 19
Browne, Edmund
  career at BP 206-7, 224, 225, 252
  education and career 118, 129, 132, 179
  directorships 169, 282
BSkyB 73
BTF (Bernard Tapie Finance) 59
Bubolz, M.M. 36
Bullock Report (1977) 51-2
Burgess, R. 9
Burt R. et al. 177
business associations 189-90
business elites
  cohesion and solidarity 240-5
  definition and qualification 2, 32, 261
  nationality of 221
  see also super-elite

business scandals 57-63, 71, 85, 228
Butler-Cox 92, 137
Buxton, Andrew 129, 283

Cable and Wireless 66, 167, 200, 272
CAC-40 (France)
  executive pay in 64-5, 229-30
  foreign investment in 57, 186
  share buy-backs 233
  specialist committees 212
  women directors 143-4
Cadbury, Sir Adrian 9, 51
  on boards 72, 81-2, 83, 84
  on executive pay 63, 227
  on networks 178-9
  recreational interests 153, 157
  on reform of corporate governance 80, 238
  on women directors 308n.15
Cadbury Report (1992) 2, 50, 73, 80, 211
Cairncross, Frances 146
Cairns, Lord Simon 179
CalPERS 71, 72, 209
Cambridge University 106-7
  alumni 147, 153
  elite attendance at 110, 114, 118, 119-20
  funding 109
  league tables 88
  and networks 178-9, 241
Camus, Albert 97
Cap Gemini 79, 270
capitalism, models of 196, 235-8, 255-8
Cappelli, P. 106, 138, 139
Carat France 145, 271
careers 123-48
Carrefour 58, 199, 200, 202, 205, 269
Carson, E. 212
Casino 78, 270
Castries, Henri de 225
CGU (now Aviva) 203, 272
chairman
  interlocking directorships 169, 142
  and nominations committees 83
  shareholder criticism of 217
  separation from CEO role 80, 81, 213-15